Ancient & Postmodern Christianity

Paleo-Orthodoxy
in the 21st Century

Essays
in Honor
of Thomas
C. Oden

Edited by
KENNETH TANNER &
CHRISTOPHER A. HALL

InterVarsity Press
Downers Grove, Illinois

InterVarsity Press
P.O. Box 1400, Downers Grove, IL 60515-1426
World Wide Web: www.ivpress.com
E-mail: mail@ivpress.com

Acknowledgments and permissions can be found on pages 279-80.

InterVarsity Press® is the book-publishing division of InterVarsity Christian Fellowship/USA®, a student movement active on campus at hundreds of universities, colleges and schools of nursing in the United States of America, and a member movement of the International Fellowship of Evangelical Students. For information about local and regional activities, write Public Relations Dept., InterVarsity Christian Fellowship/USA, 6400 Schroeder Rd., P.O. Box 7895, Madison, WI 53707-7895, or visit the IVCF website at <www.intervarsity.org>.

Cover photograph: B. Schmid/Photonica

ISBN-10: 0-8308-2654-8
ISBN-13: 978-0-8308-2654-4

Printed in the United States of America ∞

Library of Congress Cataloging-in-Publication Data

Oden, Thomas C.
    Ancient and postmodern Christianity: paleo-orthodoxy
    in the 21st century: essays in honor of Thomas C. Oden/
    edited by Kenneth Tanner and Christopher A. Hall.
        p. cm.
    ISBN 0-8308-2654-8 (pbk.: alk. paper)
    Includes bibliographical references.
    1. Theology. I. Title.
BR 50+
pcc   2002005650

P	21	20	19	18	17	16	15	14	13	12	11	10	9	8	7	6	5	4	3	2
Y	23	22	21	20	19	18	17	16	15	14	13	12	11	10	09	08	07	06		

Contents

Introduction

It is a deep pleasure for Kenneth Tanner and me to introduce and edit a series of essays presented in honor of Thomas C. Oden. I first met Tom Oden when I began my doctoral work at Drew University in the fall of 1987. As things turned out, Tom was my faculty adviser throughout my years at Drew. I must admit that I didn't know what to expect or anticipate as I entered the rigors of theological study under Tom's direction. I imagined a deep immersion in thinkers such as Schleiermacher, Bultmann, Barth and Tillich. Instead, Tom led me into a different world, one dominated by luminaries such as Athanasius, Chrysostom, Ambrose and Augustine. I had spent little time in the world of the early church, and yet Tom was convinced that unless I did so my theological education would sorely lack its indispensable foundation. Why would Oden think such a thing, I asked myself. His own life's journey provides the answer.

An Immersion in Modernity

Imagine a kid raised in a home that was deeply rooted in the pietistic tradition and the political ideals of the Democratic Party.[1] Oden's parents were devoted to the Bible and also deeply committed to liberal political philosophy and the union movement. Oden took this upbringing seriously, especially the idea that genuine faith would demonstrate itself in concrete action. During high school he organized students in the United World Federalist movement, and in college was attracted to quasi-socialist philosophy as Tom worked for the Students for Demo-

---

[1] In this essay I am freely drawing on my book, *Reading Scripture with the Church Fathers* (Downers Grove: InterVarsity Press, 1998), and from my interview with Tom Oden in *Christianity Today* ("Back to the Fathers," *Christianity Today* 34, no. 13 [1990]: 28-31; see also Christopher A. Hall, "A Long Journey Home: A Profile of Thomas C. Oden," *Catalyst* 20, no. 1 [1993]). I have also consulted Oden's "Personal Interlude," found in his *The Word of Life*, Systematic Theology (New York: Harper & Row, 1989), 2:217-19. See also Thomas C. Oden, *After Modernity . . . What?* (Grand Rapids, Mich.: Zondervan, 1990), pp. 26-29.

cratic Action at the University of Oklahoma. When Oden decided to attend the theological school at Perkins in Dallas, it wasn't because he was strongly committed to the biblical message, but rather to the hope that the church could be an effective instrument of social change.

A continuing political radicalism tinged Oden's seminary experience, but was somewhat moderated by his exposure to theological voices that demanded a greater realism. As Oden read Reinhold Niebuhr and Martin Luther, for instance, he was shocked out of his pacifism in 1955. Generally speaking, however, Oden remained committed for many years to the premises of strong government regulation and a general slate of liberal-socialist goals.

During Oden's time at Perkins he was exposed to a heavy helping of existentialist thought while studying with Joseph Matthews. Sartre, Camus, Marcel and Rudolf Bultmann became close companions. It is especially Bultmann who best symbolizes the direction of Oden's thought at Perkins. Bultmann's existentialist perspective resurrected the Bible for Oden in the early 1950s. It is difficult to overestimate the influence of Bultmann on Oden during these formative years. "As I look back at the trajectory of my adult life, one name weaves in and out almost from the beginning: Rudolf Bultmann."[2]

A sense of theological vocation was crystallizing in Oden as he left Perkins for graduate study at Yale, a vocation that continued to be shaped by existentialist categories throughout the late 1950s and early 1960s. Indeed, as Oden recalls, "As late as the mid-sixties I continued writing and speaking in defense of what I would call a moderate Bultmannian position in theology."[3] Added into the theological mix was an interest in post-Freudian psychology.

Oden remembers this period as one of novel experimentation combined with a mistrust and disdain for the past. His interaction with Scripture and other theological texts was less a dialogue than a "filtering process"; he allowed more traditional sources to speak to him "only insofar as they could meet" his "conditions," "worldview" and "assumptions as a modern man."[4] Oden experimented to a lesser or greater degree with communitarianism, politics, yoga, breathing techniques, tarot cards, paranormal phenomena and T groups—much that today is being called New Age.[5] His worldview continued to turn toward the left, a movement that changed direction only as the political and social anarchy of the late sixties undercut Oden's expectations and hopes.

---

[2]Oden, *Word of Life*, p. 217.
[3]Ibid., p. 218.
[4]Ibid., p. 219.
[5]Cf. Hall, "Back to the Fathers," p. 28.

A Change of Direction

The hedonism so deeply imbedded in Oden's thought ultimately led to a deep disillusionment with the direction his life had taken by the late sixties. Tom relates that the 1968 Democratic National Convention was a crucial turning point. "By that time I had developed a preliminary revulsion against antinomianism and anarchism, which would soon grow toward moderate political neo-conservatism. When people started throwing excrement at the police in Chicago, I got scared, and I've never been the same since."[6] He was witnessing and experiencing first hand tremendous pain, both culturally and personally. Ideas and lifestyles that were meant to lead to life had instead led to destruction and death.

For instance, Oden increasingly realized his advocacy of abortion rights demonstrated a fundamental misdirection in his own value structure. Throughout the sixties Oden was sincerely committed to liberalized abortion legislation in Oklahoma. He was shocked when he became aware that his support of individual choice as a fundamental value had led to the sacrifice of thousands of individual lives. "In the midst of all the rhetoric about freedom came the embarrassing awareness that I was condoning a moral matrix in which innocent life was being taken. That was a shock. It still is."[7] Oden's revulsion over his abortion stance in turn produced a loss of confidence in a whole series of liberal programs. Hedonism, autonomous individualism, the idolatry of the new, moral relativism and Tom's narrow empiricist worldview had run into a dead end. Where was he to turn? Oden's eyes had always been focused on the future for solutions. Soon he would find himself looking in the opposite direction.

Back to the Fathers

Oden began teaching at Drew University in the early seventies and encountered there the Jewish philosopher and true renaissance man Will Herberg. In fact, Oden remarks that Herberg "did more for me intellectually in the six years of our close friendship (1971-1977) than did any other person during that time, by requiring me to ground my thinking in classical sources."[8] It was Herberg who in no uncertain terms warned Oden that his overall understanding and perspective would be grossly misshaped unless Oden supplemented his immersion in modern sources and authorities with a concentrated exposure to the world of the early church fathers and mothers. Tom took Herberg's advice to heart and for the next five years devoted himself to an attentive study of patristic sources.

---

[6]Ibid., p. 28.
[7]Ibid., p. 28.
[8]Oden, *Word of Life*, p. 218.

During this time his consciousness underwent a dramatic shift, and Oden's theological agenda for the coming years was radically altered. He had earlier been trained to believe that theological work must be creative and novel to possess validity and worth in the church, seminary, university and broader intellectual community.

> I was mentored (especially by Bultmann, Tillich, Heidegger, and Rogers) to understand that what it meant to be a theologian was to struggle to create something new, to develop a new theology, to see things differently than any others had seen things before and thereby to offer my personal skill and subjective experience as a theologian to the emergent world. The result was that my relation to my sources became less a dialogue than a filtering process by which I permitted these sources to speak to me only insofar as they could meet my conditions, my worldview, my assumptions as a modern man. This is the modernity that ended for me in the late sixties, whose end it took some time for me to realize.[9]

The more Oden read, the more he realized that much of what he had taken for "new" was as old as the apostolic tradition itself. The early Christian theologians had intuited many ideas Oden had believed were more recent modern contributions. Tom has related to me a refreshed sense of excitement and renewal as he entered into the patristic world and was freed from the assumption that the effective and gifted theologian was by definition innovative and creative. He felt released from the need to reinvent the wheel. Indeed, most of the wheels Oden had relied on had possessed hairline fractures which sooner or later had widened under the stresses of "modernity." As Oden immersed himself in ancient sources, he discovered an antidote to his past idealization and idolization of the new. The need to create was replaced by the call to listen. As Oden puts it:

> I realized that I must listen intently, actively, without reservation. Listen in such a way that my whole life depended upon hearing. Listen in such a way that I could see telescopically beyond my modern myopia, to break through the walls of my modern prison, and actually hear voices from the past with different assumptions entirely about the world and time and human culture. Only then in my forties did I begin to become a theologian. Up to that time I had been teaching theology without ever having sufficiently met the patristic mentors who could teach me theology.[10]

People sometimes misunderstand this directional shift in Oden's thinking. By turning to the past Oden has not abandoned the modern situation. Rather, Tom remains involved in a bridge-building task, one of bringing the riches of the con-

---

[9]Ibid., p. 219.
[10]Ibid., pp. 219-20.

sensual Christian tradition into contact with the deepest questions and hopes of the modern person. Oden's work is centered on demonstrating how the living tradition of the church can help to clarify the meaning of human history in the midst of its sin and death. The burning question then becomes, in Oden's own words, "How does God's coming to us in Jesus Christ illuminate, regenerate, and transform our behavior in the midst of sin and death?"

A dream Oden experienced in the midst of the fundamental reorientation of his values and perspective sheds light on the heart of this shift. In the dream Tom is walking through the New Haven cemetery and comes across his own tombstone. The epitaph reads: "He made no new contribution to theology." A nightmare? No. Oden actually awoke refreshed and relieved. This striking image communicated to Tom that he no longer had to produce something new in order to create his niche in the theological arena. Rather, the dream indicated that Oden's calling could be fulfilled through building bridges between the classical Christian consensus and the broken, lost reality of the modern world, the world which desperately needs to encounter the Christ who is "the same, yesterday, today, and forever." Oden comments that "in my dream I was extremely pleased, for I realized I was learning what Irenaeus meant when he told us not to invent new doctrine. . . . The dream somehow said to me . . . that my calling as a theologian could be fulfilled through obedience to apostolic tradition."[11]

What can the reader expect to encounter in the essays collected in this *festschrift*? A number of essays explore patristic sources for their contribution to particular theological topics: Robert Jenson investigates the thought of the Christian East on christological issues. Christopher Hall explores the thought of St. John Chrysostom on nature and God's providence. Amy Oden, Tom's niece, contributes an essay on the importance of hospitality in the early church. Bradley Nassif explains the intricacies of Chrysostom's understanding of *theoria*. Vigen Guroian mines ancient sources for insights on learning to die well. Edmund Rybarczyk compares and contrasts the theological anthropology of Eastern Orthodoxy with classical Pentecostalism.

Three contributors, David Mills, J. I. Packer and Thomas Howard, discuss ecclesiological topics. Mills writes concerning the necessary doctrines that characterize the church. Packer makes a case for the "genuine churchliness" of today's evangelical church. Howard explores and explicates the five marks of the church. Mills and Howard have found their church home in the Roman Catholic Church, Howard some years ago and Mills more recently. Packer, of course, remains an Anglican. Robert Webber also develops a central ecclesiological

---

[11]Hall, "Back to the Fathers," p. 31.

theme, authentic worship in the midst of a changing world. Webber particularly focuses on the crisis and future of evangelical worship. Joel Scandrett draws on both John Wesley's and Wolfhart Pannenberg's understandings of the Eucharist in proposing the possibility of reclaiming eucharistic piety within the American evangelical tradition.

William J. Abraham and Geoffrey Wainwright discuss issues closely related to Methodist and Wesleyan themes. The United Methodist Church, Oden's church home, finds itself in the midst of heated debate on a number of theological and ecclesial matters. Abraham ponders the question of whether those committed to classical and apostolic faith should remain within the United Methodist Church or break away. Wainwright writes in a somewhat similar vein, particularly centering on John Wesley's thoughts on schism, heresy and ecclesial unity.

A number of essays are clustered around more general theological themes. Carl Braaten, for instance, examines what can be learned from eight critical theological disputes that have occurred in approximately the last one hundred years. Stanley Grenz and John Franke ask how the church's tradition can be wisely retrieved in evangelical circles, particularly from a nonfoundationalist perspective. Alan Padgett, like Robert Webber, investigates the connection between theological reflection and Christian worship, especially in the "postmodern university." Wolfhart Pannenberg contributes an essay on a topic close to his heart: the importance of the bodily resurrection of Jesus. Richard John Neuhaus presents an analysis of C. S. Lewis in the public square, drawing interesting connections to Thomas Oden's life and thought. Finally, Daniel Clendenin offers "A Poem of Saint Bonaventure," a meditation of sorts on the importance of the life of the mind and the heart.

Though our contributors traverse broad terrain in their essays, a common theme unites them all, sometimes expressed overtly, at other times less directly. All are thankful for the life and thought of Tom Oden. Oden's call for a paleo-orthodoxy, an orthodoxy rooted in the life and thought of the early church, resonates through the essays contributed to this volume. Yes, the conclusions and emphases of the contributors may well vary, but at heart there is the fundamental consensus that we neglect our theological forebearers to our own peril. Tom Oden couldn't agree more.

Christopher A. Hall

ONE

WITH NO QUALIFICATIONS

The Christological Maximalism of the Christian East

ROBERT W. JENSON

T here could hardly be a more direct and basic confession of Christian faith than "Jesus is Lord." Nevertheless, the history of theology is in considerable part shaped by sustained reluctance to admit immediate religious and conceptual consequences of that confession. There has been a recurrent rear-guard action against them, only broken through by interventions of the Spirit. When some—usually in itself perfectly obvious—new consequence of the proposition "Jesus is Lord" has been glimpsed, a usual first reaction has been "Oh, no! That can't be right"; and an ecclesial majority has devoted great energy and ingenuity to fending it off. The weapons of the Spirit have been initially beleaguered minorities or even individuals, and the teaching authorities who have eventually justified them.

The first great such struggle I will adduce lasted some two hundred years, from around 150 until the confession of Nicea and Constantinople.

In the Bible, there is and can be only one Lord. So if Jesus is Lord, what then? It looks like Bible-readers are committed to say that he is that Lord, that he is somehow or other to be identified with the God of Israel, with the very one he called Father and taught us to call so.

But surely, said most of the church's intellectuals from the first "apologists" to Athanasius' majority opponents, that cannot be. For Jesus inhabits our temporal world, and it is—as surely everyone of course knows!—the very definition of deity that it is immune to the temporal world's contaminations, to time's challenges and problems. Jesus has, for the decisive points, a mother and an executioner, and moreover he hangs around with mortals. Whereas God does not and indeed cannot—and now I must cite a great Christian, the martyr Justin—"speak to anyone, or be seen by anyone, or appear in any particular part of earth,"[1] never mind inhabiting a womb or hanging on the cross. So Mediterranean antiquity had taught Justin to honor deity, and so we epigones of that civilization still think. God is—obviously!—"immovable," "impassible," "invisible," "unchangeable," "unplaceable," "immaterial,"[2] and in short everything that Mary's boy and the victim on the cross is not.

Or as we might now state the same objection, God is obviously beyond and above any of the temporal stories the particular Jewish and Christian communities tell of him. Surely God is not bound to one stretch of history or one community or one religion, but lies beyond all such mundanities. Surely we have to be more widely inclusive and dialogic than that. And surely God does not actually speak to us, but must, as my denomination once officially declared, be glimpsed only in bits and pieces, as our metaphorical exertions strain through the distances of his metaphysical purity. In short, also deteriorated modernism thinks, surely God is everything that Mary's boy and the victim on the cross is not. To suit us late-comers of Mediterranean religion also, "Jesus is Lord" requires major qualifications.

In that first round in the ancient church the search for an escape from the gospel's plain consequence was channeled by a basic phenomenon of the faith, which is obtrusive in Scripture, built into the church's worship from the start, and too prominent in both to be disregarded. I have elsewhere described this phenomenon as "primary trinitarianism," the trinitarian pattern or logic of all original Christian discourse. Here I will merely point it out.

The New Testament cannot speak of God at all without somehow, as it were, touching the three bases: Father, Son and Spirit. For example at random, "For through him [Christ], we . . . have access in one Spirit to the Father" (Eph 2:18). "But it is God who establishes us . . . in Christ; . . . [and] has . . . given us his Spirit" (2 Cor 1:21-22). And so on every page of the epistles and other writings. And baptismal and eucharistic invocation of the triune name, "Father, Son and Holy Spirit," and prayer in the defining Christian pattern, to the Father with the Son in

---

[1] Justin Martyr, *Dialogue with Trypho*, p. 127.
[2] Ibid.

the Spirit, were the substance of the church's worship from the beginning.

This logic did not appear from nowhere. It distilled the plot of God's whole history with Israel, as the first believers read it in their Scripture and as they had experienced its denouement in the Resurrection and Pentecost.

Jesus notoriously addressed the God of Israel as "Father" and referred to him as "my Father," just thereby making himself out to be God's Son, and that in a way more personal and essential than the Messianic title had usually been thought to open. Perhaps what was most deeply offensive in this, even when the exact nature of the offense remained mostly subliminal, was that he thereby claimed the role of *Israel* for himself, claimed to be in his singular person a sort of Israel for Israel.

For the primary trinitarian sense of "the Son" is a pattern established in the Old Testament, if not usually with that label. The trinitarian Son is an other by whom God identifies himself, and with whom God is thereby identified, so that what God does to and for this other he does to and for himself, in a way to which the relation between parent and child is a created analogy, and so that God knows himself as the one who is related to this other in this way. Quite apart from occasional appearances of Father-Son language in the Old Testament, this is the very relation we see there between God and Israel.

Thus the old rabbis, to adduce a much cited passage, could look back on the whole of Israel's Bible and history and say, "Israel (can even say) to God, 'You have redeemed yourself. . . .' For wherever Israel was exiled, the *Shekinah* [that is, the inner-Israelite identity of God] went with them into exile; . . . and when at the end of days they return, the *Shekinah* will return with them."[3] What the Lord does to Israel he does to himself, in that the *Shekinah* shares Israel's lot and the Lord's being.

As for the Spirit, he had always been there in Israel's story with God and in the same way as he was now experienced in the church.

So back to Justin and his successors. The trinitarian logic of their Scripture and worship channeled their search for a way to interpret the identification of Jesus with the Lord: he had to be understood as the Son of the Father, and *so* to be Lord. And so far so very good. But at the same time this situation seemed to indicate a way of escape from the unwelcome implications of "Jesus is Lord." For "the Son" of primary trinitarianism appears in the New Testament under another title also, "the Word." And the one with this title they thought they recognized.

The notion of the divine "Word" or Logos was a chief item of late Mediterranean antiquity's general construal of the world, and so of the intellectual and religious apparatus which Gentile converts, and indeed some Hellenized Jews, brought with them. And in that construal the Logos functioned exactly to bridge

---

[3] *Mekhilta Y* to Exodus 12:41.

the gap between antiquity's immovable, impassible and silent deity and the temporal world in which this deity cannot be implicated. The Logos is on the one side the sense, the rationally comprehensible order, which the temporal world, despite its chaotic foundations, does exhibit. And since the world with its order derives from the divine, the Logos is on the other side the divine conception of the world; if a personal or semi-personal God is contemplated, the Logos is its rationality. Thus the Logos is on the one hand divine but on the other hand informs our temporal world. As the Logos has its origin in God, it does have an origin and so is not absolutely eternal. Yet as the sense and order of the changing world, the Logos must itself be unchanging. And so the Logos is halfway between absolute eternity and sheer temporality. Which is just what the Christian elites wanted.

The Logos, said Justin and Theophilus and their successors, is an "other God," "the next Power *after* the Father of all, a sort of Offspring." This entity, in his relative deity and relative temporality, can, if it comes to that, speak to mortals and appear to them.

So they had their escape. The Logos, they said, is that Son named in the trinitarian rhetoric and naming. In Jesus this Logos has come to inhabit the world of which he is the eternal meaning. He has become "incarnate" in Jesus, so that in converse with Jesus we may finally be rescued from ignorance of God's truth. And so far their proposition is a permanent contribution to Christian thinking. But in it they found a way in which Jesus can be said to be identified with the one Lord without—impossibly, of course—saying that God has a mother or a cross: Jesus is the incarnation of an entity who is a mini-step from God, yet so little down, so little different from real God, that from our perspective it makes no difference.

This will not do, and in the not too long run that was perceived. For it was the center of the revelation to Israel that the Lord is a ferociously jealous God, that he brooks no almost-gods, no "next" powers "after" the Father of all. "Hear, O Israel, the Lord your God is one God," is the first creed of the church also. In the Bible there is the Lord, the Creator of all things, and there are his creatures, and there is nothing in between; there is no ontological overlap, no pantheon of not-quite-gods or divine creatures.

So which is the Logos, Creator or creature? For such Bible-readers as were the ancient churchmen, the question could not be ignored, but it could be long suppressed. Until finally poor Arius pressed it so urgently that it had to be faced, whereupon the church blew apart.

The outcome is familiar. A few thinkers took up Arius's challenge and faced the church with the stark alternative: either stop worshiping the Son, because he is a creature and Christians do not worship creatures, or acknowledge that the

Son is Creator, God Almighty. For a time such radicals were a minority, yet with this stern biblical reasoning they eventually bullied the church, kicking and screaming, into the confession of Nicea and Constantinople, that the Son who is *from* God is nevertheless, or rather just so, himself *true* God, that in the case of *this* God, being from God is not incompatible with being 100 percent God.

The thought was achieved that has since enabled all specifically Christian thought on any given subject: that to *be* God the Father is first to be the Father of this Son, and just and only so to be God; that to *be* God the Son is first to be the Son of this Father, and just and only so to be God, and that to *be* God the Spirit is first to be the Spirit of this Father resting on this Son, and just and only so to be God; so that only in their mutuality *is* there God at all. God—if I may use my own jargon—is what happens between Jesus and the one he called Father, as they are freed for each other by their Spirit.

So Jesus is the Son, who is of one being with the Father, either of whom can be called Lord and neither of whom can be called the Lord without the other. From A.D. 381 on that has been the dogma of the holy catholic church. The matter is surely settled—except that it was not settled at all.

For the old pagan dogma of our civilization, that God—obviously—is impassible, inaccessible, immovable and so forth, remained unbroken on its own turf as the definition of deity. If it was now Christian dogma that God the Son is 100 percent God, does not that have to mean that *he*, God the Son, is impassible, inaccessible, immovable and so on? That is, everything that Mary's crucified child is not?

Jesus is the Son and the Son is God. The compound sentence contains two instances of "is." If it has become dogma that the "is" in "the Son is God" is not to be tampered with, then escape from the compound sentence's unwelcome implications must be sought in mitigating the other "is," in "Jesus is the Son." Within the great church, this "is" was never so denied as by the Gnostics, but in many quarters it was badly weakened. The argument was in full swing before the ink was dry at Constantinople: the second hypostasis of God, God the Son and Logos, surely cannot in his own identity have a mother and a cross; therefore Jesus, who has both, must be one and the Son another.

And in our time we go from some of their recoilings to some of our own. Surely the second hypostasis of God, God the Son and Logos, cannot have an ethnic identity, particularly not Jewish—though this one is now a bit out of fashion, having been tested in practical politics. Surely the second hypostasis, God the Logos, cannot have a gender, or anyway not male. Surely the second hypostasis of God cannot indeed be identified with *any* particular historical person, however stipulated. As a well-known and currently practicing theologian of my denomination once wrote, defending newly invented baptismal formulas,

"Surely not even Jenson would want to *identify* Jesus with the Son of God."

What happened was that after Constantinople the search for an escape from the consequences of "Jesus is Lord" simply shifted a notch. If the "is" in "the Son is God" must be left alone, the one in "Jesus is the Son" can be the target. The new move was so to mitigate the "is" between the Son and Jesus that temporality's suffering can be left to Jesus and eternity's glory to the Son.

Again we can easily translate to our own apostasies: surely we must leave the masculinity to Jesus and the androgyny to the Son, the particularity to Jesus and the universality to the Son, the victimhood to Jesus and the righteous self-acceptance to the Son—and so on again.

Perhaps, it was put forward after Constantinople, we may say that the Son so "inhabits" Jesus that the man Jesus is a temple wholly transparent to his presence, or that the Son is so personally "conjoined" with Jesus that from our point of view they cannot be told apart, or that they too will be in fact one person at the End, after the suffering is over.

Perhaps, as we would now put it, we may say that Jesus is so perfect a metaphor or avatar of the Son that from our point of view they are indistinguishable—though from, for example, an Indian or pagan Norwegian or inner-city point of view they can easily be. Or that "the Christ," who is the energy of everyone's religious aspiration, is incarnate in Jesus' teaching and example. Or that . . .

Whether Nestorius was a Nestorian or not—or whether or not there *were* any Nestorians—"Nestorianism" is of course our grab-bag label for this kind of thinking. Notoriously, Nestorianism was ruled out by a great council at Chalcedon in 451 as one extreme, and an almost entirely fictional heresy fathered on a poor innocent named Eutyches was ruled out as an opposite extreme. The Son, said Chalcedon, is as "one and the same," born of God and born of Mary; so much for Nestorianism. Yet, said the council, the two "natures" of divinity and humanity are intact in him, with each its characters and capacities; so much for Eutyches. And, so far, I suppose, so good.

And that is where my seminary education stopped—of course I was luckier than some seminarians now, who are not even introduced to the subject. Christology was taken care of, it was supposed, and we went on to other matters. Or if we lingered, it was to discuss whether something called "Chalcedonian orthodoxy" was still viable, many having declared it was not. The sad part is: at Chalcedon the history of Christology had just gotten to the interesting bits.

In fact, Chalcedon settled almost nothing. The actual subject of discussion in the period just before the council and at the council was the Christology of Cyril of Alexandria. Adulation of his theology by some and worries about it by others made up the actual matter at hand; those we call Nestorians were already a lost cause. And the council fathers fudged it.

Cyril's great concern was that the story told in the Gospels of the doings and sufferings of the one named Jesus, in all its parts and aspects, be understood as the story of God the Son. His concern was for what we would now call the *narrative* content of "Jesus is Lord." The story told in the Gospels is at once a story of majesty and victimization, of divine authority and human suffering. It is a story of the birth of Immanuel from the blood and serum of a womb, of exaltation to the Father by being hung on a cross. Not all Cyril's formulations could be fortunate; for language fails us here. But his concern was steadfast: this whole story is the story of God the Son. Jesus, the life told by the story the Gospels tell, is the Lord.

The formulas of Chalcedon do not really meet Cyril's concern, as his more percipient disciples quickly saw. The fathers of Chalcedon did attach some of Cyril's writings to their decrees as a legitimate interpretation. But they attached a letter of the then pope also, the so-called Tome of Leo, in spite of its saying the exact opposite. According to Leo, "Each nature is the agent of what is proper to it, working in fellowship with the other: the Word doing what is appropriate to the Word and the flesh what is appropriate to the flesh. The one shines forth in the miracles; the other submits to the injuries." If this is not Nestorianism, it is something rather worse. The Son does the saving, the man Jesus does the suffering. The Son does the self-affirming, Jesus does the victim part.

With this intervention the West mostly drops out of the christological story. The enormous analytical energy which Latin theology would develop in its middle centuries, insofar as it was concerned for Christology, tended to be devoted to refining and polishing Christology of Leo's type. And that is to say, at the heart of the theology Western Christians have inherited there is a retreat from the most primitive consequences of the gospel, a palpable mitigation of the confession that Jesus is Lord.

Indeed it must be said: the facility with which contemporary American and European academic and church-bureaucratic theology can separate "the Christ" or "the Logos" from Jesus, is simply the coming home to roost of chickens long incubated in Western theology. The Word does his business and the man Jesus his: the "one shines forth in the miracles, the other submits to the injuries." So Jesus is male, but never mind, "the Christ" is whatever sexuality we prefer. Jesus is Jewish, but the Logos is ethnically malleable. Jesus is voluntarily poor, but the Christ can even represent our aspirations to be rich.

Or we can run it the other way around. We can represent *Jesus* to suit us, whether as an early version of Trotsky or as a beach-boy guru or as the archetypical social worker or as whatever turns us on, while claiming at the same time to remain perfectly orthodox and biblical in our thinking about the Son.

It was in the East that the interesting discussion continued. That is, went on in a history to which my seminary education—and for that matter, except by accident, my graduate education—devoted no attention at all. It was all, we gathered, a succession of "controversies"—monophysitic, theopaschite, monergistic, monothelitic and iconoclastic—with little relevance to us.

And then there was the matter of the "neo-Chalcedonians" within the post-Chalcedon imperial church—including, as I found out only a few years ago, the Emperor Justinian himself—who labored to make Chalcedon say what in their view it should have. A few months ago at a conference, I identified myself as a neo-Chalcedonian, and shocked a colleague, who said she had never heard anyone admit such a thing.

Having mentioned myself, I may further confess that I began teaching in a seminary still with the obscure impression that this history, which stretched from, let us say, 450 to 775, a 325-year history of passionate spiritual and conceptual argument, merely marked the beginning sad decline of the Eastern churches, of their captivity to scholastic hairsplitting and imperial religious politics. I had early come upon Werner Elert's wonderful book on the monophysites and had acquired great respect for them. But then came something about "three chapters" and the monergites and the monothelites and the folks who destroyed so much art and so what?

The monophysites themselves were and are simply the most stubborn of Cyril's disciples, and having described Cyril's concern we have described theirs. They alone of the contending parties could say without equivocation such things as that when Jesus cried "My God, my God, why have you forsaken me?" this was "spoken . . . by the incarnate Logos of God himself," or that "the holy, almighty, immortal God was crucified for us and died." But even they frightened themselves when they did.

The "monergistic" controversy of the early seventh century may well have been so entangled in its own language as to be the fight about language we have been told it was. Neo-Chalcedonians within the imperial church tried to throw a bridge to the monophysites by proposing that though there were two natures in Christ—Chalcedon had settled that—these had but one "action" between them. After a relatively brief period of total confusion, the emperor in 638 forbade theological use of the language.

But the suppression of the monergistic controversy only triggered the "monothelitic" controversy. Only partly daunted by their previous failure, Neo-Chalcedonian theologians proposed, for the wooing of the monophysites, that although there are two natures in Christ there is only one *will*. And *that* touched a genuine religious nerve and started a great man and theologian into furious thought, Maximus called Confessor.

Such recorded petitionary prayers of Jesus as "Father, if it be possible, let this cup pass from me. Nevertheless, not my will but yours be done" had always been a problem. How could the Son want something different than does the Father? Theologians had been tempted to explain such passages away, even sometimes saying Jesus was play-acting to provide an example for us. But when the monothelite proposal called these prayers freshly to Maximus's consideration, he refused to dodge their plain sense. What occurred in Gethsemane and elsewhere, he said, was obviously Jesus' human decision, indeed a decision made in suffering, to defer his will to the divine will. But that locates this act of choice in his "human nature;" and that means that as there are two natures in Christ, divine and human, there must be two wills in Christ, divine and human.

After a struggle in the course of which Maximus was tortured, to earn his title "Confessor," the sixth ecumenical council condemned monothelitism and affirmed Maximus's "dyothelitism." All of which seems routine and formulaic enough, except that a remarkable dialectic had occurred in Maximus's thinking. It is hard enough to see how there can be one person who is two natures, divine and human, but how can there be a one person who has two *wills*?

I must brutally abbreviate one of the most elegant and subtle discussions in intellectual history. Maximus' analysis runs somewhat as follows: As the Son is the human Jesus, he decides to obey the Father's will for him, decisively the Father's command that he suffer for his fellows. He assents to the Father's command, in Gethsemane and otherwise, and this assent is a true act of his humanity, a painful human decision achieved with struggle. The man Jesus has willed our salvation by being obedient to the Father even to death.

But in the Son's divine nature, that is, as he is the second trinitarian hypostasis, he does not have individual decisions to make, for the divine nature is what he and the Father and the Spirit are *mutually*. The Son's divine will is simply his participation in the triune life, which is in one of its aspects a single great act of decision.

Thus the Son's individual act of suffering decision, to die for our salvation, is his *human* decision, which however *occurs* as an event in the triune life. "Thus his act of willing is, as a describable act, exactly like ours; but its ontological location transcends ours and is divine."[4] Jesus' "Let it be so" in the Garden and elsewhere is a proper human decision, but one that only occurs as God the Son's actuality in the triune life.

That is, pushing a bit but I think not too much: Jesus' painful human choice is what happens in God as the actuality of the Son. At any rate, finally Maximus can

---

[4]*Opuscula* 91.60C.

say it: the Son is the "Suffering God."[5]

And so finally enough of the history recitation. Maximus has said what had eventually to be said, and in the West has not yet been fully acknowledged: the man Jesus, exactly as his personhood is defined by the life story told in the Gospels, is the one called the Son, the second identity of God. *Jesus* is the Son, with no qualifications.

And that is: the other by whom the Father identifies himself and with whom the Father is thus identified, is Mary's boy and the victim on the cross. If we can think of God asking, "Who am I?" we must know that he answers himself, "Who I am is the Begetter of that man. Who I am is the one who sent him to the cross. Who I am is the one who raised him from the dead."

Or put it so: the story told by the Gospels, as the denouement of the story told in the Old Testament, is the story of God's determining who and what sort of God he is. And that finally is why so much rides on who this man Jesus is.

The Father has defined his deity itself by the appeal of that man, "Father, forgive them": to be God *is* to be the one who says "Yes" in that exchange. That is why there is hope of salvation. The Father has defined his deity itself by that man's hospitality to publicans and sinners: to be God is to justify the ungodly. That is why *we* have hope of salvation. It is because the Father has defined deity by that man's permission to piggyback our prayers on his, sharing his address to "Father," that we can pray with certainty of hearing. Shifting for a moment to metaphysics, it is because that Father has defined being by Jesus' promise to be with us, that a loaf and cup here and now can *be* his body and blood. And so forth through as much of the Gospels' story as needed for any homiletic or confessional occasion.

What if Jesus were in fact a sort of male Shirley MacLaine? And *he* were risen to be the Son? Then that is the kind of God there would be. Almighty Boopsie in heaven. What if Jesus were in fact a liberal politician? And he were risen to be the Son? Then standard Protestantism would be *true*. What if Jesus were in fact an unconditionally accepting therapist? One can only set one's nightmares in order.

Mary is the Mother of God. *Unus ex Trinitate mortuus est pro nobis.* One of the Trinity is a Palestinian Jew who came eating and drinking and forgave sin and prophesied implausible glory. Jesus saves. These and more sentences like them are the great metaphysical truth of the gospel, without which it is all religious palaver and wish fulfillment and metaphorical projection. Jesus really is Lord because he is one of the Trinity, and that is our salvation.

---

[5] *Ambigua*, 91.1037B. Maximus is quoting Gregory, but out of context.

Two

Nature Wild & Tame in St. John Chrysostom's On the Providence of God

Christopher A. Hall

I first met Tom Oden as a graduate student at Drew University in the fall of 1987. I was already familiar with aspects of Oden's thought but did not know what to expect in a personal encounter. As I entered Drew University's Great Hall I found my name posted on a list of new graduate students and was pleased to see that Tom had been selected as my adviser. I made my way to Wesley House, found Tom in his office and a relationship began that has continued over the years. I was immediately impressed by how well Tom combined a warm pastoral heart with a vigorous, inquiring, critical mind. I felt safe to ask the questions I needed to ask, especially regarding the relevance of the church and its tradition for modern life.

As Tom introduced me to the life and thought of the early church during my time at Drew, I progressively realized that a look backward is sometimes the wisest course for forming and framing a step forward. It is in this spirit that I offer the following thoughts on Chrysostom's understanding of divine providence as expressed and demonstrated in the natural world. I have written the essay both as a testament to my friendship and admiration for Tom Oden, and as an instance of the abiding importance of patristic perspectives for the issues that continue to face Christ's church in the modern world.

During the last years of his life St. John Chrysostom, bishop of Constantinople, found himself living in exile in the desolate village of Cucusus in the mountains of Armenia. His sufferings in exile were severe: harsh winters, separation from beloved friends, frequent illness and the constant threat of Isaurian incursions. In a letter to the deaconess Olympias, Chrysostom describes his first winter in Cucusus:

> For the winter, which has become more than commonly severe, brought on a storm of internal disorder even more distressing, and during the last two months I have been no better than one dead, no worse . . . in spite of endless contrivances I could not shake off the pernicious effects of the cold. . . . I underwent extreme sufferings, perpetual vomiting following headache, loss of appetite, and constant sleeplessness.[1]

Not only were the physical conditions in Cucusus harsh but Chrysostom faced daily the stress and sadness of separation from the church in Constantinople he had shepherded faithfully. What sense could one make of this turn of events? How were the purposes and plan of God present and active in his difficult circumstances? How was God's providential care and power manifest in a place such as Cucusus? Might even such harsh winters reveal the purposes of God?

In these last years of Chrysostom's life—which indeed would end with death in exile—Chrysostom pondered God's providence and wrote his last great theological work, *On the Providence of God*. Chrysostom addressed this work "to those troubled by the lawless deeds of recent days."[2] He describes his treatment of providence as a "medicine" at times difficult to swallow but finally restorative in its effect. It is concocted from the "word," a word equivalent to "medical instruments, medicines, food and drink, and money." It is "all these things for sick people."

> For this remedy nourishes more than bread, restores more effectively than a drug and cauterizes more powerfully than fire without causing any pain. At the same time it checks the foul-smelling tides of perverse reasonings. Sharper than iron, it painlessly cuts away the infected areas without causing any expenditure of money or deepening one's poverty. Therefore, having prepared this remedy, we are sending it to everyone. I know that all will benefit from this treatment, provided they set their thoughts on our words with thoroughness and good will.[3]

A word or two about *On the Providence of God* as a whole before we take a closer look at Chrysostom's understanding of nature as a fruitful illustration of God's providence in particular. In *On the Providence of God* Chrysostom introduces four

---

[1]Chrysostom, *Letters to Olympias*, Nicene and Post-Nicene Fathers, first series [hereafter NPNF1] (Peabody, Mass.: Hendrickson, 1994), 9:297. I have slightly modified the translation.
[2]Chrysostom, *On the Providence of God*, intro.
[3]Ibid., 1.3-1.4.

main theses that he defends and illustrates throughout the work:

1. The means one uses to interpret reality—what Chrysostom speaks of as personal disposition—determines what each person sees and understands of God's providential purposes and acts. That is to say, Chrysostom insists that one's hermeneutical stance—whether one views reality through the interpretive lens the gospel provides or not—determines how well we perceive and understand God's purposes. Chrysostom urges his readers to "learn to think and live like a Christian," enfolding life's events within the boundaries of the gospel and interpreting them accordingly. By doing so, "you will not only not be harmed by any of these events, but will reap the greatest benefits."[4]

The one who has learned to think like a Christian, the one whose thinking has been shaped by the gospel and the realities it represents, will not judge by appearances. Instead, genuine believers will remain sensible and vigilant, wary of making a premature judgment concerning God's actions or creation. They will understand that the events of this life *in themselves* are indifferent matters and take on the character of good or evil for us *according to our response to them*. Those who stumble over the events God allows to occur "would be more correct in reckoning their stumbling to themselves, and not to the nature of the events."[5]

The possible stumbling blocks life and life's arena produces do not arise from the nature of things in and of themselves, but from the inability of the observer to see reality clearly, an interpretive weakness that one can avoid through the development of a "well-disposed" character. This interpretive disposition, formed by the Holy Spirit as individuals accept the truths of the gospel and incorporate them into their lives, is the central factor in determining whether God's world will be understood or not. Those who are "worldly, difficult to lead, self-willed, and utterly carnal," will continually misread God's providence because they lack the eyes to see him at work, a vision that comes only to those who are actively exercising faith, that is, allowing their perspective to be shaped by the gospel and acting accordingly.[6]

2. Many of God's actions in the world will remain incomprehensible even to the faithful Christian. Chrysostom argues that there are limitations and boundaries imposed by the both the nature of human reason and the character of God's providence itself. A failure to observe these epistemological boundaries will result in spiritual sickness.

What, therefore, is the cause of such a sickness? A curious mind preoccupied with

---

[4]Ibid., 22:11; cf. Source Chrétiennes [hereafter SCh.], *Sur la Prov.*, 22:11, p. 262.

[5]Ibid., 14:7; cf. SCh., *Sur la Prov.*, 14:7, p. 206.

[6]Ibid., 7:1; cf. SCh., *Sur la Prov.*, 7:1, p. 108.

vain questions, one that wants to understand all the causes of everything that comes to pass and to strive contentiously with the incomprehensible and ineffable providence of God. It shamelessly scrutinizes and concerns itself with a subject which in its very nature is infinite and untraceable.[7]

Rather than prying into things that at the present time cannot be fathomed, those seeking a knowledge of God's providence should be like clay in the potter's hands, "following wherever the artist leads, not resisting, not prying into things."[8] Again and again Chrysostom derides an inappropriately inquisitive attitude as audacious, insane, obstinate, foolish, improper, mad, impudent, shameless, bold, inappropriate, ignorant, indiscrete, arrogant, ridiculous and curious.

3. The love and goodness of God is a fundamental presupposition for understanding and interpreting all of God's actions, whether seen in the incarnation, daily events or nature itself. Hence, Chrysostom's methodology for understanding providence is fundamentally deductive rather than inductive. Chrysostom insists that key revealed truths, whether in nature, Scripture or history, must be accepted as necessary presuppositions for correctly discerning God's providence. Primary among these is God's love for humanity. And where can this love most clearly be seen? In the cross. Indeed, Chrysostom delights in the way the incarnation and cross have turned the values of the world upside down. Out of seeming defeat, disgrace, suffering and the reality of death comes unimaginable victory.

In short, in the cross all the major themes of Chrysostom's understanding of providence intersect. If what appeared to be the greatest tragedy in the history of the world *is actually* the most blessed event, Christians can have an entirely different perspective on the circumstances of their own lives and the arena in which their lives are lived. The cross is "the foremost good," "a proof of God's great providence, goodness, and love."[9] The primary paradigm of the cross, then, becomes the pattern on which Christians are to mold their own understanding of God's providence at work in their lives and of how God's love and goodness manifest themselves in life between the ages.

4. Chrysostom would be quick to admit that our present situation in the world must also be interpreted in light of God's ultimate goal and end for human history. The *present* must be viewed in light of the *end*, and premature opinions as to the goodness of providence must be delayed until history itself reaches the conclusion God has set for it. Because only the end of history will finally clarify God's actions in history, our present interpretive stance must be one of patience and humility. At

---

[7]Ibid., 2:1; cf. SCh., *Sur la Prov.*, 2.1, p. 60.

[8]Ibid., 2:16; cf. SCh., *Sur la Prov.*, 2.16, p. 70.

[9]Ibid., 15, intro.; 17, intro.; cf. SCh., *Sur la Prov.*, 15, intro., p. 214; 17, intro., p. 224.

present we know only a little. Paul himself, Chrysostom reminds his reader, warned that "if anyone thinks he knows something, he does not yet know as he ought to know" [1 Cor 8:2]. "He goes on to demonstrate," Chrysostom comments, "that our present knowledge is grossly deficient and that complete knowledge is reserved for the age to come. Only a very small amount has been given to us at the present time."[10]

Hence, during this present in-between time God's providence will often remain "indescribable," "ineffable, inexpressible, and incomprehensible."[11] Chrysostom teaches, however, that this incomprehensibility does not cloud either its wonder or its promise for the future. God's character and promise are the guarantee "that in every circumstance all things that come to us from him have a favorable outcome—provided that our activities don't get in the way."[12] The prudent and wise course is to await the final outcome of events. "Above all," Chrysostom counsels, "one should not inquire too inquisitively, neither at the beginning of events nor at their conclusion. But if you are so curious and unduly inquisitive, wait for the final outcome and consider how things will turn out. Don't be troubled or disturbed at the outset."[13]

Chrysostom's view of the future, then, clearly informs and influences his attitude toward God's providential actions in this present life, including God's providence as seen in the natural world. Chrysostom knows his readers are in danger of losing heart. The church has been scattered. Persecution is rampant. Families are breaking apart. Only a perspective that includes the future within its boundaries will be broad enough to encompass these trying times without breaking under their pressure. "The true life," Chrysostom writes, "and the trustworthy and unchanging realities await us in the future. For the circumstances and events of the present life have the character of a journey, but the realities of the future await us in our true homeland."[14]

If this is indeed true, if this present life is a "journey," if God's goal for us reaches fulfillment in a life we have yet to experience fully, what are the lessons God is trying to teach us now? That is to say, the character of God's providence and of our own experience, circumstances and natural environment will become clearer to us as we recognize the character of our present time. Our expectations and interpretations of life in the present natural order must be shaped by God's goals for this in-between time. For example, pilgrims on a journey will interpret the terrain—

---

[10]Ibid., 2:13; cf. SCh., *Sur la Prov.*, 2:13, p. 68.

[11]Ibid., 8:14; cf. SCh. *Sur la Prov.*, 8:14, p. 142.

[12]Ibid.

[13]Ibid., 9:1; cf. SCh. *Sur la Prov.*, 9:1, p. 144.

[14]Ibid., 11:3; cf. SCh., *Sur la Prov.*, 11:3, p. 180.

including nature itself—differently from settlers who are attempting to construct a permanent residence. Attitudes toward trials, priorities, possessions, time and the natural world will all be affected accordingly.[15]

How might God, for example, have structured the natural world to facilitate the journey of a pilgrim? If, as Chrysostom puts it, "the present life is a wrestling school, a gymnasium, a battle, a smelting furnace, and a dyer's house of virtue," might not God have structured nature itself to aid in this process of shaping and forming Christian character? What might characterize the natural world if it is created by God to be the arena for shaping human beings more fully into the image of Christ until the fulfillment of the ages?

Near the beginning of *On the Providence of God* Chrysostom writes that he is "concocting this treatment, not only by drawing from the Divine Scriptures, but also from the events which occur in this present life and which continually take place."[16] He widens the source of his inquiry into providence because, as he puts it, he realizes there are some people "who do not pay attention to the Scriptures" and yet can still benefit from what he has to say "if only they are willing."[17] Chrysostom will augment his argument, then, from two further sources: this life's events and God's providence as demonstrated in the natural world itself.

This is not to say, however, that Chrysostom ignores or downplays God's voice in nature for those who also accept the authority of Scripture. Indeed, Chrysostom contends that God's evaluation of nature in the pages of Scripture is the primary grid one must utilize to avoid misunderstanding God's intentions in the natural order. Nature in itself contains aspects that are quite beneficial to humanity and elements that are more difficult to reconcile with God's love and goodness. Its goodness is not always immediately apparent.

> That is to say, among those things which God viewed were not only light, but also darkness. Not only fruit, but also thorns. Not only cultivated trees, but also wild trees. Not only sloping plains, but also poisonous reptiles. Not only fish, but also sea

---

[15] In Chrysostom's homilies on Ephesians he reflects on the foolishness of making a large house the center of one's dreams: "But as to us, let us not be insatiable . . . let us not be seeking out for splendid houses; for we are on our pilgrimage, not at home; so that if there be any that knows that the present life is a sort of journey, and expedition, and, as one might say, it is what they call an entrenched camp, he will not be seeking for splendid buildings. For who, tell me, be he ever so rich, would choose to build a splendid house in an encampment? . . . The present life is nothing else than a march and an encampment" (Chrysostom, "Homily 23," *Homilies on Ephesians*, NPNF1, 13:166; cf. Patrologia graeca [hereafter PG] 62.168B; cf. Chrysostom, "Homily 79," *Homilies on the Gospel of St. John and The Epistle to the Hebrews*, NPNF1 [Peabody, Mass.: Hendrickson, 1994], 14:293; cf. PG 59.429D-430A; cf. also Chrysostom, "Homily 17," *The Homilies on the Statues to the People of Antioch*, NPNF1, 9:457; cf. PG 49.177D-178A.

[16] Chrysostom, *Providence of God*, 1:4.

[17] Ibid., 1:5.

monsters. Not only calm seas, but also the unnavigable ocean. . . . Many were soon to be troubled by these realities and heresies born.[18]

Chrysostom teaches much the same message in his homilies on Genesis. He argues, as in *On the Providence of God*, that heresies are born when we refuse to accept God's judgment concerning the goodness of creation.

> When we see people of good reputation giving their opinion of things that happen, we don't contradict them, but rather fall in with their opinion and often prefer their opinion to our own. So much the more in the case of the God of all things, the Creator of everything we can see, should we do likewise: we should learn his judgment on things, subdue our own reasonings, and instead of presuming further we should be content with the knowledge that everything has been produced by a word coming from him and by his loving kindness, and that nothing has been created idly or to no purpose. Even if, through the limitations of our own reasoning, we should be in ignorance of created things, he himself in his own wisdom and thoughtful love produced all things.[19]

If God, the one who has created all things, does not hesitate to label all creation "good," this is also the interpretive stance his believing community is to assume, even before those aspects of nature that appear to be harmful.

> Therefore, having heard the prophet say to you that God saw these things and praised them, stop trying to find another test and demonstration of their goodness. Don't ask: "In what way are they good?" For the declaration of the opinion and judgment of the one who created them is more certain than the demonstration drawn from the works themselves. . . . For if you are not satisfied with this word, but want to occupy yourself with a detailed investigation of creation, you are only flinging yourself into a violent tide of evil reasonings and billows creating a great tempest.[20]

One must exercise great care in interpreting Chrysostom at this juncture. He is painting in broad strokes, and we will misunderstand him if we believe him to be saying that the Christian should avoid close observation and examination of the natural realm. His own insights into the natural world demonstrate both a fascination with nature and a willingness to hypothesize how it functions.

In his *Homilies on the Statues*, for example, Chrysostom does not hesitate to argue that God delayed in giving humanity the Scriptures because God's revelation in nature was present for all to see. He writes:

And if so useful, for what reason, say they, were they (the Scriptures) not delivered

---

[18] Ibid., 4:2-3.

[19] Chrysostom, *Homilies on Genesis* (Washington, D.C.: The Catholic University of America Press, 1986), p. 137; cf. PG 53.88A.

[20] Chrysostom, *Providence of God*, 4:7, 10; cf. SCh., *Sur la Prov.*, 4:7, 10, pp. 84, 86.

to us from the beginning? It was because God was desirous of instructing the nature of man, not by letters, but by things. . . . By means of the Creation itself. . . . For when you see the beauty, the breadth, the height, the position, the form, the stability thereof over so long a period; hearing as it were a voice, and being instructed by the spectacle, you adorn Him who created a body so fair and strange! *The heavens may be silent, but the sight of them emits a voice, that is louder than a trumpet's sound; instructing us not by the ear, but through the medium of the eyes;* for the latter is a sense which is more sure and distinct than the former" (my emphasis).[21]

Chrysostom does believe, however, that God's own declaration concerning the goodness of creation must not be sidestepped. A humble, reverent, trusting attitude before God's declaration will lead to an exploration and enjoyment of creation, but not to a stubborn, cynical questioning of its goodness.

The "evil reasonings" he warns against are engendered by an unbelieving desire to obtain a greater knowledge and insight than is possible at present. Human reason's own weakness must be acknowledged along with the limitations its frailness imposes.

Chrysostom observes that Greeks, on the one hand, are exaggerated in their praise of creation, worshiping it as a god, while groups such as the Manichaeans deride created matter as evil.[22] Both groups error in presuming autonomous human reason is capable of making a valid, cogent judgment about the inherent goodness or evil of creation. This presumption leads to no new knowledge and produces a premature and ignorant misreading and slandering of the natural world.[23]

Chrysostom's warnings about the misuse of reason, however, do not prevent him from inviting his more skeptical readers to take a close look at the created order. Indeed, the longest chapter in *On the Providence of God* is a specific attempt to demonstrate God's provident goodness from nature to those who doubt this very thing.[24] Chrysostom appears to be annoyed that he has to conduct such an exercise, relating it to the "worldly," "self-willed" and "utterly carnal" nature of at least some of his readers.[25] He plainly believes that God's providence in nature is plain for all to see. All Chrysostom asks of his audience is a willingness to listen.

---

[21]Chrysostom, "Homily 9," *Homilies on the Statues*, NPNF1, 9:401; cf. PG 49.105B-105D, 106A. Chrysostom's close observation of the natural world is apparent when he writes: "For the spider also labours, and toils, and spreads out his fine textures over the walls, surpassing the utmost skill of woman. . . . Imitate the ass in his love to his master, and the ox also! . . . for great, great indeed is the advantage that may be gained from irrational creatures for the correction of manners" (ibid., "Homily 12," p. 420; cf. PG 49.120D-121A).

[22]Chrysostom, *Providence of God*, 4:11; cf. SCh. *Sur la Prov.*, 4:11, p. 88.

[23]Ibid., 4:10; cf. SCh., *Sur la Prov.*, 4:10, p. 86.

[24]Ibid., 7:1-39; cf. SCh., *Sur la Prov.*, 7:1-39, pp. 108, 110, 112, 114, 116, 118, 120, 122, 124, 126, 128, 130.

[25]Ibid., 7:1; cf. SCh., *Sur la Prov.*, 7:1, p. 108.

For God's providence is as plain as the sun and its rays. In each situation and place, in the wilderness, in inhabited regions and uninhabited, on earth or sea or wherever you might go, you will observe the clear and sufficient, ancient and new, reminders of this providence; voices which speak more clearly than our rational voice and are conveyed from all places, teaching those willing to listen about his constant concern.[26]

Chrysostom begins by delineating the goodness of God's providence in "the visible elements of creation." He notes that "this praiseworthy and all-harmonious creation was created for no one else but you."[27] Angels had no need for the visible, created order. They existed before it ever came into being. Instead, creation was produced for the sake of humanity, and its various characteristics were specifically designed to meet humanity's varied needs and to elicit our praise for its creator.[28]

The stars, sun and moon, for example, are both beautiful and useful. They are faithful guides for those who must travel on land and sea, and also are useful for determining the time of day and the changes of the seasons. As they mark off the significant cycles of the year, people are able to organize their lives in a prudent fashion. Utility and delight flow together.[29] The sun opens the day with the beauty of the sunrise and also provides the light and heat needed for almost every aspect of nature's function and health.[30]

Chrysostom proceeds to describe other witnesses to God's providence in nature. In a single sentence he blends together the benefits of both animate and inanimate aspects of creation, and unhesitatingly groups readily identifiable goods with characteristics of the natural world one would likely view as harmful.

One learns of God's providence from tamed and untamed animals, from savage beasts and those accustomed to human touch, from both small animals and large, from the birds which appear in the winter, summer, and autumn, from four-footed creatures, fish, plants and herbs, from those which are active in the night and those which are lively during the day, from the rains, from the passing of time, from death, from life, from the hard work which is our lot, from despondency, from relaxation....[31]

What is at first glance puzzling is Chrysostom's insistence that the dark or rough elements of nature are *created by God* and not simply the result of post-Fall distortion. While we can learn of God's providence from certain post-Fall characteristics, such as death or despondency, Chrysostom indicates that the created

---

[26]Ibid., 5:2; cf. SCh., *Sur la Prov.*, 5:2, p. 92.

[27]Ibid., 7:2; cf. SCh., *Sur la Prov.*, 7:2, p. 108.

[28]Ibid., 7:3-4; cf. SCh., *Sur la Prov.*, 7:3-4, p. 110.

[29]Ibid., 7:4-12; cf. SCh., *Sur la Prov.*, 7:4-12, pp. 110, 112, 114.

[30]Ibid., 7:14-16; cf. SCh., *Sur la Prov.*, 7:14-16, pp. 114, 116.

[31]Ibid., 7:18-19; cf. SCh., *Sur la Prov.*, 7:18-19, p. 118.

order God designates as good in its pre-Fall state contained darkness as well as
light, wild trees as well as cultivated ones, ravines as well as plains, poisonous reptiles as well as human beings, sea monsters as well as fish.[32] Nature in its pre-Fall
state demonstrates a wildness that God considers good, an untamed face that can
be dangerous, much as a live wire is lethal if treated in a careless manner.

In what way, though, are these characteristics "good"? Chrysostom directly
addresses this question in his homilies on Genesis. He frames his response by first
reminding his readers that God had called all of the created order "good." Even sea
monsters? Yes, Chrysostom replies, and adds, "although you stand in ignorance of
the reason for the created things, don't presume to find fault with their creation."[33]
The "well-disposed," discerning person will humbly observe the epistemological
boundaries God has dictated, boundaries framed by his love and power.

> I mean, if you were well disposed you would be able from the creation of these
> things to get an insight into the power of your Lord and his ineffable love—his
> power, for the reason that he caused living beings like this to be created from the
> waters by his word and command, and his love, for the reason that in creating
> them he gave each of them a particular place, and assigned them a boundless area
> of the sea so that they might not hinder one another but dwell in the waters and
> provide an example to teach us the Creator's extraordinary power and cause no
> harm to the human race.[34]

God, Chrysostom preaches, demonstrates a certain "prodigality," creating some
things for the benefit of humanity, and producing others simply so that his power
might be proclaimed and glorified. Reptiles and wild beasts are products of this
prodigality, aspects of the abundance of God's creation, an abundance meant to
"overwhelm" us and teach us "that all these things were produced by a certain wisdom and ineffable love out of regard for the human being that was destined to
come into being."[35] God has created the world that is most appropriate for the spiritual and material well-being of humanity. We can readily identify certain aspects
of creation as beneficial. The benefits of other aspects will remain beyond our
grasp. This mystery should not lead, however, to skepticism, but rather be gratefully accepted as an occasion for praise.

For example, Chrysostom comments that while not all trees are fruitbearing,
they still provide "a remarkable service" and "contribute to our well-being; we make
our houses from them and gain many other advantages contributing to our well-

---

[32]Ibid., 4:2; cf. SCh., *Sur la Prov.*, 4:2, p. 82.
[33]Chrysostom, "Homily 7," *Homilies on Genesis*, p. 97; cf. PG 53.65D.
[34]Ibid., p. 98; cf. PG 53.65D-66A.
[35]Ibid., p. 99; cf. PG 53.66D.

being."[36] Even poisonous reptiles are a gift of love. "I mean, physicians get from them many things which they employ as medications capable of promoting the health of our bodies."[37] Still, Chrysostom reminds his hearers that "when reasoning fails and the intellect proves inadequate, call to your mind the greatness of the Lord, especially from the fact that his power is such that we fail to understand precisely the meaning of the things made by him. *This is the attitude of sensible minds and sober hearts*" (emphasis added).[38]

Chrysostom's overall perspective can be further clarified in light of his earlier sermons preached on the occasion of the tax riots in Antioch in A.D. 388. These sermons illustrate many of the same principles that Chrysostom develops in *On the Providence of God* over fifteen years later.

In homily 10 Chrysostom avers that nature's beauty and weakness demonstrates its utility and God's own inherent goodness. How so? God foresaw humanity's fall into sin and tendency to make an idol out of the created order.

> For God, foreseeing these things of old, destroyed, in His wisdom, this plea of theirs. On this account He made the world not only wonderful and vast, but also corruptible and perishable; and placed therein many evidences of its weakness; . . . For it was made corruptible by the command of God. But God so commanded it for the sake of our race; for since it was to nurture a corruptible man, it was necessary that itself should also be of the same character; for of course corruptible bodies were not to dwell in an incorruptible creation.[39]

Creation's goodness then is a *functional goodness*, one that reflects God's infinite love for humanity and God's desire to create an environment purposely designed to nurture a human being's awareness of and love for God. The natural world is given to humanity as a gift, filled with grace, in the sense that it is the ideal natural environment for human beings as created in the image of God to grow, develop and exercise the responsibilities given to them by God.

In his homilies on Genesis, Chrysostom speaks of humanity as a king who must wait for his palace to be prepared for his entrance.

> Let me draw a comparison with a king on the point of entering a city on a visit: his bodyguard has to be sent on ahead to have the palace in readiness, and thus the king may enter his palace. Well now, in just the same way in this case the Creator, as though on the point of installing some king and ruler over everything on earth, first erected the whole of this scenery, and then brought forth the one destined to preside

---

[36]Cf. PG 53.67B.

[37]Chrysostom, "Homily 7," *Homilies on Genesis*, p. 100; cf. PG 53.67B.

[38]Ibid., pp. 101-2; cf. PG 53.68AB.

[39]Chrysostom, "Homily 10," *Homilies on the Statues*, NPNF1, 9:409; cf. PG 49.115B, 117D-118A.

over it, showing us through the created things themselves what importance he gave to this creature.[40]

Chrysostom defines the image of God in humanity as the control and authority God gives human beings over all things on earth. He writes: "So 'image' refers to the matter of control, not anything else. In other words, God created the human being as having control of everything on earth, and nothing on earth is greater than the human being, under whose authority everything falls."[41] This gift of authority is a sign of God's love and esteem for humanity.[42]

God places Adam in the Garden of Eden, an environment specifically designed by God to communicate to him his love and care. Even in Adam's life in the garden, however, a life described by Chrysostom as one of "freedom and great affluence,"[43] he still has specific responsibilities to perform. Adam is to till the garden. This work, though "painless and without difficulty," would keep him from falling into "indulgence" and "sloth" and would develop in him "a better frame of mind." Chrysostom pictures God as a loving father "who prevents his young child from being unsettled by great relaxation and freedom from care by devising some slight responsibility appropriate to the situation."[44] These tasks will be a "stabilizing influence" in Adam's life, preventing him "from overstepping the limit."[45]

Adam can avoid possible harmful aspects of nature as he chooses freely to respond to God in faith, a thought quite similar to Chrysostom's argument in *On the Providence of God* that nothing can harm people who do not choose to harm themselves in sin. Here Chrysostom's thought coincides well with other fathers' thoughts on the meaning of creation and its relationship to humanity.

Irenaeus, for example, contends that Adam and Eve were not created as perfect human beings but rather as infants who were to grow and mature as they relied in faithful dependence on their Creator as they lived within the world God had given them. God, "who made the things of time for man," designed the created order as the arena in which this growth could take place, "so that coming to maturity in them, he may produce the fruit of immortality."[46] God creates both the world and humanity itself as grace-filled realities, where human beings as the image of God are called and created to participate in God and to freely choose to respond to him. As Chrysostom might put it, God's creation is eminently good because it is the

[40]Chrysostom, "Homily 8," *Homilies on Genesis*, p. 107; cf. PG 53.71B.
[41]Ibid., p. 110; cf. PG 53.72D.
[42]Ibid., p. 134; cf. PG 53.86B.
[43]Ibid., "Homily 13," p. 177; cf. PG 53.109D.
[44]Ibid., "Homily 14," p. 185; cf. PG 53.113D-114A.
[45]Ibid., p. 185; PG 53.114A.
[46]Irenaeus, *Against Heresies*, Ante-Nicene Fathers (Peabody, Mass.: Hendrickson, 1994), 1:466.

ideal environment for humanity to pursue its vocation.

The darker aspects of creation, such as cliffs, poisonous reptiles and unnaviga-ble oceans, function within God's providence to accomplish divine purposes for the center of creation, men and women created in the image of God.[47] Hence, the refrain throughout Chrysostom's *On the Providence of God* that the natural world and the events of daily life were produced "for no one else but you."[48]

> And all these things, Friend, are for your sake—arts and crafts for you, life's pursuits and activities, cities, villages, sleep for you, death for your sake, life for your sake, growth, so many works of nature and such a magnificent world in its present state for you, a world that will be even better in the future for your sake.[49]

In a moving passage from Chrysostom's homilies on Genesis he states:

> I mean, even if pagans shout and scream a thousand times, I will proclaim it from the housetops that all these things were created for the human race, since the Cre-ator is sufficient of himself and needed none of them; instead, it was to show his love for us that he created them all, demonstrating the great regard he has for the human race, and it was for us to move from these creatures to bring to him a proper adora-tion.[50]

To sum up: As we have already observed in mentioning Chrysostom's descrip-tion of the benefits of the stars, sun and moon, he delights in demonstrating the benefits of nature for humanity and finds evidence for God's graced providence from a wide variety of witnesses in the natural world.

Again, some are immediately identifiable as good, regardless of one's theolog-ical perspective; others are recognized as such when seen within the broader boundaries of God's purposes and designs for humanity. For example, we learn of God's providence from reptiles, birds, various forms of plant life, domesti-

---

[47]John Meyendorff argues that the view of humanity prevalent in the Christian East is based on the idea of partic-ipation in God. A human being is not "an autonomous, or self-sufficient, being; his very *nature* is truly itself only inasmuch as it exists 'in God' or 'in grace.'" Grace, then, is specifically given to aid a human being in his "natural development." Nature and grace are not in opposition, but rather "express a dynamic, living, and necessary rela-tionship between God and man, different by their *natures*, but in *communion* with each other through God's en-ergy, or grace." Meyendorff resonates with the voices of Irenaeus and Chrysostom when he writes that humanity's participation in God is not a "static givenness," but rather "a challenge, and man is called to *grow* in divine life. Divine life is a gift, but also a task which is to be accomplished by a free human effort" (John Meyen-dorff, *Byzantine Theology* [New York: Fordham University Press, 1974], pp. 138-39). Chrysostom might well add that God in his providence faithfully and continually provides the arena for the challenging growth God calls us to in his grace and love.

[48]Chrysostom, *Providence of God*, 7:2, 22, 24, 31; cf. SCh., *Sur la Prov.*, 7:2, p. 108; 7:22, p. 120; 7:24, p. 122; 7:31, p. 124.

[49]Ibid., 7:33; cf. SCh., *Sur la Prov.*, 7:33, p. 126.

[50]Chrysostom, "Homily 6," *Homilies on Genesis*, p. 88; cf. PG 53.60D.

cated animals and the seasons of the year. Even the most ordinary creatures point to a wise and loving Creator. "For what," Chrysostom asks, "is smaller and more ugly than the bee? And what is more ordinary than ants and cicadas? Nevertheless, even these emit a clear voice concerning the providence, power, and wisdom of God."[51]

More harsh realities also demonstrate the providence of God. Savage beasts, death, despondency and sickness are all tools that God uses to form human character and to bridle unruly passions that would blur the understanding and distract one from the true purpose of life. That is to say, God uses pain and suffering, occasionally caused by the operations and structure of nature itself, to refocus our attention and help us to rearrange priorities that too often echo a stunted, self-centered perspective.[52]

Conclusion

How might Chrysostom's thoughts on God's providential ordering of the natural world inform our ecological perspective today? Time and space allow for only tentative explorations. Two aspects of Chrysostom's providential theology seem immediately relevant:

First, Chrysostom argues that the image of God is reflected in humanity's control and authority over the natural world. As Chrysostom expresses it, "God created the human being as having control over everything on earth . . . nothing on earth is greater than the human being, under whose authority everything falls."[53] This authority and control is a gift of love, given to humanity to be exercised responsibly. Indeed, the exercise of a responsible dominion, Chrysostom believes, rebukes the fallen human tendency toward irresponsibility, laziness and self-indulgence. Responsible care for the environment is to be a "stabilizing influence" in our lives, forcing us to look beyond ourselves toward the well-being of our broader world with all its varied inhabitants. To exploit or ignore that environment is to deface God's own image in us.

Second, God has exhibited, as Chrysostom puts it, an amazing "prodigality" or extravagance in God's creation of the world. Certain characteristics of the natural order—the seasons and their rhythms, for example—have been created to facilitate humanity's life and understanding of God's love and care. Other aspects of nature—reptiles and wild beasts come to mind—illustrate the abundance of God's creation, an extravagant prodigality designed to "overwhelm" us and teach us

---

[51]Chrysostom, *Providence of God*, 7:20; cf. SCh., *Sur la Prov.*, 7:20, p. 120.

[52]Ibid., 7:18-20, 34; cf. SCh., *Sur la Prov.*, 7:18-20, p. 118; 7:34, p. 128.

[53]Chrysostom, "Homily 8," *Homilies on Genesis*, p. 107; cf. PG 53.71B.

"that all these things were produced by a certain wisdom and ineffable love out of regard for the human being that was destined to come into being."[54]

Even if we struggle to identify all of nature's utility and benefit, we are called to preserve it in its entirety. Hence, both the wild and tame aspects of the natural world must be preserved and protected. In fact, Chrysostom appears to teach that the wild, the rugged, the untamable, the inexplicable characteristics of nature—those creatures and places that possess no immediately discernible utility and benefit for humanity—must be particular objects of our care, as we are apt to misread their meaning. They too point to the glory, wisdom and love of God. All species and areas—from the elephant to the spider, from the polar ice caps to the plains of North America—find their ultimate source and raison d'être in the mind and prodigal heart of God. It is all good and is to be preserved as such.

---

[54]Ibid., p. 99; cf. PG 53.66D.

THREE

GOD'S HOUSEHOLD OF GRACE

Hospitality in Early Christianity

AMY ODEN

T he Christian tradition has much to say about hospitality. Christians for centuries have tried to understand hospitality and its faithful expressions. Brothers and sisters in Christ who have gone before us believed the practice of hospitality was central to the Christian life. They told stories about it, lifted up examples of it, preached about it, praised it. Most importantly, they understood it to be a dynamic of God's household of grace.

The good news is that Christians are rediscovering hospitality as a virtue and a practice within the Christian life. Conversations, scholarship and conferences on hospitality in the last few years have brought attention to the ways a developed notion of hospitality might contribute to Christian community and identity as well as to mission, spiritual growth and even contemporary worship.[1] The voices lifting up hospitality are lively and hopeful, and I believe they are on to something. As the

---

[1] In 1983 Abraham J. Mahlerbe wrote, "The practice of early Christian hospitality has received some attention in the last decade, but its theological implications as perceived by the early church still await serious attention" (*Social Aspects of Early Christianity* [Philadelphia: Fortress, 1983], p. 67). That can no longer be said. Christine Pohl's most recent book reflects this trend (see *Making Room: Recovering Hospitality as a Christian Tradition* [Grand Rapids, Mich.: Eerdmans, 1999]).

conversation broadens, it is important to bring historical voices to the table, listening to what our ancestors learned and lived with regard to hospitality.

This essay will present some initial findings from early Christian sources on hospitality. The notion of welcoming the stranger can be found throughout early Christian writing and preaching. This essay will focus on two important insights in early Christian texts on hospitality. The first is that Christians must recognize themselves as strangers in the world. The second is that Christians must recognize strangers as Christ. Examples and discussion of each of these recognitions follow.

Many early Christian texts insist that Christians understand themselves first as strangers in order to then extend hospitality in the world. This is sometimes accomplished through the deliberate confusion of the roles of host and guest. Particularly in stories about hospitality offered, it is sometimes hard to tell who is giving and who is receiving. For example, Palladius tells the story of Elias, a solitary ascetic who lived near a road.[2] When a large group of visitors stopped by looking for refreshment, Elias was eager to offer hospitality but only had three loaves of bread to feed them all. Miraculously two loaves were plenty to fill all twenty guests and the loaf that was left fed Elias for twenty-five days. Elias the host became the recipient of abundance as a result of his visitors. This reversal of roles is a common theme in early Christian stories of hospitality.

Even when a role-reversal theme is not present, early Christians talk about Christian identity in terms of the stranger, the sojourner or the foreigner.[3] Christians of the first three centuries certainly understood themselves to be aliens and pilgrims in this world with citizenship in another.[4] Given their political location in the Roman Empire, it is not surprising that stranger status would be a primary way Christians understood themselves and their place in the world.

The stranger status at the heart of Christian identity has biblical roots as well as cultural and political ones. Remembering that "we were strangers in Egypt" is central to Christian identity because it is central to the salvation history told in the

---

[2]Palladius, *The Lausiac History* 51, trans. Robert T. Meyer, Ancient Christian Writers 34 (New York: Newman Press, 1964), p. 133. See chapter four for the full account.

[3]For a useful discussion of this phenomenon in early Christian writing, see Rowan A. Greer, "Alien Citizens: A Marvelous Paradox," in *Broken Lights and Mended Lives: Theology and Common Life in the Early Church* (University Park, Penn.: Pennsylvania State University Press, 1986). Also see W. H. C. Frend, *Martyrdom and Persecution in the Early Church: A Study of a Conflict from the Maccabees to Donatus* (Oxford: Basil Blackwell & Mott, 1965); Robert L. Wilken, *The Christians as the Roman Saw Them* (New Haven, Conn.: Yale University Press, 1984). For a case study, see Richard Valantasis, "The Stranger Within, The Stranger Without: Ascetical Withdrawal and the Second Letter of Basil the Great," in *Christianity and the Stranger: Historical Essays*, ed. Francis W. Nichols (Atlanta: Scholars Press, 1995), pp. 65-81.

[4]For a discussion of the eschatological dimensions of hospitality, see Thomas W. Ogletree, *Hospitality to the Stranger: Dimensions of Moral Understanding* (Philadelphia: Fortress, 1985), pp. 7ff.

Hebrew Bible.[5] God saved his people from their alien, slave status in Egypt. In delivering them God reminds them of who they truly are, his own chosen people far from home. Salvation history reinforces a central aspect of identity as alien, foreigner enslaved in a strange land or sojourner wandering in a foreign desert.

This theme continues through the New Testament writings. The letter to the Hebrews emphasizes the faithfulness of the Hebrew patriarchs in their status as "strangers and foreigners on the earth, for people who speak in this way make it clear that they are seeking a homeland" (11:13-14). They sought a true home, remaining strangers on earth all their lives.[6]

Early Christians frequently remind one another that their true allegiance is not with the powers of this world, and they must hold a sort of double consciousness, seeking to be good citizens in their communities yet never fully at home in the world. Christians under arrest often identify themselves not by referring to their nationality or province or even their family of origin, but by reference to Jerusalem or God as authoritative sources of identity. This was virtually unintelligible in the early empire. Eusebius tells the story of the martyr Pamphilius in *The Martyrs of Palestine*. When brought before judge Firmilianus, the martyrs give the names of prophets as their own, then Pamphilius claims Jerusalem as his homeland.

> He [Firmilianus] heard in reply the name of some prophet instead of his proper name. For it was their [Christians'] custom, in place of the names of idols given them by their parents, if they had such a name, to take other names; so that you would hear them calling themselves Elijah or Jeremiah or Isaiah or Samuel or Daniel. This way they themselves were inwardly true Jews, and the genuine Israel of God, not only in deeds, but in the names which they bore. When Firmilianus had heard some such name from the martyr, and did not understand the force of what he was saying, he asked next the name of his country. But he gave a second answer similar to the former, saying that Jerusalem was his country, meaning that of which Paul says, "Jerusalem which is above is free, which is our mother," and, "You have come to Mount Sion, to the city of the living God, the heavenly Jerusalem." This was what he meant. But the judge, thinking only of the earth, sought diligently to discover what that city was, and in what part of the world it was situated. He applied tortures to find out the truth. But the man, with his hands twisted behind his back, and his feet crushed by strange devices, asserted firmly that he had spoken the truth. And being questioned repeatedly what and where the city was of which he spoke, he said that it was the country of the pious alone, for no others should have a place in it, and that it

---

[5]For other references in the Hebrew Bible to stranger status see Genesis 23:4, 47:4, 9; Leviticus 19:34, 25:23; 1 Chronicles 29:15; Psalm 39:12.

[6]For other references in the New Testament to stranger status see Ephesians 2:19; Hebrews 13:1; 1 Peter 1:1, 2:11.

lay toward the far East and the rising sun. . . . But the judge being perplexed, was impatient, thinking that the Christians were about to establish a city somewhere, inimical and hostile to the Romans. So he inquired much about this, and investigated where that country toward the East was located. But when he had lacerated the young man with scourgings for a long time, and punished him with all sorts of torments, he realized that his persistence in what he had said could not be changed, and passed against him the death sentence. This was what was done to this man. And having inflicted similar tortures on the others, he sent them away in the same manner.[7]

The reigning power, in this case, judge Firmilianus, can only imagine cities located geographically, not spiritually. He completely misunderstands the identity these Christians profess, and in frustration he punishes them. This disconnect between Christian identity and earthly, pagan powers is similarly expressed in Tertullian's now famous question, "What has Athens to do with Jerusalem?"[8]

The *Epistle to Diognetus* expresses this paradox of Christian identity. Written as a defense of Christians in the face of pagan misunderstanding, the letter explains that Christians are at once citizens and foreigners.

But, inhabiting Greek as well as barbarian cities, according as the lot of each of them has determined, and following the customs of the locals in respect to clothing, food, and the rest of their regular daily life, they [Christians] display to us their wonderful and admittedly striking way of life. They dwell in their own countries, but simply as sojourners. As citizens, they share in all things with others, and yet endure all things as if foreigners. Every foreign land is to them as their native country, and every land of their birth as a land of strangers.[9]

Moreover, Christians' sense of cultural alienation was often expressed through identification with exiles and refugees. Because Christians were at times under threat from civil authorities, the act of harboring refugees who were brothers and sisters in Christ became imperative. Sheltering strangers was essential to the survival of Christianity in a hostile empire. Christians became well-known within the larger culture for their practices of hospitality and were often cited as examples of morality on this account. When Julian (the apostate) came to power in the middle of the fourth century, his attempts to revitalize pagan traditions drew heavily on the positive press Christian practices of hospitality had received, what he called the

---

[7]Eusebius, *The Martyrs of Palestine* 11, Nicene and Post-Nicene Fathers (hereafter NPNF) 2.1, ed. Philip Schaff and Henry Wace (New York: Christian Literature, 1890).

[8]Tertullian, *Prescription Against Heretics* 7, Ante-Nicene Fathers: The Writings of the Fathers Down to A.D. 325, ed. Alexander Roberts and James Donaldson (New York: Christian Literature, 1884), 3:443.

[9]*Epistle to Diognetus*, Ante-Nicene Fathers: The Writings of the Fathers Down to A.D. 325, ed. and trans. Alexander Roberts and James Donaldson (New York: Christian Literature, 1884), 1:26.

"humanity evinced by Christians towards strangers."[10] It is not a far step from understanding oneself to be a stranger in the world to identifying with other political, economic and social strangers, and vice versa.

After the reign of Constantine, Christianity enjoyed a new location of privilege and power within the culture. Yet Christians continued to use the language of stranger status to describe their identity, though with different shadings and nuances. One way some Christians expressed this status was through identification with the poor and outcast. It is not uncommon in Christian literature of the fourth and fifth centuries for Christians to enact their alien status most powerfully in economic terms. In hagiography, poverty is a standard bearer of Christian identity, signaling that this is a *real* Christian. This identification with the poor or the stranger can also be cast as an identification with Christ, who became poor and outcast on the behalf of all.

Paula (347-404) represents an early model of Christian life that many Roman matrons were to emulate. They eschewed the privileges of their rank and family status, renounced Rome and took on the identity of strangers in a foreign land. Paula went on the arduous journey to Palestine and, after visiting various holy sites, settled at Bethlehem to join Jerome in the wilderness. In a letter to her friend Marcella in Rome, Paula is eager to distance herself from the cultural mores that confer status, claiming instead to be no longer a person of importance. The lack of social distinction demonstrates stranger status.

> To these places we have come, not as persons of importance, but as strangers, that we might see in them the foremost men of all nations. . . . Among all this will be found what is, perhaps, the greatest virtue among Christians—no arrogance, no overweening pride in their chastity; all of them vie with one another in humility. Whoever is last is reckoned as first. In their dress there is no distinction, no ostentation. The order in which they walk in procession neither implies disgrace nor confers honor.[11]

Another example demonstrates that Christians no longer under political threat continued to identify themselves as citizens of another realm, as pilgrims on their way to the Holy City. John Chrysostom (c. 347-407), the great preacher at Constantinople, calls his listeners to embrace their identity as sojourners here:

> Don't you know that we live in a foreign land, as though strangers and sojourners? Don't you know that it is the lot of sojourners to be ejected when they don't think they will be, when they least expect it? This is also our lot . . . but seeing we are by

---

[10]Sozomen, *Ecclesiastical History* 15.16, NPNF 2.2 (New York: Christian Literature, 1890).
[11]Paula *Letter of Paula and Eustochium to Marcella About the Holy Places*, trans. Aubrey Stewart (London: Adam Street, 1889), p. 10.

nature sojourners, let us also be so by choice; that we be not there [with God] sojourners and dishonored and cast out. For if we are set upon being citizens here, we shall be so neither here nor there; but if we continue to be sojourners, and live in such wise as sojourners ought to live in, we shall enjoy the freedom of citizens both here and there.[12]

Chrysostom speaks plainly to his congregation: Christians are strangers by nature, and Christians are also sojourners by choice, or can be. Chrysostom enjoins Christians to choose stranger status as their identity in order to see through this world into the larger life in God.

In one of his sermons, the *Letter to the Hebrews*, Chrysostom draws on Paul and Abraham as examples of the stranger status for those who know themselves to be sojourning here.

The first virtue, indeed, the whole of virtue, is to be a stranger to this world, and a sojourner, to have nothing in common with things here and let go of them, as we would from anything strange to us. This is just like those blessed disciples did, of whom he says, "They wandered about in sheepskins, and in goat-skins, being destitute, afflicted, tormented, of whom the world was not worthy" (11:37-38).

So they called themselves "strangers," but Paul went beyond this. For he did not merely call himself a stranger, but said that he was dead to the world, and that the world was dead to him. "For the world," he says, "has been crucified to me and I to the world" (Galatians 6:14). But we, being both citizens and very much alive, busy ourselves about everything here as citizens do. What the righteous were to the world, namely, "strangers" and "dead," that we are to Heaven. And what they were to Heaven, alive and acting as citizens, that we are to the world. On this account, we are dead, because we have refused that which is truly life, and have chosen this which is but fleeting. On this account, we have provoked God to wrath, because when the blessings of Heaven have been set before us, we are not willing to be separated from things on earth. Instead we act like worms, we turn about from the earth to the earth, and again from this to that. In short, we are not willing to look up even for a little while, nor to withdraw ourselves from human affairs, but as if drowned in stupor and sleep and drunkenness, we are stupefied with delusions. . . .

The saints were "strangers and sojourners." How and in what way? And where does Abraham confess himself "a stranger and a sojourner?" Probably indeed even he himself confessed it, but David both confessed "I am a stranger" and "As all my fathers were" (Psalm 39:12). For those who dwell in tents and who have to buy even their own burial places, evidently were in some sense strangers, as they didn't even have a place to bury their dead.

---

[12] John Chrysostom, "Homily 16 on 2nd Corinthians," NPNF 1.12, p. 359. Cf. "Homily 12 on Matthew," NPNF 1.10, p. 78; "Homily 23 on Ephesians," NPNF 1.3, p. 166.

What then? Did they mean that they were "strangers" from the land that is in Palestine? Of course not. But they were strangers in respect to the whole world and with good reason, because they saw therein none of the things they truly longed for, but everything foreign and strange. They certainly wished to practice virtue but here there was so much wickedness, and things were quite alien to them. They had no friend, no familiar acquaintance, save only some few.

But how were they "strangers?" They had no concern for things here. And this they showed not by words, but by deeds. In what way?

He said to Abraham, "Leave what seems to be your country and come to one that is foreign." He [Abraham] did not cleave to his relatives, but let go as unconcernedly as if he were about to leave a foreign land. He said to him, "Offer up your son," and he offered him up as if he had no son, as if he had divested himself of his nature, so he offered him up. The wealth he had acquired was common to all passers-by, and this he accounted as nothing. He yielded the first places to others. He threw himself into dangers. He suffered troubles innumerable. He built no splendid houses, he enjoyed no luxuries, he had no care about dress, which all are things of this world, but lived in all respects as belonging to the city yonder. He showed hospitality, brotherly love, mercifulness, forbearance, contempt for wealth and for present glory, and for all else.[13]

For Chrysostom, Christian identity as stranger entails the proper ordering of desire. Strangers, he says, know that the "things they truly long for" are not in this world. Abraham evidences that by his willingness to yield his place, risk danger, share his wealth and show hospitality.

Augustine of Hippo, preaching to his congregation in Roman North Africa, continues this claim. In this sermon on the Gospel of Luke, Augustine claims that Christians are strangers on Earth, and that is the ground of hospitality.

Acknowledge the duty of hospitality, for by this some have attained unto God. You take in some stranger, whose companion in the way you yourself also are, for we are all strangers. This person is a Christian who, even in his own house and in his own country, acknowledges himself to be a stranger. For our country is above, there we shall not be strangers. For every one here below, even in his own house, is a stranger. If he is not a stranger, let him not pass on from here. If pass on he must, he is a stranger. Let him not deceive himself, he is indeed a stranger. Whether he wills it or not, he is a stranger. If he leaves that house to his children, he leaves it one stranger to other strangers. Why? If you were at an inn, wouldn't you leave when another comes? You do the same thing even in your own house. Your father left a place to you, you will some day leave it to your children. You don't live here as one who will

---

[13]Chrysostom, "Homily 24 on Hebrews," in *Homilies on John and Hebrews*, trans. G. T. Stupart. NPNF 1.14, pp. 473-74.

live forever, nor will those to whom you leave it live forever. If we are all passing away, let us do something which cannot pass away, so that when we shall have passed away, and we come to that place where we no longer pass away, we may find our good works there. Remember, Christ is the keeper, so why do you fear you might lose what you spend on the poor?[14]

Augustine makes clear the connection between stranger status and identification with Christ. These early Christian voices reflect the profound conviction that Christian identity is rooted in otherness. Before Christians can truly offer hospitality, they must understand their marginal position.[15]

If the first step of being hospitable is remembering who we are as Christians, the second necessary step is recognizing the other, the stranger standing before us.[16] On first glance, the poor at the gate or the stranger at the door may seem to be just that, the supplicant wanting something. The stranger may seem suspicious or even dangerous. The stranger's presence can be disorienting.[17] But if we look a little closer, we will see our initial reading of the situation is wrong. Over and over again, early Christian voices remind us to be prepared for surprises. The apparent stranger at our door is not simply the poor, the stranger, the widow or the sick, but Christ himself. For those with eyes to see, hospitality offered to another is always hospitality offered to Christ. Receiving others, we receive Christ; rejecting them, we reject Christ.[18]

---

[14]Augustine, "Sermon 61," in *Homilies on the Gospels*, NPNF 1.6, p. 446.

[15]For a contemporary discussion, see Christine D. Pohl, "Hospitality From the Edge: The Significance of Marginality in the Practice of Welcome," *The Annual of the Society of Christian Ethics*, ed. Harlan Beckley (Boston, Mass.: Society of Christian Ethics, 1995), pp. 121-36. Also see Pohl's, *Making Room: Recovering Hospitality as a Christian Tradition* (Grand Rapids, Mich.: Eerdmans, 1999).

[16]The presence and identity of the stranger has been addressed with insightful reflections by several recent writers. See Christine D. Pohl, "Hospitality, Dignity and the Power of Recognition," in *Making Room: Recovering Hospitality as a Christian Tradition* (Grand Rapids, Mich.: Eerdmans, 1999), pp. 61-84; Thomas W. Ogletree, *Hospitality to the Stranger: Dimensions of Moral Understanding* (Philadelphia: Fortress, 1995); Parker Palmer, *The Company of Strangers: Christians and the Renewal of America's Public Life* (New York: Crossroad, 1981); Henri Nouwen, *Reaching Out: The Three Movements of the Spiritual Life* (New York: Doubleday, 1975); John Koenig, "Hospitality, Strangers, and the Love of God," *New Testament Hospitality: Partnership with Strangers as Mission and Promise* (Philadelphia: Fortress, 1985), pp. 1-14; *Christianity and the Stranger: Historical Essays*, ed. Francis W. Nichols (Atlanta: Scholars Press, 1995).

[17]Ogletree reminds us not to romanticize the stranger, for that trivializes the genuine risk of hospitality (see *Hospitality to the Stranger*, pp. 41-43).

[18]The identification of the stranger with the divine is commonplace in classical literature. Visitation of gods disguised as humans, or *theoxenia*, is a frequent motif in Greek literature. See J. H. Rose, "Divine Disguisings," *Harvard Theological Review* 49 (1956): 63-72; S. Murnaghan, *Disguise and Recognition in the Odyssey* (Princeton, N.J.: Princeton University Press, 1987); "The Theme of Divine Visits and Human (In)Hospitality in Luke-Acts: Its Old Testament and Graeco-Roman Antecedents," in *The Unity of Luke-Acts*, ed. J. Verheyden (Leuven: Leuven University Press, 1999), pp. 263-68; Julian Pitt-Rivers, "The Stranger, the Guest and the Hostile Host: Introduction to the Study of the Laws of Hospitality," in *Contributions to Mediterranean Sociology: Mediterranean Rural*

Early Christians turn to the Gospel of Matthew to ground the recognition of the stranger:

> "Lord, when was it that we saw you hungry and gave you food, or thirsty and gave you something to drink? And when was it that we saw you a stranger and welcomed you, or naked and gave you clothing? And when was it that we saw you sick or in prison and visited you?" And the king will answer them, "Truly I tell you, just as you did it to one of the least of these who are members of my family, you did it to me." (Mt 25:37-40 NRSV).

To recognize Christ, we must have eyes to see. To recognize Christ in the guest at the door is not easy, for the guest may not look like the Christ we expect. We rarely expect Christ. The Matthew passage emphasizes that the Christ who comes will be needy, hungry, thirsty—a Christ known by "the least of these." Eyes that can only see Christ in the triumphant or powerful will fail to recognize the Christ present in the stranger and the poor. Only proper recognition makes union with Christ possible. This recognition changes everything. Jesus' followers on the road to Emmaus (Lk 24:13-35) powerfully portray this experience of recognition and surprise when they unexpectedly encounter Christ as traveler and guest.

Because the guest is actually more than just a guest (i.e., Christ), there is another surprise as well. Christ becomes the host and the host becomes the guest. When we attend to the guest, we are not left unchanged. We become the guest of the heavenly host, who receives us into his life. But again, this depends on our having eyes to see. The Greek word used to express hospitality, *xenos*, connotes shared identity and partnership. It can mean "guest," "host" or "stranger." The semantic fluidity conveys the blurred identities of guest and host heightened by the recognition of Christ.

Ambrose (c. 339-397) was a Roman lawyer who became bishop of Milan in 374. He promoted the independence of the church in the face of civil power and was best known for his preaching. In one of his letters, Ambrose makes explicit the identification of Christ with the guest.

> Love hospitality, whereby holy Abraham found favor, and received Christ as his guest, and Sarah already worn with age gained a son. Lot also escaped the fire of the destruction of Sodom. You too can receive Angels if you offer hospitality to strangers. What shall I say of Rahab who by this means found safety?[19]

---

[18] *Communities and Social Change*, ed. J.-G. Peristiany (Paris: Mouton, 1968). For treatment of this theme in an eastern religious tradition, see Teigo Yoshida, "The Stranger as God: The Place of the Outsider in Japanese Folk Religion," *Ethnology* 20 (1981): 87.

[19] Ambrose, "Epistle 63," in *Selected Works and Letters*. trans. H. De Romestin, E. De Romestin and H. T. F. Duckworth, NPNF 2.10, p. 472.

Similarly, in a sermon on the book of Acts, John Chrysostom makes this identification between the stranger and Christ explicit.

> Pay attention! It is in your power to entertain Paul's Master for your guest, and you refuse. For "he that receives one of these least," he said, "receives me." By how much the kindred may be least, so much the more does Christ come to you through him. For whoever receives the great, often does it from vainglory also, but the one who receives the small, does it purely for Christ's sake. It is in your power to entertain even the Father of Christ as your guest, and you refuse! For, "I was a stranger," He says, "and you took me in," and again, "To one of the least of these of my family, you have done it to me." Though it may not be Paul, yet if it is a believer and kindred, although the least, Christ comes to you through that one. Open your house, take him in. "Whoever receives a prophet," He says, "shall receive a prophet's reward." Therefore too the one that receives Christ, shall receive the reward of whoever has Christ for a guest. Do not disbelieve His words, but be believing. Christ has said, "Through them I come to you." So that you may not disbelieve, He lays down both punishments for those who do not receive, and honors for those who do receive, since He would not have done this, unless both the person honored and the person insulted were Himself. "You received Me," He said, "into your lodging, I will receive you into the Kingdom of My Father. You took away My hunger, I take away your sins. You saw Me bound, I see you loosed. You saw Me a stranger, I make you a citizen of heaven. You gave Me bread, I give you an entire Kingdom, that you may inherit and possess it."[20]

Later in the same sermon, Chrysostom returns to the theme of recognizing Christ in the stranger. A Christian's house can be Christ's resting place. Chrysostom ends this portion with an exasperated note—Christ isn't asking that we kill our best calf; he's only asking for the minimum: feed the hungry, give clothes to the naked, shelter the stranger.

> Do you want to put us to shame? Then do this. Surpass us in generosity. Have a room, to which Christ may come. Say, "This is Christ's space. This building is set apart for Him." Even if it is just a basement and tiny. He won't refuse it. Christ goes about "naked and a stranger." It is only a shelter He wants. . . . Abraham received the strangers in the place where he himself lived. His wife stood in the place of a servant, the guests in the place of masters. He didn't know that he was receiving Christ, didn't know that he was receiving Angels. Had he known it, he would have lavished his whole substance. But we, who know that we receive Christ, don't show even so much enthusiasm as he did who thought that he was receiving humans. "But many of them are impostors and ungrateful," you will say. And for this the greater your reward when you receive for the sake of Christ's name. For if you know indeed that

---

[20]Chrysostom, "Homily 45 on the Acts of the Apostles," in *Homilies on Acts of the Apostles*, trans. J. Walker and J. Sheppard, NPNF 1.11, pp. 275-77.

they are impostors, don't receive them into your house. But if you don't know this, why do you accuse them lightly?" Therefore I tell them to go to the receiving house." But what kind of excuse is there for us, when we do not even receive those whom we know, but shut our doors against all? Let our house be Christ's general receiving place. Let us demand of them as a reward, not money, but that they make our house the receiving place for Christ. Let us run about everywhere, let us drag them in, let us seize our prize. Greater are the benefits we receive than what we confer. He does not require you to kill a calf, but only to give bread to the hungry, raiment to the naked, shelter to the stranger.

Perhaps in the plainest terms of all, Chrysostom concludes that if we cannot receive the stranger as Christ, we should not receive the stranger at all. In "Homily 14 on 1 Timothy," he preaches:

> Observe, the hospitality here spoken of is not merely a friendly reception, but one given with zeal and full of life, with readiness, and going about it as if one were receiving Christ Himself. The widows should perform these services themselves, not commit them to their handmaids. For Christ said, "If I your Master and Lord have washed your feet, you ought also to wash one another's feet." (John 13:14) And though a woman may be very rich, and of the highest rank, vain of her birth and noble family, there is not the same distance between her and others, as between God and the disciples. If you receive the stranger as Christ, be not ashamed, but rather glory. But if you receive him not as Christ, receive him not at all. "He that receives you," He said, "receives Me." (Matthew 10:40) . . . If you give to the poor, don't disdain to give it yourself, for it is not to the poor that it is given, but to Christ, and who is so wretched, as to disdain to stretch out his own hand to Christ?[21]

In the Gospels, Jesus says it is necessary to have eyes to see and ears to hear to recognize the kingdom of God. Hospitality may be a mark of that kingdom, and strangers may be its bearers.

Early Christians express a profound appreciation for two initial movements of hospitality. First we recognize our own status as strangers. Second, we recognize the stranger as Christ. Strangers offer an opportunity to receive Christ and participate in God's grace. Hospitality becomes more than private virtue; it is a means of grace whereby we are received into the household of God just as we receive others into our own lives and communities. This dynamic movement of grace permeates the practice of hospitality.

Early Christian thought on hospitality is a rich resource for the recovery of hospitality in Christianity today.

---

[21]Chrysostom, "Homily 14 on 1 Timothy," in *Homilies on Galatians, Ephesians, Philippians, Colossians, Thessalonians, Timothy, Titus and Philemon*, trans. James Tweed, NPNF 1.13, pp. 454-55.

Four

Antiochene θεωρία in John Chrysostom's Exegesis

BRADLEY NASSIF

It is an honor for me to celebrate the achievements of Thomas Oden with a chapter on early Christian exegesis.[1] Ancient Christian exegesis lies at the very heart of Thomas Oden's vision of postmodern orthodoxy. His monumental twenty-seven-volume Ancient Christian Commentary on Scripture series pioneers new ground that is sure to make a major contribution toward a renewed understanding of the continuing relevance of the church fathers. It was in the context of the ecumenical meetings of the Society for the Study of Eastern Orthodoxy and Evangelicalism that I first met Dr. Oden when he served as a featured speaker for our annual gathering in 1996. As an Eastern Orthodox theologian I found his perspectives refreshingly similar to the "living tradition" of the Antiochene tradition in which I was reared. Readers who are familiar with Dr. Oden's works on postmodern orthodoxy will readily see how this chapter elucidates some of the ways in which this is so. In important ways

---

[1]I want to thank my wife, Barbara Nassif, for her meticulous editorial work in this chapter. Her love and dedication motivated me to make numerous editorial revisions that I would have otherwise overlooked. Any remaining shortcomings are, or course, my own.

Dr. Oden follows in the footsteps of the early church fathers and exemplifies the neo-patristic movement of their modern Orthodox successors—the late Frs. George Florovsky, John Meyendorff and Alexander Schmemann. As such, Dr. Oden speaks to us not only as a scholar with rigorous academic standards but also as a compassionate pastor and inspiring interpreter of Christian orthodoxy and spirituality. I affectionately dedicate this essay to Thomas Oden, who by nearly all estimates stands as one of the most influential theologians of our time.

Purpose and Relevance

A handful of scholars[2] over the course of the past hundred years have attempted to demonstrate that behind the Antiochene Fathers' search for the literal meaning of Scripture lies a deceptively simple hermeneutic that governed their efforts to bridge the spiritual and historical approaches to biblical interpretation. This "spiritual" hermeneutic, known as θεωρία ("fuller sense," "deeper insight"), lies at the center of the Antiochenes' concern for a unified reading of the historical and christological meanings of the Bible. Their application of θεωρία in biblical exegesis required them to find what can appropriately be called "spiritual" interpretations which, for them, were not to be confused with Alexandrian allegory. Unlike their Alexandrian adversaries who employed allegorical exegesis to find deeper meanings in the Bible, the mystical meanings of the Antiochene exegetes were said to have been based on and congruent with the literal sense of the text. But very few scholars have investigated this overlooked feature of Antiochene exegesis. The handful of specialists who have researched it thoroughly (noted above) universally concur that this was very likely "the chief exegetical feature" of the School of Anti-

---

[2]For an overview of the history of scholarship on this lesser-known feature of Antiochene exegesis see Bradley Nassif, " 'Spiritual Exegesis' in the School of Antioch," in *New Perspectives on Historical Theology: Essays in Memory of John Meyendorff*, ed. Bradley Nassif (Grand Rapids, Mich.: Eerdmans, 1996), pp. 344-77. The article extensively examines the contributions of only nine authorities who have written on this subject over the past century and critiques the secondary literature in which the subject appears. The major authors are Heinrich Kihn, "Über 'Theōria' und 'Allegoria' nach den verlorenen hermeneutischen Schriften der Antiochener," *Theologische Quartalschrift* 20 (1880): 531-82; Alberto Vaccari, "La *teōria* nella scuola esegetica di antiochia," *Biblica* 1 (1920): 3-36; "La 'teōria' esegetica antiochena," *Biblica* 1 (1934): 94-101, in reply to P. J. M. Bover, "La 'teōria' antioquena definida, por Julian de Eclano," *Estudios Biblicos* 12 (1933): 405-15; F. A. Seisdedos, "La 'te?ria' antioquena," *Estudios Biblicos* 11 (1952): 31-67; Paul Ternant, "'La 'teōria' d'Antioche dans le cadre des sens de l'Ecriture," *Biblica*, 34, pts 1, 2, 3 (1953): 135-58; 354-83; 456-86; Francis S. Rossiter, "Messianic Prophecy According to Theodoret of Cyrus and Antiochene θεωρία" (Ph.D. dissertation, Pontifical Gregorian University, Rome, 1949); Bertrand de Margerie, "Histoire, 'Theoria' et tradition dans l'École d'Antioch," in *Introduction a l'histoire de l'exégèse* (Paris: Cerf, 1980), 1:188-213; John Breck, "The Hermeneutic Problem," "The Patristic Setting for 'Theoretic' Hermeneutics," "*Theōria*: An Orthodox Hermeneutic" (pts. 1, 2, 3), in *The Power of the Word in the Worshipping Church* (New York: St. Vladimir's Press, 1986), pp. 25-116; *The Legacy of St. Vladimir's*, ed. John Breck, John Meyendorff, and Elaine Silk (New York: St. Vladimir's Press, 1990), pp. 141-57; Bradley Nassif, *Antiochene θεωρία in John Chrysostom's Exegesis* (Ph.D. dissertation, Fordham University, N.Y., 1991).

och. What made it so prominent was their unceasing efforts to discover the Scriptures' christological content for its soteriological purpose within the framework of salvation history. Bertrand de Margerie summarizes the current state of research on the presence of θεωρία in the writings of the Antiochene Fathers, and the need for obtaining a more precise understanding of its definition in the School of Antioch.

> The complexity of the material available undoubtedly shows that we still await the definitive work which will give us an exact understanding of the meaning of Antiochene θεωρία, and the different meanings of the hermeneutic found in the authors of the School of Antioch, and even within a single author.[3]

There are two modest results that I seek to accomplish in this article: (1) My primary goal is to fill a gap in the paucity of scholarship that exists today on the study of spiritual exegesis in the School of Antioch by focusing on selected writings of St. John Chrysostom.[4] (2) A secondary goal is to suggest ways in which the Antiochene approach to polyvalences in the biblical text are relevant to modern theories of hermeneutics. I will explain my rationale for these goals below and suggest their potential contributions for scholars and pastors today.

I select Chrysostom chiefly because he is a well known, reliable and widely read representative of the Antiochene School. There are more extant manuscripts of Chrysostom to analyze than any other patristic author in antiquity—hundreds of his original manuscripts survive. This was largely due to his immense popularity in the Byzantine Church. Shortly after his death and throughout the subsequent thousand-year history of the Byzantine Empire, Chrysostom ("the golden-mouthed") was revered and imitated by virtually all the patriarchs of Constantinople as the greatest pastor of the Eastern church fathers.

In focusing on the Chrysostomian corpus I will examine a selection of previously neglected homilies that exemplify his characteristic use of θεωρία in scriptural exegesis. I will mostly study the New Testament homilies rather than the Old Testament or selected treatises since that is where one can obtain the most information on how the hermeneutic was actually applied. The results will provide the textual documentation that is required for making a new contribution to the secondary literature on the history of exegesis. It will suggest a revision in the tradi-

---

[3] de Mergerie, *Introduction a l'histoire*, 1:194.

[4] The author who deserves credit for doing the most sustained work on Chrysostom's hermeneutics is Robert C. Hill. When researching this topic, however, I was surprised to discover that over the past thirty years Hill had examined a great many of the technical terms and concepts of Chrysostom's exegesis except θεωρία. This essay will hopefully compliment fourteen of his fine publications that can be found listed in *St. John Chrysostom: Commentary on the Psalms*, trans. Robert C. Hill (Brookline, Mass.: Holy Cross Orthodox Press, 1998), 1:42-43.

tional portrayals of John Chrysostom from that of a "rigid literalist" to a "mystical literalist" exegete of Scripture. As we will see, the Antiochene Father valued not only the literal meaning of a text (i.e., the recovery of an author's original intent within the historical circumstances of his day), but he self-consciously pursued deeper spiritual meanings that corresponded to that historical method within the framework of salvation history. In short, John Chrysostom's theoretic exegesis reflects what can be described as an "Antiochene mysticism" that was rooted in the distinctive hermeneutical principles which characterized Antioch as a literalist, salvation history school of exegesis.

My secondary goal of suggesting ways in which the Antiochene approach to polyvalences in the biblical text are relevant to modern theories of hermeneutics cannot be developed in a complete or systematic way here. Yet by showing how a major author in the Antiochene School consciously or unconsciously dealt with issues of polyvalence, modern theologians will have new primary sources to work with in assessing the relevance of Antiochene exegesis today. This is important because notable patristic specialists on Alexandrian exegesis have promoted allegory as hermeneutically fruitful for biblical exegesis today.[5] Very few patristic or modern scholars, however, have seriously reflected on the role of Antioch in contemporary theology. Modern theologians outside the field of patristics are dominated by the perspective that Antioch has nothing new to say because it was a rigidly literalist school of biblical interpretation, much like that of the historicists in our own day who stand in the Enlightenment legacy. Admittedly this is the prevailing view of Antiochene exegesis. I believe it is wrong, however, mainly because it is a caricature that has been based on a lack of familiarity with the Antiochenes' use of θεωρία and its related vocabulary of mystical exegesis. There is no doubt that Alexandria has a great deal to say to the contemporary discussion over "meaning" in biblical texts[6] or that Antioch was indeed a literalist school of exegesis insofar as it pursued an author's original intent and recognized the presence of metaphorical language. What I wish to advocate, however, is that Antiochene exegesis needs to be understood more comprehensively than it has been to date. Once it has been understood more comprehensively, it surpasses both of these schemes (allegory and historicism) for contemporary relevance by its balanced inclusion of both historical and christological approaches to exegesis.

This is not to say that the Antiochene Fathers applied their hermeneutics con-

---

[5]One of many examples is Andrew Louth, *Discerning the Mystery* (New York: Oxford University Press, 1983).

[6]As argued by David Steinmetz: "The medieval theory of levels of meaning in the biblical text, with all its undoubted defects, flourished because it is true, while the modern theory of a single meaning, with all its demonstrable virtues, is false" (David Steinmetz, "The Superiority of Precritical Exegesis," *Theology Today* [April 1980], p. 38).

sistently, or that their exegesis never contained a fanciful allegorical departure from their own hermeneutic principles, or that if one accepts the more comprehensive vision of Antiochene hermeneutics there will be exegetical uniformity among all exegetes today, or even that Chrysostom's interpretations are more accurate than those of modern biblical exegetes. But I propose that the Antiochene *approach* to exegesis offers a balanced corrective to the known abuses of allegorical exegesis and the spiritual barrenness of much of modern historical criticism. It does so by establishing the biblical authors' original intent within the historical circumstances of their day while also seeking, where relevant, the fuller soteriological relevance (θεωρία) of each text by placing it within the whole of salvation history with Christ as its origin and goal.[7] Antiochene exegesis also acknowledges that the true meaning of Scripture is a *theological* one that was arrived at not by being allegorical or antihistorical, but by wedding theology and history. Any rigid separation of these complementary approaches inevitably fails to keep text and community together, as has occurred in our post-Enlightenment era.

Chrysostom's Exegesis

Hermeneutical description of θεωρία. According to John Chrysostom the main purpose of Scripture is to bring salvation to all who read it. The hermeneutical question for us to ask, then, is "What were the exegetical goals that served Chrysostom's soteriological concerns?" This is the key question I will answer throughout this essay. The older and still prevailing explanations of his interpretive aims by such excellent scholars as Frederick Chase and Chrysostom Baur have defined Chrysostom's exegesis almost exclusively as a search for the plain meaning of the text. Even the new biography by J. N. D. Kelly promotes this view, although he acknowledges the spiritual dimension in Chrysostom's exegesis without exploring it.[8]

As noted previously this conventional portrayal of Chrysostom's exegesis remains indisputable as far as it goes, but it is too narrow. For all its merits the image of John Chrysostom as a bare literalist has so exaggerated the Antiochene distinctives of his interpretive goals that it has overshadowed significant portions of his exegesis revealing deeper sensitivities to the spiritual treasures which lie hidden within the sacred text. To be sure, under the rubric of θεωρία Chrysostom occasionally lapses into incredulous allegorical explanations and at times surpasses

---

[7]For a comparison between θεωρία and allegory, typology and the *sensus plenior* of Scripture, see Nassif, " 'Spiritual Exegesis' in the School of Antioch," pp. 366-73.

[8]Frederick Chase, *Chrysostom: A Study in the History of Biblical Interpretation* (Cambridge: Deighton, Bell, 1887), pp.115-50; Chrysostom Baur, *John Chrysostom and His Time*, trans. M. Gonzaga, 2nd ed. (Westminster, Md.: Newman Press, 1988), 1:315-28; J. N. D. Kelly, *Golden Mouth: The Story of John Chrysostom, Ascetic, Preacher, Bishop* (Ithaca, N.Y.: Cornell University Press, 1996), p. 60.

a biblical author's understanding of his own prophetic words. But even then Chrysostom employed θεωρία as an inspired perception of the divine activity in Scripture that was discernible within the words and events of salvation history, christologically centered. Quite unlike Theodore of Mopsuestia, Diodore of Tarsus and Julian of Eclanum's application of θεωρία as a literal method of messianic exegesis,[9] Chrysostom applies the hermeneutic of θεωρία to the interpretive task of disclosing the soteriological significance of such literary vehicles as typology, narrative or a broad range of literary forms such as metaphors, proverbs, parables, allegories and even biblical names, places and events. In this capacity θεωρία functions as a technical term that points to a fuller soteriological meaning which was believed to have coinhered in the literal sense of the text through the work of the Holy Spirit.

In the broadest sense Antiochene θεωρία in John Chrysostom's exegesis can be simply described as a faculty of insight into the deeper meaning of divine revelation within the boundaries of salvation history. The following cumulative description inductively derived from an analysis of Chrysostom's New Testament homilies is more precise. My exegesis of selected homilies below will reflect one or several aspects of it. That definition is as follows:

> Depending on which Chrysostomian passage is under study, θεωρία in John Chrysostom's exegesis can be described as the divine revelation or mystical illumination of spiritual realities which attends the processes of inscripturation, interpretation, or homiletical discourse within the framework of Incarnation history (οἰκονομία). History is not placed in opposition to θεωρία but serves as the foundation and basis for it. In some instances Chrysostom maintained that a fuller meaning was known to the biblical author, while in others it was not. Patterned after God's considerate way of communicating with His creatures (συγκατάβασις) through Scripture and the Incarnation, θεωρία is a rarely applied principle of theological exegesis chiefly because of the spiritual immaturity of Chrysostom's audience. Yet θεωρία quite often occurs in his typological exegesis as a faculty of spiritual illumination even though Chrysostom frequently avoids an explicit hermeneutical discussion about it. Under the enlightening power of θεωρία, Chrysostom perceived the spiritual connection

---

[9]These Antiochene authors interpreted such texts as Psalm 16:10; Hosea 1:10, 11:1; Joel 2:28, Micah 5:2; and Zechariah 9:9 as prophecies that the prophets knowingly applied both to Israel and to the messianic age under one literal hyperbolic mode of expression. This method of messianic exegesis—known variously as "double fulfillment," "multiple fulfillment," "generic prophecy," etc.—is what separates their use of θεωρία from Chrysostom's and illustrates the need for obtaining a more precise understanding of the hermeneutic within the Antiochene School. Chrysostom, on the whole, uproots these prophecies from their historical setting and interprets them as direct prophecies of Christ (e.g., *Homiliae in epistulam 1 ad Corinthios* 34; *Homiliae in epistulam ad Romanos* 16; *Homiliae in Acta apostostolorum* 4, 1; 5, 1; *Homiliae in Matthaeum* 8) (See Nassif, " 'Spiritual Exegesis' in the School of Antioch," pp. 366-73).

which exists between the usual meaning of words and their fuller spiritual content by contemplating the soteriological significance of biblical language on the plane of salvation history (whether that be historical events and places, prophecies, figures of speech, etymologies, or names) and drawing from such facts the moral and soteriological teachings they contain. (author's definition)

As indicated above, it is important to underscore the fact that the hermeneutic of θεωρία failed to achieve high visibility in Chrysostom's exegetical method—unless we consider θεωρία as the spiritual perception or fulfillment of all biblical types, in which case it would be a quite prominent feature in Chrysostom's works from start to finish even though he failed to call attention to it every time it occurred in the text. Due to the spiritual nature of the narratives themselves, and especially because of the lack of spiritual maturity on the part of his hearers, Chrysostom seldom made public use of θεωρία.[10] The failure to account for his spiritual sensitivities toward his flock has likely contributed to Chrysostom's modern reputation as a sober-minded exegete concerned only with the literal meaning of the Bible.

What soteriological truths were contained in θεωρία for Chrysostom, and how was his search for them demonstrated and accomplished by the method of exegesis he employed? In his exposition of Psalm 9:7, Chrysostom gives us a rare statement of his hermeneutical theory. Terse comments are made concerning θεωρία, the literal meaning of Scripture and the goal of exegesis.

> But if you feel it necessary to give in addition some kind of figurative interpretation [ἀναγωγή] we have no objection. For it is possible to interpret some passages theoretically [θεωρῆσαι]. Others, in contrast, are to be understood solely according to a strictly literal interpretation, for example, "In the beginning, God made heaven and earth" (Gen. 1:1). Others again in a sense different from the actual words, for example, "Spend your time with the hart you love, with the filly that has won your favor," and "Let those things be yours alone, and let no stranger share them with you. Your well is for you to drink from" (Prov. 5:17-19). . . . I mean, if you take this passage as it occurs and do not depart from the surface meaning but stay at that level, it reflects little humanity—the counsel to share water with no one. The sense, however, is talking about a wife . . . she is called a "well" and "hart" on account of the purity of the marriage relationship. . . . In other passages, however, it is necessary to accept both the sense of the words as they stand and the meaning that plainly arises from them, as in the following instance: "Just as Moses lifted up the serpent" (Jn. 3:14). Here we must believe the actual fact (for there is no doubt it is a fact) and, in addition, the

---

[10]As late as the tenth century Chrysostom's great patriarchal successor, Photios, notices Chrysostom's avoidance to explain "the deeper teaching" (βαθυτέρας θεωρία) of Scripture and attributes it to the practical and soteriological requirements of his congregation (Codex 174, 119b, *Bibliotheca*).

sense that was signified by the fact, namely a type of Christ.[11]

Explicit in this passage is the Antiochene pastor's recognition of three kinds of biblical language: the literal, metaphorical and typological. Each has its own meaning, but none is separable from its literal and historical reference. Literal passages include such statements as Genesis 1:1. Metaphors such as Proverbs 5:19 contain fuller meanings (ἀναγωγή, θεωρῆσαι) which have a "sense different from the actual words," and it is the interpreter's task to draw out the appropriate metaphorical θεωρία of the text in order to obtain its true sense. Finally, the typological sense is an additional secondary meaning resting on the literal. It is a symbolic prophecy of the Messiah through figurative history couched in narrative form, as in John 3:14. An analysis of how these distinctions are played out in actual exegesis will help define the features of Chrysostom's theoretic exegesis. We will see that θεωρία could be active in both the words and events of the biblical text through metaphors, types and other literary forms, as well as in the mind of the interpreter as a faculty of spiritual insight. To illustrate I will select homilies that illuminate Chrysostom's use of θεωρία in his interpretation of typology and the unity of the Testaments, etymological exegesis of scriptural names, Gospel harmonization, the diverse literary forms of Scripture and homiletical discourse.[12]

θεωρία in typology and the unity of the Testaments. In Chrysostom's typological interpretation θεωρία functions as a mystical perception of the interior unity between the Old and New Testaments. It is a means of hermeneutically processing the historical and theological patterns of unity between the Testaments in the types and antitypes which were prefigured and fulfilled.[13] The Antiochene pastor carries this out by means of a Spirit-inspired search for events that are both historical and typological. He sees at least two kinds of prophetic oracles in Scripture when he draws what became a classic distinction in the history of exegesis between verbal and typological prophecy:

---

[11]*Expos. in Ps.* 9, Patrologia cursus completus: Series graeca 55.126, 127, ed. J.-P. Migne (Paris, 1844-1864), (idiomatically translated). Hereafter the series will be identified by PG.

[12]The following texts are only a selection from the Chrysostom corpus. For a complete treatment of every New Testament homily that uses the technical term θεωρία see Bradley Nassif, *Antiochene θεωρία in John Chrysostom's Exegesis* (Ph.D. dissertation, Fordham University, N.Y., 1991). Each passage was located with the assistance of the TLG data base.

[13]The extent to which Chrysostom applied θεωρία to his interpretation of the liturgical rites has not been fully explored, though its typological legacy can be traced in the Byzantine liturgy. In the liturgical exegesis among the Antiochenes in general, Bornert briefly commented that "history (ἱστορία) is not opposed to the higher contemplation (τῇ ὑψηλότερᾳ θεωρίᾳ); quite the contrary, it is the foundation and basis of it" (R. Bornert, *Les commentaires byzantins de la divine liturgie du VIIe au XVe siècle* (*Archives de l'Orient chrétien* 9) (Paris: Institut français d'études byzantines, 1966), p. 72. It appears, however, that θεωρία as a spiritual illumination of the mind to see the correspondences between OT prophecy and NT fulfillment was everywhere assumed or implied whenever sacramental typology was employed (see Bradley Nassif, "θεωρία in Liturgical Exegesis" in *Antiochene θεωρία*, pp. 248-56).

Prophecy in type is that which takes place in deeds or in historical realities; other prophecy is one in words. For God has persuaded some by highly insightful words, while He has bolstered the certitude of others, the less sophisticated, through the vision of events.[14]

Typological prophecy is expressed by historical facts (διὰ πράγματον προφητεία) and serves to enlighten the eyes of the dull and less sophisticated; verbal prophecy persuades the spiritually mature by highly insightful words. It is by means of θεωρία that Chrysostom discerns the deeper revelatory function of the shadow (σκία) of the historical events as images of their antitypes. Chrysostom's most striking remarks on this point occur in Homily 15 on Hebrews. There θεωρία is expressly tied to a typological exegesis that discerns in the Jewish sanctuary an interior unity between the Old and New Testaments. In Hebrews 9:1-9 the apostle Paul (the alleged author) stated that the Levitical ritual was appointed by God and given to Moses under the guidance of the Holy Spirit. In commenting on these verses Chrysostom describes the liturgical instruments prescribed by the Levitical ordinances for the old sanctuary. He then suddenly veers away from the surface meaning of those historical facts and engages in a spiritual exegesis of the higher meaning of the biblical text through a brief but precious comment about St. Paul's exercise of θεωρία in his own interpretation of the Old Testament.

> Up to now there is certainly no higher vision [οὐδαμοῦ ἐνταῦθα θεωρία]. But from this point on he [Paul] "theorizes" and says [λοιπὸς δὲ θεωρεῖ καὶ φησί], "The Holy Ghost signifies that the way into the Holiest of all was not yet made manifest while the first tabernacle was standing." ... There is also something else which he indicates when he says "which [was] a figure for the time then present." Namely, it became the type. ... Observe how he calls the body a tabernacle, a veil, and heaven: "By a greater and more perfect tabernacle. Through the veil, that is, His flesh" (Heb. 10:20). ... Why, then, does he [say] this? Because he wants to signify one thing or another. I mean, for example, that heaven is a veil, for as a veil it walls off the Holy of Holies; the flesh [is a veil] hiding the Godhead; and the tabernacle [is a veil] likewise holding the Godhead.[15]

In these homiletical remarks Chrysostom ascribes the hermeneutical function of θεωρία to the Spirit's role in the divine revelation, inscription and interpretation of the Old Testament. The Spirit first ordained Israel's cultic ritual as a divine revelation which contained a higher proleptic message for the Christian era. The cultic practices of the Levitical institution contained the promises that were related to

---

[14]*De Poenitentia* 6, PG 49.320.

[15]*Homiliae in epistulam ad Hebraeos* 15, PG 63.118.

God's purposes in history. "The Holy Spirit signifies" the higher meaning of the old tabernacle through the scriptural words recorded by the author who inscribed its liturgy in the book of Exodus. The Spirit then continued his revelatory work in the new dispensation by interpreting the θεωρία of the biblical text to the apostolic author who himself also discerned (θεωρεῖ) the theological unity between the Testaments. The divine purpose was partially fulfilled in the earthly tabernacle but fully realized in Christ who tabernacled among his people. Chrysostom believes that Christ himself provided the hermeneutical key that enabled Paul to see the whole of Scripture in its inspired unity and to acquire an integrated understanding of its parts. The biblical author appears to him as one who cooperated with the Spirit synergistically in order to apprehend the interior revelatory work of the divine Author who used the pattern of the old earthly tabernacle to impart deeper spiritual truths to the people of God under the New Covenant. Only as the apostle read such texts under the enlightening power of θεωρία could he perceive the unity between the Testaments. Had the apostolic author stopped short of drawing out the mystical sense of the Hebrew ordinances, there would have been no θεωρία ("Up to now, there is certainly no higher vision [θεωρία]"). Yet the fact that he did so by discerning the revelatory activity of the Spirit in the Exodus narrative, "from this point on he (Paul) 'theorizes' [θεωρεῖ] and says . . ." Hence, the hermeneutical rule of Chrysostom's exegetical tutor, Diodore of Tarsus, clearly reappears here: "The literal reading of the text reveals some truths while the discovery of other truths requires the application of θεωρία."[16]

Chrysostom's point is that history, as a medium of revelation, contains a deeper soteriological significance (θεωρία) that can only be discerned by a mystical insight (θεωρεῖ) which has as its foundation the literal sense. In Chrysostom's spiritual exegesis, therefore, it is essential for the interpreter—whether apostolic or post-apostolic—to conform to the hermeneutic activity of the Spirit who inspired and interprets that deeper meaning to the mind of the exegete.

In Homily 12 on Hebrews we can see how Chrysostom further employs θεωρία as a hermeneutical process for discerning the theological relationship between type and antitype. He starts by drawing attention to how Paul's pastoral sensitivities led him to gradually prepare his readers for understanding the differences between the Old and New Covenants beginning at the very outset of the epistle to the Hebrews. In chapter one Paul (the alleged author) discussed who the Son was, what he did and how Christians should obey him. Paul often wanted to expound the differences between the Covenants, declares Chrysostom, but the apostle first had to go to great

---

[16]Diodore of Tarsus, *Praef. Comm. Ps.* 118, trans. Karlfried Froehlich, *Biblical Interpretation in the Early Church* (Philadelphia: Fortress, 1984), p. 87.

lengths to prepare his readers for such knowledge by clearing away their despondency through fearful reproof and gentle encouragement. Finally, in chapter seven, Paul arrived to the place where he could now introduce his readers to the true meaning of the New Testament's fulfillment of the Old. Thus by patiently following Paul's thought through a chapter-by-chapter exposition of the book of Hebrews, the spiritual knowledge of Chrysostom's audience had likewise been prepared for the deeper truths they were about to hear with "ears in their full vigor. For he who is depressed in spirits would not be a ready hearer." Reminiscent of God's gracious accommodation to human weakness (συγκατάβασις), Chrysostom announces that the apostle expounded the differences between the Covenants by means of the pedagogical device of the Melchizedek typology:

> And what does he say? "For this Melchizedek, King of Salem, Priest of the Most High God." And what is particularly noteworthy is that he shows how great the difference [between the two covenants] is by the type itself. For, as I said, he constantly confirms the truth from the type, from things past.[17]

Having prepared his congregation for what was about to follow in the homily, Chrysostom moves on to specify the controlling hermeneutic that governed Paul's typological exegesis of the Old Testament: "Having concisely set down the whole narrative, he looked at it mystically [μυστικῶς αὐτὴν ἐθεώρεσε]." This explanatory comment is of supreme importance for understanding the relationship between typology and θεωρία in the hermeneutics of Chrysostom. The manner in which θεωρία attended the interpretive process is seen in how Chrysostom expounded Hebrews 7:2ff.:

> And first from the name. "First" (he says) "being by interpretation 'King of righteousness'": for Sedek means "righteousness"; and Melchi, "King": Melchizedek, "King of righteousness." Do you see his precision [ἀκρίβειαν] even in the names? But who is "King of righteousness," save our Lord Jesus Christ? . . . He then adds another distinction, "Without father, without mother, without genealogy, having neither beginning of days nor end of life, but made like unto the Son of God, he remains a Priest always . . . see how he explains it mystically [ὅρα πῶς αὐτὸ Τεθεώρεκεν]? . . . "But made like unto the Son of God." Where is the likeness? . . . If the likeness were to exist in all respects, there would no longer be type [τύπος] and reality [ἀλήθεια]; but both would be type. [Here] then just as in representations [εἰκόσιν] (by painting or drawing) there are some aspects that are similar and others that are different. By means of the lines indeed there is a similarity of features [χαρακτῆρον], but when the colors are put on, then both the similarity and the difference is plainly shown.[18]

---

[17]Ibid., Homily 12, PG 63.97.
[18]Ibid.

Chrysostom's exegesis of the Melchizedek figure beautifully illustrates the typological application of θεωρία. The Old Testament is seen as a shadow for the reality that came fully in Christ. Chrysostom notices that the writer of Hebrews attested that Melchizedek was "without beginning" and "without end" and was "made like unto the Son of God." It was not that Melchizedek set the pattern and Jesus followed it. Rather, the historical events surrounding Melchizedek were so providentially arranged that they contained certain truths which applied far more fully to Christ than to Melchizedek. For the apostolic author the Old Testament writer was referring to the Son's eternal nature. With regard to Melchizedek himself the Genesis narrative was simply a matter of record. Yet with Christ the biblical facts about his name, genealogy and receipt of tithes from Abraham were not only historically true, but they also had significant spiritual dimensions that required the apostle to employ θεωρία in order to understand the true import of the Melchizedek narrative contained in the Old Testament Scriptures: "Having concisely set down the whole narrative, he [Paul] looked at it mystically [μυστικῶς αὐτὴν ἐθεώρεσε]." Later in the homily Chrysostom again makes recourse to the hermeneutic of θεωρία by adding, "'Without father, mother, genealogy , etc.' . . . see how he explained it mystically [τεθεώρεκεν]?"

Chrysostom believed that the apostle's mystical insight enabled him to perceive that Christ was the antitype who fulfilled the proleptic history which was embedded in the narrative of Genesis 14:9. Implicit in Chrysostom's interpretation is his assumption that a deeper typological meaning resided in the Old Testament, but that the later apostolic interpreter may not have comprehended the full implications of its reference to the New Covenant had he not recognized the completed revelation of God's purposes in history through Christ. By means of θεωρία the apostolic author read the Old Testament by the light of the New Testament in order to find the deeper meaning of the Spirit's revelatory work in salvation history. θεωρία enabled Paul to recognize divine realities for what they were, guiding him into the Old Testament's spiritual meaning by exegeting the literal sense of the text and then integrating its deeper purpose with the New Covenant ministry in Christ.[19]

θεωρία and Biblical Names

In addition to a typological use of θεωρία, Chrysostom's interpretation of biblical

---

[19]q.v. Adversus Judaeos, PG 48.923 for "the higher vision of the type" (θεώρημα τοῦ τύπου) of Melchizedek. Only those who had the capacity for seeing the Spirit's revelatory work in salvation history could discern it (Homiliae in epistulam ad Romanos 2, PG 60.409). See also Chrysostom's theoretic exegesis of the "allegory" of Hagar and Sarah (Homiliae in epistulam ad Galatas commentarius chap. 4, PG 61.6621).

names offers fascinating insight into his Antiochene mysticism. Chrysostom believed etymology was an aspect of grammar that was especially useful for ascertaining a fuller theological significance. In his closing remarks on the genealogical section of Matthew, Chrysostom draws attention to the spiritual treasures that can be found in the etymologies of the biblical names which the Evangelist listed. More than mere appellations, the root meaning of names could at times reveal a sacred person's function in the overall plan of God's revelation (οἰκονομία) that was not immediately obvious at the surface level of the text.

> And also with regard to the very names, if anyone were to attempt to translate even their etymologies he would derive a great deal of deeper insight [θεωρίαν]. This is of great importance with regard to the NT as, for example, from Abraham's name, from Jacob's, from Solomon's, from Zerubbabel's. For it was not without purpose that these names were given to them. But lest we seem tiresome by going on at great length let us pass these things by and proceed to what is urgent.[20]

Here Chrysostom plainly professes that the theoretic sense of biblical names is a matter "of great importance with regard to the New Testament." In the context that immediately precedes this passage Chrysostom expounded the religious reasons for Matthew's threefold division of the genealogies. Matthew's narrative not only served to explain their messianic meaning but also recounted the names of great personalities in biblical history whose very etymologies inferred the presence of higher spiritual truths. Through the names of Abraham, Jacob, Solomon and Zerubbabel the Scriptures conveyed fuller theological meanings (θεωρία, not ἀλληγορία) that could be grasped through an etymological study of the language. Just what those truths were Chrysostom does not say, for he judged it to be more expedient for his flock to understand the foundational truth of the virgin birth than to apprehend the etymologies contained in the genealogy. Chrysostom's pastoral judgment of when to explain the θεωρία of biblical names was informed by the degree of spiritual maturity in his flock.[21]

θεωρία and Gospel Harmonization

Chrysostom sees a further use of θεωρία in helping to resolve apparent contradic-

---

[20]*Homiliae in Matthaeum* 4, PG 57.41.

[21]*Homiliae in epistulam ad Hebraeos* 12 above also illustrates the hermeneutical control which Chrysostom placed on his mystical exegesis of "Melchizedek." The loftier sense derived from and conformed to the literal meaning of the name and, unlike allegory, went no higher than what could be paralleled on the plane of salvation history. See also *Homiliae in epistulam ad Romanos* 31, PG 60.671. Nineteenth century translators of *Homiliae in Matthaeum* 4 and *Homiliae in epistulam ad Romanos* 31 have mistakenly confused θεωρία with allegory (see George Provost's translation in Nicene and Post-Nicene Fathers 10, p. 21 n. 6; George B. Stevens in Nicene and Post-Nicene Fathers 11, p. 56 n. 1).

tions among the Gospel writers. A close reading of the parallel accounts of the four Gospels presents Chrysostom with critical problems that require a harmonizing explanation (άρμονία) to reconcile apparent discrepancies in the biblical record. His efforts to harmonize those discrepancies rest on the dual assumption that the Gospels are in complete theological agreement and that such agreement is in fact supported by their differences in details such as time, place and sequence of events.[22] To this end he formulates the principle of harmonization which states that if two accounts seem irreconcilable, they either describe two separate incidents or else the differences are attributable to the individual style and purpose of each Gospel writer.[23] Thus Chrysostom holds there were two separate cleansings of the Temple. John placed the cleansing early in the ministry, but the Synoptics placed it during Passion Week.

In Homily 36 on Matthew, Chrysostom encounters the difficulty of harmonizing Matthew 11:2-3 with Luke 7:18. In Matthew the Evangelist tells us that the disciples of John the Baptist spoke only about the works of Jesus, while Luke included the miracles. Chrysostom asserts that the difficulty of reconciling those two accounts can be most easily resolved by engaging the text at the deeper level of a contemplative analysis of the historical characteristics of the narratives: "However, this contains no difficult matter, but only requires deeper spiritual insight [άλλά θεωρίαν μόνον]."[24] To achieve that "deeper spiritual insight" (θεωρία) Chrysostom relied on literary, historical and theological facts to harmonize the divergent Gospel accounts.

In Homily 34 on John, Chrysostom connects the various literary forms of Scripture with θεωρία. He draws attention first to the initial confusion which the disciples had over the meaning of Jesus' words: "My food is to do the will of Him who sent Me, and to accomplish His work" (John 4:34). Their bewilderment, he maintains, was intentionally designed according to a divine pedagogy. By communicating through dark sayings Jesus evoked perplexity in the minds of his disciples that, in turn, predisposed them for advancing to the higher meaning of his words:

> He did so because He wished first to make them more attentive, as I have said, as a result of their perplexity, and to dispose them to listen carefully to His words, by reason of such enigmatic statements [εἰνιγματαον].[25]

---

[22] Homiliae in Matthaeum 1, PG 57.18.

[23] Homiliae in Matthaeum 4, PG 57.45. This text differs from Origen's efforts to resolve divergent accounts by explaining them in terms of the union of the soul with the Logos (Commentarii in evangelium Joannis bk. 10, Fathers of the Church 80 [Washington, D.C., 1947-], p. 299).

[24] Homiliae in Matthaeum 36, PG 57.413.

[25] Homiliae in Joannem 34, Fathers of the Church 33, p. 334 (PG 59.194).

Such a pedagogical device may at first seem to be nothing more than the tactful skill of a wise teacher. However, in that same text Chrysostom goes on to announce that Jesus wished to convey a higher θεωρία by the ordinary use of figurative language:

> See once again how by references to ordinary things [τοῖς συντρόφοις ὀνόμασιν] He leads them up to the higher vision [ἀνάγει πρὸς τῶν μεγίστων θεωρίαν αὐτούς]. By saying food He signified nothing else than the salvation of the men who were going to come to Him. Now the field and harvest signify the same thing; namely, the multitude of souls ready to receive their preaching. By "eyes" He here meant both those of the understanding and those of the body, for as He saw the crowd of Samaritans already on their way and the receptiveness of their dispositions, He said they were fields already white. Just as the ears of corn are ready for harvesting when they are white, so these people also, He meant, were prepared and fitted for salvation. . . . What end did these figures of speech [τρόπαι] accomplish for Him? For He used them not only here, but all through the Gospel. And the Prophets similarly have made use of the same device, uttering many metaphorical sayings [μεταφορικῶς]. What in the world, then, is the reason for this? . . . Do you see how, while the words refer to sensible objects, the significance is spiritual, and by the words themselves He distinguished the things of earth from the heavenly?[26]

What is so striking about this passage is the extent and variety of literary forms that Chrysostom identifies as being capable of expressing the spiritual meaning of the text. Not only was figurative language used in the Gospel of John but also throughout the Old Testament. The literary forms include enigmas (αἴνιγμα), metaphors (μεταφόρα), parables (παραβολή) and proverbs (παροιμία). This homily is the only explicit example in Chrysostom's New Testament homilies where he affirms that various figures of speech are vehicles for expressing θεωρία.

The hermeneutical implications of these passages bring into sharp focus the Antiochene's application of θεωρία to the interpretation of symbolic discourse. Chrysostom's method for finding the spiritual content of the different kinds of figurative speech contained in the Bible, especially metaphors, proceeds on the assumption that each symbol has a figurative and mystical reference. The earthly referent conveys the meaning of its spiritual counterpart and determines the kind of truth which θεωρία reveals to the receptive listener.

Some figures are so highly saturated with lofty meaning that the hearer is perplexed because of his or her own lack of spiritual preparation for receiving it. Chrysostom explains to his congregation that Jesus raised the minds of his disciples to higher planes of soteriological insight by inducing them to contemplate the spiri-

---

[26]Ibid. For the ordinary use of metaphors which have no deeper meanings see Chase, *Chrysostom*, pp. 180-94.

tual counterpart that belonged to the figurative sense of his words. In order to apprehend the θεωρία of the Gospel, therefore, one first had to recognize the literal meaning in its actual, ordinary, cultural situation. Then, through a contemplative vision of the literal sense the relevant points of similarity between the earthly symbol and its deeper spiritual reality could be known. The spiritual sense was established by its natural points of similarity with the literal earthly symbol. The hermeneutical restraints on Chrysostom's spiritual exegesis were thus controlled and defined by the nature of the narrative itself.

θεωρία and Homiletics

No analysis of Chrysostom would be complete without reference to his use of θεωρία in homiletical discourse. The fundamental presuppositions he brought to his sermons included the belief that Scripture was uniformly inspired by God and that part of the homiletical task required that the pastor conform proclamation of the Word to the nature and manner in which it was given. Paul's first epistle to Timothy provides the occasion for Chrysostom to comment on the nature of Scripture and the theoretic exegesis which must accompany its true exposition. Paul exhorted, "Pay close attention to yourself and to your teaching, persevere in these things, for as you do this you will insure salvation both for yourself and for those who hear you" (1 Tim 4:16). Chrysostom exhorts the Christians living in Antioch to obey Paul's injunction. "For these things are not said to Timothy only, but to all. And if such advice is addressed to him, who raised the dead, what shall be said to us?" He declares that Paul urged Timothy to inquire into the Scriptures with the same exegetical purpose with which Paul himself had interpreted the sacred text. The congregation in Antioch was to follow the apostolic example, for even St. Paul constantly searched the prophetic Scriptures in order to obtain the salvific truth they contained:

> Hence we find him constantly appealing to the testimony of the prophets and theorizing [θεωροῦντα] into their writings. Paul, then, applies this to reading, for it is no small gain that is to be reaped from the Scriptures. But we are lazy and hear with carelessness and indifference. What punishment do we not deserve![27]

Chrysostom's reference to the Old Testament Scriptures as "prophets" is a literary instance of synecdoche or possibly metonymy. His point is that the apostle Paul carefully searched out the theological meaning of the words and events recorded in the prophetic Scriptures by "theorizing" or "divining" (θεωροῦντα) as it were, the deeper soteriological import of their oracles. To Chrysostom's dismay,

---

[27]*Homiliae in epistulam 1 ad Timotheum* 13, PG 62.566.

however, most Christians were too careless and indifferent to make the effort to learn these divine teachings.

The spiritual preparation required for discerning the deeper truths of revelation is stressed in Chrysostom's reflections on the Transfiguration recorded in Matthew 17:1-3. He maintains that the theoretic significance of the Transfiguration was more readily apprehended by Jesus' disciples because the event was first preceded by prophetic preparation. The predictive element came from Matthew 16:28: "Truly I say to you, there are some of those who are standing here who shall not taste death until they see the Son of Man coming in His kingdom." "The kingdom indeed," said Chrysostom, "He shows in the vision."[28] The Transfiguration was not intended for all of Jesus' disciples. It was primarily for the benefit of Peter, James and John who "were superior to the rest." By prophesying to them of the glorious event, Jesus "leads them on the gentler way." The tender care that was shown to the three disciples had as its goal a profound revelatory purpose (θεωρία):

Why, then, does He foretell it? So that they might be more prepared to grasp the higher vision [περὶ τὴν θεωρίαν] by His foretelling it; and in those days being filled more intensely with desire to understand it, they might arrive at that meaning with their mind alert and reflective (οὕτα νηφούστῃ καὶ μεμεριμνημένῃ τῇ διανοίᾳ παραγένωντα).[29]

The content of that "higher vision" (θεωρία) is spelled out in Chrysostom's exegesis of the biblical text. It is the private epiphany of Christ's deity to the chosen disciples that was revealed in the context of a typological and eschatological event: The deity of Christ was revealed through the radiance of his glory that showed through the ordinaries of his human flesh, while the typological figures of the eschaton were symbolized by the appearance of Moses and Elijah. In Homily 21 of *Ecloga de Imperio Potestate et Gloria* Chrysostom asks, "What does 'transfigured' mean? It means that He disclosed a little of the Godhead and showed them the indwelling deity."

Finally, the seventh homily on John exhibits an organic connection between revelation, inscripturation and homiletical discourse in Chrysostom's application of θεωρία. Commenting on John 1:9, "That was the true light which, coming into the world, enlightens every man," Chrysostom begins the homily by explaining the reasons why it is prudent to impart deeper knowledge to Christians discreetly, a little at a time:

Dearly beloved children, the reason why we feed you little by little [κατὰ μέρος] with

---

[28] *Homiliae in Matthaeum* 56, PG 58.549.

[29] *Homiliae in Matthaeum*, PG 58.550.

thoughts [νοήμασι] from the Scriptures, and have not poured them all out at once, is that we might make it easy for you to hold fast on those already given to you. . . . And I say this for, when constructing a building when the first stones are not yet firmly fastened together if a man sets others upon them, he renders the wall altogether unsound and easy to throw down. But, if he waits for the cement to set first, and then places the rest upon it gradually, he completes the whole house with safety, making it not a temporary structure, or easily destroyed, but durable. Let us also imitate these builders and let us build up your souls in the same way. For we are afraid lest, when the first foundation has just been laid, the adding of the next teachings [θεωρημάτων, better rendered "higher doctrines"] may weaken the former, because your understanding is not sufficiently strong to hold all together firmly. . . . What is it, then, that is read out to us today? "It was the true light that enlightens every man coming into the world." . . . he [John] appealed to our imagination and dispatched it to that Existence preceding every beginning, an existence which comes to no end and has no beginning. . . . John, the Son of Thunder, as he sounded forth on his spiritual trumpet, did not inquire further when he heard the word "was" from the Spirit. And you, who do not share in his grace but merely give voice to your weak reasonings, strive contentiously to surpass the measure of his knowledge? . . . [L]et us be obedient to God, and let us remain faithful to those things which He has commanded us. Let us not beyond that be unduly inquisitive.[30]

In the above passage, νοήμασι presumably referred to the scriptural thoughts Chrysostom had previously preached in homilies one to six. His use of θεωρημά-των, however, connoted not simply the "next teachings" of his sermon but the "higher doctrines" of the Gospel of John. When Chrysostom spoke of the gradual unfolding of scriptural teaching in his preaching, the theoretic meaning was identified as the divinity and coeternality of the Son with the Father. The hermeneutical inference is that the source of this truth came from the Holy Spirit, who revealed it to the apostle John when he composed his Gospel under divine inspiration, and that such truth could be known by Chrysostom's contemporaries on the basis of a grammatical-historical exegesis of John 1:1. Chrysostom urged those curious souls (perhaps Arians) who foolishly inquired into the incomprehensible nature of God to observe the apostle's own silence in this matter, for even after John received the divine knowledge he sought to learn no more than what had been revealed. Moreover, Chrysostom saw himself as participating homiletically in the biblical text by patterning his sermons after the manner in which revelation had been given. Just as a builder carefully lays one brick at a time in constructing a wall, patiently allowing each layer to dry, so also Chrysostom taught his congregation by carefully placing in their minds one θεώρημα at a time. Such language echoes God's gracious act

---

[30]*Homiliae in Joannem* 7, Fathers of the Church 33, pp. 75-76 (PG 59.85).

of accommodation (συγκατάβασις) in salvation history (θεώρημα). Chrysostom's use of the term οίκονομία to describe the Word of God inferred that pastoral preaching itself was viewed as a mystical event. The manner of the divine pedagogy of God's self-revelation in Scripture provided the Antiochene pastor with a model by which to pattern his own homiletical discourse. In this way Chrysostom made good homiletical use of θεωρία by expounding the hermeneutic not only as an inspired event of revelation but also as a pastoral model for the proclamation of the Word.[31]

---

[31]q.v. *Homiliae in Joannem* 4 and 30; *Homiliae in epistulam ad Hebraeos* 9, PG 63.76; and *Homiliae in epistulam 2 ad Corinthios* 3, PG 61.409. A fascinating project that is deserving of a separate monograph is a history of the influence of Chrysostom's (and other Antiochenes') use of θεωρία on the Syriac tradition of biblical exegesis. A notable start in this direction can be seen in Cornelia Molenberg's dissertation, *The Interpreter Interpreted: IšoBar Nun's Selected Questions on the Old Testament* (Rijksuniversiteit Groningen, Netherlands, June 1990), pp. 359-81. Also noteworthy is the strong influence that the Antiochene methods of messianic interpretation exerted on Irish exegesis in the west from the seventh to twelfth centuries. Diodore and Theodore's theory of a twofold historical sense (θεωρία) reappears in early Irish scholars. See the brief observation of James P. Mackey, *An Introduction to Celtic Christianity* (Edinburgh: T & T Clark, 1989), pp. 428-29.

FIVE

LEARNING HOW TO DIE WELL

Lessons from the Ancient Church

VIGEN GUROIAN

With the advent of a new millennium we on the North American continent are anticipating an increase of the average human life span to fourscore or more years. In this century the accomplishments of scientific medicine have been truly astonishing, and there are many reasons why we all should be grateful for these advances. But with these marvelous achievements come technologies that give us the capacity to control and manipulate life and death processes beyond the wildest dreams of our ancestors. It is no exaggeration to say that a society resembling Aldous Huxley's *Brave New World* may soon be within our reach and might even suit our desire. In such a society reproductive technologies and eugenics could ensure that every human being is "predestined" to be "useful" to society. And what Dr. Kevorkian has named obitiatric and thanatologic medicine might be carried on in hospitals as human being are exited from life the way we now put dogs and cats to "sleep."

In addition to the available technologies, ideological currents that challenge traditional religious prohibitions against radically altering human nature or medically ending human life are swirling all about in the culture. Today's medicine is not yet consciously antagonistic toward biblical faith, nor does it deliberately seek to subvert or contravene religiously inspired moral and legal limitations on what humans do with their bodies and biology. Nevertheless, the medical profession is under increasing pressure to use the new technologies in ways that challenge these limits.

In his hilarious but deeply troubling short story "The Death of Justina," John Cheever introduces his readers to a character named Moses, who rebels against our culture's aversion to death and disrespect of the dead. Moses makes this stunning comment at Justina's funeral: "How can a people who do not mean to understand death hope to understand love, and who will sound the alarm?"[1] Moses' unsettling statement is reminiscent of that chilling scene in Aldous Huxley's novel when John, the so-called Savage, is called to the Park Lane Hospital for the Dying to visit his dying mother, Linda. In this facility, the "patients" are put out of their misery in the pleasantest way possible, with plenty of soma, canned music, perfume mists, television and other amenities. In *Brave New World*, care for the dying has been perfected into a clinical and sanitized form of warehousing bodies until they may be utilized by society one last time—as phosphorous extracted by cremation. Love and attachment and feelings of loss are discouraged in *Brave New World*, and marriage and parenthood have been abolished. Suffering has been isolated and death is not mourned; both are sequestered to places where, apart from the attendants, the living needn't be.

The Culture of Death

I think Moses is right. At the heart of our culture's moral sickness is a growing aversion to death and the dying, and this may be traced to a commensurate diminishment of abiding love in human relations. There spreads through society a willingness to impose death on the sick and dying in order to cause the least discomfort and distraction to the healthy and the living. With such attitudes in mind, Pope John Paul II has rightly warned that ours is becoming a culture of death. There is a compelling need for Christians to be far better educated about what the faith says about the meanings of sickness and death.

From the beginning the Christian church has understood death as the counterpoint of life within the broad scope of God's providence. God's unbounded and steadfast love in Jesus Christ remedies our mortality. In our day, however, the church has not said enough about death, and is failing to persuade society to guard life and love adequately in the medical environment.

I will present, first, a religious view on the meaning of death that draws especially from Eastern Christian theology and liturgy. Second, I will examine the ancient sources of the church's long-standing interest in the healing arts. Third, I will illustrate with a true story how this theology of death and care for the dying

---

[1]John Cheever, "The Death of Justina," in *Stories of John Cheever* (New York: Ballantine, 1980), p. 515.

applies to our own day, urging the Christian churches to assume a much greater role and responsibility for preparing people to die well.

Death and Christian Belief

Not according to God's will but by sin has sickness unto death come to define the human condition, says the ancient tradition. Because of sin the entire race of Adam and Eve has been disconnected from God's immediate life-giving energies. We are like run-down batteries that finally lose their charge. All humanity is under this condition of mortality: no one is exempt. Original sin is the intractable habit of making the wrong moral choices and doing damage to the human environment. It is passed on from generation to generation, much like alcoholism, and its effects are deadly. St. Paul writes in his epistle to the Romans: "Sin came to life, but I died" (7:9 NKJV).

The fear of death threads through the entire fabric of human life. It drives human beings to desperate and often selfish acts. Sometimes it moves them to end their own lives so that they do not suffer the agony of death's onset. The ancient fathers of the church named the death that we die due to sin "corruptible death." They often cite the Wisdom of Solomon, a Greek intertestamental text included among the so-called Apocrypha of the Old Testament. "God created us for incorruption, and made us in the image of his own eternity, but through the devil's envy death entered the world," says the Wisdom of Solomon (2:23-24 RSV). Drawing on this, St. Athanasius recounts the story of the advent of corruptible death in his tract titled *On the Incarnation*.

> God set them [Adam and Eve] in His own paradise, and laid upon them a single prohibition. If they guarded the grace and retained the loveliness of their original innocence, then the life of paradise should be theirs without sorrow, pain or care and after it the assurance of immortality in heaven. But if they went astray and became vile, throwing away their birthright of beauty, then they would come under the natural law of death and live no longer in paradise, but, dying outside of it, continue in death and corruption.[2]

Thus, because of sin human existence comes under the strict determinism of nature's law. In other words, sin throws human existence into nature's cycle of life and death, into the entropy of natural existence that draws every living thing toward extinction. Sin activates our creaturely proclivity to fall into the darkness and nothingness out of which we were lifted into light and life by God's creative doing. Corruptible death, therefore, is a profound tragedy that has befallen the

---

[2]*St. Athanasius on the Incarnation: The Treatise De Incarnatione Verbi Dei*, trans. a Religious of C.S.M.V. (Crestwood, N.Y.: St. Vladimir's Seminary Press, 1982), pp. 28-29.

image of God. A hymn of the Byzantine Burial Rite lends powerful expression to this:"I weep and I wail when I think upon death, and behold our beauty, fashioned in the image of God, lying in the tomb disfigured, dishonored, bereft of form. O marvel! What is this mystery which doth befall us? Why have we been given over unto corruption, and why have we been wedded to death?"[3]

Only for the human being is death contrary to nature because in man's case mortality is a consequence of sin. At the close of the Armenian Church Service for Burial of the Dead, the priest gives voice to the deceased as the coffin is carried in procession out through the doors of the sanctuary. The deceased laments his fallen and corruptible state and prepares to meet "the Righteous Judge," adding the inevitable and strong penitential note in all Eastern Christian funeral and burial rites.

Let the whole world look upon me and witness my woes....
I have sinned and am condemned to oblivion
I have dug my own grave. I have plotted against myself.
I have betrayed, I cheated....

Once I was light and now I am in darkness and the shadow of death.
How shall I recount my sins, they are so numerous....

Hurry, O my person, flee from evil, desire goodness.
Collect yourself, before Death's sleep overcomes you.
Commit yourself to the Righteous Judge.
Lord have mercy. Lord, have mercy. Lord, have mercy.[4]

As reflected so poignantly in this Armenian hymn, the ancient tradition is quite clear that the death we know in a fallen world is not what God intended for human beings. St. Gregory of Nyssa writes: "From the nature of the dumb animals, mortality is transferred to a nature created for immortality."[5] God created Adam and Eve for eternal life, not to endure personal extinction, insists Gregory. Had the first couple not sinned, the parents of the race would have passed on to eternal life with God after the duration of their temporal lives. This passage into eternal life would not have entailed the radical rupture of body and soul and the demise of the person

---

[3]Service Book of the Holy Orthodox-Catholic Apostolic Church, ed. and trans. Isabel Florence Hapgood (Englewoood, N.J.: Antiochian Orthodox Christian Archdiocese, 1975), p. 386.

[4]Canon for the Burial of Laypersons according to the Sacred Rites of the Armenian Orthodox Church, trans. Very Rev. Ghevont Samoourian, Armenian Orthodox Theological Research Institute, unpublished. A portion of this recessional hymn may be found in The Rituals of the Armenian Apostolic Church (New York: Armenian Prelacy, 1992), p. 145.

[5]I am using Georges Florovsky's translation here as it appears in The Collected Works of Georges Florovsky, vol. 3: Creation and Redemption (Belmont, Mass,: Nordland, 1976), p. 106. This may be found in English translation also in The Great Catechism (chap. 3) in Gregory of Nyssa: Selected Works, Nicene and Post-Nicene Father of the Christian Church, 2nd ser. (Grand Rapids, Mich.: Eerdmans, 1979), 5:483.

that we see in death. However, Jesus Christ, the only begotten Son and express image of the Father, reversed the entropy and corruption that sin activated in humankind. Only the incarnate Son of God, who lived and died in our human flesh, was capable of renewing human nature by restoring the image of God within us through his sinless life and freely-willing death on the Cross. By these things Christ healed humankind so that all might be whole and inherit eternal life. Christ by his good death transformed death back into a passage to eternal life. This is the sure conviction of the ancient tradition.

The Medicinal Metaphor in the Ancient Tradition

From this theological perspective we are invited to think of the redemptive act of God in Jesus Christ as a kind of divine therapy. God's love and compassionate care have cured our diseased and mortally sickened human nature. In Fr. Georges Florovsky's words: "Redemption is not just man's reconciliation with God. Redemption is the abolition of sin altogether, the deliverance from sin and death. . . . The death of Our Lord was the victory over death and mortality, not just the remission of sins, nor merely justification of man, nor again a satisfaction of an abstract justice."[6] Florovsky's view is rooted deep within the ancient tradition and is forcefully reflected especially in the liturgies of the Orthodox Church. Salvation is understood as healing and also growth toward perfection. God's medicinal prescription of salvation in Christ remedies the carcinogenic effects of sin and cures the mortal sickness that corrupts our whole being. The fourteenth-century Byzantine theologian Nicholas Cabasilas evokes this meaning of healing in his great work of sacramental theology, *The Life in Christ*. There he explains:

> Many are the remedies which down through the ages have been devised for this sick race; it was Christ's death alone which was able to bring true life and health. For this reason, to be born by this new birth [of baptism] and live the blessed life and be disposed to health and, as far as lies in man, to confess the faith and take on oneself the passion and die the death of Christ, is nothing less than to drink of this medicine.[7]

This is a wonderful image of salvation in Christ through faith and baptism by water and the Spirit. Cabasilas plumbs the deep etymology of salvation. Its Greek root is *sozo* from *saos*, which literally means healthy. The Hebrew equivalent is *yasha*, which is to rescue from danger. The second-century church father Clement of Alexandria leads us in this same direction when he states: "The Word of the Father, who made man, cares for the whole nature of His creature; the all-sufficient

[6]Florovsky, *Creation and Redemption*, pp. 103, 104.
[7]Nicholas Cabasilas, *The Life in Christ*, trans. Carmino J. deCatanzaro (Crestwood, N.Y.: St. Vladimir's Seminary Press, 1974), p. 94.

Physician of humanity, the savior, heals both body and spirit."[8] Clement maintains that "the whole nature of His [God's] [human] creature" needs to be healed. Gregory of Nyssa may exceed all of the Greek fathers in his vivid description of the Christian Eucharist as medicine for a mortally sickened human nature, a remedy for corruptible death. In his Great Catechism St. Gregory states:

> Those who have been deceived into taking a poison use another drug to counter its harmful effects. Moreover the antidote, just like the poison must enter a man's system, so that its healing effect may be thereby spread throughout his whole body. Such was our case. We had eaten something that was disintegrating our nature. It follows, therefore, that we were in need of something to restore what had been disintegrated; we needed an antidote which would enter into us and so by its counteraction undo the harm already introduced into the body by the poison.
>
> And what is the remedy? It is that body which proved mightier than death and became the source of our life. For, as the apostle says, a little yeast makes the whole lump of dough like itself [see 1 Cor 5: 6]. In the same way, when the body that God made immortal enters ours, it transforms it entirely and makes it like itself. It is just like mixing poison with something wholesome, where everything in the mixture is rendered as worthless as the poison. Similarly the entry of the immortal body into the body that receives it transforms it in its entirety into its own immortal nature.[9]

If we venture to say that medicine has gained inspiration from the Christian ethos, it is equally true that Christian theology has taken from medicine metaphors that help to identify the mystery of salvation in Christ. And these in turn imprint deep within the Christian imagination a value to medicine. In contrast to the juridical and forensic metaphors that are dominant in Roman Catholicism and Protestantism, Eastern Christian writers employ medicinal metaphors to explain salvation; true faith brings about an inner change, or cure, that enables persons to pursue perfection. This perfection is no mere moralism. While it includes good works, it is primarily a process of inner transformation and healing of the sinful self. This process is engendered by faith, so that the human person may increase in divine similitude.

Ancient Christian Anthropology and Medicine

This medicinal interpretation of redemption is rooted in a Christian anthropology that will not make a sharp distinction between body and soul. Rather, the ancient tradition emphasizes that the unity of the two constitutes the whole person. God

---

[8]Clement of Alexandria, *The Instructor* 1.2, in *Fathers of the Second Century, Ante-Nicene Fathers* (Peabody, Mass.: Hendrickson, 1994), 2:210.

[9]Gregory of Nyssa, *Catechetical Oration* 37, in *Documents in Early Christian Thought*, ed. Maurice Wiles and Mark Santer (Cambridge: Cambridge University Press, 1975), p. 194.

breathed the breath of life into the man whom he made from dust and the man became a living soul (see Gen 2:7). The body without a soul is a corpse, and the soul without a body is a ghost. Only when they are perfectly one is the person alive and present. This notion of the human person as a psychosomatic unity was alien to the Hellenic mind. And my experience in the college classroom and in church parishes leads me to conclude that it is nearly as strange to many modern people, including Christians. Many in the churches embrace the Hellenic dualism that the soul is immortal but the body perishes. My undergraduate students at Loyola College—the vast majority of whom have attended Catholic parochial schools—are surprised to hear that the soul is by nature no more immortal than the body, and in the living person indistinghishable from the body. They have a hard time believing that Christianity defines personal identity as a unity of body and soul.

The earliest Christian creeds boldly insist that the final resurrection is a bodily resurrection. And it is precisely because the ancient church understood that salvation pertains to the whole human being, body and soul as one, that it was interested early in scientific medicine and valued it as an important human art aiding the process of our temporal journey to God. In the fourth century St. Basil the Great commented at length on the important place of medicine among the other arts and sciences that God uses to help us sustain our earthly existence and advance toward our heavenly home. In his *Long Rules* for monastic living, Basil declares:

> Each of the arts is God's gift to us, remedying the deficiencies of nature, as, for example, agriculture, since the produce which the earth bears of itself would not suffice to provide for our needs; the art of weaving, since the use of clothing is necessary for decency sake, and for protection from the wind; and similarly for the art of building. The same is true, also, of the medical art. In as much as our body is susceptible to various hurts, some attacking from without and some from within by reason of the food we eat, and since the body suffers affliction from both excess and deficiency, the medical art has been vouchsafed us by God, who directs our whole life, as a model for the cure of the soul, to guide us in the removal of what is superfluous and in the addition of what is lacking. Just as we would have no need of the farmer's labor and toil if we were living amid the delights of paradise, so also we would not require the medical art for relief if we were immune to disease, as was the case, by God's gift, at the time of Creation before the Fall.[10]

According to St. Basil, medicine functions within the catastrophic effects of the Fall and is a partial remedy for those effects. Rational or scientific medicine cannot

---

[10]Basil of Caesarea *The Long Rules* Q.55, in *Saint Basil: Ascetical Works*, trans. M. Monica Wagner, *The Fathers of the Church* (New York: Fathers of the Church, Inc., 1950), 9:330-31.

save the human being from death, but it can contribute to a healthy and meaningful life, so long as human beings do not put their whole hope in it. St. Basil's advice
is especially pertinent in our day when so may people mistakenly make an idol of
medicine and expect their physicians to be priests and shamans also. He continues:

> So then, we should neither repudiate this art [of medicine] altogether nor does it
> behoove us to repose all our confidence in it; but, just as in practicing the art of agri-
> culture we pray God for fruits, and as we entrust the helm to the pilot in the art of
> navigation, but implore God that we may end our voyage unharmed by the perils of
> the sea, so also, when reason allows, we call in the doctor, but not leave off hoping in
> God.[11]

How Even Death Becomes a Prescription for Life

The ancient tradition is able to guard against inflated expectations in the curative
power of scientific medicine because it finds reason for hope even in death. The
Cross and Resurrection have transformed even death into a medicine of salvation.
Nowhere that I know of in Christian liturgy is this more movingly portrayed than
in the central part of the Armenian funeral service for the home. We first encounter a series of penitential and intercessory hymns that are dialogical in character.
Both the deceased and the congregation are lent voices. The deceased pleads with
God for healing because sin—which is the infective source of all sickness and of
mortality itself—requires supernatural cure even after death. By willing submis-
sion to the judgment and mercy of Christ, the sins of the deceased may be washed
away forever.

> When my days are consumed, help me, O Lord, lover of mankind.

> You, who have assumed the tortures and death on the cross, help me, O Lord, lover
> of mankind.

> Through the intercession of the ever-virgin Holy Mother of God, help me, O
> Lord, Lover of mankind. . . .

> As a sinful person, I cry to you, O Heavenly father, help me in my distress, I, who
> am dead in my sins, help me.

> I have been wounded by the invisible enemy, O Healer of the sick, cure my malady. I,
> who am dead in my sins, help me.

> I have gone astray like the lost sheep, O seeker of the enslaved seek me, the wan-
> dered, I, who am dead in my sins, help me. . . .

---

[11]Ibid., p. 336.

O Lord, open the door of your mercy for us, and make us worthy of your luminous lodgers with your Saints.

In the abode that you prepared for your Saints, O Savior, accept us also as adopted children into the discipleship of life.

When you sit in your judgment, O formidable judge, have mercy upon your creatures, through the intercession and prayer of Holy ascetics.[12]

These hymns embrace the entire meaning of salvation understood both as rescue from danger and healing of the whole person. After several more hymns, a litany and prayers, the deacon chants the following verses from Psalm 39 as the mourners are reminded that they share the fate of the deceased under a common condition of mortality.

Behold, Thou who has made my days a few handbreadths, and my lifetime is as nothing in Thy sight. Surely every man stands as a mere breath! Surely man goes about as a shadow! Surely for naught are they in turmoil; man heaps up, and knows not who will gather. (vv. 5-6)[13]

A reading from St. Paul's second epistle to the Corinthians follows immediately and complements the psalmist's meditation on the brevity of our lives. The apostle invokes God the Father who is merciful and comforts us in our afflictions so that we may comfort others. He reminds his reader of the Son, Jesus Christ, who has shared in human suffering and by his death and resurrection heals humanity of the sickness and mortality of sin.

Blessed be the God and Father of our Lord Jesus Christ, the father of mercies and God of all comfort, who comforts us in all affliction, so that we may be able to comfort those who are in any affliction, with the comfort with which we ourselves are comforted by God . . . rely[ing] not on ourselves but on God who raises the dead . . . (2 Cor 1:3-11)[14]

These three elements of the Armenian Funeral Rite—penitential and intercessory hymns, psalm, and Pauline blessing—exemplify the three principal steps of the ancient Christian church's pedagogy of dying well in Christ. The first recalls

---

[12]*The Rituals of the Armenian Apostolic Church* (New York: Armenian Prelacy, 1992), pp. 123-24. This text is abbreviated and misleadingly lists this text as a single hymn. I have introduced ellipses and additional spacing where there is more text that is left out of this translation but which may be found in the recent translation of the complete Canon and Services that I have listed under footnote 4.

[13]*Rituals of the Armenian Apostolic Church*, p. 124. This text leaves the impression that this reading of the psalm follows immediately. Once again *Canon for the Burial of Laypersons* cited in footnote 4 should be consulted for the full text of the service for the home.

[14]*Rituals of the Armenian Apostolic Church*, p. 125. I have abbreviated the rite which actually includes the entire text of 2 Cor 13:3-11.

our mortality in the light of God's enduring love. The second seeks meaning in our suffering in light of the crucifixion and resurrection of Christ. The third envisions salvation as cure of sin and healing of body and soul leading to eternal life. If this simple pedagogy were practiced more often and consistently in the Christian churches, medicine might be infused anew with an ethos of healing and life.

A Modern Story of Death and Dying

Medicine needs better patients, and the church can and should help provide them. In contemporary medical ethics the character of the patient often is ignored. All too frequently medical ethics is fixed in quandary ethics that focus on the decisions, agency and acts of the physician. Even when issues of character are taken up, the professional care provider is the focus of attention, not the patient. But much good could be accomplished if the church were to attend to the rest of us who may never be professional care providers but will be patients at some point, at least when we are dying.

In a recent book *The Measure of Our Days: New Beginnings at Life's End*, physician Jerome Groopman tells a disturbing story that illustrates the importance of character and internal resources when facing the prospect of personal demise.

Kirk Bains was a highly successful businessman who made a small fortune in speculative investment ventures. Before coming to Dr. Groopman, Bains had been to the top hospitals in cancer treatment and was told repeatedly that nothing could be done for him. But Bains was a fighter. He told Groopman on their first meeting: "You've seen my records from Yale and Sloan-Kettering. . . . They think I'm too sick for their research studies. So you cook up some new magic. Make me a guinea pig, I take risks all the time. That's my business. I won't sue you."[15]

Groopman decided to run the standard tests. But he also trusted his intuition, believing that it is at least as important to know the story of the patient as to know clinically what he suffers from. The test results were as grim as the reports said. He explained to Kirk Bains the difficulty of his case. And the conversation turned in this direction:

> "I had hoped it would be a replay of *The Exorcist*," Kirk painfully quipped. "Remember how the priest took the demon out of the child, a bloody, ugly creature? I thought the surgeon would do the same. Maybe I'd have been better off with a priest than a doctor. Never thought I'd need the clergy. But that's what everyone is recommending now."

> "Are you affiliated with a church?" I always try to learn the scope of religious feeling, the ties of the patient and his family to faith. God, whether positive, negative, or

---

[15]Jerome Groopman, *The Measure of Our Days* (New York: Penguin, 1998), p. 7.

null, is an essential factor in the equation of dying.

"Episcopalian. I celebrate Christmas. The food. The music. Decorating the tree. Giving gifts. That's fun. But the religion—I can't take much stock in a church founded because Henry VIII wanted a younger wife."

My response was a skeptical look.

"Let me put it in my own terms. I'm not a long-term investor. I like quick returns. I don't believe in working for dividends paid in heaven."[16]

Dr. Groopman decided to try a radical and unorthodox combination of treatments. The night before the surgery, Groopman visited Bains in his hospital bed. He noticed that Bains was troubled and agitated.

"Are you thinking you could die tonight?" . . . "You won't, Kirk," I said confidently.

"So you're a prophet, not a wizard. Shall I call you St. Jerome?" . . . "I didn't expect to be so afraid, Jerry," Kirk paused, reaching for his thoughts. . . . "Maybe it's because I know this is my last chance and I'll probably die, and after death . . . it's just nothingness."

I absorbed his words and tightened my grip on his hand. I now understood why he had insisted on treatment, and I realized it would be wrong to readdress that decision tonight.

"So then it would be the same as before we were born?" I softly replied. "Is that terrifying, to be unborn? That's what my father used to say to comfort me as a child when I asked him about death."

"See if you still find that enough comfort when you're the one in this bed. Nothingness. No time. No place. No form. I don't ask for heaven. I'd take hell. Just to *be*."[17]

Kirk Bains's imagination is strong and vivid, and it is terrorizes him. The church he neglected or which neglected him might have helped form in him a religious imagination better equipped to cope with the futility of his physical condition. Dr. Groopman himself is not unaware of the importance of imagination and how it is formed. He comments:

"I thought about how we all develop our inner pictures of death and an afterlife, from stories and words we hear as children, which form our first image. As we pass through life, we redraw these images, hoping that at the end we will be prepared for what awaits."[18]

---

[16]Ibid., pp. 13-14.
[17]Ibid., pp. 23-24.
[18]Ibid., p. 25.

My friend Rev. Charles Kratz, an Episcopal priest, first brought Dr. Groopman's story to my attention. Rev. Kratz commented that he has seen many Kirk Bainses in his fifty-plus years as a priest, and he also knows how miserably his church has failed to address these matters of mortality and personal demise in the pulpit or at the bedside. "I couldn't help thinking," said Fr. Kratz, "that we clergy are to blame. Look at what kind of a person and patient we left for this doctor to deal with."

The conversation Dr. Groopman cites constitutes a crucial moment in the life and death of Kirk Bains: he is open to counsel, but Dr. Groopman's father's religious views do not allay Bains's fears or satisfy his needs. Of this scene Rev. Kratz said: "Maybe something might have been accomplished with the right religious counsel at that moment. But we rarely get to be there at those moments. And by this time, it is almost too late for people like Kirk Bains, short of a divine act of grace."

Dr. Groopman is himself shaken by this conversation with Bains. He spends several paragraphs ruminating over it. He recalls his father's death. And he acknowledges that is probably why he rarely visits that memory; it is a nearly unbearable reminder of the personal nature of death.

> After he died, it was impossible for me to imagine my father as disintegrated into nothingness. . . . It was too painful, to stark an image in my mind, that his body, the warm expansive body that had snuggled me in bed when I was fearing the shadows of the night, held me in the water when I learned to swim, embraced me with surprising strength when I succeeded, and embraced me with even greater strength when I had failed. That that body was now inanimate matter. . . . And nothing more. . . . I hoped I would not lie terrified in bed, like Kirk.[19]

The radical treatment prescribed by Dr. Groopman worked for a time, the tumors shrank and the cancer went into remission. Kirk Bains was given four months of relatively comfortable living. But did he use this gift? Dr. Groopman stayed in touch with Bains and his wife during this time. When the cancer came back, he visited Bains in the hospital just after an initial radiation treatment.

> "I'm sorry the magic didn't work longer," I finally offered to Kirk.

> "It did more than anyone expected, Jerry. But you shouldn't feel sorry. There was no reason to live anyway. . . . You read newspapers?" Kirk asked abruptly. . . . "I don't read newspapers anymore. I don't know how to. Or why I should," Kirk paused and his voice lowered. "Newspapers used to be a gold mine for me. They're filled with what to you looks like disconnected bits of information. A blizzard in the Midwest, the

---

[19]Ibid., pp. 25, 26.

immigration debate in California. . . . For you, Jerry, those articles are about the lives and fortunes of individuals and nations. For me, they mean nothing beyond information for deals and commodity trading. I never really cared about the world's events or its people. Not deep down inside. . . .

And when I went into remission I couldn't read the papers because my deals and trades seemed pointless. Pointless because I was a short-term investor. Like I told you Jerry, I had no patience for the long term. I had no interest in creating something, not a product in business or a partnership with a person. And now I have no equity. No dividends coming in. Nothing to show in my portfolio," Kirk grimaced with pain.

"How do you like my great epiphany? No voice of God or holy star but a newspaper left unread in its wrapper." . . .

"Jerry, you realize I'm right. The remission meant nothing because it was too late to relive my life. I once asked for hell. Maybe God made this miracle to have me know what it will feel like."[20]

Groopman says he felt "the crushing weight of Kirk's burden." He continues pensively, "There is no more awful death than to die with regret, feeling that you have lived a wasted life—death delivering this shattering final sentence on your empty soul."[21]

It's a terrifying tale of modern death. The story is a challenge, not primarily to medicine but to the Christian faith. There will always be patients like Kirk Bains who believe in nothing or very little and who come to the medical practitioner with the demand, "Save me! Save me in whatever way you can!" But in the future there be increasing numbers of others who will come to physicians with the equally ferocious demand, "If you can't fix me, then put me out of my misery!"

So much of what constitutes dying a good death depends not on the health care setting or the medical skills of the care providers but the religious and moral resources of the dying. My good friend Sr. Sharon Burns, R.S.M., taught theology for many years, but for the past fifteen years has worked as a chaplain at Stella Maris Hospice in Towson, Maryland. She told me how much it helps when her patients have religious formation equipping them with beliefs that can carry them through. She says these people can be healed deeply during their dying. At Stella Maris the stories, symbols and rituals of the Christian faith are brought to a prominence in the daily routine that the secular culture does not permit. Much in the way of penance and forgiveness, reunion and reconciliation can be accomplished in

---

[20]Ibid., pp. 35-37.
[21]Ibid., p. 37.

the lives of Stella Maris patients in a relatively brief period of time. Love, so often hindered and sometimes discouraged in more typical health care environments, is given and returned by staff and family at Stella Maris. Suffering is not isolated but shared in a manner that reflects the great pastoral counsel of St. Paul in 2 Corinthians.

Churches also need to more conscientiously prepare people for dying. Indeed, the ancient fathers of the church valued and commended an unremitting remembrance of death as one of the principal virtues of the Christian life. This is a virtue long neglected in Christian teaching and sorely needed today. "The unremitting remembrance of death is a powerful trainer of body and soul," wrote St. Hesychios of Sinai. "Vaulting over all that lies between ourselves and death, we should always visualize it, and even the very bed on which we shall breathe our last, and everything connected with it."[22] While a secular world might view this as a call to morbidity, Christians should receive this advice in the joyful light of their resurrection faith. Death and resurrection are inevitably and necessarily woven together in the Christian imagination. This pedagogy of the remembrance of death is already present in the liturgies of the church. I mean especially the theology and spirituality communicated through baptism, the Eucharist and the rites of burial. Thus, for example, near the conclusion of the Byzantine rite of burial, the mourners are asked specifically to exercise this remembrance of death. "As we gaze on the dead who lieth before us, let us all accept the example of our own last hour."[23]

Care of the dying has been a deep concern of the church from the earliest centuries, but so too has the preparation of Christians to meet their deaths. Much has been written in the annals of medical ethics about virtues that physicians and health care professionals need in order to care properly for the terminally ill and dying. Yet surprisingly little has been said about the character that the church must cultivate in persons so that they make good patients.[24] If there is a lesson to be learned from the story of Kirk Bains, it is medicine cannot cure our mortality and we must be prepared to accept this truth with courage and hope in order to be best served by our physicians. The resources the Christian faith has to help people live toward their dying in freedom, courage, patience and hope cannot be instantaneously transmitted to the sick person whose flesh is already ravaged and whose is mind tormented by disease. The meaning that faith sup-

---

[22]St. Hesichios, "Watchfulness and Holiness," in *The Philokalia*, ed. and trans. G. E. Palmer, Philip Sherrard, and Kallistos Ware (London: Faber & Faber, 1970), 1:178.

[23]Service Book of the Holy Orthodox-Catholic Apostolic Church, p. 390.

[24]By "good patient" I do not mean a simply cooperative or compliant patient, as the term has come to mean in common medical parlance. I mean a patient that is formed and habituated in patience, fortitude and faith among other virtues valued and invoked in the Christian sacraments.

plies for living and dying must be claimed over a lifetime.

Physicians have always needed good patients to be good healers. The situation has not changed in our day. In fact, this may be more necessary than ever before. How else will physicians be able to shift their goals at the appropriate time from cure to being present for their patients as death approaches? The physician's most important obligation is to be present throughout for the sick or dying person, to never abandon the patient. This can be accomplished successfully only if doctor and patient collaborate. As Christian ethicist Stanley Hauerwas has wisely said in *Suffering Presence*: "It is important, then, that the one who is dying exercise the responsibility to die well. That is, the person should die in a manner that is morally commensurate with the kind of trust that has sustained him or her in life. . . . A good death is a death that we prepare for through living because we are able to see that death is but the necessary correlative to a good life."[25]

Good care for the terminally ill and dying begins with care for the healthy and living. Through the church's own best standards, that care is the fundamental responsibility of the church, not of medicine. By the example of Christ and all the martyrs and saints, it is the responsibility of the church to prepare people to die well, while they are still living, through the sacraments, prayer and preaching. If the church and those of us who are its living members could look to this pedagogy and preparation more conscientiously, then we might stand to make a great contribution toward strengthening the humane ethos of medicine.

---

[25]Stanley Hauerwas, *Suffering Presence* (Notre Dame, Ind.: University of Notre Dame Press, 1986), pp. 96, 98.

Six

What Are You, O Man?

Theo-Anthropological Similarities in Classical Pentecostalism & Eastern Orthodoxy

EDMUND J. RYBARCZYK

If the fall of the Berlin Wall was exciting for citizens in the West, it was even more so for Christians in the West. Marxist communism had finally been proven to be the economic, political and religious disaster that it was. Protestant missions agencies were eager to take the gospel into the "dark" regions formerly under Soviet control. After all, for many conservative Protestants, Russia was the great "Gog and Magog" of Ezekiel 38—39 and Revelation 16:12; the archetypal anti-Christian nation to be used by Satan. Chief among these mission-minded Western groups were the classical Pentecostals (herein after simply Pentecostals).[1]

---

[1]Classical Pentecostals are distinguished from both evangelicals and charismatics, though they share more in common with those groups than they have by way of distinction. Pentecostals share with evangelicals the following beliefs: the universality of sin and the ensuing need for God's forgiveness, Jesus as the only way to salvation, the Bible as God's inspired and authoritative revelation, and a commitment to proclaiming the gospel. Classical Pentecostals are unique in that they have emphasized the following: Spirit-baptism followed by speaking in tongues, the healing power of Christ's atoning work, the necessity of spreading the gospel in light of Christ's imminent return, an egalitarian ecclesial structure, and the importance of a sanctified life. In the United States the major classical Pentecostal denominations include the Reformed (also called Baptistic) and Wesleyan Holiness groups. The Reformed group consists of the Assemblies of God, the Christian Missionary Alliance, and the International Church of the Foursquare Gospel. The Wesleyan Holiness group consists of the Church of God in Christ, the Church of God (Cleveland, Tennessee), the Church of the Nazarene, the Church of God (Anderson, Indiana)

What many of these missionaries did not know and what they remain slow to recognize is that the so called "dark" Eastern European regions had been affected by the gospel as early as the ninth century, when the brothers Cyril and Methodius brought Orthodoxy from Byzantium to the Slavs.[2] For their part, in the seventeenth and eighteenth centuries the Russians believed that Russia was the supreme Christian country, and spoke of Russia as fulfilling eschatological prophecies about the spread of the gospel. In the minds of those Russian Orthodox, Christianity would be birthed around the globe through "Mother Russia." Thus when Western Christian missionaries and parachurch agencies began to enter these long-standing Eastern Orthodox countries in order to shine the light of the gospel,[3] the Orthodox Church hierarchs reacted with horror and outrage.[4] Who were these insensitive Western cowboys? Had they no respect or shame? For their part the Westerners have been slow to even admit that the Orthodox were ever even Christian.[5] Moreover, due to their own cultural free-market milieu, the Westerners were both surprised and insulted when their intentions were maligned and their activities were suppressed. There was insensitivity and stereotyping on the part of both camps.

Today the stereotyping and acrimony continue to abound. The Orthodox Church leaders in formerly Soviet bloc countries jealously guard territories that they believe "belong" to them. They have made use of political and social means to

---

and the Pentecostal Holiness Church. A further distinction resides with Oneness Pentecostalism, a movement that separated from the Reformed Pentecostals in 1916. Oneness denominations do not hold to the Chalcedonian trinitarian formulae and include the United Pentecostal Church International and the predominantly black Pentecostal Assemblies of the World. Whereas charismatics believe in the immanence of the Spirit's operations through a believer, they do not emphasize tongues as the evidence sine qua non of Spirit-baptism as do most Pentecostals. Charismatics see themselves as Spirit-filled believers, but they have remained in traditional non-Pentecostal denominations. See Timothy P. Weber, "Evangelicalism," in *Evangelical Dictionary of Theology*, 10th ed., ed. Walter A. Elwell (Grand Rapids, Mich.: Baker, 1994), pp. 382-84; Peter D. Hocken, "Charismatic Movement," in *Dictionary of Pentecostal and Charismatic Movements*, ed. Stanley M. Burgess and Gary B. McGee (Grand Rapids, Mich.: Zondervan, 1988), pp. 130-60; David A. Reed, "Oneness Pentecostalism," in *Dictionary of Pentecostal and Charismatic Movements*, ed. Stanley M. Burgess and Gary B. McGee (Grand Rapids, Mich.: Zondervan, 1988), pp. 644-51; David K. Bernard, *The Oneness of God* (Hazelwood, Mo.: Word Aflame, 1983).

[2]It was these brothers who invented the Slavic alphabet in order to spread the gospel.

[3]To be more accurate, Pentecostals first began to enter Eastern European countries as early as 1908. World War I slowed considerably the Pentecostals' efforts. See Cecil M. Robeck Jr., "A Pentecostal Witness in an Eastern Context," address given at the "Building Bridges, Breaking Walls," international conference, Prague, Czech Republic, September 12, 1977.

[4]Eleanor Randolph, *Waking the Tempests: Ordinary Life in the New Russia* (New York: Simon & Schuster, 1996). The Orthodox are aghast at the surging religious pluralism. Randolph quoted a priest named Otets Nikolai, "the main task of [Orthodox] Christianity is to preserve the purity of the faith because the church is attacked on all sides by these variations and they are appearing like mushrooms" (p. 313). See also Niels C. Nielsen Jr., ed., *Christianity After Communism: Social, Political, and Cultural Struggle in Russia* (Boulder, Colo.: Westview Press, 1994).

[5]Robeck, "Pentecostal Witness," pp. 27-32.

inhibit the Pentecostals' activities. In the most shameful cases they have physically assaulted Pentecostals.[6] The Orthodox leaders of the East tend to view the Pentecostals as quasi-Christian enthusiasts who lack any kind of defined ecclesiology. Having no historical connection to the apostolic succession of the priesthood and lacking any kind of accountability to the established Orthodox territorial jurisdictions, the Pentecostals tend to be viewed as unscrupulous mavericks. On the other hand Pentecostals tend to look at the Orthodox as those who are stuck in the quagmires of empty religious ritual and state-church relationships that are largely passé in the West. Because there has been little careful study of the Orthodox by either evangelicals or Pentecostals,[7] the latter view the former as both hopelessly bound to ancient custom and unwilling to allow the laity to have a genuine role in the work of the kingdom of God. The great bulk of the acrimony and stereotyping, on both fronts, is due to sin and ignorance. Sin makes us naturally xenophobic. Xenophobia naturally makes us disinterested in learning about those who are different from ourselves. And to complete and perpetuate the cycle, ignorance feeds into the pathology of sinfulness.

Together with the cultural, historical and ecclesiastical problems mentioned above, there are varied and important theological issues that stand between Pentecostals and the Orthodox. These will not be developed here, but they certainly need to be addressed by any future interested representatives: the virgin Mary, the sacraments,[8] the priesthood, salvation (specifically how salvation is wed to the church), ecclesiology (just what is the church?), icons, and church tradition.

Despite the aforementioned cultural tensions and theological differences, the Eastern Orthodox (hereafter simply Orthodox) and the Pentecostals share a great many features, features that warrant notation here but which are too regularly ignored in the attempt to criticize or exclude the other. First, although it is obvious,

---

[6]Recently (March 2001) Pentecostal pastors and leaders in Tbilisi, Republic of Georgia, were assaulted by Basili Mkalavishvili and one hundred or so of his followers on property where the Pentecostals intended to build a Bible school. The Pentecostals were kicked, punched and beaten with wooden rods. Mkalavishvili is a former Orthodox priest who had been excommunicated in 1995 for anti-Christian activity. See Assemblies of God electronic *News and Info* reports on March 30 and April 20, 2001. Robeck notes that Orthodox persecution of Pentecostals occurred in Armenia and Russia prior to WWI. "A Pentecostal Witness in an Eastern Context," pp. 11, 14, 17, 19, 25.

[7]My own dissertation, "Beyond Salvation: An Analysis of the Doctrine of Christian Transformation Comparing Eastern Orthodoxy with Classical Pentecostalism" (Fuller Theological Seminary, 1999), is an attempt to address this gaping lacuna. Another is the ACUTE report on evangelicalism and Orthodoxy, Timothy Grass, ed. (Carlisle, U.K.: Paternoster, 2001). The evangelical scholar Daniel B. Clendenin, who both lived and taught in Russia, has edited some Orthodox literature, but has done very little to synthesize, or make fine distinctions between, evangelicalism and Orthodoxy. See Clendenin, *Eastern Orthodox Theology: A Contemporary Reader* (Grand Rapids, Mich.: Baker, 1995); *Eastern Orthodoxy: A Western Perspective* (Grand Rapids, Mich.: Baker, 1994).

[8]More appropriately understood within Orthodoxy as the *mysteries*—vehicles whereby the life of God is communicated to believers.

neither is beholden to the Roman Catholic Church. In that aspect both groups believe their respective ecclesial structures are more organic (involving the laity and the Spirit's operations within the laity) and less institutionalized (i.e., hierarchically structured) than that of the Roman Catholics. Also pertaining to Christian service both Pentecostals and Orthodox allow their local ministers/priests to marry and have children; ordained service is not the exclusive privilege of a select or celibate minority.

Second, both traditions understand themselves to be Christendom's great pneumatologists. The Orthodox maintain their pneumatological identity especially in light of their unequivocal opposition to the insertion of the *filioque* clause into ancient Christian creeds.[9] By holding to what they believe is the most accurate interpretation of Scripture and the ancient creeds—and the most accurate *experience* of Scripture and the ancient creeds[10]—the Orthodox believe they are, after all, the ones who maintain right belief and worship (*ortho* meaning "right" or "correct;" *doxa* meaning "glory" or "worship"). Pentecostals believe they are the rightful custodians of pneumatology because they believe they, since the early part of the twentieth century, have been reintroducing the dynamic life of the Spirit to the larger church. The Pentecostals believe their experience of the Spirit's presence and power is like that experienced by the apostles in the book of Acts.

Third, both groups are theologically conservative and assert the following tenets of faith: Jesus Christ is God's only means of salvation; Jesus was born of the virgin Mary; following Nicea and Chalcedon, Jesus is fully human and fully divine; God is a triune being; and the Christian canon is inspired of the Holy Spirit and is therefore the primary and authoritative source for Christian life and thought.

Those features are important. One would think such important issues might be pivotal for shared Christian worship, missions and activism. Unfortunately, the fact of the matter is that the cultural, historical, ecclesial and political issues loom more important in the minds of each sides' respective leaders. In that regard both the Pentecostals and the Orthodox have allowed themselves to become over-

---

[9]Because they believe the *filioque* clause (lit., "and [from] the Son") jeopardizes the very life of the church and the means of salvation, almost every substantial Orthodox publication written with an eye toward the West includes a critique of this issue. For example see Vladimir Lossky, *In the Image and Likeness of God*, ed. John H. Erickson and Thomas E. Bird (Crestwood, N.Y.: St. Vladimir's Seminary Press, 1985); John Zizioulas, *Being as Communion: Studies in Personhood and the Church* (Crestwood, N.Y.: St. Vladimir's Seminary Press). Kallistos (Timothy) Ware qualified that there are varied opinions among the Orthodox concerning the extent of heresy deriving from the *filioque* clause. See Kallistos Ware, *The Orthodox Church* (Baltimore, Md.: Penguin, 1964), pp. 213-17.

[10]John Meyendorff summarized the Orthodox on tradition and said, "tradition is not a continuity of ideas only, but also of experience." John Meyendorff, *Christ in Eastern Christian Thought*, 2nd ed., trans. Yves Dubois (Crestwood, N.Y.: St. Vladimir's Seminary Press, 1987), 10.

wrought by the world's values: triumphalism, superiority and self-interest that cannot tolerate accomodation of others. The dynamic Spirit-inspired yeast of God's kingdom is supposed to penetrate and transform the loaf of the world, but sadly that yeast is too regularly taken and shaped into the rigid mold of the world. Instead of the yeast being the impelling force shaping the bread, the bread throttles the life of the yeast, making it become like itself.

This then is the present state of affairs in Eastern Europe between these two traditions that together comprise about seven hundred million of the two billion who call themselves Christians.[11] (Matters may be less caustic in Western Europe and the United States, but mutual ignorance is still the rule.) It is distressing that mutual suspicion and stereotyping resides between these two, especially since it is the case that they are alike in other ways that are, frankly, striking.

Of chief concern for this study, the Pentecostals and the Orthodox define the human person in a similar way.[12] In distinction to much of twenty-first century Protestantism that sees the human intellect as the defining feature of the *imago Dei*, the Pentecostals and Orthodox emphasize that humanity's spiritual nature, the core of what it means to be fashioned in God's image, transcends mental capacity. "They became futile in their thinking, and their foolish minds were darkened" (Rom 1:21), informs both Orthodoxy's and Pentecostalism's understanding that the whole human is unable to clearly perceive the truth about life and existence. It is no mere accident that each group has traditionally been wary of the interpretive truth claims of the natural sciences: the human mind is itself fallen and therefore not always to be trusted. To hold that either the Orthodox or the Pentecostals are resistant to scientific claims—though, certainly they both are—simply because they are premodern country bumpkins is to fail to understand each has a theological commitment that forcefully shapes their perspective. The very core of human existence is itself corrupted and darkened by sin.

As will be apparent herein, each tradition defines humankind's spiritual nature in categories befitting each one's own historical and cultural matrix. The failure to interpret either Orthodoxy or Pentecostalism apart from those respective historico-cultural backgrounds will leave one with a truncated understanding. A few

---

[11]Roman Catholics number about one billion. D. B. Barrett, "Global Statistics," in *Dictionary of Pentecostal and Charismatic Movements*, ed. Stanley M. Burgess and Gary B. McGee (Grand Rapids, Mich.: Zondervan, 1988), pp. 810-30. Also see Cecil M. Robeck Jr., "Pentecostal Origins in Global Perspective," in *All Together in One Place: Theological Papers from the Brighton Conference on World Evangelization*, ed. Harold D. Hunter and Peter D. Hocken (Sheffield, U.K.: Sheffield Academic Press, 1993), pp. 166-80.

[12]I do not mean that the Orthodox and Pentecostals are decisively unique in their positions. Other branches of the Christian family tree could make similar claims. What I am arguing is that the anthropology of both groups decisively and emphatically characterizes the whole range of their spirituality in a way that surpasses that of most other Christian traditions.

introductory remarks in this regard will suffice.

The Orthodox, in their anthropological definitions, employ Greek ontology and the language of iconography. Like an icon that shines forth something of the reality of the subject portrayed, human beings have an innate and God-given capacity to shine forth, to emit, something of whom God is in a myriad of ways. In this regard the Orthodox believe the energy of the Holy Spirit works or shines in and through our own energy. God's life works in and through our lives. This is a coworking the Orthodox call synergy. Because he shone forth God in perfect fashion (Jn 1:5, 14, 18), Jesus Christ was (and is) the perfect icon, the perfect image, of the Father. By the grace of God and his Spirit we can come to resemble what Jesus is by nature: deified humanity. To this end, and from creation, it was God's intent that we undergo *theosis*,[13] the process of becoming like God in powerful, mystical and even charismatic ways.[14] In all of this, God's *being* is the Orthodox foundation for interpreting all of life.

Generally speaking, Pentecostals follow their Western Catholic and Protestant heritage concerning anthropology, although they rarely realize or admit that they are products of this heritage! In a manner that succinctly summarizes the Pentecostals' own position, Melanchthon said, "To know Christ is to know his benefits."[15] The traditional fourfold[16] Pentecostal gospel is structured around Christ's works and benefits in his various offices as Savior, Healer, Spirit baptizer and soon coming King. Neither God's inner-trinitarian being nor Jesus' divine-human nature have as much import for how humans are like God as those issues do in Orthodoxy, although some reflection is made thereupon.[17]

More critical for Pentecostals is God's *purpose*. To that end, and following a rather literal scriptural hermeneutic, the Holy Spirit has come to instill love and power in us for personal transformation and Christian service. Jesus died for our

---

[13] *Theosis* is often translated as either "divinization" or "deification." Those terms do not mean that human beings become gods, but that they become Godlike after the pattern of the perfect iconic God-man himself, Jesus Christ (cf. Col 1:15).

[14] A study of Orthodox saints and heroes will sustain my analysis. The Holy Spirit en-gifts (en-gifted) these people with ministry gifts and abilities strikingly similar to those attested to in Pentecostal and Charismatic circles.

[15] Philipp Melanchthon, *Melanchthon and Bucer*, Library of Christian Classics 19, ed. Wilhelm Pauck (Philadelphia: Westminster Press, 1969), pp. 21-22, quoted in Millard J. Erickson, *Christian Theology* (Grand Rapids, Mich.: Baker, 1985), pp. 675.

[16] Wesleyan-Holiness Pentecostal groups hold to a fivefold gospel, adding Christ as sanctifier to the mix.

[17] For example, the Christ-as-moral-example model is little employed in Pentecostalism. Jesus is more regularly cited as a model for the believer's own spiritual experiences of water baptism, anointing by the Spirit, empowerment by the Spirit, and resurrection. Jesus was, William G. MacDonald said, "Pentecostal, the charismatic par excellence." William G. MacDonald, "Jesus Christ," in *Dictionary of Pentecostal and Charismatic Movements*, p. 481. One should not overstate the case, but Jesus' ontology (his divine-human nature, his personhood vis-a-vis God the Father and his representative role on behalf of creation itself) is little studied or appreciated in Pentecostalism.

sins. It now remains that we can become like and serve in a manner after the Spirit-empowered apostles. This divine-human coworking is an important dimension of the work of God's kingdom. Pentecostals, like the Orthodox, believe there is nothing we can do to save ourselves but that our own "amen" to Christ's transforming work is necessary for our sanctification.[18] In all of this, God's doing is the primary Pentecostal foundation for interpreting all of life. As beneficiaries of Western pragmatism, it is rather natural for them to see their faith as a seamless garment consisting of American can-doism and Christianity.[19]

The Eastern Orthodox on Being Human

The Psalmist cried out, "What is man, that Thou dost take thought of him?" (Ps 8:4 KJV). To no small extent the Orthodox respond by quoting that verse's next clause, "And the son of man, that Thou dost care for him?" That is, the Orthodox maintain that humankind is made in the image of the Son of man. Each person is created as an image of *the* Image. Again, we do not *have* something(s) within us that constitutes the *imago Dei;* we *are* an image.[20] In this regard it was not Adam who was the great archetype after whom the rest of the human race was fashioned; it was Jesus of Nazareth who serves that role. Put differently, when God looked ahead from timeless eternity into the future time of creation, he envisioned Jesus of Nazareth. Seeing that perfect paradigmatic figure, he fashioned the human race.[21] Thus the incarnation had been God's eternal intent for the second person of the Trinity. The West, including the Pentecostals, tends to see the incarnation as a remedy for fallen humanity, but the East interprets the incarnation as God's eter-

---

[18]Sanctification is a process that has both moral and spiritual dimensions. These two trajectories—the moral and the spiritual—form an important dialectic in Pentecostal history. It has been rather presupposed that moral purity will foster spiritual sensitivity. Simply stated, the fewer hindrances between a believer and the Holy Spirit, and the less encumbered one's conscience is by sin and guilt, the greater propensity there will be for the Spirit to use and work through that believer.

[19]Grant Wacker develops some of the history of Pentecostal pragmatism in "Character and the Modernization of North American Pentecostalism" (a paper read at the Society for Pentecostal Studies meeting, Lakeland, Florida, 1991).

[20]Lars Thunberg, "The Human Person as the Image of God: Eastern Christianity," in *Christian Spirituality*, vol. 1: *Origins to the Twelfth Century*, ed. Bernard McGinn, John Meyendorff, and Jean Leclercq (New York: Crossroad, 1988), pp. 298-300.

[21]Plato had written about the existence of *paradigmata*: thoughts in the mind of God that have a kind of self-existence as thoughts and that serve as the models for all created entities. Gregory Palamas (A.D. 1296-1359) especially developed the ramifications of this line of thought for Orthodox theology. Palamas argued that God exists both as he is in himself (here we can think of God's essence), and as he relates to creation (in terms of God's created energies). The end result is a clever model that sustains the biblical dialectic of God's transcendence and imminence, but which does not devolve into pantheism. God is thus truly both creator and sustainer, pervading his entire creation but not becoming it. See John Meyendorff, *A Study of Palamas*, trans. George Lawrence, 2nd ed. (London: Faith Press, 1974); Robert E. Sinkewicz, *Saint Gregory Palamas: The One Hundred and Fifty Chapters* (Toronto: Pontifical Institute of Mediaeval Studies, 1988).

nally intended and perfect plan, and not a kind of accident (in the philosophical sense) due to sin. In Jesus Christ, God intended both that created matter and divine personhood be united, and that time and eternity be united. Thus Jesus Christ is a cosmic Christ. And as I will develop, it follows in Orthodoxy that each of us is called to a cosmos-embracing dimension of existence.

With regard to what constitutes the *imago Dei* it is important to delineate Jesus' divine-human nature. Contrary to docetism, he was not God simply appearing in a human body. His nature was not simply that of the *Logos*, as Apollinarius held.[22] He was not simply an upright Jew who obediently followed the leading of the Holy Spirit, as the ancient adoptionists held or as do some contemporaries who hold to some derivation of Spirit christology. Neither was he simply a human being who merited our salvation by cooperating with the *Logos*. He was both human and divine. His body was human and his soul was human, but his *hypostasis* was divine. He was a divine person indwelling humanity; one person with two natures. Vladimir Lossky clarified that God's *Logos* "became an *hypostasis* of human nature without transforming himself into the *hypostasis* of a human person."[23] That is, he was an individualization of the species, a person within the species, without his divine *hypostasis* ceasing to be the person of the triune Godhead himself. The Word of God thus "enhypostasized" human nature. Just as the three *hypostases* of the Godhead interpenetrate one another yet remain distinct, the two natures in Christ interpenetrated one another.

In the person of Jesus Christ we have the archetypal model for all human beings. He is the perfect living emblem of humanity and divinity. The "last Adam" (1 Cor 15:45) was the prototype for all who seek to variously become like God, to fulfill God's plan for their lives and to present that identity to creation. Maximus the Confessor (d. 662) said, "communion with the *Logos* is precisely the natural state *(logos physikos)* of true humanity."[24] Through his incarnation he divinized human nature. Indeed, for the Orthodox, Chalcedon's christology is not only a careful statement of Christ's dual nature, it is as I wrote elsewhere "the Church's assertion that Jesus Christ was the theandric one who, in His own being, united all of humanity to God's divinity."[25]

Building on both the witness of Scripture concerning the triune existence of God, and the patristic ecumenical reflection on and development of that, the

[22]Reinhold Seeberg, *Textbook of the History of Doctrines*, trans. Charles E. Hay (Grand Rapids, Mich.: Baker, 1954), 1:245.

[23]Vladimir Lossky, *In the Image and Likeness of God*, eds. John H. Erickson and Thomas E. Bird (Crestwood, N.Y.: St. Vladimir's Seminary Press, 1985), p. 118.

[24]Meyendorff, *Christ in Eastern Christian Thought*, p. 210.

[25]Rybarczyk, "Beyond Salvation," p. 108.

Orthodox church believes it has been given language and terminology for defining human personhood. Just as Christ is an *hypostasis* indwelling nature (though in his case, two natures), so also is a human being an *hypostasis* indwelling the nature of the species.[26] And just as the *Logos* had the ability to transcend himself and indwell human nature, human beings also have the ability to transcend themselves, "to participate in the nature of God, as well as that of others."[27] In this regard the Trinity is itself a model of and for human existence. We were created not only to be social beings, just as the Trinity is an eternally self-giving social being, we were created with personhood that is able to transcend itself. We are able to participate in others, in life and in the created universe.[28]

Again, the triune God and God the *Logos* are foundational for Orthodoxy's anthropological definitions. Regarding the Trinity, we were made to exist with regard to others. We were created in such a way that we can only be fulfilled within relationships. John Zizioulas said, "The substance of God, 'God,' has no ontological content, no true being, apart from communion."[29] It follows then that human beings are genuinely whom they were created to be when they are in communions of mutual love. Regarding the *Logos*, Jesus was by nature what we are to become by grace: deified humanity. Following Irenaeus, Athanasius had said, "For he was made human so that we might be made divine. And he revealed himself through a body so that we might receive an understanding of the invisible Father. And he endured the mistreatment of humans, so that we might inherit immortality."[30] Elsewhere Athanasius said, "For He has become Man, that He might deify us in Himself."[31] We were created to experience *theosis*: to become like God after the likeness of his Word. Just as there was a perfect cooperation, a perfect synergy, between the two natures of Christ, so also there is supposed to be a perfect synergy between our nature and the grace of the Holy Spirit.[32] This fellowship of existence, this transformation of human personhood in all its dimensions, will nevertheless

---

[26]Lossky, *Image and Likeness*, p. 118.

[27]Rybarczyk, "Beyond Salvation," p. 109.

[28]The Orthodox make this dynamic claim but do little to express or define it. Do we transcend ourselves in shared work? In our genetic code? Through the transference of social mores and norms? By being sociologically charismatic? In our mystical moments? Perhaps it is all of this or other dynamics, but I have yet to read this described in specific ways.

[29]John D. Zizioulas, *Being as Communion: Studies in Personhood and the Church* (Crestwood, N.Y.: St. Vladimir's Seminary Press, 1985), p. 17.

[30]Athanasius *De Incarnatione* 54, in *Patrologia Cursus Completus*, series *Graecae* 25, ed. I. P. Migne (Turnholti, Belgium: Typographi Brepols, 1978), col. 192.

[31]Athanasius *Ad Adelphium* 4, in A Select Library of Nicene and Post-Nicene Fathers of the Christian Church (hereafter NPNF), 2nd series, vol. 4, ed. Archibald Robertson, trans. Philip Schaff and Henry Wace (Grand Rapids, Mich.: Eerdmans, 1978).

[32]Ware, *Orthodox Church*, p. 244.

render us fully human, fully whom it is that we are as unique creations.[33] Athanasius believed that in the eschaton our own state of existence will ultimately surpass Adam's original state, because the last type, Christ, surpasses the first type, Adam.[34]

These somewhat technical and rather philosophical definitional boundaries are emphatically maintained by the Orthodox, not only because they believe they are true but because they believe they have tremendous ramifications for theological anthropology. Perhaps the differences between East and West can be simplified by way of a broader assessment. As I see it, the primary differences between East and West concerns the definitional points of departure. In the West, Christians tend first to consider what it is to be human and then imagine how the transcendent God could indwell a person among us. How can he still be God if he is truly human? is a fair summarization of the theological questions and debates in Western Christian history. (This even succinctly summarizes the historical reason for the addition of the *filioque* clause.)[35] In the East, Christ's identity is posited first, and then all of created human nature is explained in light of him. For the East's part, How can he still be human if he is truly God? is a fair summarization of theological questions and debates in the East's history. (The monophysite and monothelite controversies sustain my summary here.)[36]

At the expense of being redundant, Christ incarnate and the Trinity are paradigmatic in Orthodoxy for understanding human personhood. The resulting thrust of this is that the Orthodox consistently make their anthropological formulations about human beings as they existed *before the Fall*. To define human beings as they are after the Fall, the Orthodox believe, will have one reproduce the effects of the Fall and make those effects normative. It follows then that Orthodoxy has a more positive view of human personhood than that of the Protestant West,

---

[33] Meyendorff, *Christ in Eastern Christian Thought*, pp. 210-12.

[34] Athanasius *Orationes contra Arianos*, 4.2.67; in NPNF 4:385.

[35] While *filioque* may have been assumed in the West as early as in the third century with Tertullian, and certainly was being advocated by Augustine early in the fifth century, it was not until the seventh century (in part due to the language barriers) that there was an awareness of the difference in the use of doxological and theological terms between the East and the West to describe the inner-Trinitarian life of the Godhead and the procession of the Spirit. At the local councils of Toledo (446-447, 589 and 633) the Franks in the West relied on the Athanasian Creed (also known as the *Quicunque Vult*) in their battle with Arianism. The Franks wanted to make clear their assertion that the Son was in no way inferior to the Father and the Athanasian Creed aided them in this because it argued for the Spirit's double-procession. Although these councils did not prompt an official alteration of the Nicene Creed to include *filioque*, they make evident its acceptance in the West. See Michael Fahey, "Son and Spirit: Divergent Theologies between Constantinople and the West," in *Conflicts About the Holy Spirit*, ed. Hans Küng and Jürgen Moltmann (New York: Seabury Press, 1979), p. 6.

[36] Both the monophysites and monothelites emphasized Jesus' divinity to the detriment of his humanity. An abiding commitment of monophysitism is God's immutability: the Word could not become human by nature, for that would imply a change in God's own nature. See Meyendorff, *Christ in Eastern Christian Thought*, p. 39.

wherein human sinfulness is assumed throughout theological systems.[37] (The implications of such an anthropology certainly must have profoundly affected the development of Eastern European societies, though an analysis on that line cannot be made here.) As will become apparent below this more optimistic view of humanity does not imply that Adam and Eve were perfect before the Fall.

Some specific features of human identity as they appear in Orthodox theology deserve notation and description. Together with the West the Orthodox would list the moral nature, the conscience, free will, the emotions, the soul (spirit) and the intellect as constitutive dimensions of being human. Rather unique to Orthodoxy are the characteristics of *nous* and the potential for growth. Because the latter two are novel, further description follows.

When the divine *Logos* created the universe, he did not merely make it, wind it up like a clock and then leave it to run on its own. Following and developing ancient Stoic thought, the Orthodox teach that God's very act of creating suffused the universe—both corporeal and incorporeal—with his own identity as a rational, ordering and loving Being.[38] As both creator and sustainer he marked creation with an imprint of himself. On every created thing was placed a divine seal that placed everything into an intimate relationship with God.[39] Within and on human beings this imprint, this seal, is especially discussed as nous, the superior faculty through which human persons enter into communion with God.[40] *Nous* is not understood in a unanimous manner by Orthodox theologians, but it is consistently cited as the constitutive dimension of the *imago Dei*.[41] Often it is part and parcel of the rational capacity. More regularly, it incorporates a spiritual dimension or capacity by which a

---

[37]Here I must show my own Western bias and ask, to what extent does Scripture itself define human personhood prior to the Fall? The Orthodox can develop their anthropology based on extrabiblical philosophical commitments, but they must declare those commitments for what they are. In other words, despite how aesthetically beautiful and symmetric their model is and despite its internal coherence, at some point their position is tenuous, speculative and sustained only by church tradition.

[38]I develop and critique this element of Orthodox theology in my dissertation, "Beyond Salvation." For further study see Julia Annas, *Hellenistic Philosophy of Mind* (Berkeley: University of California Press, 1992); and, A. A. Long, *Hellenistic Philosophy: Stoics, Epicureans, Sceptics* (London: Duckworth, 1974).

[39]Vladimir Lossky, *Orthodox Theology: An Introduction*, trans. Ian and Ihita Kesarcodi-Watson (Crestwood, N.Y.: St. Vladimir's Seminary Press, 1978), pp. 53-58.

[40]Lossky, *Mystical Theology of the Eastern Church* (Crestwood, N.Y.: St. Vladimir's Seminary Press, 1976), p. 27; Kallistos Ware, *Orthodox Way*, rev. ed. (St. Vladimir's Seminary Press, 1995), pp. 48-49.

[41]The patristic fathers especially tended to locate the image of God within the human *nous*. See Thunberg, "The Human Person as the Image of God," p. 295. Hierotheos S. Vlachos also shows the difficulty that the Orthodox fathers had in defining the image (*Orthodox Psychotherapy*, 2nd ed., trans. Esther Williams [Levadia, Greece: Birth of the Theotokos Monastery, 1995], pp. 41, 118-21). Meyendorff said there is no consensus among the Orthodox fathers as to the exegesis of Genesis 1:26-27 and the meaning of image (*Christ in Eastern Christian Thought*, p. 114). Lossky followed the teaching of Gregory of Nyssa and said that the image of God in people is "necessarily unknowable, for, reflecting the plenitude of its prototype, it too must possess the unknowability of the divine being" (*Orthodox Theology*, p. 23).

person, Kallistos Ware says, "understands eternal truths about God or about the *logoi* or inner essences of created things, not through deductive reasoning, but by direct apprehension or spiritual perception . . . *a kind of intuition* that St. Isaac the Syrian calls 'simple cognition.' "[42] As such, *nous* is understood to be the energy or eye of the soul. It produces thoughts and conceptual images.

The *nous* was not destroyed in the Fall, but its capacity was obfuscated. It is capable of being shaped and affected by either virtue or vice. When a person follows after evil passions the *nous* can be darkened (Mt 6:22-23; Rom 11:10), sickened, wounded, made apathetic to the things of God and perverted. Conversely, the *nous* can be restored through the grace of God that is variously available in the sacraments, godly living and especially through ascetic disciplines (fasting, vigils, meditation, self-control and the like). In the end the *nous* can be healed so that the person, Hierotheos Vlachos said, "becomes a temple of the Holy Spirit."[43]

The concept of synergy deserves reiteration at this point. A person becomes a Christian when he or she gains entrance into Christ (through water baptism, for the Orthodox), but he or she is not therefore fully Christlike in the core of whom he or she is. That process of becoming Christlike—again, the process of *theosis*—is one that the believer will undergo across the span of one's life and even into eternity.[44] A critical goal in this synergistic process is the experience of *theoria*, a participatory contemplation of God that transcends physical vision. Lossky clarified that *theoria*, the vision of God which Adam and Eve themselves enjoyed before the Fall, involves a "certain participation in the incorruptible state, a stability of the being participating in the creative nature of the Logos."[45] The Orthodox argue that this contemplative-participatory experience is like that event witnessed by the apostle Paul who said he was caught up to the extent that he did not know whether he was in or out of his body (2 Cor 12:2).[46]

The *nous* may thus be understood as a God-given capacity through which mystical encounter with God is possible. Gregory Palamas believed that God had created the human mind in such a way that it alone of God's creation could transcend itself and participate in the divine. Human beings, created in the image of God,

---

[42]Ware, *Orthodox Way*, p. 48 (emphasis added).

[43]Vlachos, *Orthodox Psychotherapy*, p. 49.

[44]The Orthodox do not teach the doctrine of purgatory. They are reticent to discuss eschatology as it pertains to individuals. Nonetheless, we can summarize the Orthodox position: while an individual can be in the presence of heaven, it may remain for him or her to say "yes and amen" to the appeals of the Holy Spirit and the will of God on into eternity.

[45]Lossky, *The Vision of God*, 2nd ed., trans. Asheleigh Moorhouse (London: Faith Press, 1973), p. 59.

[46]John Meyendorff, *Gregory Palamas: The Triads*, trans. Nicholas Gendle (New York: Paulist, 1983), pp. 34, 38, 53.

thus have an "organ of vision" that, when it receives divine grace, is able to transcend itself and commune with God.[47] Sometimes in the process of spiritual and ontological healing, the Christian will have dramatic spiritual encounters such as having ecstatic visions, hearing heavenly voices or experiencing theophanies. More often than not the believer will have to learn to patiently wait on God in prayer, worship and stillness. Through all of this believers will gradually learn both to better understand their own self and recognize the presence of Christ in other persons and the physical universe. "Because the process of *theosis* includes one's physical body, one cannot be perfectly deified until after the resurrection."[48] In all of this, we can neither save nor transform ourselves. It is the work of God.

A second rather novel feature in Orthodox theological anthropology is the potential for growth. This feature is not a "something" latent within us, but it is nevertheless a constitutive dimension of what it means to be human. As noted above, the Orthodox hold that we are able to transcend ourselves. But this transcendent activity can only happen with our assent. We can choose, we must choose, to exercise our *autexsousia*, our inner self-determination. That self-determination can be used for the kind of evil that is apparent in idolatry and selfishness. Or our self-determination can be exercised toward godliness, growth in knowledge and wisdom. God, ever respectful of human free will, does not force or coerce anyone to live in communion with him. He offers his grace, and we accept that gratefully.

This potential-for-growth feature is an important aspect of the larger Orthodox theology concerning the image and likeness of God. Although contemporary biblical scholars have reasoned that image and likeness (Gen 1:26-27; 5:1-3; 9:6; Ps 8) are Hebrew synonyms,[49] Orthodox theologians since the patristic era have maintained that these two words are distinct components of God's plan for the human race. We have been created in God's image; it now remains that we become like him. "God the creator," Ware said, "set Adam's feet upon the right path, but Adam had in front of him a long road to traverse before reaching his journey's end."[50] (God's intention that we become like him through our free will aided with his divine grace rules out Augustinian models of predestination.)

Important for this study, and as the previous explication has implied, the Orthodox do not believe that a human person's ability to experience God in profound subjective-mystical ways is a take-it-or-leave-it dimension of Christian the-

---

[47] Meyendorff, *Gregory Palamas*, pp. 32, 35. Meyendorff said Palamas was little concerned to enter the physiological debates about where the mind—*nous*—was precisely located (p. 6).

[48] Rybarczyk, "Beyond Salvation," p. 93. See Vlachos, *Orthodox Psychotherapy*, p. 354.

[49] For example see Anthony A. Hoekema, *Created in God's Image* (Grand Rapids, Mich.: Eerdmans, 1986), pp. 9-32.

[50] Kallistos Ware, "The Mystery of the Human Person," *Sobornost* 3:1 (1981): 62-69.

ology or Christian spirituality. (We should qualify that the Orthodox see the words *theology* and *spirituality* as synonyms; this is not unlike the position of Pentecostals.)[51] Instead, it was for the precise purpose of our subjective-mystical, participatory, communion with God—a communion that itself will transform a person after the likeness of God—that we were created. God did not create beings whom he merely hoped would live morally upright lives, though certainly he intended that. God did not create people whom he merely hoped would worship him as their creator, though he certainly intended that too. Instead, the very mystical-personal experience of communion that the triune God enjoyed from eternity was the driving force behind both why God created us after his image and likeness and why he became incarnate. And we should reiterate God gave us an innate capacity for sharing in the communion—the *Sobornost*, as the Russian Orthodox put it— that belongs to God as he is. In all of this the intuitive-spiritual-mystical dimension of human personhood is at the forefront in Orthodoxy. In striking ways, though rooted in an entirely different matrix, the Pentecostals aver the same.

The Classical Pentecostals on Being Human

Pentecostalism has undergone subtle but profound changes in the last fifty years. Scholars have noticed how Pentecostals, at least in the United States, have become "evangelicalized."[52] While this has had its positive effects,[53] it has also come at a clear cost. The days when entire congregations waited in a holy and expectant silence, the days when congregations were taught how to hear the Spirit's voice, and the days when the charismatic gifts were actively present among the laity—in the corporate worship services—are all on the wane. The effect of this corporate identity shift on anthropological formulation is that the subjective, intuitive and mystical dimensions have been muted. When recently I addressed an assembly of Pentecostal educators to the effect that Pentecostalism is an essentially Westernized intuitive-mystical Christian phenomenon, they looked at me with raised eyebrows! Much of Western Pentecostalism has become indistinguishable from the

[51]Simon Chan, a Pentecostal theologian, develops how and why theology and spirituality are interwoven in *Spiritual Theology: A Systematic Study of the Christian Life* (Downers Grove, Ill.: InterVarsity Press, 1998). A Church of God (Cleveland, Tennessee) Pentecostal theologian, Steven Land, follows Barth on the relation between theology and spirituality (pp. 36-37) and then later develops the integration of theology and spirituality in his third chapter. See Steven Land, *Pentecostal Spirituality: Passion for the Kingdom* (Sheffield, England: Sheffield Academic Press, 1993).

[52]Cecil M. Robeck Jr. shows how Pentecostal cooperation with Fundamentalists brought about certain and clear changes within Pentecostalism ("The Assemblies of God and Ecumenical Cooperation," in *Pentecostalism in Context: Essays in Honor of William W. Menzies*, ed. Wonsuk Ma and Robert P. Menzies, Journal of Pentecostal Theology Supplement Series 11 [Sheffield, England: Sheffield Academic Press, 1997]).

[53]Depth and maturity are coming to characterize Pentecostal theology and institutions of higher education. And without question the Pentecostals have been increasingly accepted by other Protestant traditions.

charismatic movement, or evangelicalism more generally. I make that caveat regarding change because the following delineation of Pentecostal theological anthropology will be largely rooted in the past. I happen to believe the original subjective, intuitive and mystical dimensions remain latent within contemporary Pentecostal denominations and congregations. However, unless Pentecostal leaders and pastors can learn to reconfigure and re-present the heartbeat of the original Pentecostal ethos within the twenty-first-century context, the spiritual vibrancy of Western Pentecostalism will die the same sociological death as that of the Methodist and Holiness movements.

Pentecostals do not have the kind of immediate philosophical heritage that pervades Orthodox theology,[54] and it is probable that they would have rejected it if it were available. Their theological sourcebook is the Bible, plain and simple.[55] And by and large they interpret it in a plain and simple—literal—manner.[56] Thus it follows that Pentecostals consistently define human beings as they are after the Fall. There is some speculation made about what Adam and Eve might have been like prior to the Fall, but it is recognized as being primarily speculation.[57] Whereas the Orthodox emphasis is on the ontology of the Trinity and the *Logos* in creation—in short, the "who" of creation—the Pentecostal focus is on the "why" of creation.[58] And the "why" pertains to God's purpose. The physical universe is not an accident,

---

[54]Indeed they do have a philosophical heritage that unquestionably informs their own identity. But they have not even begun to realize that they do have one or how it shapes them. I develop this in my dissertation, "Beyond Salvation."

[55]The extent to which early Pentecostals understood themselves to represent a distinct epoch in history is widely attested. Generally speaking, they believed that their own era was that prophesied by Joel (Joel 2:28-32) and Peter (Acts 2:14-21) as the end of history. Whereas the apostles were the first bookend of Christian history, the Pentecostals represented the last bookend. That which transpired in between was nominally Christian at best, save a few exceptional persons and seasons. Obviously, this historical perspective is both naive and triumphal. The present extent of that older Pentecostal historical viewpoint varies by denomination, geographical location and individual. Generally speaking, Pentecostals would admit that they have a heritage in the Reformation, Methodist, Holiness and Higher-Life movements. The fact that they draw a tremendous amount of their theological heritage from both Anglicanism and Roman Catholicism would be only admitted with great reticence if at all.

[56]Here a fuller analysis of Pentecostal hermeneutics would be warranted. Suffice it to say that they do *not* always read the Bible literally. One only needs to hear them explain Daniel or the Revelation to know this. Donald Dayton fairly summarized the Pentecostal hermeneutic as a "subjectivizing hermeneutic." In that regard Pentecostals shaped their own identity by reading the New Testament and seeing how the modern believer's spiritual experiences replicate those in the biblical texts (Dayton, *Theological Roots of Pentecostalism* [Peabody, Mass.: Hendrickson, 1987], p. 24). To see the multifaceted character of Pentecostal hermeneutics, see Gary B. McGee, "Early Pentecostal Hermeneutics: Tongues as Evidence in the Book of Acts," in *Initial Evidence: Historical and Biblical Perspectives on the Pentecostal Doctrine of Spirit Baptism*, ed. Gary B. McGee (Peabody, Mass.: Hendrickson, 1991), pp. 96-118.

[57]Myer Pearlman, *Knowing the Doctrines of the Bible* (Springfield, Mo.: Gospel Publishing House, 1937), pp. 68-77. A kind of speculation by negation is made. If we are sinful now, Adam was not. If we are selfish, hateful, xenophobic, idolatrous and the like now, Adam was not.

nor did God create in a haphazard fashion.[59] God had a clear plan when he created. "This plan included the very sequence by which He created, the organization of the universe, the manifold variety of creatures with their corresponding characteristics and instincts, and the providential purpose of humanity's salvation."[60]

When God created Adam and Eve in his image, he wanted them to glorify him in all they did, to have fellowship with him, and to complete his purposes for them, specifically as the latter were found exercising dominion over creation. Whereas Protestants are divided as to whether dominion and purpose constitute an element of the *imago Dei*,[61] Pentecostals do see that as important. So it follows that fulfilling God's intent for one's life will assist one in realizing and fulfilling what it means to be in God's image. In light of Christ's commissioning the church to spread the gospel, it is now the case that discerning God's purpose for one's life will either have immediate, or implicit, involvement in the fulfillment of that commission. Unlike Athanasius and the ensuing stream of Orthodox theologians who held that the Trinity (and specifically the *Logos*) is foundational for understanding human existence, Pentecostals largely maintain that human beings are preeminent among all God's creations because it was God's intent that they should be. In all of this, again, action and doing are critical concepts for explaining human existence. Sin, for its part, hinders and prevents a person from fulfilling God's purpose for one's life.[62]

Central to Pentecostal definitions of what it means to be human is the dimension of moral nature. This emphasis demonstrates that Pentecostals are clearly products of Western Christendom; both the Roman Catholic and Protestant trajectories emphasize the moral nature. "Of all the differences between man and the lower animals," Pearlman said, "the moral sense or the conscience is by far the most important . . . the most noble of all the attributes of man."[63] Adam and Eve were created morally innocent, but it was God's intent that they should develop and

---

[58]A contemporary example of this emphasis is Timothy Munyon, "The Creation of the Universe and Mankind," in *Systematic Theology: A Pentecostal Perspective*, ed. Stanley M. Horton (Springfield, Mo.: Logion, 1994), pp.215-53.

[59]These, among other reasons, help to account for the consistent Pentecostal aversion to theories of evolution. It is also the case that to a large extent the biblical creation narratives are explored and considered precisely because of the threat posed by evolution (and I could add, abortion). Pentecostals otherwise have had little regard for the implications of God's act of creation.

[60]Rybarczyk, "Beyond Salvation," p. 259.

[61]Millard J. Erickson, *Christian Theology*, 11th ed. (Grand Rapids, Mich.: Baker, 1994), pp. 498-515. For his part Erickson concluded that the *imago Dei* does not incorporate the element of dominion.

[62]Bruce R. Marino, "The Origin, Nature, and Consequences of Sin," *in Systematic Theology, A Pentecostal Perspective*, ed. Stanley M. Horton (Springfield, Mo.: Logion, 1994), p. 255; Pearlman, *Knowing the Doctrines*, pp. 129-38; Ernest W. S. Williams, *Systematic Theology* (Springfield, Mo.: Gospel Publishing House, 1953), 2:129-33.

[63]Pearlman, *Knowing the Doctrines*, p. 117.

mature. It was for that latter reason that God placed the tree of the knowledge of good and evil in Eden and then prohibited them from eating of it. God knew their obedience to his commandment would facilitate their moral growth. E. S. Williams held that whereas Adam and Eve were created sinless, they were not yet holy. "Holiness," he said, "and character result from choices and decisions. Man could not develop morally were there nothing to resist. In innocence moral character was undeveloped, because not tested."[64]

Adam and Eve's morality was the determining factor for their immortality. Thus it follows that they would live forever if they only obeyed God's law. Their immortality was not located in their finding their being in God's own being. That is, they were not created immortal to the extent that they participated in the life of God, as the Orthodox would state it. Because of sin, Jesus came to live and die for us. He was the perfectly moral human being who died for our sins so that we might have immortality. Christ was both the ransom and the ransomer (Mt 20:28; Mk 10:45; 1 Tim 2:6).[65] Again, the juridical emphasis of Western Christendom is clearly perceived here.

A second emphasis in Pentecostal theological definitions of human personhood is the soul. While every creature was created with a quality of soul consistent with its own species, only human beings' souls were created to live eternally. In a way that very much resembled many Orthodox descriptions of the soul, Myer Pearlman said the God-breathed soul is, "the life-giving and intelligent principle animating the human body, using the bodily senses as its agents in the exploration of material things and the bodily organs for its self-expression and communication with the outside world."[66] Important for this study's purpose, Pentecostals emphasize that the soul is not simply the eternal element of human existence, but that it is the spiritual quality that can relate to the spiritual dimension.

There is no unanimity among Pentecostals whether human beings comprise body and soul (the dichotomist position) or body, soul and spirit (the trichotomist position). Following the efforts of the larger evangelical movement's biblical studies, Pentecostals would increasingly affirm that we do not *have* a soul but we *are* a soul. And this anthropological understanding is affecting how Pentecostals do ministry today. The maturation of Pentecostal ministry and outreach has seen Pentecostals move away from the traditional "get 'em saved before Jesus comes" emphasis to a more holistic understanding. The needs of the whole human person

---

[64]E. S. Williams, *Systematic Theology*, 2:123-15. See also 119-20; and Pearlman, *Knowing the Doctrines*, p. 109.

[65]Pearlman, *Knowing the Doctrines*, pp. 191-214; Daniel B. Pecota, "The Saving Work of Christ," in *Systematic Theology: A Pentecostal Perspective*, ed. Stanley M. Horton (Springfield, Mo.: Logion, 1994), p. 349.

[66]Pearlman, *Knowing the Doctrines*, p. 104.

must be addressed in Christian ministry. That important development notwith-standing, Pentecostals remain very much attuned to the spiritual nature of the human person. This is, as I mentioned above in a footnote, the result of their belief in the availability—and normative nature—of spiritual experience. Most espe-cially, that experiential realm has been rooted in the arena of charismatic gifts.

Jesus Christ sends his Spirit to us today for the same reason that he sent his Spirit to the apostles: to empower his followers for Christian ministry. Empower-ment is the primary focus of the Pentecostal distinctive of baptism with (or in) the Holy Spirit (hereafter simply "Spirit baptism").[67] But, and this is an important point, the Spirit does not simply benefit the believer from without as though suc-cess in the pastorate, mission field and mercy or healing ministries were God's pri-mary aim. (To Pentecostals, God himself indeed may be a pragmatist, but his involvement in life is aimed at far more than success!) The Spirit also comes to in-dwell the believer in intimate, dynamic, loving and transformative ways.[68] The his-torical intramural debates between Pentecostal denominations hinge on this intimate dimension of the Spirit's presence. They have addressed questions such as Is Spirit-baptism for empowerment alone? Or does it necessarily include deep and personal transformation? The Wesleyan-Holiness Pentecostals tend to see the sanctifying effects of the experience as primary. (They would argue the need to be sanctified before one can be Spirit baptized. However, the lines of demarcation are being blurred in that camp.)[69] The Reformed (baptistic) Pentecostals tend to see the transforming effects of the experience as secondary. Nevertheless, millions of Pentecostals in both camps have consistently testified that the experience of Spirit baptism changed them in the core of who they are.

The theology of Spirit baptism, narrowly, and the charismatic gifts, more broadly, have direct implications for Pentecostalism's theological anthropology. Again, "doing" Christian ministry informs how Pentecostals think about the "being" of human existence. Though the emotions are included in the affections, they do not totally define them. Instead, "the affections are included with the mind

---

[67]There is little appreciation for how the Spirit's outpouring on Pentecost formed the Christian community as the church, the body of Christ. See Simon Chan, "Mother Church: Toward a Pentecostal Ecclesiology," *Pneuma* 22, no. 2 (2000): 177-208.

[68]For this reason many Pentecostals are hesitant to follow the Augustinian model of the Trinity in which the Spir-it is the love that spirates from the relationship between the Father and the Son. Such a position seems to dep-ersonalize the Spirit in ways inconsistent with the New Testament's testimony. Pentecostals are too attuned to the personal dimensions of the Spirit to speak of the Spirit in such an abstract way.

[69]I examined seventy-five years of the Church of God's (COG) weekly literature and seven different COG theo-logians on this matter in the unpublished paper "The Transformation of Sanctification: The Church of God (Cleveland, TN) and its Doctrine of Sanctification," Fuller Seminary, 1996. The past fifty years have seen a con-sistent and marked move toward the Reformed (Baptistic) position on sanctification within the COG.

in how the soul perceives and experiences life."[70] Pentecostals would describe the affections and intuition as comprising the seedbed of visceral knowing and willing. Pentecostals know the passages in Scripture that describe the various bodily organs' experiences and emotions should not be taken literally. The kidneys, heart and intestines do not think. However, such Scriptures do describe how it is that the soul operates through the bodily organs.[71] Paul Pipkin says the heart "is a tricky thing—it is the seat of all our affections, our passions, and our appetites," and "[it] is impressionable, it is pliable, it is sensitive, it may be broken and wounded and crushed—and it may be hardened."[72] Arne Vick writes, "God is a spiritual Being, so it follows that our communication with Him in worship must be a spiritual exercise. 'Deep calleth unto deep'—the depths of the human spirit respond to the infinite deep of the Spirit of God." Sometimes words cannot even express what the human soul needs to express to God.[73]

Pentecostals emphasize that God created human nature expressly with an affective dimension. Those who deny the affections often overemphasize the intellect as a means of knowing. The mind can pridefully usurp the intellectual-affective integration with which God created men and women. When the mind fails or refuses to grasp the things of the Spirit (invisible and eternal things which can only be apprehended by the soul), the heart is supposed to bring such vain and doubting thoughts under its domain.[74]

Steven Land argued that the affections are a critical, Spirit-infused element within Christian existence. Land emphasized that Christianity's experiential dimensions—dimensions which Pentecostalism has long emphasized—have for too long been neglected in formal theology. He said:

> If God is the living God, the God who in Trinitarian communion is spirit; if the church is a living organism of charisms and signs; and, if salvation is a living relationship with this God among these people who live in last days' expectancy and urgency—if all this is the case, then theology must be a discerning reflection upon this living reality, these divine-human relations. Theology requires not only discursive reasoning but also the engagement of the whole person within the communion of charisms.[75]

---

[70]Rybarczyk, "Beyond Salvation," p. 270.

[71]Pearlman, *Knowing the Doctrines*, p. 107.

[72]Paul H. Pipkin, "Know Your Heart," *Pentecostal Evangel: The Weekly Magazine of the Assemblies of God* [United States], June 17, 1962, pp. 4-5.

[73]Arne Vick, "Pentecostal Worship," *Pentecostal Evangel*, March 3, 1966, p. 10.

[74]Cf. J. T. Boddy, "Divine Rationality," *Pentecostal Evangel*, May 14, 1921, pp. 1, 3; Pearlman, *Knowing the Doctrines*, p. 50; Williams, *Systematic Theology*, 1:159.

[75]Land, *Pentecostal Spirituality*, p. 34.

The affections are not just the emotions, although those are involved. Affections are "abiding dispositions which dispose the person toward God and the neighbor in ways appropriate to the source and goal in God."[76] They ought also be understood as "construals of and concerns for the world. As such," continued Land, "they are also 'reasons' for action."[77] Those who have encountered Christ's Spirit in the affective dimensions of their inner being are, Land said, "truly liberated and not merely informed."[78] "The "peace of perfect love (which 'casts out fear,' 1 Jn. 4:18)," he said, "[is] maintained by walking in love with no inner resistance or 'hold outs.' ""The Spirit [searches] the heart and, by the Word, [points] out what [is] not like Christ and therefore carnal."[79] In all of this Land reasoned that the head and heart, or the intellect and the affections, should not merely be balanced in the Christian life; they should be integrated.[80]

On the basis of his own exegetical study of the Pauline corpus, Gordon Fee also evinced the traditional Pentecostal awareness of and emphasis on the deep, if uneasily defined, dimensions of human existence. As the apostle Paul wrote, it is in the human spirit that God's Holy Spirit takes up residence.[81] Fee argues that this divine-human dynamic can be expressed as a S/spirit phenomenon. Indeed, if Paul's own literary emphasis hits the definitional mark, to be a Christian is less a matter of being forgiven (though no one would denigrate that) and more a matter of being indwelt by God's Spirit. Fee said:

> Any careful reading of Paul's letters makes it abundantly clear that the Spirit is the key element, the *sine qua non*, of all Christian life and experience. To put that in theological perspective, it needs to be noted that, contrary to historic Protestantism, "justification by faith" is not the central theme of Pauline theology. That is but one metaphor among many, and therefore much too narrow a view to capture the many-splendored richness of God's eschatological salvation that has been effected in

---

[76]Ibid., p. 136.

[77]Ibid. We should add that Land, consistent with his own Pentecostal heritage, framed his discussion of the affections within an apocalyptic hermeneutic. That is, for him the imminence of Christ's return is the telos toward which the affections are oriented.

[78]Ibid., p. 123.

[79]Ibid., p. 130.

[80]Ibid., p. 133. In a manner consistent with the historical-cultural ethos of Pentecostalism that I previously described, Land did not place the locus for the human affections in relation to God's own being (or even in the *imago Dei*). Instead, Land rooted those in how it is that God (or his kingdom) comes to us. He said, "What God has said and done, is saying and doing, will say and do is the source and telos of the affections" (Ibid., p. 134).

[81]Fee develops Paul's flexible use of *pneuma*. Fee concludes that in fourteen instances (1 Thess 5:23; 1 Cor 2:11; 5:5; 7:34; 14:14; 16:18; 2 Cor 2:13; 7:13; Gal 6:18; Rom 1:9; 8:16; Philem 25; Phil 4:23; 2 Tim 4:22) Paul uses *pneuma* to refer simultaneously to the divine Spirit and the human spirit. Thus, in Pauline literature there is a dynamic interaction between the Spirit of God and a believer's spirit. See *God's Empowering Presence: The Holy Spirit in the Letters of Paul* (Peabody, Mass.: Hendrickson, 1994).

Christ. . . . For [Paul] "salvation in Christ" is the activity of the triune God. . . . But it is God the Spirit who has effectively appropriated God's salvation in Christ in the life of the believer and the believing community. Without the latter, the former simply does not happen.[82]

For its part the experience of conversion is made subjectively real by an "*experiential appropriation* of Christ—the Holy Spirit's presence within the believer." This appropriation can produce "some radical changes in the believer."[83] To his discussion about conversion Fee adds that Paul frequently "implies there are further, ongoing appropriations of the Spirit's empowering," (Gal 3:5; 1 Thess 4:8; Eph 5:18; Phil 1:19). In all of this Fee believes Pentecostals recapture the heart of the New Testament pattern of Christian religious experience.[84]

I could continue to exemplify the Pentecostal emphasis within theological anthropology by further noting various writers and scholars on the topic of the a-rational dimensions of human existence. For our purposes it will suffice to note the great archetypal example in this regard: the Pentecostal practice of praying in tongues. Following the apostle Paul's mention of the practice in Romans 8:16-27 and 1 Corinthians 14:14, Pentecostals believe that the Spirit can pray through the believer's spirit. As Pentecostals describe it, this can happen through praying in tongues or groaning and travailing in prayer.[85] The end result is that God's Spirit may accomplish any number of things even though the believer may not even know for what he or she was praying. In order to understand Paul's discussion on this practice, we need to view life through a set of interpretive lenses not unlike those of the apostle Paul. Fee summarized well this viewpoint:

> While such an understanding runs counter to the heavily Enlightenment-influenced self-understanding of Western Christendom, Romans 8:27 offers the theological key to such edification. It is a matter of trusting God that the One to whom we thus pray by the Spirit 'knows the mind of the Spirit, that the Spirit is praying on behalf of the saints what is according to God' [= in keeping with his purposes.] Paul is obviously at rest much more than later Christians with the Spirit's edifying one's spirit, without such edification needing to be processed in the cortex of the brain.[86]

---

[82] Gordon Fee, *Listening to the Spirit in the Text* (Grand Rapids, Mich.: Eerdmans, 2000), pp.37-38. Fee notes that "justification by faith" only appears in three of Paul's letters (Gal, Rom, Phil), letters wherein Paul is arguing against the imposition of Jewish law on Gentile converts (p. 37, n. 12).

[83] Fee, *God's Empowering Presence*, p. 854.

[84] Ibid., p. 863. See pp. 854-64.

[85] For a cogent presentation of this practice see Fee's "Toward a Pauline Theology of Glossolalia," in *Listening to the Spirit in the Text*, pp. 105-20.

[86] Fee, *Listening to the Spirit in the Text*, p. 116-17.

Conclusion

In developing the theo-anthropological similarities between these two Christian traditions, I have consistently followed rather didactic, though sometimes uneven, delineations of both Eastern Orthodox and classical Pentecostal writers. Another way to have expressed this would have been to include the descriptions and portrayals found within their prayer books, their devotional literature and their doxologies. Both Orthodox ascetic studies and popular Pentecostal literature are full of imagery and prose depicting the visceral, intuitive, experiential and even mystical dimensions of human personhood, especially as that is located in relationship to God. A person attending either an Orthodox liturgy or a genuine Pentecostal church service will be struck by the extent to which both traditions are attuned to the a-rational dimensions of human nature.

Together the Orthodox and Pentecostals have in common an experience-laden spirituality that stems from and is located in their anthropological understandings. Both traditions are emphatic that God longs to indwell and work through persons who are submitted to and open to his Spirit. Both traditions are emphatic that when a believer opens him- or herself to the presence of God (or alternately, that when God opens a believer to himself!) that person will be transformed. Both traditions affirm that the believer who is open and submitted to God will more likely produce spiritual fruit and fulfill God's will. Such an intuitive-affective-spiritual dimension is neither an added bonus within the Christian life nor simply an oddity on the theological fringes to be studied. To know and be known by the resurrected Christ can involve encounters in the experiential dimension that are only explained with great difficulty.

While both traditions see the divine-human cooperation as a component of salvation, neither is historically interested in simply "getting people saved." There are, of course, exceptions to that rule. In the worst cases the Orthodox can be criticized for assuming that all water-baptized peoples in their ethnic populations are therefore genuine believers. In the worst cases contemporary Pentecostals indeed have a tendency to hold evangelistic "salvation" rallies but then do little to follow up or disciple those who raised their hands for Jesus. Nevertheless, the leaders within both traditions are adamant that salvation is the beginning point in Christianity, not the culmination. And as both express it the life in Christ comprises subjective, experiential and even mystical dimensions that transcend the usual definitions of what it means to be a Christian.

With the fall of the Berlin Wall, perhaps a new season is dawning after all. Perhaps these two traditions that share a similar dynamic and apostolic vision of the human person can begin to better appreciate the depths and riches of one another's own Christian characters. So that God's Spirit may be not grieved (Eph 4:30-32), I pray that the greater dividing walls of suspicion and stereotypical assumption may also come tumbling down. So that Christ may be lifted up (Jn 12:32) and that the reconciling work of the gospel may be modeled (Eph 2:13-16), I pray that Orthodox and Pentecostal leaders will take the risks that are necessary to better understand one another.

N E C E S S A R Y   D O C T R I N E S
Why Dogma Is Needed & Why Substitutes Fail

D A V I D   M I L L S

Many perfectly serious Christians hate, just hate, to be thought of as "dogmatic." You know the sort of people I mean. They end a discussion of first principles by earnestly reassuring everyone of their deep respect for all those who disagree with them, with an eagerness that suggests not so much a respect for differences as a fear that others may think them too sure of their position.

I have heard some very conservative Christians end such a discussion—of first principles, mind you—by declaring all views on the subject are of equal value and then looking around with the perky smile of someone who expects to be praised. I once heard (I am not making this up) a man finish explaining the inescapable necessity of believing in the divinity of Christ with "Of course, this is only my opinion." If I remember rightly, I could hear a sigh of relief from the others.

What Makes Them Nervous
It is the specifically Christian doctrines that upset this sort of Christian. Such Christians are themselves on many other matters very dogmatic people: they believe that eating ground glass is stupid, that you should not run in front of moving trucks and that hitting babies is wicked. They believe these, the last especially, to be eternal and unchangeable truths and will say so in public.

But for some reason they do not like to say in public anything exclusively Christian. Like those who boast of their belief in the authority of Scripture but are so afraid of being thought of as fundamentalist or literalist that they rarely quote a word from the Bible, these Christians believe in a gracious God who loves man-kind, but they do not talk about how grace is given to men, or who exactly this Jesus is who gives it, or how he is related to the Father and the Spirit, or (especially to be avoided) how those who have received God's grace are supposed to live, or (even more to be avoided) what actions will separate us from that grace, or (most to be avoided) why he is the only Savior of men.

They like their doctrines "filed by title," with the content left unspecified. They like to talk about the incarnation but are less comfortable saying "he was made man," because that implies "he, and no other, was made man" and "he, and not Allah or Buddha or any of the Hindu pantheon, was made man," and these imply "I, though an unworthy sinner, know the truth, and you don't."

As I said, it is Christian doctrine that quiets their voices, lowers their eyes, removes the conviction from their faces and drives them to find some alternative to saying out loud the stark and inevitably divisive words of the Christian doctrines. They may believe them, but they do not speak as if they do. It would be useful to reflect on why they do this, but in this essay I want instead to explain why their usual alternatives to doctrinal conviction do not work.

When they explain their objection to doctrine, they usually insist that a concern with right doctrine destroys both the unity of the church and her ability to serve the world. They will point to the obvious faith of other Christians and say they do not want to be parted from the others by a mere difference of a few words, and they will declare that the world's needs are far too great to spend time disputing a few abstract concepts.

At the same time and as a sort of theological support for this rejection of theol-ogy, they usually suggest that believers need a more immediate and fluid relation to God, uninhibited by doctrinal restrictions. On the liberal side, the former Episco-pal bishop of Newark once said in his straightforward way—he at least never minded being thought dogmatic—that doctrines are merely "images that bind and blind us all." On the conservative side, various charismatic leaders have been fond of saying that "theology divides, but experience unites" and dismissing theological arguments as "mind games." Both treat dogma as something that less enlightened people hold to. Dogma is for spiritual and moral dullards, people who do not have the liberal's vision or the charismatic's revelation. People who cannot let go of the past cling to doctrines.

The same attitude is seen among mainline Christians' ritual appeals to "unity in diversity and diversity in unity," "dialogue" and "koinonia." In its mildest form it is seen in the pained look that crosses a mainline Christian's face when someone is so ill-mannered as to suggest that something might be true, even if he is careful not to add that something else is therefore wrong. This attitude can also be seen in the pitying look many a charismatic leader will give anyone who wants to judge some charismatic phenomenon by the words of the Fathers. The critic will be told that he is "quenching the Spirit" or even "resisting the Sprit" because he wants to discern what the Spirit is doing, using the truths the Spirit has revealed to us in Scripture.

Actually many questing and questioning liberals are not nearly so hostile to doctrine as they honestly believe. One is allowed—in fact expected—to be dogmatic about liberal causes, but to demand dialogue when the liberal cause has not yet been won.

So dozens of Episcopal bishops want the church to continue to talk about approving homosexuality (which has not yet been officially approved), but demand that every parish in their dioceses accept women priests (which has been officially approved). The issue on which they have not yet got their way is to be settled through dialogue; the issue on which they have gotten their way is a triumph of justice and true Christianity, and dialogue therefore is forbidden.

And even their appeal to dialogue on the still contentious issue depends on a very dogmatic assertion of the nature of the church as a body that should not be divided by doctrinal disagreements. When they plead for more dialogue, as if they were asking for something doctrinally neutral, they implicitly declare that the continued institutional unity of the body is more important than its unity in doctrine, which is to say, they insist on their own doctrine of the church without admitting it.

Divisive Doctrine

When I use the word *doctrine* I mean a statement about reality, natural and supernatural, a description of what one believes to be true, not what one feels or suspects or intuits or hopes or wishes. Doctrine explains how the world began, why it is the way it is now and where it is going. By *dogmatic* I mean a type of conviction that the Christian holds with certainty but the world takes for arrogance.

The Christian doctrines are both elaborate and specific, even in the short form of the Nicene Creed. The Christian doctrine is not just "Jesus is God's Son," but that he is "one Lord Jesus Christ, the only-begotten son of God, begotten of his Father before all worlds, God of God, Light of Light, very God of very God, Begotten, not made, being of one substance with the Father" and so on. This statement about reality is both complex and detailed.

These doctrines are so elaborate because they express in propositions the truths of God's revelation, which comes to us first in a Person and then in a very long book, understood and articulated by many very learned, wise and holy men who had to answer some very dangerous errors so precisely that no one could make that mistake again, even by accident. (In other words, so that in the future that belief would be a heresy, not an honest mistake.)

They are so specific because God acted through specific people and events. He did not send fallen man a philosophy of life; he sent his only Son. And he did not send his Son as a spirit who spoke from the clouds but made him incarnate of the virgin Mary. And this God-man did not teach people for a few years and then disappear; he suffered, died, was buried and rose again on the third day. The doctrines are specific because the reality is specific.

Because Christian doctrine is both so elaborate and specific, modern American Christians tend to feel the whole collection is a bit overdone or academic or of interest only to people who care about that sort of thing. They mean well: they love Jesus, but they simply do not see why they should worry about doctrine. It looks irrelevant. True religion can't be that complicated.

But there is another irony, similar to the dogmatic people who hate dogma. Christians who dislike doctrine because it is so complicated will spend thousands of dollars and hundreds of hours to learn all about the intricacies of the law or the chemical processes of the digestive system or the way a jet engine works—because they can see the point of that intricacy. They are fascinated by the complexity of the things they care about. They expect the law to be complex, but for some reason they expect religion to be simple.

Chesterton's Monk

Religion ought to be even more complex than law. It has to answer many more questions because it deals with even more aspects of human life. As G. K. Chesterton put it in *Orthodoxy*:

> This is why the faith has that elaboration of doctrines and details which so much distresses those who admire Christianity without believing in it. When one believes in a creed, one is proud of its complexity, as scientists are proud of the complexity of science. It shows how rich it is in discoveries. If it is right at all, it is a compliment to say that it's elaborately right. A stick might fit a hold or a stone a hollow by accident. But a key and a lock are both complex. And if a key fits a lock, you know it is the right key.

This is also why Christians insist on thinking about their faith. If you have the key to the code, you will use it to decode the messages you receive. You will use it to find out what you should know. "Suppose," Chesterton wrote in his entertaining book *Heretics*, "that a great commotion arises in the street about something, let us say a lamp-post, which many influential persons desire to pull down."[1] A monk is asked

---

[1] *Heretics*, the "prequel" to *Orthodoxy*, is a collection of short articles on contemporaries such as H. G. Wells, George Bernard Shaw and Rudyard Kipling.

his opinion and is knocked down for beginning, "Let us first of all consider, my brethren, the value of Light. If Light be in itself good—" Everyone, Chesterton continues, rushes for the lamp-post and pulls it down in ten minutes, and then

> they go about congratulating themselves on their unmediaeval practicality. But as things go on they do not work out so easily. Some people have pulled the lamp-post down because they wanted the electric light; some because they wanted old iron; some because they wanted darkness, because their deeds were evil. Some thought it not enough of a lamp-post, some too much; some acted because they wanted to smash municipal machinery; some because they wanted to smash something. And there is war in the night, no man knowing whom he strikes.

So, Chesterton concludes, "gradually and inevitably, today, tomorrow, or the next day, there comes back the conviction that the monk was right after all, and that all depends on what is the philosophy of Light. Only what we might have discussed under the gas-lamp, we now must discuss in the dark."

Doctrine, in other words, is like light: the more of it you have, the better you can see. Those who insist on elaborate and complex doctrines merely prefer walking in the full light of day to groping about and stumbling through the gloom. We want to know not just that "God is love," which can mean nearly anything, but that the second person of the Trinity died for our sins and still rose from the dead. The first does not help us see; the second is, if you will, a light unto our paths.

Doctrine Is for Sinners

Were we perfect, we would not need doctrine, though I think even the perfect might well write creeds just for the joy of putting into words what they know about their God. The Bible itself begins with the representative man and woman walking and talking with God in the garden, and ends with the redeemed crowded round his throne singing his praises. Neither are said to have written systematic theologies, but the latter at least sing him praises that are essentially doctrinal.

We are fallen creatures and are therefore far more likely to err than to get things right. We need doctrine, and yet it does not seem to do us much good. It seems pointless at best and pernicious at worst. Doctrinal differences have broken friendships, destroyed families, divided churches and even brought nations to war. Doctrinal certainty has led perfectly normal people to kill and torture other people. When the world finds the church increasingly irrelevant to its needs and interests, and when souls are driven away from Christ by the sight of Christians brawling over words, a concern for doctrinal precision and the inevitable squabbles seems to be a luxury the church cannot afford.

There is a legitimate case to be made against doctrine. One can argue quite persuasively that Christians should abandon it before their arguments hurt more people and waste more time and money when they should be ministering to the world.

Most people today feel as if this view of doctrine ought to be true, but it isn't. The church neither can be unified nor can it witness effectively to the world without a common doctrine. Doctrine is another name for reality, and churches will stay together and act effectively only if they live according to right doctrine, for otherwise reality will eventually destroy them.

If Christians are to be one body in any meaningful sense, and if they are to get anything useful done, they have to be dogmatic. To stop worrying about right doctrine is a luxury the church cannot afford.

The Unity of the Church

First, the church needs doctrine to ensure its unity. Almost all the Western churches are deeply divided on fundamental questions, and those responsible for keeping them alive usually propose four alternative sources of unity: a common ethical standard, a common religious experience, a common ecclesiastical process, and a common institution. None, however, can create unity when the members disagree on doctrine. The mainline churches have all tried the four alternatives in the last three decades, to no avail.

Each of the four alternatives, judiciously applied, protect a church from the disintegrating pressures suffered by any fallen human institution. Working together or praying together or talking together do sometimes reveal a doctrinal unity obscured by superficial contradictions, differences in language, personal ambitions and hatreds or unquestioned assumptions. But these practices can only discover and protect a unity that already exists, as happens when Baptists and Roman Catholics meet to protest abortion and find that, though one is holding a rosary and the other a big floppy Bible marked to show that Rome is the whore of Babylon, they love and serve the same Lord.

The four alternatives never create unity, though. If anything, by replacing a common doctrine they make division all the more likely by making everyone's personal preferences, tastes and opinions much more important. You can pray with a person whose musical tastes you dislike if you are both bound by the same creed, but if you are not bound by a transcendent authority who demands that you kneel at his side, you might as well leave him for someone whose CD collection is similar to yours. You will define "common" in the most convenient way.

A Common Ethical Standard

The first alternative that mainline Christians usually propose is a *common ethical standard.* It is thought that however much people differ from one another in doctrine, they all recognize the same moral laws. If they disagree about the resurrection, they will nevertheless agree that murder and adultery and selling nuclear weapons to developing nations are wrong. One does not hear this suggestion very often these days, though several mainline leaders have recently suggested that environmentalism will bring the church together.

A common ethical standard cannot produce unity because a common ethical standard requires a common doctrine. People act in certain ways because they believe certain things to be true. If they did not believe these things, they would act differently. In one of Chesterton's Father Brown stories, "The Crime of the Communist," the master of an Oxford college tells Father Brown he prefers the old adage "For forms of faith let graceless zealots fight; he can't be wrong whose life is in the right." That can't be true, Father Brown replies:

> How can his life be in the right, if his whole view of life is wrong? That's a modern muddle that arose because people didn't know how much views of life can differ. Baptists and Methodists knew they didn't differ very much in morality; but then they didn't differ very much in religion or philosophy. It's quite different when you pass from the Baptists to the Anabaptists; or from the theosophists to the Thugs. Heresy always does affect morality, if it's heretical enough. I suppose a man may honestly believe that thieving isn't wrong. But what's the good of saying that he honestly believes in dishonesty?

In mainline churches, different doctrines have already led to irreconcilable ethical standards. Those who accept St. Paul's teaching believe sex outside marriage is sinful; those who don't, don't. Those who believe that everyone is created in the image of God oppose abortion on demand; those who believe in the ultimate importance of individual choice support it. Those who believe creation reveals God's will believe homosexuality a perversion; those who believe creation less significant than "God's inclusive love" believe it an honorable life. Without a common doctrine, there is no common ethical standard and no unity.

A Common Experience

The second candidate usually invoked to replace doctrine is a *common religious experience.* All people, it is thought, have some sense of the divine, some feeling for the "wholly other" or some "ultimate concern," though they express it in the forms of their culture and experience. Traditional doctrines are only inherited expressions of this sense, more or less helpful and relevant. When we get behind these cultural forms to the experience they express, we find that we all worship the same God.

A common religious experience cannot produce unity because we cannot define "religious experience" in any usefully limited way—after all, people have sincerely claimed divine guidance to torture babies. "Experience" is a not a specific enough experience to appeal to. To be able to say that one person has experienced God but another (the baby-torturer, for example) has not requires a doctrine, which defeats the purpose of appealing to experience in the first place.

More important, on the testimony of religious people themselves, they do not experience the same divinity. People who know and follow their religion are usually more convinced of its unique truth, not less. The cultural forms and inherited doctrines of each are different because a different god is worshiped in each.

The proponents of common religious experience respond by claiming to understand peoples' experience better than the people themselves or by making some implausible claims—for example, that Christianity, which asserts that God became a specific man who was raised bodily from the dead to make men and women sons of God, is really the same as Buddhism, which looks forward to the extinction of the self.

The diversity of religious experiences in mainline churches suggests that different gods are being worshiped. Some members experience God only in Jesus; others experience him or her or (I suppose) it in the deities of pagan religions or in the depths of their own psyches or even (this has been proposed by a tenured professor of theology at the Episcopal Divinity School in Cambridge) in passionate and varied sexual episodes. Some experience God as the transcendent Father, others as the immanent Mother. Without a common doctrine there is no common religious experience, and no unity.

A Common Process

The third alternative, increasingly invoked as the first two fail, is a *common process*, particularly of "dialogue" and (the new, improved version of dialogue) "conversation." Unity, it is thought, is not to be found in our answers but in our questions, in opening ourselves to each other's unique insights, in coming to know each other better and in affirming each other's experiences and beliefs. Just talking to each other will by itself heal our divisions.

This alternative also fails. A common process cannot produce unity, because dialogue, if it is sincere, must eventually discuss the members' basic beliefs. About the fundamentals, people will either will agree or disagree. Dialogue cannot heal division where the source of division is a doctrinal difference neither side can give up.

In the mainline churches the process of dialogue has only delayed the official recognition of fundamental differences. Their members may possibly respect each other more (though possibly not), but respect is not unity. Two men fighting a duel may respect each other greatly, but they are still trying to kill each other. When a process of dialogue has come to some conclusion in an ecclesial legislative body—such as the votes in the Church of England and the Episcopal Church to ordain women—it has only shown how profoundly divided they are.

Even in conservative circles Christians are asked to dialogue on women's ordination and homosexuality. Some people believe that male headship is scriptural; others that male headship is a cultural product that does not apply universally. Some people believe that the experiences of homosexual people do not change the scriptural judgment of homosexual acts; others believe that the experiences are more revealing than Scripture. Once these differences are clarified, there really isn't much more to be said. Without a common doctrine, dialogue can only lead to disagreement and division, but not to unity.

A Common Institution or Heritage

The fourth alternative to doctrine as a source of unity, invoked when even the third has failed, is a *common institution*. Unity in doctrine, ethical standards, religious experiences and institutional process is seen to be impossible, but it is thought that those who hold irreconcilable doctrines can be held together by shared allegiance to the church or its tradition or ethnic heritage. Hope is held out that doctrinal opponents might someday agree if only they put the unity of the institution ahead of their doctrine.

Anglicanism, for example, is said to be comprehensive or inclusive (defined as doctrinally agnostic, which as a matter of historical fact is simply untrue). Its mission is to prove that people of profoundly divergent beliefs can live together in harmony. Doctrinal ambiguity is said to be of the "genius of Anglicanism," which would have surprised the Reformers who died at the stake for their doctrinal clarity and sent others thereto for theirs.

Institutional unity is, admittedly, unity of a sort. It means that no matter what is preached each Sunday from the pulpit of the various churches, they will all have the same name on the sign outside, and their members share the same newspapers, seminaries and pension fund. But this kind of unity simply draws the largest possible boundary to include everyone it wants to include, and true and useful unity is more than the agreement to go about under the same name.

Unity is not a matter of external signs. I am not united with an atheist because we both wear deck shoes and button-down collars, nor the pope with a Hindu priest because they both wear colored clothes to lead worship. It is a matter of what the signs—which often look alike—symbolize, in other words what doctrines they express.

No institution with a mission can afford such radical diversity or such a depleted definition of itself. John Ashcroft and Hillary Clinton could both join the same club, but not the same political party. A chess club could include those who believe Scripture eternally authoritative and those who believe it must be revised to satisfy new demands, but a church cannot.

External, nondoctrinal unity inevitably dissolves when a crucial issue is addressed and specific action taken. People will prove at some point to have principles that they expect their church to share and to use its influence to further them. At this point (except for the terminally unprincipled, of whom there are many, especially among the clergy) members divide, and some refuse all appeals to save the institution by withdrawing their demands.

Mainline churches have devised a legal unity in which people grow farther from each other while maintaining a nominal membership in a common body—until liberalism, which in its newest forms is inherently intolerant, acquires enough political power to purge the unenlightened. Even the most ardently "inclusive" Episcopal liberals have decided that some Episcopalians are going to have to conform or leave because their doctrinal commitments are too different and therefore too divisive to be included.

Without a common doctrine, an institution is merely a marriage of convenience, one that will almost certainly lead to divorce. Actually, as the liberals now in power lose tolerance for those who hold to the traditional, received view of sex and orders, the marriage of convenience is just as likely to lead to murder, because one partner does not want to divide the estate and would like to keep it all for himself.

The Usual Alternatives

The alternatives to doctrine as a source of unity are unable to hold together the people of a church. Without a common doctrine, a common ethics simply does not exist; a common experience produces behaviors too diverse to call unity; a common process leads to disagreement and division, if it leads anywhere; and a common institution is not unified in any meaningful sense. Mainline Christians, and Anglicans especially, now know from painful experience that none of these can hold a church together.

If the alternatives have failed, perhaps doctrine has more value than people have granted. For if mainline churches are to be united, both internally and with their sister churches around the world, they must first return to a common doctrine. Then all these things—an agreed ethical standard, a shared experience of the divine, meaningful dialogue and a common loyalty to the church—will be added unto them.

The Church's Ministry

If doctrine is necessary to hold the church together, it is also necessary for the church to get anything done. The church cannot act effectively without knowing what it believes. It cannot convince its own members to work together or convince others to join them, if it cannot give them a reason.

The church cannot proclaim a word of judgment or speak a word of healing unless it can speak dogmatically, unless it can say with confidence, "Thus saith the Lord." Otherwise its words are just opinion, of no more value or interest than anyone else's. The church cannot speak a word of invitation or demand repentance and offer change and salvation unless it can say with confidence, "Thus saith the Lord." The church is not alone in offering salvation, and its version is often less appealing and more demanding than most versions the world offers. All it has to offer, its only selling point, is that the story it tells is true. To reach and to serve the world, the church must be dogmatic.

An Advocate of Dialogue

A parish I once attended had a sentimental liberal for an interim rector. For him doctrine seriously held was divisive. He did not care what you believed, as long as you were not so crass as to think your belief true for anyone else.

He was a great advocate of dialogue and a firm believer in the institution of the Episcopal Church. He winced slightly at statements of definite belief and even scriptural quotations, suggesting in a soft, patient voice that we should keep listening to each other before coming to any decision, recognizing our diversity and being willing to give up our own personal agenda to maintain community.

His elegant correction was usually enough to end debate, but it did not answer the questions that needed to be answered. He could not avoid making decisions on the basis of a clear and articulated doctrine. When the diocesan convention was voting on the ordination of practicing homosexuals, his response was "That's going too far," but he could not explain why it was going too far. Giving a reason would have meant appealing to doctrine, a practice he diligently taught the parish to avoid. Not having a doctrine of human nature, or at least not having one he was willing to admit to, he could only respond with a prejudice to a proposal that would either encourage immorality or liberate an oppressed people. He could not answer the crucial question of whether a revealed moral law excludes homosexual behavior or an inclusive God affirms it. To suffering people he had nothing of value to say, either of correction or encouragement. Recognizing our diversity and working to maintain community did not help him say anything useful to the problems his people faced.

Challenging Secular Moralities

Without doctrine the church cannot challenge secular moralities, even when it is unified in condemning them. The world has its own doctrines, which only other doctrines, true doctrines, can challenge. And the world is usually very clear about what it believes, and what it believes is usually attractive enough to capture the unsuspecting, the naive and the gullible if the church is not equally clear.

Take the example of the evil of pornography, about which nearly all Christians, whatever their theological commitments, will agree. Speaking to the *New York Times* a few years ago, Christie Hefner defended the way her father, the pornographer Hugh Hefner, treated women in the pages of *Playboy*. (Hefner had left Christie and her mother when Christie was three and rarely saw her afterward.) "In a world in which infidelity, coercive sex in and out of marriage and dishonesty between the sexes are problems that men and women are concerned about," she said, "this is a man who has been open in his relations and lived a highly moral life." This is a doctrine of human nature. It holds that any human relation is justified if it is open and honest. If young women want to sell pictures of their naked bodies and Hefner wants to buy them and sell them to others, their arrangement is "highly moral."

This is a clear, coherent and consistent doctrine of human nature, and only an equally clear, coherent and consistent doctrine of human nature can stand against it. Only another doctrine can demonstrate to the curious young man why he should leave *Playboy* on the newsstand and forgo the pleasures of staring at the naked bodies of beautiful young women, and thereby protect himself from the magazine's training in evil. He must have a reason not to do what his hormones and culture urge him to do.

A church without doctrine, however much it instinctively understands the evil of pornography, cannot condemn the pornographer's "morality" of openness and honesty. Without doctrine, it cannot propose an alternative morality or show why the pornographers' doctrine of human nature is actually destructive of human nature.

To Stop the Pornographer

Instinct and prejudice are not adequate responses to evil, especially when evil presents itself so winsomely. It is not enough to say that such things are bad. You must be able to show why they are bad, and why they must be opposed. "That's going too far" will not stop the pornographer, the racist or the abortionist; nor will it rally others to resist them.

To charges of exploitation, the pornographer responds that the women freely choose to show their bodies and are well paid for it. A church without doctrine—a church that offers only more dialogue—can offer no convincing rebuttal. With no settled view of men and women, it cannot say with conviction that such a trade in pictures, no matter how free or consensual, exploits women, endangers women and children, and defiles men.

A world without doctrine, in other words, is a world that easily justifies the most brutal exploitation. Without doctrine the church cannot denounce exploitation and can battle evil with only pious hopes for dialogue and high-minded appeals to openness and commitment, or with a condemnation it has no right to give, because it has no reason to give it. The world therefore treats it with indifference if not contempt.

Without doctrine the church appeals to a vague and undefined divinity supposedly underlying all "religious" experiences—a god to which Mr. Hefner can appeal for justification as confidently as any rector.

All Is As It Should Be

I have been identifying the need to have doctrine, but of course not just any doctrine will do; we need the Christian doctrine. By this I mean the Christian doctrine as given and illustrated in Scripture and articulated by the undivided church and those who follow in the "Great Tradition." Every Christian has a doctrine, and unless it is the Christian doctrine it will almost certainly be a bad and destructive one.

My former parish had a second interim rector, a process theologian for whom the traditional Christian doctrines prevented people from recognizing new truths (his in particular). "All is as it should be," he began one notable sermon. God willed the Fall, he went on, "in order that man should live in a world of risk." Only in a world of risk will humans will grow into maturity. But apply his doctrine to a mother whose child lies dying of leukemia. Tell her in her agony that all is as it should be. Tell her that God willed a world in which the fruit of her womb would die; that she should be grateful she is growing into maturity; that as they lower her boy's casket into the ground, she should rejoice she lives in a world of risk.

This is not the religion of the cross and the resurrection. Its god watches passively while people suffer, offering them nothing but meaningless suffering and then personal extinction. Our God came down from heaven to be tortured to death for the salvation of each one of us. There is a difference.

Hindu or Christian

Without doctrine the church cannot explain pain and suffering or offer any hope for redemption and release. It can respond only with prejudice or with theories that, however high-minded and rhetorically intoxicating, cannot heal or reconcile or renew. Healing, reconciliation and renewal require truth, and truth is another word for doctrine.

The religion closest to the contemporary rejection of doctrine—the religion that believes, in Bishop Spong's words, in "a divine power that unites us as holy people"—is Hinduism. It was the British Empire, acting on Christian beliefs about the worth of each individual, that prohibited Hindus from burning widows to death upon their husbands' funeral pyres.

Burning widows was a culturally coherent practice, to which neither of my interim rectors could legitimately have objected. If a doctrinally agnostic Christianity guided society, burning wives on their husbands' funeral pyres might well be the price to be paid for continuing the dialogue or for growing to maturity in a world of risk.

There, as the women roast to death, they might take comfort in the fact that all is as it should be, while their friends are prevented from saving them by stern commands to set aside all personal agendas and listen respectfully to those who think widows make very nice candles.

EIGHT

A STUNTED
ECCLESIOLOGY?

J. I. PACKER

About a half-century ago North American evangelicals began to speak of *the evangelical church*. They still do. The phrase denoted, and denotes, the worldwide fellowship of congregations and Christians that profess evangelical beliefs and maintain an evangelical style of piety and pastoral care, centering on conversion, Bible-reading, evangelism, fellowship with God in assurance and trust, and fellowship with other believers in the shared joy of born-again life. The currency of the phrase marks the mutation of the former self-image of evangelicals as the marginalized faithful remnant within liberal-led Protestantism into a sense of being truly the core of God's church on earth. Evangelicalism is more and more viewing itself as the main stream in relation to which nonevangelicals, whether so by adding to the biblical faith or subtracting from it, are deviating eddies, and evangelical vocation is more and more seen as involving prayer and labor for the leavening and reinvigorating of nonevangelical communities by evangelical truth. This mutation continues to broaden and deepen. It shows a remarkable recovery of confidence and, so I think, of churchliness too.

What is in the mind of evangelicals when they speak of *the evangelical church*? They are not using the singular noun in what would be a secular way, that is, to signify a statistical and organizational collective, though of course the global evangelical fellowship is that and may be so viewed if sociology is one's concern. But in fact their use of this phrase is voicing the same sort of claim to authenticity as

Roman Catholic and Orthodox Christians express when they identify themselves as belonging to the church. This small-c use of the word *church* (large C reduces it to a group label) carries the thought of the one body of Christ on earth, of which all believers are in some sense members, but which takes its most proper form in the circle of communion to which each of the adjectival qualifiers (Roman Catholic, Orthodox, and now evangelical) is pointing. Believers using any one of these three distinguishing labels for self-identification express thereby, in an informal and subtextual way, their belief, not that God is content to have three communities of saints side by side but that here is the particular road that ideally all God's people would be taking together. The ecumenical exchanges of the past century have brought an awareness of this churchly inkling (often not more, but never less) as undergirding the sometimes perplexing phenomenon of separation justifying itself; and when evangelicals speak of *the evangelical church*, the same inkling is involved. There is here, in fact, a recognizable renewal of the sense of churchly reality that lay at the heart of the sixteenth-century reformation.

A comparable renewal has taken place among evangelicals in Britain, and I see myself as a product of it. English by birth, Canadian by choice, Christian by conversion and Calvinist by conviction, I speak as an evangelical who finds his home in the worldwide Anglican church family precisely because historic Anglicanism in its essence represents evangelical churchliness so well. (Present-day Anglicanism in the West is dreadfully out of shape and out of sorts, but that is another story.) In what follows, however, I attempt to generalize about all global evangelicalism as it is today. This, be it said, is a tall order, for since World War II evangelicalism has become a massive network of pulsating energies, largely charismatic in style and constantly adjusting its cultural forms. Statisticians say there are something like half a billion evangelicals in the world, twice as many as there are Orthodox and almost half as many as there are Roman Catholics, and to speak representatively for this multinational pluriform constituency is not an easy task. But I will try my best, and I apologize in advance to any evangelicals who may feel I am off key as far as they are concerned.

What does *evangelical* mean on evangelical lips? It is an umbrella word covering and connecting belief, spirituality, purpose and action both personal and corporate. The quadrilateral account of evangelicalism as biblicist, cross-centered, conversionist and evangelistic has gained wide acceptance in recent years. I myself profile evangelicalism in terms of six belief-and-behavior principles, thus:

☐ enthroning holy Scripture, the written Word of God, as the supreme authority and decisive guide on all matters of faith and practice

☐ focusing on the glory, majesty, kingdom and love of Jesus Christ, the God-man who died as a sacrifice for our sins and who rose, reigns and will return to judge humankind, perfect the church and renew the cosmos

☐ acknowledging the lordship of the Holy Spirit in the entire life of grace, which is the life of salvation expressed in worship, work and witness

☐ insisting on the necessity of conversion (not of a particular conversion experience but of a discernibly converted condition, regenerate, repentant and rejoicing)

☐ prioritizing evangelism and church extension as a life project at all times and under all circumstances

☐ cultivating Christian fellowship on the basis that the church of God is essentially a living community of believers who must help each other to grow in Christ

I think this profile remains accurate, and will assume it in the rest of this essay.

The evangelical emphasis on the uniqueness of holy Scripture as the verbalized revelation of God and on its supreme authority over God's people is sometimes misunderstood as a commitment to the so-called restorationist method in theology. This method sets tradition in antithesis to Scripture and places the church's heritage of thought and devotion under a blanket of permanent suspicion, thus reducing its significance to zero and encouraging all who seek truth and wisdom from Scripture to dismiss tradition as mere morbid pathology and a hydra-head of destructive mistakes. There is no denying that individual evangelicals of highest integrity, if sometimes limited learning, have followed this method, at least in their own view of what they were at. But the authentic evangelical way has always been to see tradition as the precipitate of the church's living with the Bible and being taught by the Holy Spirit through the Bible—the fruit, that is, of the ministry that the Holy Spirit has been fulfilling in the church since Pentecost, according to Jesus' own promise. Seeing it so, mainstream evangelicals value highly what they see as the positives of tradition, as witnesses their constant drawing of inspiration from the thought and service of such past leaders as (for instance) Augustine, Bernard, Luther, Calvin, Edwards, Whitefield, Wesley, Spurgeon, Carey and Hudson Taylor. Similarly, they treasure the hymns of such as Isaac Watts, Charles Wesley and John Newton, and many also value liturgical forms from the classic Anglican Book of Common Prayer and the literature of Celtic spirituality—all of which are elements in the tradition of the church. Jaroslav Pelikan's felicitous description of tradition as "the living faith of the dead" in contrast to traditionalism, "the dead faith of the living," is, so far, a thoroughly evangelical estimate.

Because evangelicals know that Christian minds, like Christian hearts, are as yet imperfectly sanctified, they expect some of the Christian community's traditions to prove mistaken and misleading, and they see the need to test all of them accordingly. But because evangelicals know that the Holy Spirit's guidance into truth was and is a reality, they expect to discover that tradition is full of truth and wisdom, and to find that even controversy in the church's past, however bewildering and unhappy in the short term, brought clarity out of confusion about what honors God, benefits souls and builds the church. Thus they treat tradition as an archive of past ventures in expounding and applying the Bible, and so as a resource to help them in their own exegetical and theological work.

Evangelicals do not regard tradition or any part of it as infallible, any more than they view present-day expositions of Scripture from pulpits, platforms and podiums, and in printed pages as in any way infallible. Their goal is canonical interpretation, that is, understanding reached by letting the corpus of canonical writings elucidate itself from within, as the various books link up with and throw light on each other. Evangelicals know that the Bible, thus canonically interpreted, must itself be the assessor of all attempts to expound and apply it. So, as the eighth of the Anglican Thirty-nine Articles says, even "the Three Creeds" (Apostles', Nicene and Athanasian) "ought thoroughly to be received and believed" not simply because the church commends them but because "they may be proved by most certain warrants of Holy Scripture."

Evangelicals value tradition, then, as a repository of God-given insight—that is, of ripe skill in listening to what the Bible says and verbally reproducing it in ways that transcend the limitations and relativities of particular cultural backgrounds. Thus evangelicals value Nicene trinitarianism and Chalcedonian Christology and Augustine's analysis of sin and grace, all of which were wrought out in the Greco-Roman intellectual world; and they value also the Reformers' christocentric bibliology, soteriology and ecclesiology, which were wrought out in the intellectual world of Europe's Renaissance. The evidence for that is the long series of theological treatises and textbooks affirming the general Reformational point of view that have been written during the past half-millennium; though coming from a wide variety of geographical and denominational sources, they are extraordinarily similar in substance on all of these basic themes.

I am making a case for the genuine churchliness of today's evangelical church, a churchliness that is directly in line with that of the churches who separated from Rome at the time of the Reformation. It is a case, I believe, that urgently needs to be made, both because this recovered churchliness is a significant fact that is often overlooked and because much evangelicalism is in a state of cognitive dissonance about it, affirming churchliness yet retaining an ethos and mindset that seems to observers to deny it. Roman Catholic, Orthodox, high Anglicans and leading ecumenists often say that evangelicals have an inadequate view of the church. Is that true? In theory, no, but in practice the answer often appears to be yes.

Churchliness means recognizing the centrality of the church and the primacy of the corporate in the purpose of God. The corporate means the negating of individualism in conscientious togetherness of life and action in, through, under and for our

Lord Jesus Christ. Locally, that means mutual involvement, openness, dependence and ministry within the congregation; ecumenically, it means realizing brotherhood with all Christians worldwide, plus "all the company of heaven" as the historic Anglican Prayer Book puts it, in ongoing adoration of the Father and the Son through the Spirit. The local-church aspect of this is adumbrated in Ephesians 4:11-16, the universal church aspect is reflected in Hebrews 12:22-24 and Revelation 7:9-12, 14:1-5.

To be sure, the gospel message individualizes, and faith is always an individual, personal matter, and in the God-centered relationships of love and service formed within Christian community each person's individuality and selfhood is deepened and enhanced. At the same time, however, through the ministry of the Holy Spirit, the self-sufficient individualism to which sin in our spiritual system gives rise should be step by step snuffed out, and the glory of God in and through the community's life should increasingly become the focus of each believer's longings and prayers. This process is precisely a growing into and an expressing of churchliness. Is it a regular mark of evangelicals, as it certainly was of the magisterial Reformers? I, for one, have to say: nothing like sufficiently. And that is in effect to say that evangelical churchliness is as yet a stunted growth.

Confessionally and conceptually, evangelical ecclesiology is full and strong. Consider, for instance, the account of the church given by the Amsterdam Declaration, representing the common mind of some eleven thousand evangelists and church leaders gathered together in the opening year of the third millennium:

> The church is the people of God, the body and bride of Christ, and the temple of the Holy Spirit. The one, universal church is a transnational, transcultural, transdenominational and multiethnic family, the household of faith. In the widest sense the church includes all the redeemed of all the ages, being the one body of Christ extended throughout time as well as space. Here in the world, the church becomes visible in all local congregations that meet to do together the things that according to Scripture the church does. Christ is the head of the church. Everyone who is personally united to Christ by faith belongs to his body and by the Spirit is united with every other true believer in Jesus.

The classic exponents of Reformation ecclesiology, John Calvin of Geneva and Richard Hooker of England, would have nothing major to add to that. Yet, as was said, observers will feel there is cognitive dissonance here: evangelicals who subscribe to such statements do not seem in practice to rate churchliness a factor in full-orbed Christian discipleship, and rarely do they display a personal formation that is fully churchly. Strong individuality within an equally strong frame of corporateness is indisputably the New Testament ideal for Christian living—why then do evangelicals, strong as they are on individuality in Christ, appear weak when it comes to the corporate awareness that should flow from seeing the church as central in the plan of God? What is the problem here?

In broadest terms this problem of today has three sources. First, evangelicalism was always in part reactionary against Roman Catholicism, and reaction restricts and constricts those reacting. Evangelical rejection of the Catholic mode of churchliness, which is essentially sacramentalist, breeds a tendency to undervalue churchliness as such. Out goes the baby with the bath water. Second, reinforcing this, European pietism, which has decisively shaped English-speaking evangelicalism since the eighteenth century, was very much a reaction against the deadness of state churches, and in effect redefined churchliness as close fellowship among spiritually lively groups—a view that evangelicals readily embrace, without considering its sectarian overtones. Third, twentieth-century wrenching of leadership out of evangelical hands and away from evangelical principles, which has significantly deadened some older denominations, has given new appeal to the pietistic (even separatist) path. This is how Christian concern to cultivate spiritual life has come to hinder the converted from developing a fully churchly heart.

To be more specific, there are five elements in the characteristic evangelical mindset of our time that work against thorough realization of what has been called the "abundance ecclesiology" of Paul's letter to the Ephesians, where the church is declared to be the fullness of Christ, the beloved bride for whom he laid down his life, and to grow as a single new man in Christ (you can hardly have a more corporate image than that!), moving always into the maturity that is the measure of Christ's own stature (see Eph 1:23, 5:25-27, 4:11-16). All five are matters of proper Christian priority that have unhappily triggered improper reactionary antitheses. They are as follows.

Factor one is evangelical *salvation-centeredness.* No one should fault evangelicals for their loving attention to the task of unpacking the gospel message that "Christ Jesus came into the world to save sinners" (1 Tim 1:19). Nothing is more important than that the gospel is fully grasped, and exploring it and emphasizing it is a thoroughly churchly activity. But is has led to a habit of human-centered theologizing, which sets needy humans center stage, as it were, brings in the Father, the Son and the Holy Spirit just for their saving roles, and fails to cast anchor in doxology, as Paul's expositions of the gospel lead him to do (see Rom 11:33-36, 16:25-27; Eph 3:20-21; 1 Tim 6:13-16; cf. Rev 5:9-14). Too often we evangelicals relegate the truth of the Trinity to the lumber room of the mind, to be put on display only when deniers of it appear, rather than being made the frame and focus of all adoration. The church then comes to be thought of as an organization for spiritual life support rather than as an organism of perpetual praise; doxology is subordinated to ministry, rather than ministry embodying and expressing doxology, and church life is thought out and set forth in terms of furthering people's salvation rather than of worshiping and glorifying God. The antithesis is improper and false, to be sure, but the human-centered mindset is real and is one facet of a stunted churchliness.

Factor two is evangelical *word-centeredness*. No one should fault evangelicals for valuing Scripture and doctrine and preaching in the way that they do—or, at least, used to do, for catechism, and adult Bible schools, and serious learning of the historic faith, are currently in eclipse among us, to our own great loss. But our stress on text and talking has marginalized and dumbed down the sacraments, so that their message about the crucified and living Lord as the life of the church is muffled, and the Eucharist becomes an extra tacked on to a preaching service rather than the congregation's chief act of worship, as Calvin and Luther and Cranmer thought it should be. The word-sacrament antithesis, most certainly, is also false, but evangelicals' disproportionate word-centeredness is a fact, and is a further facet of a stunted churchliness.

Factor three is evangelical *life-centeredness*—using "life" in the spiritual sense whereby, in historic pietism as in holy Scripture, it means responsive, satisfying personal fellowship with God, the fruit of regeneration in the heart and the first installment of the coming bliss of heaven. No one should fault evangelicals for flagging this as the most vital matter of all, doubly not when they, and those to whom they speak, belong to moribund congregations or denominations that settle for something less than spiritual life in their adherents. Martin Bucer, the Strasbourg reformer, who midwifed Calvin's understanding of the Lord's Supper and helped Cranmer to envision a pastorally adequate Church of England, was the pioneer evangelical thinker in this area: he urged that the spiritually lively folk should meet separately as *ecclesiola in ecclesia* (the little church within the church), to maintain their spiritual vitality in fellowship together. English Puritanism and German Pietism took this up in a big way. The perennial trouble, however, is that, by a process as understandable as it is regrettable, growing care for the health of the smaller body reduces concern for the quickening and renewing of the larger unit. Evangelicals have hewed to Bucer's line diligently enough for the small group that meets to pray, study the Bible and share experience to be labeled an evangelical institution, and this unhappy process has been observed to take place in these groups over and over again. Such a narrowing of care is a seedbed of sectarianism and ought never to occur—but it does; and it has to be listed as one more facet of modern evangelicalism's stunted churchliness.

Factor four is the *parachurch-centeredness* that is nowadays virtually an evangelical trademark. No one should fault evangelicals for creating a plethora of parachurch ministries; they are needed if the work of the kingdom is to get done. Parachurch agencies supplement the ministrations of the church with auxiliary activities and specialist skills that local congregations lack. Missionary societies were first in this field, followed by societies for specialized service at home, and from these beginnings has grown today's vast mix of parachurch bodies, ranging from the very small to the very large (Campus Crusade, Focus on the Family, the International Fellowship of Evangelical Students, the Billy Graham Evangelistic Association, and such like). Everyone should be glad they are there and rejoice in the work they do. But, sadly, by the same narrowing process that was described above, these agencies of God's kingdom draw interest, prayer, enthusiasm and money away from the wider-ranging, slower-moving, less glamorous realities of congregational life, so that the parachurch body comes to have pride of place in supporters' affections and in effect to be their church. Here again the antithesis is improper in theory but potent in practice and must appear as yet a fourth facet of evangelicalism's stunted churchliness.

Factor five is the *independent-church syndrome*, which matches parachurch-centeredness but goes further. Evangelicals have created many independent congregations in recent years, and I would be the last to criticize them for doing so: after all, church-planting as such is a sign of health and growth. Nor should we fault the theology behind independent churches, which is that Christ the Lord himself must rule and guide each congregation by his Word and Spirit as directly as possible. Yet a problem lurks here. Independent congregations are such through declining connectional bonds with other congregations—such bonds, I mean, as synods, councils, superintendent ministers, bishops and court systems provide. Abuse of these bonds, as seen, for instance, in American Anglicanism's current agony under rogue bishops, is an argument not for abolishing authority networks but for constitutionalizing them more wisely and electing operatives for them more discerningly. No antithesis should be posited between connectional structures and the congregation's responsibility to follow the will of Christ, for structural links holding congregations together as the apostles' personal ministry once did would seem to be part of his will, whatever local problems may arise from acknowledging this. Links of this kind, within an agreed frame of creedal soundness, are signs of the organic, space-time continuity of the body of Christ on earth, the catholic visible church of which each congregation is an outcrop, sample and microcosm; such signs should not be cast off. When they are, sectarianism seems to threaten, and another aspect of stunted churchliness has made its appearance.

My hope is that in this new century the churchliness of evangelicalism will become evident. As my analysis shows, the difficulty here is more practical than theoretical. Evangelical ecclesiology is not stunted, but evangelical churchliness as a mindset and an ethos is, and without rethinking and adjustment this will continue, so that the credibility of the evangelical claim to mainstream status as church will remain suspect and perhaps be forfeit. Will the evangelical church gain credibility through change at these key points? Or will it continue partly at least to deny its name? We wait to see.

Nine

Recognizing the Church

A Personal Pilgrimage & the Discovery of Five Marks of the Church

THOMAS HOWARD

I was brought up in an evangelical household. To say this is to say something good.

My father was a layman, not a preacher; but he was a devoted and assiduous daily student of the Bible. He and my mother exist to this day in my imagination as the very icons of the godly man and woman. It was a wonderful thing—that sage, earnest, transparent, Bible-centered faith. I owe the fact that I am a believer today, and that my whole pilgrimage, steep and tortuous as it has been sometimes, has been toward the center, not away from it, to the faith and prayers and example of my father and mother.

I believe that I and my five brothers and sisters, all of whom, now, in our seventies, are Christians who want to follow the Lord wholly, would all testify to this godly influence of our parents. The household was a household suffused with the Bible. We sang hymns daily—hundreds of them over the years, so that probably all six of us know scores of hymns by heart. We had family prayers twice a day, after breakfast and after supper. Our parents prayed with us at our bedside, the last thing at night. We all went to Sunday school and church regularly.

There is only one agenda in a fundamentalist Sunday school: the Bible. The Bible day in and day out, year in and year out. Flannelgraph lessons, Sword drills, Scripture memory: everything was focused directly on the Bible itself. I am grateful for every minute of this, now, sixty years later. Because of this the whole of Scripture, from Genesis to Revelation, is ringing in my ears all the time. Hundreds of verses, in the language of the King James Version, are there, intact, in my memory. I hope that, if my memory fails and I lose my wits in my old age, perhaps these verses, from so long ago, will remain there and bring me solace.

The Christian believers among whom I grew up were very forthcoming about the faith. They spoke easily and informally about "the Lord." When you were among them you knew you were among people of "like precious faith," as St. Peter phrases it. Many of the guests in our household had been overseas missionaries, some of them interned in concentration camps by the Japanese during World War II. Our ears were full of stories of how God had been faithful in all sorts of extremities. It would be hard to find a better ambiance, I think, than this good and trusty evangelicalism of my youth.

The Pilgrimage Begins

But I speak as one whose pilgrimage has led him from the world of Protestant evangelicalism to the Roman Catholic Church. One way or another, all of us whose nurture has been in one of the sectors of Protestantism where the Bible is honored, where the gospel is preached without dissimulation and where Jesus Christ is worshiped as God and Savior—all of us, desire to be faithful to the ancient faith that we profess, and to be found obedient to the will of God. Certainly such fidelity and obedience have motivated us so far, and we want to be able to give an accounting of ourselves when it comes to our turn at the divine tribunal, for we must all appear before the judgment seat of Christ.

Why then, would anyone want to leave such a world? Was not that a rendering of the ancient faith almost without equal? Surely to leave it would be to go from great plenty out to famine and penury?

Of my own case I would have to say that I did not want to leave it. Certainly I was restless as a young man, like all young men, and any grass across any fence tended to look very green. I did, out of mere curiosity, draw back from the little church of my parents and my childhood when I returned to my hometown after graduating from college and putting in my time in the army. I visited the local Presbyterian church, and the Methodist and the Lutheran and the Episcopalian.

Only this last one held any great attraction for me—I think it was a matter of aesthetics more than any other single factor. The Episcopal liturgy is the most elegant thing in the world, and this is to be attributed to their prayer book, which has since been supplanted by a modern translation, but which in 1960 was still the old Book of Common Prayer, with its matchless Shakespearean prose. Episcopal churches tend to be Gothic, with stained glass and cool, dark interiors. Episcopal hymnody is virtually the best in the world, if we are speaking of a rich treasury of hymns drawn from the era of Isaac Watts and Charles Wesley, as well as from ancient Christendom. I was attracted by all of this. There was also a strange note of nostalgia in it, since I knew that my mother had been "saved" out of Episcopalianism into fundamentalism in about 1915, but that she still retained an undying love for Episcopal hymns and liturgy. Somehow that nostalgia had communicated itself to me.

The next step in my pilgrimage was made easy. I found myself teaching at a boys' school in England, so this put me in the neighborhood of the Church of England. There is a robust evangelical wing in this old church. So I did not have to "leave" anything. I could have all this and heaven too, so to speak. I was received into the Church of England in 1962 and found myself among the best crowd of all, I thought: evangelicals who took the liturgy and the atmosphere of Anglicanism for granted. I loved it.

When I returned to the United States and married, my wife, who was a wise and holy woman, was fairly quickly received into the Episcopal Church—or the Anglican Church, as many prefer to call it—and our two children were raised as Anglicans. Fortunately, we found ourselves, both in New York in the early years of our marriage and then in Massachusetts, in parishes where the Scripture was honored and the gospel was preached and sturdy fellowship was central.

Liberalism and Worship

Two questions, I think, spring into the minds of people, when they hear of someone opting into Anglicanism. First, what about the liberalism in these big Protestant denominations? And second, doesn't one have to settle into worship that is dull and lifeless since it is all canned and rote, leaving behind the wonderful spontaneity and freshness that marks the worship in the evangelical and Pentecostal churches?

On the first question, there is only one answer, and that is yes, one does have to learn to live in a denomination that has very largely given itself over to an extremely liberal interpretation of Scripture and now, alas, of sexual morality. The good and faithful souls in these Protestant denominations suffer over this, of course, and will tell you that they are trying to bear witness in the situation, and that the church historically has been plagued always with heresy and sin, and that we can't keep splitting and splitting as we evangelicals have done in the interest of doctrinal or moral purity. You end up with an ecclesiastical flea market that way, such people might urge.

On the second question, about canned and rote worship, we come to an immense issue. What is at stake here is the rock-bottom question as to what worship is and how you do it. Put briefly, the question comes to this: Worship is the thing that we were created for—to know God, and knowing him to bless him and adore him forever. This is what the seraphim and the cherubim and all the angelic hierarchy do ceaselessly. This is what the creation is doing: the Psalms call upon winds and mountains and seas and frosts and hail and sun and stars to worship the Most High. We believe that in some very literal sense the entire creation, each part of it after its own unique mode, "worships" him. But you and I belong to the species whose dignity entails leading the praises of our world.

To worship God is to ascribe worth to him. It is an activity distinct from teaching and fellowship and witnessing and sharing. It is an act, not an experience. We come to church primarily to do something, not to receive something; although of course in the ancient worship of the church we do indeed receive God himself, under the sacramental species of bread and wine. But our task in worship is to offer the oblation of ourselves and our adoration at the Sapphire Throne.

Obviously this is a daunting and an august task. Fortunately we are not left to our own resources, nor to the whim of the moment, nor even to our own experience. The faithful have been worshiping God since the beginning, and there is help for us. All of us, even those of us who come from the so-called free churches where spontaneity is supposed to be the rule, are accustomed to borrowing secondhand, canned words to assist us in worship. I am speaking of hymns. When we sing "Amazing Grace" or "O, For a Thousand Tongues to Sing," we are borrowing John Newton's and Charles Wesley's words. And we discover that far from cramping or restricting our worship, these secondhand words bring us up to a level quite unattainable by our own spontaneous efforts. They take us away from ourselves.

That is another crucial point in ritual worship: people who are fellowshiping and sharing with each other are characteristically facing each other. People who are worshiping are, all together, facing something else, namely, the Sapphire Throne. The liturgy of the church brings us into these precincts. Our Lord Jesus Christ was accustomed to this kind of worship—indeed, when he joined his parents and fellow Jews in weekly worship, he entered into the ritual. No one had ever heard of spontaneous public worship. The early church, in great wisdom, realized that this is a principle that goes to the root of the mystery of our being. Spontaneity is a good and precious thing. The Lord loves any lisping, stammering, broken and halting words we can offer to him, as he loves the buzzing of bumblebees and the braying of donkeys. But when we come together for the particular act of offering our corporate, regular, recurring adoration to him, then we need a form.

The Question of Church

During my twenty-three years as an Anglican I discovered the world of liturgy and sacrament and the church year. But also as I read in theology and church history and in the tradition of Christian spirituality, I found myself increasingly acutely conscious of a question: But what is the church?

Every Sunday at the Anglican liturgy I found myself repeating, "I believe in one, holy, catholic, and apostolic church." These are words from an era that all of us— Roman, Orthodox, Anglican, Protestant and unaffiliated—must take seriously, since all of us, whether we are pleased to admit it or not, are the direct beneficiaries of the work of the men who hammered out those words. You and I may think, in some of our less reflective moments, that all we need is the Bible and our own wits. *Sola Scriptura*. Just me and my Bible. But that is an impertinent notion. Every Christian in every assembly of believers in this world is incalculably in the debt of the men who succeeded the apostles. For they are the ones who, during those early centuries when the church was moving from the morning of Pentecost out into the long haul of history, fought and thought and worked and wrote and died so that "the faith once for all delivered to the saints" might indeed be handed on. Heresiarchs popped up out of the weeds left, right and center, and all of them believed in the "verbal inspiration" of Scripture. It was the church, in its bishops and councils, that preserved the faith from the errors of the heresiarchs and other zealots, and that shepherded the faithful along in the Way, as it was called.

An Unrecognizable Church

You and I, insofar as we are familiar with modern Protestantism and, *a fortiori*, with evangelicalism and Pentecostalism, are familiar with a state of affairs that would have been unimaginable to our fathers in the faith in those early days. I am referring to the oddity that, even though we all say we believe in the final and fixed truth of divine revelation, we are nevertheless all at odds when it comes to deciding just what that truth is.

Oh, to be sure, we all agree on the so-called fundamentals of the gospel—but of course those fundamentals have been articulated and distilled for us by the church that wrote the creeds. The Mormons and the Jehovah's Witnesses and the modernists all toil away at the pages of the Bible, but you and I would say they are not getting the right things out of that Bible. Why do we say that? Because whether we acknowledge it or not, our "orthodox" understanding of the Bible has been articulated for us by the church. All sorts of notions, for example, have cropped up about the Trinity, about the mystery of our Lord's divine and human nature and so forth. The reason you and I are not Nestorians or Eutychians or Apollinarians or Docetists or Arians or Montanists is that the church guarded and interpreted and taught the Bible; and we, the faithful, have had a reliable and apostolic voice in the church that says, "This is what holy Scripture is to be understood as teaching, and that which you hear Eutychius or Sabellius teaching from the Bible is not to be believed."

But I was speaking of the question that began to force its way into my mind during those years: What is the church? What may have appeared as a digression just now, when I referred to the men who worked so hard to preserve the faith, and the bishops and councils who settled on the right understanding of revelation, was not a digression at all. When I heard myself repeating the words from the Nicene Creed at the liturgy, "I believe in one, holy, catholic, and apostolic church," I was, of course, saying words that are not directly from any one text in the Bible, and yet that have been spoken in all of Christendom for a millennium and a half now and in some sense constitute a plumbline for us.

The Creed is not Scripture; that is true. But then all of us, whether we come from groups that repeat the Creed or not, would agree, "Oh yes, indeed; that is the faith which we all profess." Some would add, "But of course, we get it straight out of the Bible. We don't need any creed." The great difficulty here is that Eutychius and Sabellius and Arius got their notions straight out of the Bible as well. Who will arbitrate these things for us? Who will speak with authority to us faithful, all of us rushing about flapping the pages of our well-thumbed New Testaments, locked in shrill contests over the two natures of Christ or baptism or the Lord's Supper or the mystery of predestination?

This question formed itself in the following way for me, a twentieth-century Christian: Who will arbitrate for us between Luther and Calvin? Or between Luther and Zwingli, both appealing loudly to Scripture and each with a view of the Lord's Table that categorically excludes the other's view? And who will arbitrate for us between John Wesley and George Whitefield—that is, between Arminius and Calvin? Or between J. N. Darby (he thought he had found the biblical pattern for Christian gathering, and the Plymouth Brethren to this day adhere to his teaching)—and all the denominations? Or between the dispensationalists and the Calvinists on the question of eschatology?

A piquant version of this situation presented itself to us loosely affiliated evangelicals, with all of our independent seminaries and Grace Chapels and Moody Churches and so forth. When a crucial issue arises—say, what we should teach about sexuality—who will speak to us with a finally authoritative voice? The best we can do is to get *Christianity Today* to run a symposium, with one article by J. I. Packer plumping for traditional morality, and one article by one of our lesbian feminist evangelicals (there are some), showing that we have all been wrong for the entire 3,500 years since Sinai, and that what the Bible really teaches is that indeed homosexuals may enjoy a fully expressed sexual life. The trouble here is that J. I. Packer has no more authority than our lesbian friend, so the message to the faithful is "Take your pick."

This is not, whatever else we wish to say about it, a picture of things that would be recognizable to the apostles or to the generations that followed them. The faithful in those early centuries were certainly aware of a great Babel of voices among the Christians, teaching this and teaching that on every conceivable point of revelation. But the faithful were also aware that there was a body that could speak into the chaos and declare, with serene and final authority, what the faith that had been taught by the apostles was. Clearly we evangelicals had been living in a scheme of things altogether unrecognizable to the apostles and the fathers of the church.

"I believe in one, holy, catholic, and apostolic church," I found myself saying in the Creed. What church? What is the church? What was the church in the minds of the men who framed that Creed? Clearly it was not the donnybrook that the world sees nowadays, with literally thousands of groups, big and small, all clamoring and all claiming to be in some sense the church.

Five Recognizable Marks of the Church

As an Anglican I became aware that I, as an individual believer, stood in a very long and august lineage of the faithful, stretching back to the apostles and fathers. The picture had changed for me: it was no longer primarily me, my Bible and Jesus (although heaven knows that is not altogether a bad picture: the only question is, is it the whole picture?). Looming for me, as an Anglican, was "the faith," ancient, serene, undimmed, true. And that faith somehow could not be split apart from "the church." But then, what was the church?

I realized that one way or another I had to come to terms with the church in all of its antiquity, its authority, its unity, its liturgy and its sacraments. Those five marks, or aspects, of the church are matters that all of us, I think, would find eluding us in the free churches. I speak as a Roman Catholic, for that is where my own pilgrimage has brought me in my quest for this church in all of its antiquity, authority, unity, liturgy and sacraments. Let me touch on each of these briefly.

The antiquity. First, the antiquity of the church confronts me. As an evangelical I discovered while I was in college that it was possible to dismiss the entire church as having gone off the rails by about A.D. 95. That is, we, with our open Bibles, knew better than old Ignatius or Polycarp or Clement, who had been taught by the apostles themselves—we knew better than they just what the church is and what it should look like. Never mind that our worship services would have been unrecognizable to them or that our church government would have been equally unrecognizable or the vocabulary in which we spoke of the

Christian life would have been equally unrecognizable. We were right, and the Fathers were wrong. That settled the matter.

The trouble here was that what these wrong-headed men wrote—about God, about our Lord Jesus Christ, about his church, about the Christian's walk and warfare—was so titanic and so rich and so luminous that their error seemed infinitely truer and more glorious than my truth. I gradually felt that it was I, not they, who was under surveillance. The "glorious company of the apostles, the noble army of martyrs, and the holy Church throughout all the world" (to quote the ancient hymn, the *Te Deum*) judge me, not I them. Ignatius, Polycarp, Clement, Justin, Irenaeus, Cyprian, Cyril, Basil, the Gregorys, Augustine, Ambrose, Hilary, Benedict—it is under the gaze of this senate that I find myself standing. Alas. How tawdry, how otiose, how flimsy, how embarrassing seem the arguments that I had been prepared so gaily to put forward against the crushing radiance of these men's confession. The church is here, in all of its antiquity, judging me.

The authority. Second, the church in its authority confronts me. That strange authority to bind and loose that our Lord bestowed on his disciples has not evaporated from the church—or so the church has believed from the beginning. If you will read the story of those decades that followed Pentecost, and especially that followed the death of the apostles, you will discover that the unction to teach and to preside in the church that passed from the apostles to the bishops was understood to be an apostolic unction. I, for example, could not start up out of the bulrushes and say, "Hi, everybody! The Lord has led me to be a bishop! I'm starting me a church over here." The whole Christian community—bishop, presbyters, deacons and laity—would have looked solemnly at me and gone about their business.

The Holy Spirit, in those days, did not carry on private transactions with isolated souls and then announce to the church that so-and-so had been anointed for this or that ministry. The unction of the Holy Spirit and the authority of the church to ordain for ministry were not two random enterprises. The Holy Spirit worked in and through the church's ministry and voice. To be sure, he could do what he wanted to do, as he had always done, being God. Under the Old Covenant we could say that he worked in and through Israel; but of course you find these extra characters like Job and Jethro and the Magi coming across the stage from outside the Covenant, yet nonetheless undeniably having been in touch with God. God can do what he wants, of course.

But the church understands herself to be the appointed vessel for God's working, just as the Incarnation was. Her authority is not her own. She arrogates nothing to herself. Her bishops and patriarchs are the merest custodians, the merest passers-on, we might say, of the deposit of faith. As a Roman Catholic, I am of course acutely conscious of this. When someone objects to me, "But who does the Catholic Church think she is, taking this high and mighty line" (about abortion or about sexual morality or about who may or may not come to the Lord's Table), the answer is, "She doesn't think she's anything particular, if you mean that she has set herself up among the wares in the flea market as somehow the best. She has her given task to do—to pass on the teaching given by the apostles, and she has no warrant to change that. She is not taking her cues from the Nielsen ratings or from a poll or even from a sociological survey as to what people feel comfortable with nowadays. She didn't start the church, and it's not her church."

As a free-church Christian one can, of course, make up one's mind about lots of things. Should I fast or not? Well, that's for me to decide. Should I give alms? Again—a matter for my own judgment. Must I go to church? That, certainly, is my own affair. Need I observe this or that feast day in the church year? I'll make up my own mind. Piety and devotion are matters of one's own tailoring: no one may peer over my shoulder and tell me what to do.

Indeed, no one may do anything of the sort—if we are speaking of ourselves as Americans who have constitutional rights. But if we are speaking of ourselves as Christian believers, then there is a touchstone other than the U. S. Constitution by which our choices must be tested.

Our Christian ancestors knew nothing of this sprightly individualism when it came to the disciplines of the spiritual life. They fasted on Fridays, or they went to church on Sundays. Some Roman pope did not make these things up. They took shape in the church, very early; and nobody dreamed of cobbling up a private spirituality. And likewise with all sorts of questions. Should women be ordained as priests? It is, eventually, not a matter of job description or politics, nor even of common sense or public justice. The question is settled by what the church understands the priesthood to be—with cogent reasoning given, to be sure. It is not a question to be left interminably open to the public forum for decade after decade of hot debate.

The church is here, in all of its authority, judging us.

The unity. Third, the church in its unity confronts me. This is the most difficult and daunting matter. But one thing eventually became clear: my happy evangelical view of the church's "unity" as being nothing more than the worldwide clutter that we had under our general umbrella, was, for good or ill, not what the ancient church had understood by the word *unity.* As an evangelical I could pick which source of things appealed most to me: Dallas Seminary, Fuller Seminary, John Wimber, Azusa Street, the Peninsula Bible Church, Hudson Taylor, the deeper life as taught at Keswick, Virginia Mollenkott, John Stott or Sam Shoemaker. And in one sense variety is doubtless a sign of vigorous life in the church. But in another sense, of course, it is a disaster. It is disastrous if I invest any of the above with the authority that belongs alone to the church. But then who shall guide my choices?

Once again we come back to the picture that we have in the ancient church. Whatever varieties of expression there may have been—in Alexandria as over against Lyons or in Antioch as over against Rome—nevertheless, when it came to the faith itself, and also to order and discipline and piety in the church, no one was left groping or mulling over the choices in the flea market.

Where we Protestants were pleased to live with a muddle—even with stark contradiction (as in the case of Luther versus Zwingli, for example)—the church of antiquity was united. No one needed to remain in doubt for long as to what the Christian church might be or where it might be found. The Montanists were certainly zealous and earnest, and had much to commend them: the difficulty, finally, was that they were not the church. Likewise with the Donatists. God bless them for their fidelity and ardor and purity, but they were not the church. As protracted and difficult as the Arian controversy was, no one needed to remain forever in doubt as to what the church had settled on: Athanasius was fighting for the apostolic faith, against heresy. It did not remain an open question forever.

There was one church and the church was one. And this was a discernible, visible, embodied unity, not a loose aggregate of vaguely like-minded believers with their various task forces all across the globe. The bishop of Antioch was not analogous to the General Secretary of the World Evangelical Fellowship or the head of the National Association of Evangelicals. He could speak with the full authority of the church behind him; these latter gentlemen can speak only for their own organization. He was not even analogous to the Stated Clerk of the Presbyterian Church or the Presiding Bishop of the Episcopalians, neither of whom is understood by his clientele to be speaking in matters of doctrine and morality with an undoubted apostolic authority.

This line of thought could bring us quickly to the point at which various voices today might start bidding for our attention, each one of them with "Hey—ours is the apostolic voice—over here!" To answer each one is not my task here. I would only want to urge you to test your own understanding of the church against the church's ancient understanding of itself as united, as one. What is that unity? It is a matter that has perhaps been answered too superficially and frivolously for the last two hundred years in American Protestantism. The church in its unity is here, judging us.

The liturgy. Fourth, the liturgy of the church confronts and judges me. That seems like an odd way of putting it: in what sense can anyone say that the liturgy "judges" me? Certainly it does not condemn me or pass any sort of explicit judgment on me. But if only by virtue of its extreme antiquity and universality, it constitutes some sort of touchstone for the whole topic of Christian worship.

Often the topic is approached as though it were a matter of taste: John likes fancy worship—smells and bells—and Bill likes simplicity and spontaneity and informality. There's the end of the discussion. And certainly, as I mentioned before, God receives any efforts, however halting and homespun, which anyone offers as worship, just as any father or mother will receive the offering of a limp fistful of dandelions as a bouquet from a tiny child. On the other hand, two considerations might be put forward at this point.

First, what did the church, from the beginning, understand by worship—that is, by its corporate, regular act of worship? The book of Acts gives us little light on the precise shape or content of the Christians' gatherings: the apostles' doctrine, fellowship, the breaking of bread and the prayers are mentioned. St. Paul's Epistles do not spell out what is to be done. We have to look to other early writings if we are curious about the apostolic church's worship. And what we find when we do so is the Eucharistic liturgy. This, apparently, was what they did as worship. If we think we have improved on that pattern, we may wish to submit our innovations for scrutiny to the early church in order to discover whether our innovations have in fact been improvements.

Which brings us to the second consideration: the content of the Eucharistic liturgy. From the beginning the church seems to have followed a given sequence: readings from Scripture (including the letters from Paul and Peter and John), then prayers and then the so-called *anaphora*—the "offering," or, as it was also called, the Great Thanksgiving. This was the great Eucharistic prayer, which took on a fairly exact shape at the outset and which you may still hear if you will listen to the liturgy in any of the ancient churches. Psalmody, canticle and hymns also came to be included, and certain acclamations like the *Kyrie eleison!* The whole presents a shape of such rich perfection that one wonders what exactly is the task of the "coordinators of worship" on the staff of various churches. The worship of the ancient church is far from being a matter of endless tinkering, experimenting and innovating. The entire mystery of revelation and redemption is unfurled for us in the church's liturgy. That liturgy is here in all of its plenitude, majesty and magnificence, judging us.

The sacraments. Fifth and finally, the sacraments of the church confront me. The word *sacrament* is the Latin word for the Greek *mysterion*, "mystery." Indeed, we are in the presence of mystery here, for the sacraments, like the Incarnation itself, constitute physical points at which the eternal touches time or the unseen touches the seen or grace touches nature. It is the Gnostics and Manichaeans who want a purely disembodied religion.

Judaism and its fulfillment, Christianity, are heavy with matter. First, at creation itself, where solid matter was spoken into existence by the Word of God. Then redemption, beginning, not with the wave of a spiritual wand or mere edicts pronounced from the sky, but rather with skins and blood—the pelts of animals slaughtered by the Lord God to cover our guilty nakedness. Stone altars, blood, fat, scapegoats, incense, gold, acacia wood—the Old Covenant is heavily physical.

Then the New Covenant: we now escape into the purely spiritual and leave the physical behind, right? Wrong. First a pregnancy, then a birth. Obstetrics and gynecology, right at the center of redemption. Fasting in the wilderness, water to wine, a crown of thorns, splinters and nails and blood—our eternal salvation carried out in grotesquely physical terms. Then pure spirituality, right? Wrong. A corpse resuscitated. And not only that, a human body taken up into the midmost mysteries of the eternal Trinity. And bread and wine, body and blood, pledged and given to the church, for as long as history lasts. Who has relegated this great gift to the margins of Christian worship and consciousness? By what warrant did men, fifteen hundred years after the Lord's gift of his body and blood, decide that this was a mere detail, somewhat embarrassing, and certainly nothing central or crucial—a show-and-tell device at best? O tragedy! O sacrilege! What impoverishment for the faithful!

May God grant, in these latter days, a gigantic ingathering, as it were, when Christians who have loved and served him according to patterns and disciplines and notions quite remote from those of the ancient church find themselves taking their places once again in the great Eucharistic mystery of his one, holy, catholic and apostolic church.

Ten

The Crisis of
Evangelical Worship

Authentic Worship in a Changing World

Robert Webber

P ostmodern philosopher Hans Georg Gadamer effectively argued that we do
our interpretive work out of our prejudice, dialogue and historical consciousness.
Following his advice I will begin this presentation with an appraisal of my own
prejudices, dialogue and historical consciousness. I will then clarify the audience to
whom I am speaking, and after that I will explore the crisis of evangelical worship:
Authentic worship in a changing world.

Prejudice, Dialogue, Historical Consciousness
The word *prejudice* is not used by Gadamer in the negative and pejorative sense of
unacceptable attitudes. Rather, prejudice refers to the subliminal influences that
have shaped our mindset—those ways of thinking communicated to us through
our family of origin, education and general group consciousness. Gadamer calls us
to a conscious awareness of these influences, to an intelligent and examined life. I
am certainly not aware of all my prejudices, but I want to mention a few I have
examined and consider important to the shaping of my mindset.

The first seven years of my life were spent in the heart of the African jungle
where my parents were missionaries. My parents returned to the States where my

father pastored a congregation associated with the American Baptist Church. I was educated at Bob Jones University (fundamentalist), Reformed Episcopal Seminary (Calvinist), Covenant Theological Seminary (Presbyterian) and Concordia Theological Seminary (Lutheran). I have taught at Covenant College (five years), Covenant Seminary (three years), Wheaton College (thirty-two years), and while still a member of the Episcopal Church, I am now Myers Professor of Ministry at Northern Baptist Theological Seminary. This history undeniably puts me in a camp of interdenominational evangelical influences and names my prejudices with a degree of clarity.

Second, I have also been shaped by what Gadamer calls dialogue. Dialogue, as I understand it, is genuine conversation with those who live a set of prejudices different from your own. I want to mention two such dialogues that have enriched and expanded my horizons. First, while doing graduate studies at Concordia Seminary, I was a member of an ecumenical prayer and study group, 50 percent of whom were Catholic priests or seminarians. Here I was introduced to persons characterized by warm Christian piety and deep devotion to Christ and the church. My experience with Catholic clergy brought me to a new and appreciative reading of Catholic thought and to a continued personal friendship with my brothers and sisters in the Roman tradition. The next life-changing experience was the opportunity to teach missionaries Orthodox theology at a school established by the Slavic Gospel Mission. My exposure to the works of Georges Florovsky, Vladimir Lossky, Alexander Schmemman, Timothy Ware and John Myendorff introduced me to the most important theological reading of my life.

And then there is the matter of historical consciousness. My graduate work was in the area of historical theology, where I was exposed to the great fathers, doctors and reformers of the church. While I have sought to appreciate all of these leaders within their own cultural paradigm, my interests have always been drawn to the thought of the common era, to the formulators of the classical Christian tradition, to the foundational thought of the Rule of Faith, the Apostles' Creed, the Nicene Creed and the Chalcedon Creed.

Now where has prejudice, dialogue and historical consciousness placed me? I am an evangelical with a love for the whole church, a distaste for modernity and a commitment to the thought and practice of classical Christianity, which I think should be recovered and contextualized into a postmodern world. This is the set of glasses I wear when I think about authentic worship in a changing world.

To Whom Do I Write?

My second introductory concern is to address the audience to whom I speak. While I want to borrow from the whole church, I am keenly aware that I speak to a very small minority within it. I am not speaking to the Roman Church nor am I speaking to the Orthodox Church. My audience is Protestant, and within Protestantism my audience is primarily limited to those who identify themselves as evangelicals. This term needs to be defined.

As I see it, there are four ways in which the word *evangelical* is used. First, the linguistic use is drawn from the Greek word *evangelion* and refers simply to a commitment to the gospel. In this sense all Christians can be referred to as evangelical because all adhere to the gospel. Second, theologically the word *evangelical* is used of all who confess the historic creeds of the church—the Apostles' Creed, the Nicene Creed and the Chalcedon Creed. These creeds define classical Christianity and tighten the boundaries of evangelicalism. The third use *evangelical* refers to those movements of reform and renewal within the church. So far as I know, the word was first used by Erasmus when he jeeringly referred to Luther as "that evangelical." Since Luther, awakenings of the church have been called evangelical movements. For example, the evangelical movement attached to John Wesley in England and Jonathan Edwards in America. This more recent use of *evangelical* has given the word a decidedly Protestant flavor and has limited its use particularly to movements of reform and renewal that seek to get behind a tired experience of faith to a refreshing discovery of the simple yet powerful message of basic Christianity. The fourth use of *evangelical*, which is the most complicated and much more limiting than the three previous uses, is the sociological use.

In order to understand the sociological use of *evangelical*, it is first necessary to explain its sociological use as peculiar to the twentieth century. Let me begin with a crude but nevertheless quite accurate sociological use of the word. An evangelical is a "son of a fundamentalist." Current evangelical parentage goes back to the liberal-fundamentalist controversy in the beginning of the twentieth century. After 1925 the fundamentalists, defeated by liberalism, retreated from the mainline churches and began a new movement of churches, schools, mission agencies and publishing houses. This first phase of fundamentalism was characterized by anti-intellectualism, anti-ecumenism and anti-social action. A second phase of fundamentalism developed after World War II. Many children of fundamentalism wanted to distance themselves from their parentage. In the mid-1950s Harold Ockenga, then the young pastor of Park Street Church in Boston, coined the term *neo-evangelical* and called for new initiatives in scholarship, ecumenical dialogue and social action. This "new" evangelicalism is identified with Billy Graham and the new schools, mission agencies, churches and publishing houses spawned after World War II. The word *evangelical* stuck. The history of the word's evolution is beyond the scope of this presentation, but let it be sufficient to say that the word in its broadest sense is used by those who do not want to be identified as fundamentalists or liberal Protestants.

Regarding worship, these evangelicals of the last fifty years can be divided in two groups: traditional evangelicals and contemporary evangelicals. Traditional evangelicals are those who have not been directly affected by the worship renewal of the twentieth century. Their worship is quite the same as it was in the 1950s: primarily a sermon along with traditional forms of music such as hymns and choirs. Contemporary evangelicals, on the other hand, have been affected by the rise of the contemporary worship movement of the 1960s, 1970s and 1980s. Their worship is either seeker-centered or seeker-sensitive. Like its traditional parentage, contemporary evangelical worship is still sermon-centered, but it has exchanged traditional hymns and choirs for contemporary instrumentation, singing of choruses, worship teams and an atmosphere of intimacy. These two approaches to worship represent two cultures. Traditional worship represents the booster culture of people born before the end of World War II. Contemporary worship represents the boomer culture, people born after World War II but before 1981. Obviously not everybody fits neatly into these two categories. There are boosters who are attracted to contemporary worship and boomers who are drawn to the more traditional forms of worship. While these two groups represent two distinct histories, they also have become the center point for intense conflict in an increasing number of churches. Furthermore, the conflict has spread beyond the walls of the evangelical church into nearly every major denomination and fellowship of churches. While it is these groups to whom this presentation is directed, it has ramifications for all the churches torn by the conflict over traditional and contemporary forms of worship.

Now that I have explained my prejudices, dialogues and historical consciousness that are part of my interpretive background and have identified the particular evangelical audience to whom I write, I am prepared to identify the crisis of evangelical worship.

The Crisis of Evangelical Worship

In terms of strengths, evangelicals bring a deep, heartfelt commitment to Christ, a loyalty to the authority of Scripture and a desire to meet the needs of people. The most obvious weakness of the evangelical community is an antihistorical bias that shapes its inadequate theology of worship, its programlike nature, and its overemphasis on an accommodation to culture.

Inadequate theology of worship. The average evangelical does not have a theology of worship. For evangelicals, worship is not *leiturgia*, but *kerygma*. Evangelicalism by its very nature is an evangelizing community. The primary mandate that gives shape to the evangelical ethos and mission is the Great Commission. What is

called worship in the evangelical community is outreach. What drives contemporary evangelicalism is the market. The questions generally asked by evangelicals are
Who is the audience? How can we target their needs? What is it that attracts the
audience? How can we sell Jesus to our target market?

I recently attended an evangelical market-driven megachurch. The building and
the grounds were beautiful and compelling. There was an enthusiastic buzz among
the people gathered on the patio. (I overheard one person say, "Wow! This is just
like Disneyland!") The service began with a light jazz piece that gathered the people. A few songs focusing on love were sung by a worship team. There were a few
announcements and then the sermon. The theme of the sermon was "Love is time
and time is love." If, the preacher urged, you want to have a good relationship with
your spouse and children, you need to love them and loving them means giving
quality time. The response to the sermon was to promise to give fifteen minutes of
quality time to each member of your family this week. I liked the sermon and felt
empowered by it. But nowhere in that sermon was the gospel. It was peppered
with verses and frequent reference was made to God, but there was no mention
made of Jesus or the Holy Spirit. I feel confident that that church believes and proclaims the gospel, but it was nowhere evident in its worship. Its worship was not
about God or the *missio Dei*. It was all about how you can help yourself to have a
better and more fulfilled relationship with your family. As good and helpful as that
is, it isn't what worship is all about.

Worship as program. My second critique of this popular kind of evangelical worship is that the content lends itself to a program, to an entertainment form of worship. Worship is not the unfolding of God's mission but a variety of acts of worship
offered as musical or dramatic events designed as entertainment to catch the attention of the "audience." This presentational form or program of worship is a natural
outcome of its culturally conditioned, Enlightenment-oriented, self-focused style.
The program is simple and almost always follows a threefold pattern: music that
puts the crowd in the right mood, a sermon oriented toward an intended accomplishment, and a response focused toward the desired outcome. This pattern does
not follow the biblical fourfold pattern of gathering, hearing the Word, celebrating
at the Table, and going forth to love and serve the Lord.

I have been in communities where worship has been intentionally pro-
grammed. In one church the worship leader repeatedly announced each new act of
the program by saying, "now the next part of our package is . . ." In another church
the pastor had deliberately shaped the worship event according to a Phil Donahue
TV program and proudly announced that they had achieved participatory worship.

Accommodation to culture. A third critique of evangelical worship is its overemphasis on relevance achieved through an accommodation to culture. Evangelical-ism, following the Enlightenment culture asks, What is in it for me? Its approach to worship is self-focused. It focuses on knowledge, experience, self-help or empowerment. The person who focuses on knowledge asks, What did I learn? What new "aha" did I get? How does the discovery of the authorial intent of the passage speak to me? In this scenario authentic worship is verified by its pedagogi-cal value. If the worshiper has been edified, educated or informed by God's Word, then, according to this paradigm, true authentic worship has happened.

Next, those who focus on subjective experience ask, Did I experience the pres-ence of God? Was my heart strangely warmed? Did the worship experience make me feel good? In this scenario worship is verified as authentic when the worshiper is made to feel good or has felt conviction or the comforting presence of God.

A third culturally bound self-focused approach regards worship as authentic when it accomplishes emotional or physical healing. When worship touches the worshiper's pain or results in the alleviation of the worshiper's anxieties, then it is authentic.

Another self-focused understanding of worship occurs when worship is authenticated by its empowerment value. If it empowers the worshiper to live a life that is holy, socially useful or directed toward the accomplishment of this or that mission, then worship is regarded as authentic. In these scenarios, worship is authenticated by what it accomplishes. If it has edified the saint, saved the sinner, healed the brokenhearted or empowered mission in the world, then it must be good, biblical and authentic worship.

This instrumental or causation approach to worship can be illustrated in both traditional and contemporary worship. For example, traditional worship of the 1950s has been influenced by either the rationalism of the Enlightenment or the subjective emotionalism of the impulses of nineteenth-century romanticism. Wor-ship influenced by rationalism is heady and intellectual; it is sermon-driven and aimed primarily toward growth in biblical knowledge and a life lived out of biblical principle. Worship influenced by emotion is primarily evangelistic and aimed at an emotional response culminating in the invitation to receive and to live in a warm-hearted relationship with Jesus. These traditions, like the Enlightenment and romantic impulses with which they identify, are self-focused. The cultural identifi-cation is "what's in it for me?" Questions about an authentic biblical or historical understanding or practice of worship are seldom asked.

Next, contemporary worship that emerged among evangelicals after the revolu-tion of the 1960s continues the same preoccupation with culture, but with a new twist. The emphasis falls on a pop-culture style of worship, characterized by a need-oriented, market-driven awareness. This approach to worship has resulted in the megachurch movement, which has attracted thousands of people to the faith. Despite its numerical accomplishments and the spiritual refreshment that these churches have brought to many, its approach to worship is still a cultural accommodation. This culturally conditioned worship has led many churches into a antihistorical rejection of all tradition, and a reductionism in worship that heralds popular chorus music as the new sacrament of God's presence; regards Scripture reading, intercessory prayer and communion as offensive to the seeker; and makes the sermon a presentation of Christianity 101. Worship and evangelism are confused. Contemporary worship leaders still ask, What does our worship accomplish?

I realize that I have given the worst possible examples of the crisis in evangelical worship. There are numerous smaller and mid-sized evangelical worshiping communities that are appalled by this current evangelical scene. So why then did I use these examples? For the simple reason that the megachurch these examples largely represent is holding itself and is being held up by the church-growth movement as the bright light of the future church. Unfortunately, many evangelicals as well as mainline Protestant and some Catholic churches are looking to the megachurch market model for leadership.

The Future of Evangelical Worship

Since I have suggested that the crisis of evangelical worship is related to its lack of a theology of worship, its approach to worship as a program and its accommodation to culture, my prescription for the future is that these trends be reversed. I suggest evangelicals first work toward a trinitarian view of worship; second, recover the historic process of worship; and third, develop a more appropriate relationship to culture.

Recover a Biblical Theology of Worship

Worship from the very beginning of the church has been in the name of the Father, the Son and the Holy Spirit. This is not the time to try to develop a full view of trinitarian worship, so I will suggest a possible direction for an evangelical worship that is triune in nature.

Worship of the Father. The Arians, who were major opponents of the Trinity in the fourth century, were characterized by the saying "I know God as He is known to Himself." St. John Chrysostom, the fourth-century bishop of Constantinople, wrote it "is an impertinence to say that He who is beyond the apprehension of even the higher powers can be comprehended by us earthworms or compassed and comprised by the weak forces of our understanding." In his five discourses on the incomprehensibility of God (*De Incomprehensible*), Chrysostom asserts, "he *insults* God who seeks to apprehend his essential being." When God, he argues, is even incomprehensible in his works, how much more is he incomprehensible in his essential nature. And, if God is unknown in his transcendent majesty, even to the cherubim and seraphim, how much more unknown is God to humanity!

The notion of God's incomprehensibility is certainly attested in Scripture. The visions of God like that of Isaiah (Is 6:1-6), Daniel (Dan 10:5-8) and John (Rev 4—5) speak in the language of poetry and metaphor, not in propositions that can be dissected and analyzed. Paul speaks of God as unapproachable light (1 Tim 6:6), and in the great doxological cry to the Romans Paul cries, "O the depth of the riches both of the wisdom and knowledge of God! How unsearchable are his judgements, and his ways past finding out" (Rom 11:33 KJV).

Throughout history this sense of the incomprehensibility of God is clearly expressed in worship. We find it in the great words of the *Gloria in Excelsis Deo*, the *Te Deum*, the *Kyrie*, and the *Sanctus*. We find it in the attention given the great vaults of space, in the quiet sounds of contemplation and prayer in the powerful use of light and shadow, and in the visions of heaven.

Father worship evokes the sense of God's mystery and our response of awe, wonder and reverence. As Rudolph Otto said in *The Idea of the Holy*, "before God becomes for us a rationality, absolute reason, a personality, a moral will, he is the wholly nonrational and 'other', the being of sheer mystery and marvel."[1] This worship of God, the source of all being who is the mystery beyond being, is offered by us in our feeble, fumbling and faulty language of praise. For it is only in the language of praise that we can approach what we cannot know.

Worship of the Son. While we confess we worship one God, we recognize God in three persons. For this reason we are able to distinguish the revelatory work of God most fully expressed in the Incarnation, the Word made flesh (Jn 1:14). Unlike the mystery of God's otherness, the work of God in history is knowable. While we don't confess to know everything about God's revelatory presence in history, we do acknowledge that our worship of God in this instance lies in the realm of intelligibility. The Eastern church fathers summarized God's work in history with the three words—*creation, incarnation, recreation*, whereas the Western church has used the words *creation, fall, redemption*. While there are different emphases in these theologies, what is common to them is the biblical record of creation; the fall; the account of how God initiated a relationship with Abraham; called a people into being in Israel; became incarnate in Jesus; was crucified, buried and resurrected to forgive sin and overcome death. He ascended into heaven and established the church by the gift of the Spirit to witness to the overcoming of the powers and principalities. He now sits at the right hand of God to intercede for us continually and will return to restore the created order where his shalom will rule forever and

---

[1]Rudolf Otto, *The Idea of the Holy*, 2nd ed. (London: Oxford University Press, 1970), p. 193.

ever in the new heavens and the new earth.

This litany, the Christian metanarrative, is characterized by a particular story we confess to be not just *our* story, but even in the face of a pluralistic world it is *the* story for all people. This story forms us as a community, gives shape to our ethic and makes us an eschatological people (not just a people who have an eschatology).

Common images of the narrative of God's activity in history, and the creation of God's special community of people who are to remember God's action, be shaped by it and live in it, are found in New Testament descriptions of the worshiping communities such as Acts 2:42-47 and 1 Corinthians 12—14. We are admonished not to forsake worship but to gather to exhort each other to good works (Heb 10:25). This worship is for the edification of the saints (Eph 4:12). It has to do with God's revelation, which is not mere knowledge for the sake of knowledge but the record of God's truth for guidance, wisdom and a life that pleases God and brings glory to God's name. This metanarrative in which we are immersed in public worship shapes our personal worship so that all of life is a "living sacrifice, holy and acceptable to God" (Rom 12:1).

History attests to the significant role given to the worship of the Son in public worship. Sermons, hymns, choruses, prayers, litanies, Eucharistic prayers, anthems and the like sing, proclaim, enact and extol God's work of creating the world and redeeming it—all of it—to the glory of God. This is the *missio Dei* that worship signifies and re-presents to the glory of God and to the formation of a people who testify by their very existence to the glory of God and grace. Therefore, when we worship the Son, we do so in the language of a knowable narrative. We remember, proclaim and enact the story that tells the truth about the mystery of life.

Spirit worship. While Father worship evokes mystery and Son worship recalls a knowable narrative, Spirit worship is apprehended primarily through the concept of presence. We encounter the very presence of God in the experience of the Spirit through the language of symbol.

We confess, of course, that God is present everywhere by virtue of creation. But we also acknowledge that the presence of God is made available in greater intensity through visible and tangible sign. In the Old Testament, God was present on the mountain, then in the tabernacle, especially in the holy of holies at the ark and between the cherubim. In the New Testament, God becomes present in the Word made flesh. Jesus is the image of God (Col 1:15): what is invisible has been made flesh.

God has been earthed and concretized into our historical reality. The God who cannot be contained in all the universe is voluntarily confined in the womb of woman, was born of her and participated in our earthly life constricted by time, space and history. This incarnational theology affirms that the God who is immaterial actually communicates to us through materiality. Thus the enfleshed God continues to be present to us by the power of the Spirit in visible and tangible ways.

This God, we confess, dwells within the church. God's people are the temples of the Holy Spirit. Consequently, the primary locus of God's presence in worship is in the assembly. When we gather to worship we become the actualized church, the body of Christ mystically united with the head of the church, Christ. In this assembly, the priesthood of all believers, there are distinct visible signs of God's presence—tangible ways that Spirit worship happens.

Historically the church has acknowledged the work and worship of the Spirit in the visible signs of Word, ministry and sacraments. The Spirit attends the reading and preaching of the Word; the Spirit empowers the pastor; the Spirit communicates through water, bread, wine and oil (to name the chief visible signs). For this reason the act of gathering, the presence and work of the ordained pastor, the reading and preaching of the Word, the rite of baptism, the celebration of the Eucharist, the anointing of oil, and the hands raised in benediction are not empty symbols but performative symbols that participate in the reality they re-present.

A goal then for evangelical worship is to become triune: to worship the mystery of the Father in the language of praise, to thankfully remember and enact the work of the Son in the language of story, and to worshipfully receive the empowering presence of the Holy Spirit through visible and tangible sign. In this way the church and each believer personally are drawn into an experience of union with the triune God, a momentary existential experience of the eschatological kingdom yet to come in its fullness.

The Process of Worship

The next prescription for evangelical worship is to recover the historic fourfold pattern of worship as the unfolding story of gathering, hearing God's Word, thankfully celebrating God's redeeming work at the table, and going forth to serve God in every area of life. If evangelicals are to recover this fourfold pattern, they will have to break with their proclivity toward programs and performances. Fortunately, a recovery of the biblical understanding of worship in both content and process will already undermine the presentational nature of worship. But evangelicals will need to pay more attention to the internal process of each of these phases in the fourfold pattern. This task includes first the recovery of the gathering as the acts by which the community is formed as the body of Christ. In the gathering, greater attention needs to be paid to the reality of Christ, the head of the church who is made mystically present in the congregation's act of centering so that a prayerful lingering in God's presence occurs. Second, there is a need to recover the dialogic nature of the Word. In reading and preaching there is a real presence of Jesus through a speech communication. There is a need to probe how the congregation can become more interactive with the Word. There is a need to return psalm singing, talk-back sermons and bidding prayer to the service of the Word. The third need is to recover the celebratory nature of the Eucharist. The current practice of the Lord's Supper is a funeral dirge. The sense of resurrection can be retained through prayerful singing and the simultaneous act of the laying on of hands with an anointing for healing. Finally, there is a need to recover the sense of God's presence in the going forth. More attention needs to be paid to the way the benediction is communicated and how people are sent forth.

Hopefully recovering the historic fourfold pattern of worship will result in a more clear distinction between worship and evangelism. The hallmark of evangelical Christianity is evangelism, not worship. The primacy given to evangelism turns what should be worship into an evangelistic event. This distorts the nature of worship from what it signifies to what it accomplishes. It then turns worship into a program or performance as opposed to the unfolding narrative of the mission of God. The recovery of the fourfold pattern as the distinct structure of *leiturgia* should help clarify the distinct nature of worship from the programmatic nature of evangelistic events.

Worship and Culture

There is one more question that we must deal with—evangelical worship in the changing world, a world shaped by postmodern culture. I have already suggested authentic worship is characterized by a triune content and a fourfold process. But worship is to be contextualized into the culture we are a part of. The questions are, What are the influences of a postmodern culture that are to be taken into account by evangelical worship, and what will an authentic biblical worship contextualized into this culture look like?

Postmodern cultural changes. The term *postmodernism* has been used in nearly all disciplines of thought, including postmodern philosophy, science, literature, politics and economics. The various ways in which the word has been used speaks to the complexity of thought implied by the term. My usage of the term is limited to those revolutions that are currently creating a postmodern culture. I can do no more in this presentation than refer to the revolutions and hint at the changes that appear to be emerging for the evangelical worshiping community.

First, consider the sociological changes resulting from technological and digital forms of communication. The world which was once lands and cultures foreign to our experiences is now on our doorstep. The result is the rise of pluralism, knowledge of many competing metanarratives and new questions about the uniqueness of Christian worship. At the very least, evangelicals will need to become more clear about the Christian metanarrative, how it is shared by the whole church, what this means for relations between Catholics, Orthodox and Protestants, and how the Christian story relates to the metanarratives of world religions.

Second, the revolution in historical understanding has shifted society away from the nineteenth-century evolutionary theory of history. Evangelicals have been influenced by the evolutionary view of history that regards the past as irrelevant to the future. The boomer generation, a product of the 1960s revolution, turned its back on all tradition and introduced contemporary and seeker-oriented worship as a brand new start for Christianity. Generation X and Millennial young people, who constitute the next generation of leaders in the evangelical church, do not share their parents' convictions. They question the future and honor the past. They are characterized by a nostalgia for the past, a return to the liturgies of the ancient church, a longing for substance and depth.

Third, the scientific revolution, introduced by Einstein's theory of relativity and quantum physics, has created a new worldview. The Newtonian mechanistic worldview with its emphasis on an understandable world has been changed to a much more dynamic and interrelated view of the world characterized by complexity and mystery. This interconnected view has resulted in a new emphasis on community; a more humble posture regarding our ability to know, and a new interest in ecology and the survival of a natural order in which humans can thrive.

The fourth revolution affecting the emergence of a postmodern culture is the shift taking place in philosophy. The interconnected understanding of all things questions the previous notion of the absolute distinction made between object and subject, and the subsequent conviction that it is possible to arrive at objective propositional truth. Postmodern science collapses the subject and object into a philosophical theory of coinherence. The new science should lead us into a more humble stance of mystery and ambiguity.

A fifth revolution, proceeding from the scientific and philosophical changes, is the religious revolution. Modern science and philosophy fostered religious skepticism and convinced atheism, but postmodern science and philosophy have the opposite effect. The new interest in transcendence, in a spiritual reality and in getting in touch with one's own spirituality is an obvious response to the recovery of mystery.

Finally, the communication revolution is shifting us from a near exclusive emphasis on print to a greater use of the visual. We have become a world of graphics and symbols. This shift has sparked new interests in imagination and creativity.

These six revolutions—the sociological, historical, scientific, philosophical, religious and communications—are only the most obvious changes taking place. How, we must ask, will evangelical worship be influenced by these changes?

The Impact of Postmodern Cultural Change on Evangelical Worship

In summary, postmodern trends are moving society toward a recovery of the supernatural, a desire to be connected to the past, a concern for intercultural affirmation, a longing for community, an openness to mystery and an affirmation of a more visual and symbolic form of communication.

In order to determine the impact of these postmodern trends on the next generation of evangelical leaders, I conducted a survey in the fall of 1999 among 176 twenty-somethings from 38 states, 41 denominations and 14 countries. The respondents were all committed evangelical Christians, active in the church and likely to have positions of clergy and lay leadership in the church by 2010. The goal of the survey was to discover the direction of the next generation of leaders.

The survey consisted of about forty characteristics of worship that were to be placed in columns designated "very important to me," "important," "neutral," "unimportant" and "very unimportant." The results were very interesting, to say the least.

First, the survey showed that there seems to be a general reaction against the contemporary style of worship developed in the 1970s, 1980s and 1990s. Eighty-seven percent of those surveyed listed "entertainment" worship as a style that least interested them. Forty-eight percent registered a negative attitude toward contemporary worship and the style of music generally associated with it such as band (63 percent), drums (59 percent), keyboard (56 percent) and guitar (38 percent).

On the other hand, the survey demonstrated that the twenty-something evangelical leaders of tomorrow are characterized by the following nine interests:

1. The strongest and deepest desire of the twenty-something worshiper is to have a genuine encounter with God (88 percent).

2. This longing for an encounter with God is not merely individualistic, but one that takes place within the context of genuine community (88 percent).

3. It follows that there is high concern to recover depth and substance in worship (87 percent).

4. There is a deep desire to return to a more frequent and meaningful experience of communion. Here is where a deep, substance-filled encounter with God is most fully experienced on the personal level (86 percent).

5. Another significant way we are encountered by God shows up in the demand for challenging sermons (69 percent) and more use of Scripture (49 percent).

6. Worship in the future will be more participatory. Worship is not a lecture or a concert done *for* us. Authentic worship is done *by* us. We are the players, God is the audience (73 percent).

7. This generation wants a more creative use of the senses (51 percent). The current communication revolution has shifted us toward a participation that is more visual.

8. Worship will become more quiet, characterized by more contemplative music and time for quiet personal reflection and intimate relationship with God (58 percent).

9. Worship will focus more on the transcendence and otherness of God (45 percent) even as the demand for an encounter with the nearness of God remains high (88 percent).

Conclusion

This essay has dealt with evangelical worship, its lack of a theology of worship, its failure to have an adequate order of worship and its attachment to culture. My concern has been to analyze the crisis of evangelical worship and to suggest an agenda for authentic evangelical worship in a postmodern world. I admit the difficulty of this endeavor, and I hesitate to offer an answer to a movement that despite its weakness in worship, is growing numerically and in influence throughout North America. So instead of an answer, I will summarize my thoughts as a suggested direction.

First and foremost, evangelicals need to recover an authentic biblical worship. This is worship that is not outreach but upreach. It is not driven by what is accomplishes but by what it signifies or represents. Its focus is on God and God's saving mission to the world accomplished in Jesus Christ by the power of the Spirit. Worship celebrates the *missio Dei*. It prays, sings, preaches and enacts it.

Second, evangelicals need to discover the unfolding process of worship. Worship is not a program but an unfolding process of gathering under divine call; listening to the living, active, life-giving voice of God in the Word of God read and preached; enacting the Christian narrative at the Table in a response of praise and thanksgiving; and a going forth with the promise of God's presence in every area of life.

To these two directions—recovery of a biblical content and process of worship—I suggest a critical listening to the text of culture. The impulses arising from the revolution in our postmodern culture support the recovery of an ancient worship with a contemporary flair. The continual task of contextual adaptation asks how we can take the ancient classical paradigm of worship, the paradigm common to the whole church and to all worshiping communities, and faithfully re-present it into a postmodern culture. My prejudices, my dialogue with the church and my historical consciousness suggest that this is the direction we evangelicals should consider taking in order to do authentic evangelical worship in a changing world.

What an evangelical brings to the table is the experience of transformation, a commitment of will, an enthusiastic discipleship, a desire for spiritual formation and a dynamic, infectious sharing of the gospel story with others. I simply suggest we add to these strong characteristics of evangelicalism the historical content and process of worship carefully contextualized into our postmodern world. I think it would result in a dynamic worship rooted in the biblical story, shaped by the test of history and spiritually expressive in a postmodern culture.

Eleven

Reclaiming Eucharistic Piety

A Postmodern Possibility for American Evangelicals?

Joel Scandrett

If, therefore, we have any regard for the plain command of Christ, if we desire the pardon of our sins,
if we wish for strength to believe, to love and obey God, then we should neglect no opportunity of receiving the
Lord's Supper; then we must never turn our backs on the feast for which our Lord has prepared for us.
We must neglect no occasion, which the good providence of God affords us, for this purpose.
This is the true rule: So often are we to receive as God gives us opportunity.
— JOHN WESLEY, "THE DUTY OF CONSTANT COMMUNION"

This essay, dependent in large part on a series of lectures by Wolfhart Pannenberg,[1] suggests the possibility of a reclamation of eucharistic piety by American evangelicals in the twenty-first century. In doing so, it neither presumes to prescribe an agenda for liturgical reform nor presupposes that all evangelicals will share the perspectives which it entails; its goal is simply to suggest that a reclamation of eucharistic piety—that is, *the recovery of the Eucharist as the central symbol and event within the life of the Christian community*—might be both a timely and advantageous option for American evangelicals.

Critical Assumptions

In posing such a suggestion, I make several important assumptions. First, as the term *reclamation* indicates, I am assuming that eucharistic piety has a precedent

---

[1]Wolfhart Pannenberg, *Christian Spirituality* (Philadelphia: Westminster Press, 1983).

in the history of American evangelicalism. This precedent can perhaps be seen most clearly in the personal piety of John Wesley. As evinced by the quote above and as pointed out by Randy Maddox,[2] Wesley was devoted to weekly and sometimes (during the Christmas and Easter seasons) daily communion throughout his adult life. For Wesley the Lord's Supper was "the 'grand channel' whereby the grace of the Spirit is conveyed to human souls, and . . . the first step in working out our salvation."[3] So great was Wesley's commitment to the centrality of eucharistic worship that he published a sermon, "The Duty of Constant Communion," in which he strongly advised the American Methodists to celebrate the Lord's Supper every week. He also edited his Sunday liturgy in such a way as to ensure the place of the Eucharist in Sunday worship.[4]

Thus while the suggestion of eucharistic piety might be perceived as an innovation from the viewpoint of contemporary evangelicals, it is, I would contend, quite the opposite. It is the suggestion of a return to and a recovery of something that has been set aside or forgotten. In particular, it suggests the discovery of new significance in the Eucharist through the rediscovery of an older perspective.

Second, this essay assumes the validity of the ancient phrase lex orandi, lex credendi. This phrase expresses the time-honored conviction that Christian worship and Christian belief are inextricably related to and unavoidably influenced by one another. In suggesting the possibility of reclaiming eucharistic piety, I call attention to the fact that Christian belief is not only propositional but also perspectival and practical, and that both Christian perspective and praxis are profoundly informed by the symbolic structures that constitute Christian worship. A more contemporary expression of this notion is captured in the work of George Lindbeck, who likens religious tradition to something more like a culture or language than merely a set of doctrinal propositions. Says Lindbeck:

> A religion can be viewed as a kind of cultural and/or linguistic framework or medium that shapes the entirety of life and thought. . . . Like a culture or language, it is a communal phenomenon that shapes the subjectivities of individuals rather than being primarily a manifestation of those subjectivities. . . . Its doctrines, [narratives], and ethical directives are integrally related to the rituals it practices, the sentiments or experiences it evokes, the actions it recommends, and the institutional forms it develops.[5]

---

[2]Randy Maddox, Responsible Grace (Nashville: Abingdon, 1994), p. 202.
[3]Ibid.
[4]Ibid., p. 206.
[5]George Lindbeck, The Nature of Christian Doctrine: Religion and Theology in a Postliberal Age (Philadelphia: Westminster Press, 1984), p. 33.

Third, this essay assumes the reality of the postmodern situation. As Henry Knight has demonstrated,[6] the demise of modernity in both intellectual and cultural spheres raises critical challenges to the ways in which evangelical theology has traditionally been conceived. The suggestion of reclaiming eucharistic piety is one that interprets the postmodern situation as an opportunity to recover an important premodern perspective. In particular, this suggestion is in hearty approval of the postmodern shift from individualism toward a more communitarian perspective and from rationalism to personalism[7] in apprehending the Word of God. With these several assumptions in mind, we turn now to the heart of the argument.

The Problem of Penitential Piety

In a collection of lectures published under the title *Christian Spirituality*,[8] German theologian Wolfhart Pannenberg discusses the importance of the Protestant rediscovery of the Eucharist:

> People are prone to look for something new, and all too often the new lacks the profound, substantial meaning enshrined in traditional forms. What is most significantly new, therefore, sometimes occurs as a new look at something one has known long since. The rediscovery of the Eucharist may prove to be the most important event in Christian spirituality of our time, of more revolutionary importance than even the liturgical renewal may realize.[9]

Pannenberg's emphasis on rediscovery highlights a dual concern: first, that certain aspects of the Eucharist's significance once apprehended by Protestants have subsequently been neglected, and second, that certain realities within the present socio-historical situation provide opportunity for a renewed appreciation of the Eucharist. In both cases, rediscovery entails being awakened to ways of understanding the significance of the Eucharist that have all too often remained unacknowledged within the history of Protestantism.

Pannenberg begins with a critical survey[10] of the development of a form of piety that became pervasive throughout the Reformation and post-Reformation periods, especially within the Pietist traditions: that of *penitential piety*. By the late medieval period, penitential confession had become a normal and pervasive aspect of Western Christian life and consciousness. The central feature of this practice—

---

[6]Henry Knight, *A Future for Truth: Evangelical Theology in a Post-modern World* (Nashville: Abingdon, 1997).

[7]As identified in ibid., pp. 53, 96. "Personalism" is my choice here and alludes to the "I-Thou" encounter with Christ of Karl Barth. Cf. George Hunsinger, *How to Read Karl Barth* (New York: Oxford University Press, 1991), pp. 40-42.

[8]See Pannenberg, *Christian Spirituality*.

[9]Ibid., p. 31.

[10]Ibid., pp. 13-30.

upon which the mediatorial function of the medieval church was founded—was a *fundamental awareness of separation from God because of sin*. It was to this mentality that the Reformers addressed their message of liberation from sin and guilt—of justification by faith.

For Luther, justification by faith was grounded in the "real—and in some sense 'mystical'—participation of believers in Christ *extra nos*, outside of ourselves."[11] This union takes place when believers entrust themselves to Christ in an act of total self-abandonment. In doing so, believers come to share by faith in Jesus' life, spirit and righteousness, and are granted "a continuous new existence . . . *extra nos in Christo*,"[12] outside of ourselves in Christ. While this spiritual union with Christ does not preclude the believer from remaining a sinner and thereby continuously in need of forgiveness, such forgiveness is continuously provided by God because of the unity of the believer with Christ by faith. God counts the unity of the believer with Christ against the intrinsic sinfulness of the believer. Thus for Luther the imputation of righteousness—or *forensic justification*—was grounded in and inseparable from the idea of a real, "mystical" participation of the believer in Christ by faith.

However, as early as Melanchthon, and increasingly during the post-Reformation period, the idea of forensic justification came to be separated from the idea of union with Christ. As a result of this separation, the promise of divine forgiveness came increasingly to be understood in terms of a spiritual *actualism* or *extrinsicism*. Instead of enjoying a relation of continuous forgiveness, which flows from the believer's union and identity with Christ by faith, the believer must repeatedly accept divine forgiveness each time he or she slides back into sin. This shift in the understanding of justification meant a loss of continuous Christian identity rooted in a relationship of union with Christ, and thereby raised the very real question of how Christians are different from other sinners in relation to God.

By Pannenberg's account, Pietism attempted to resolve this question through the idea of a once-for-all conversion and regeneration. From this perspective, contrary to that of Luther, "the identity of new life in Christ occurred *within* the individual rather than *outside ourselves* by faith in Christ."[13] However, this internalization of identity with Christ raised in turn the problem of a new form of self-righteousness, one which relied on the notion of a datable, once-for-all conversion as the basis of new life in Christ. In reaction to this, says Pannenberg:

---

[11]Ibid., p. 20.
[12]Ibid., p. 21.
[13]Ibid., p. 22.

> Revivalist movements since the middle of the eighteenth century stressed . . . the need for repeated conversion and forgiveness, but this inevitably resulted in the actualism of an ever-repeated cycle of sin and forgiveness. This came to dominate Lutheran piety and other Protestant traditions as well.[14]

The theological articulation of this cycle of sin and forgiveness was found in the Lutheran distinction between law and gospel. While the original distinction in medieval thought flowed naturally from the medieval practice of confession and absolution, the great accomplishment of the Reformation was to replace the absolution of the priest with the promise of Christ himself, thereby overcoming the medieval need for mediation and granting immediacy to God in Christ. However, just as the gospel was now no longer mediated through a priest, neither was the priest any longer required to call believers to repentance. Consequently, the significance of penance was expanded far beyond its original sacramental context to permeate all of Christian life. And as identity with Christ became increasingly subjectivized through Pietism, so the ideas of law and gospel became increasingly fixed as bipolar coordinate principles of Christian consciousness.

So it was that a new form of piety emerged within the Protestant pietist tradition, a piety that radically internalized the experience of new life in Christ while failing to retain the older conviction of an abiding union with Christ. Instead, the coordinate principles of law and gospel—sin and forgiveness—came to constitute the two poles of Christian experience between which the believer's self-consciousness constantly vacillates: the first, of an immediate and pervasive awareness of guilt in failing to keep the divine law; the second, of the forgiveness of guilt offered in the reconciling work of Christ. This polarity of the opposed principles of law and gospel, radically internalized, led eventually to a form of piety that, says Pannenberg, *especially in its late revivalist forms, made meditation on guilt and sinfulness the basic and permanent condition for communion with God.*[15] This Pannenberg calls *penitential piety.*

Pannenberg raises two main points of criticism in evaluating the development and impact of penitential piety within Protestant Christianity, the first in relation to the believing individual and the second in relation to the believing community. The negative impact of penitential piety on the individual believer is that, by construing Christian spirituality as an irreducible tension between the internal coordinate principles of law and gospel, the believer becomes trapped in a state of continuous self-alienation. Having lost the understanding of union with Christ as

---

[14]Ibid.
[15]Ibid., p. 20.

the intrinsic ground of spiritual existence—that ground which Luther assumed in his dictum *simul justus et peccator*—penitential piety reduces Christian spirituality to the constant internal negotiation of guilt consciousness. Such self-alienation leads in turn to a highly subjective, nearly exclusive focus on the individual as the living stage upon which the drama of redemption unfolds.

This reductive tendency within penitential piety is manifested on the corporate level as well, especially in the structures and orientation of worship within the Christian community. This is perhaps nowhere more evident than in the preeminent role the sermon has come to take in much of Protestant worship. With the rise of an increasingly optimistic anthropology in the Enlightenment and modern periods, the role of the preacher as the conveyor of divine law also increased in importance. While such preaching held a natural place within the penitential ethos of the late medieval period—and in this context was a powerful message of liberation—its role became increasingly vital, and therefore central, to the preservation of penitential piety in the face of the new anthropology. In particular, as the understanding of the self to be intrinsically sinful decreased within Western culture, the preaching of the law became a principal means of *producing* guilt consciousness so as to preserve the law-gospel scheme of penitential piety. This required, however, that preaching take on an increasingly strident character in order to produce a sufficient consciousness of sin such that the law-gospel scheme could remain effective. This pattern has continued to the present, with profound consequences. Says Pannenberg:

> The penitential mentality of the Protestant tradition . . . is continually affirmed by the tenacious survival of the law-and-gospel scheme in Protestant homiletics. Such a mentality in the preacher serves merely to pin down baptized Christians to a contrite consideration of their sinfulness. It is as if they were sitting not within the church but without. It achieves little more than to support a vicious circle of indeterminate guilt consciousness.[16]

The history of the Eucharist in pietist Protestantism is also telling. In direct contrast to the increasingly central and dominant position the sermon came to hold in Protestant worship, the Eucharist was reduced in both role and significance to little more than an occasional, vestigial memorial of Christ's death, and was performed primarily as a means of reassuring individual believers of the forgiveness of sins. In this way, it too was made subservient to the cause of preserving the law-gospel scheme of penitential piety, and the broader spectrum of its significance was thereby lost.

---

[16]Ibid., p. 26.

The Promise of Eucharistic Piety

Such is, by Pannenberg's account, the present-day outcome of a forensic concept of justification no longer embedded in the vision of real participation in Jesus Christ. In summing up his critique, Pannenberg concludes that penitential piety, its lasting influence in Protestant theology and spirituality notwithstanding, "is unfit as a truly contemporary form of Christian piety that could claim to embody the spirit of liberation that has motivated and accompanied the gospel proclamation throughout history."[17] In its place Pannenberg argues for the recovery of *eucharistic piety*[18] not only as a means of redressing the inadequacies of penitential piety but also as a form of piety better suited to meet the spiritual challenges of the contemporary situation.

Concretely speaking, the call to eucharistic piety is a call to recover a more fully orbed understanding of the Eucharist and, in so doing, to allow the Eucharist a more central place in the life and worship of the Christian community. Pannenberg identifies several interrelated principles that constitute such a renewed appreciation of the Eucharist, principles which he believes to be vital to this "truly contemporary" form of Christian piety.

Principle 1. Eucharistic piety entails *a recovery of union with Christ* as the central and unifying feature of Christian life. This union is realized in two dimensions: first, the individual, vertical dimension of communion with Christ, which corresponds to the love of God; and second, the corporate, horizontal dimension of communion with other believers, which corresponds to the love of neighbor. It is this twofold relational communion that constitutes the foundation of Christian life and identity, and is uniquely symbolized and enacted in the Eucharist. Pannenberg says:

> There is no other place or event in the worship of the church where the very foundation of its life can be comparably commemorated and symbolized, as well as reenacted, than in the event of celebration and communion. . . . [T]he essence of the church is communion of the faithful on the basis of the communion with Jesus Christ that each individual member shares. Every celebration of the Eucharist reenacts the reality that constitutes the foundation of the church, and that happens not only in the sense of memorial but also in the symbolic power of the Eucharist, where the essence of the church itself is alive, present, and effective.[19]

Several important implications follow from this principle: First, by reestablishing union with Christ as the central constitutive relation of Christian life and iden-

---

[17]Ibid., p. 29.
[18]Ibid., pp. 31-49.
[19]Ibid., p. 40.

tity, eucharistic piety reverses the original removal of union with Christ from the law-gospel scheme of penitential piety. Eucharistic piety reestablishes the law-gospel polarity on its former foundation of union with Christ by faith.

Second, in reestablishing this ground of union with Christ, eucharistic piety militates against the state of self-alienation in which the believer is trapped by the guilt consciousness of penitential piety. By restoring the law-gospel polarity to its original context of union with Christ by faith, eucharistic piety seeks to place the very real challenge of the Christian call to holiness in its proper place, thereby liberating the believer to pursue the imitation of Christ while continuously resting in the knowledge of the grace of God.

Third, in seeking to free the believer from guilt consciousness, eucharistic piety also seeks to reverse the intrinsically individualistic character of penitential piety. As alluded above, the loss of the awareness of union with Christ results in an inability to maintain the communal, horizontal character of Christian identity. The constant internal negotiation of guilt consciousness produces a highly individualized and subjective notion of the work of the Holy Spirit. This places the locus of the Spirit's activity primarily if not exclusively within the individual believer and in terms of the believer's own experience, rather than that of the entire body.

Thus penitential piety carries a persistent tendency to overlook the significance and role of the community—the body of Christ—as a mediating matrix through which the Spirit can function to produce spiritual maturity, both in the individual and in the relationships of which the body is comprised. Moreover, there follows a persistent tendency to downplay the communal dimension of the Christian life in general. Other than Sundays and special services, the Christian spiritual life is a relatively autonomous, individualized, and internalized experience.

Through its emphasis on twofold communion with Christ and other believers, eucharistic piety seeks to reintroduce the horizontal, communal dimension of Christian spirituality which the liberated individual is now freed to embrace. In doing so the individual is opened to ways of participating in the growth and maturity of the Christian community as a whole, ways which were not sufficiently recognized within the scheme of penitential piety.

Principle 2. Eucharistic piety entails the recovery of an awareness of *the symbolic character of Christian community*. This symbolic character is twofold: first, the church is a symbol-shaped and symbol-using community; second, the church is itself a symbol. Says Pannenberg:

> The Christian church is a symbolic community. It is not only that the church uses
> symbols that unite all Christians, like the cross, or that the ministries of the church

are symbolic in representing the people as political offices do. In the case of the church the community itself is symbolic. The Christian community symbolizes another community, . . . the kingdom of God.[20]

As mentioned above, one consequence of penitential piety has been the reduction of the Eucharist to little more than a vestigial ritual by which the substitutionary atonement of Christ is recalled. In this way it has been relegated to the role of mirroring the law-gospel scheme of penitential piety. However, another, and perhaps greater, reduction has been that of Christian worship itself. In making the sermon its central and dominant feature, Christian worship comes close to losing its symbolic character altogether. Just as penitential piety reduces Christian spirituality to an individual affair, so Christian worship tends to be perceived as little more than an aggregate of individuals who gather because of a common desire, rather than a united community infused with the presence and persona of Jesus Christ.

In direct contrast to this tendency, Pannenberg makes what is perhaps his most unequivocal statement on the subject:

> The Eucharist, not the sermon, is in the center of the church's life. . . . The sermon should serve, not dominate, in the church. It should serve the presence of Christ which we celebrate in the Eucharist.[21]

Eucharistic piety both recognizes and practices the presence of Christ in the worshiping community by making the Eucharist the central act and event of Christian worship. In so doing it reintroduces and reinforces the fact that the Christian community not only uses symbols, but is itself symbolic of the kingdom of God.

Principle 3. Eucharistic piety entails the recovery of the full spectrum of the Eucharist's *symbolic significance* for Christian life, worship and identity. In seeking to reverse the reductionism of penitential piety, eucharistic piety recognizes the significance of the Eucharist to be far greater than merely a memorial of blood atonement. Its full range of significance is manifold and includes the following, each of which has profound implications for Christian spirituality:

☐ *The Eucharist as a united body.* The Eucharist is the preeminent symbol and expression of the relationship of spiritual communion and community that the believer has with both Christ and believers everywhere. These communitarian implications have already been discussed in some detail and require no further comment.

---

[20]Ibid., p. 35.
[21]Ibid., p. 40.

□ *The Eucharist as perfect sacrifice.* The Eucharist is the preeminent symbol of the sacrificial act of Christ's death, not only as the perfect sacrifice for sin on our behalf but also as the perfect model of a sacrificial self-giving to all of humanity. While penitential piety has emphasized the first of these aspects, it has neglected the second, resulting in a piety that tends to value Christ's death for the private benefit of the individual or a select few, rather than a sacrifice intended for the whole world.

□ *The Eucharist as an eschatological meal.* The Eucharist is the preeminent symbolic anticipation of the full realization of the kingdom of God in human history as well as a recognition of its present reality. Each celebration of this meal within the Christian community is made in proleptic anticipation of that consummating event which the Revelation of John describes as "the marriage supper of the Lamb" (Rev 19:9). Because this event is definitive for all of human history, this anticipation has significance for all of humanity and is not limited to the Christian community.

In reflecting on these three dimensions of eucharistic symbolism, it becomes evident that the character of eucharistic piety is inherently inclusive in its orientation. In light of the full spectrum of the Eucharist's significance, the horizontal, relational dimension of Christian community can be seen to be an ever-expanding, all-embracing community rooted in the love of God in Jesus Christ. Beginning first with the believer in communion with Christ and moving next to believers in communion with one another, eucharistic piety seeks to extend itself as a community of love that welcomes all into gracious communion with God in Jesus Christ by faith. In this way it understands its purpose to be one of unlimited scope and everlasting duration.

At this point it is important to note that all of the above elements were fully present in John Wesley's eucharistic theology. As Paul Sanders delineates,[22] Wesley understood the Eucharist to be an *anamnesis* of Christ's redemptive death, a symbol of His body and blood, a means of grace in which Christ is truly present through the Holy Spirit, an eschatological meal that both recognizes the presence of the kingdom of God and anticipates its full realization, a symbol of the communion of the saints, and a twofold celebration both of Christ's everlasting sacrifice and of our self-offering in return to him. The similarity between Pannenberg's eucharistic piety and Wesley's eucharistic theology are striking and, I hope, reassuring to those for whom Pannenberg's suggestions might seem foreign.

Implications for Evangelicals

How are we to assess Pannenberg's critique of penitential piety in relation to evan-

---

[22]Paul Sanders, "Wesley's Eucharistic Faith and Practice," *Anglican Theological Review* 48 (1966): 157-74.

gelical Christianity? Setting aside altogether the question of the accuracy of Pannenberg's historical account, it is difficult to know precisely to what degree his critique is applicable to American evangelicalism. Because the critique is extremely broad and thematic, it lacks much of the historical particularity necessary to make a careful evaluation. However, given his allusions to "later pietism" and "mid-eighteenth century revivalism," it certainly appears that he intends to include the American evangelical tradition within his broad survey. And insofar as evangelicals are within that broader pietist and revivalist stream, they too are included.

It appears that evangelicals might be vulnerable to Pannenberg's critique of penitential piety in at least several respects. First and foremost it is striking to note the degree to which the demise of Wesley's own eucharistic theology and piety in America parallels the demise of Luther's eucharistic theology and piety in Europe. In both cases we see a fullness of an understanding of the Eucharist that is lost in subsequent generations. The history of the Lord's Supper in American Methodism shows that from its inception American Methodists began to depart from the presence-filled sacramentalism of Wesley and to reduce their understanding of the Eucharist to that of an occasional memorial of the blood atonement of Christ at Calvary.[23] In so doing, the emphasis on the need for personal holiness in the Wesleyan tradition became *separated* from Wesley's eucharistic practice and theology of spiritual communion with Christ. This trend can arguably be found in other streams of American evangelicalism as well. To the degree that it is, it appears to confirm Pannenberg's thesis.

Second, evangelicals appear to be vulnerable to Pannenberg's critique of penitential piety, especially as it gives rise to guilt consciousness. Unfortunately, the roots of this phenomenon can also be found in the theology of John Wesley, though they appear in the theology of other early American evangelicals as well. As Randy Maddox points out, the law-gospel scheme formed an important aspect of Wesley's theology of atonement that from the beginning was open to the possibility of distortion. Maddox says:

> The second possible distortion of [Wesley's] understanding of the Atonement is more serious (and, unfortunately, more frequent in popular piety). It portrays God/Father as unmerciful until after Christ propitiates the Divine wrath and constrains God to love us. It must be admitted that Wesley's language sometimes suggests this second distortion.[24]

The fact that such a possible distortion was already present in Wesley's theol-

---

[23]Paul Sanders, "An Appraisal of John Wesley's Sacramentalism in the Evolution of Early American Methodism" (Ph.D. diss., Union Theological Seminary [N.Y.]).

[24]Maddox, p. 105.

ogy furthers the suggestion that Wesley's emphasis on personal holiness became distorted when separated from his eucharistic practice and theology in the American situation. The specter of an unmerciful, wrathful God becomes all the more grim when it is no longer framed by the relation of union with Christ by faith. Consequently, the quest for personal holiness comes increasingly to be understood strictly according to the terms of the law-gospel scheme. That such a theological construction might result in a profound and abiding guilt consciousness should come as no surprise. In this respect Pannenberg's thesis appears to be offering an important critique of both the Wesleyan tradition and those other evangelical traditions that evince similar theological inclinations.

In response to Pannenberg it might be argued that evangelicals attempt to break the law-gospel problem through the doctrine of a subsequent work of grace in the believer. Within the Wesleyan tradition this is seen in the doctrine of Christian perfection. While the perfected believer maintains the awareness of being *simul justus et peccator*, the state of entire sanctification entails such a degree of conformity to Christ that the cycle of sin and forgiveness in penitential piety is effectively broken.

Analogously, the charismatic doctrine of baptism in the Holy Spirit might also be proffered as an attempt to *recover* a form of piety that includes a dimension of spiritual communion, thereby solving the law-gospel problem. A clear example of the development of such a perspective can be seen in Asa Mahan's *Baptism of the Holy Ghost*, published in 1870 by Phoebe Palmer. Among the "consequences" Mahan lists as resulting from Spirit baptism, he includes a more intimate "fellowship with the Father, and with his Son Jesus Christ," a "deep and permanent spiritual blessedness" and a "unity of the Spirit" among believers.[25]

While these perspectives may hold promise for reducing the effects of penitential piety's guilt consciousness, it must be pointed out that they are, at least within the Wesleyan *ordo salutis, subsequent* to the founding of the believer's relationship with Christ. To whatever degree they may succeed in alleviating guilt consciousness, they do so as an after-measure and do not resolve the basic problem of the loss of an understanding of spiritual union with and participation in Christ, which, by Pannenberg's account, must *precede* any law-gospel polarity. The problem of the believer's fundamental identity is still at issue.

Third, and related, evangelicals are confronted by Pannenberg's critique of penitential piety's inherent individualism. While evangelicals place strong emphasis on the need for spiritual maturity, such maturity is generally understood in individualistic terms. The role of the Christian community as both contributor to and

---

[25]Cited by Donald W. Dayton, *Theological Roots of Charismaticism*, Studies in Evangelicalism 5 (Metuchen, N.J.: Scarecrow, 1987), p. 89.

beneficiary of the individual's spiritual progress is often ignored. Within the Wesleyan tradition the primary emphasis is on sanctification as an essentially *individual* process. Purity is primarily a matter of individual victory over sin. Within the charismatic tradition, primary emphasis is given to the essentially *individual* event of baptism in the Holy Spirit, with less emphasis on the communal activity of the Spirit. Power is primarily a matter of individual experience.

Fourth, the patterns of worship in evangelical churches also reflect the impact of penitential piety. As mentioned above, the law-gospel scheme has played an important role in evangelical piety. Liturgically speaking, the preeminence of the sermon as a means of conveying the divine law continues to play a central role in evangelical worship, and to the extent that it does so, it runs the risk of perpetuating the guilt consciousness of penitential piety. However, charismatic worship does not completely conform to Pannenberg's analysis. While the preaching of the law may still be present, it is balanced or modified by a more pronounced awareness and practice of the presence of the Holy Spirit. Nonetheless, a strong emphasis on the sermon as the means of conveying divine law continues to characterize both traditions.

Eucharistic Piety: A Postmodern Possibility?

Having stated these criticisms, it is important to note that some evangelicals are well situated to take advantage of the benefits of eucharistic piety. First, Wesleyans and charismatics retain a strong experiential and personal emphasis in their piety. This experiential characteristic safeguards them to some degree from the rationalistic excesses of the more Reformed or fundamentalist wings of evangelicalism, which tend to place an emphasis on Scripture and downplay personal experience. This experiential emphasis of Wesleyans and charismatics is complemented by an emphasis on personal encounter and relationship with God through Christ in the Holy Spirit. This experiential "personalism" grants Wesleyans and charismatics a relatively greater accessibility to the idea of union with Christ inherent within eucharistic piety.

Second, personalism and freedom from rationalistic biblicism also render Wesleyans and charismatics more open to the symbolic character of Christian community and worship. As we have seen, eucharistic piety is inherently defined as an encounter of the believing community with the living Christ through the celebration of the Eucharist. This emphasis on encounter and relationship are, it seems to me, entirely congruent with Wesleyan and charismatic spirituality.

In addition, certain aspects of Pannenberg's three eucharistic themes are already very much at the heart of Wesleyan and charismatic piety. The Wesleyan tradition's emphasis on self-denial in the service of others is closely related to

Pannenberg's understanding of the Eucharist as a *perfect sacrifice* that Christians
are to imitate. The charismatic emphasis on the presence of the Holy Spirit and
the eschatological return of Christ is closely related to Pannenberg's understanding of the Eucharist as an *eschatological meal*. However, both traditions still need
to be informed by a deeper appreciation of the Eucharist as symbolic of the *united
body*.

There are also several current cultural factors that make the possibility of
reclaiming eucharistic piety a more realistic option for the future of Wesleyan and
charismatic traditions. First is the very real development of postmodern perspectives regarding human thought, identity and community. With the increasing
rejection of the universalizing claims of modern philosophical perspectives comes a
renewed recognition of the degree to which all human knowledge and identity is
inevitably situated in, constructed by and mediated through particular socio-historical contexts. This development is mirrored on the social level by an emphasis
on the place and importance of the particular community in the development of
both identity and worldview. This postmodern, community-oriented perspective
is highly congruent with and uniquely accessible to many of the features of Pannenberg's eucharistic piety.

Second, the rediscovery of the sacramental traditions and eucharistic piety
within Wesleyan and charismatic circles—not to mention other evangelical
groups—appears to be on the rise. The cases of Stan White and the Evangel
Assembly of God in Valdosta, Georgia, in 1990[26] and of Charles Bell and the San
Jose Vineyard Christian Fellowship in 1993[27] both draw attention to the "rediscovery" of ancient liturgical practices within Pentecostal and charismatic churches.
Vinson Synan believes that these occurrences indicate a "convergence" of Protestant (Bible-based), Catholic (liturgical and sacramental) and charismatic (Spirit-
filled) traditions within the larger ecumenical situation.[28]

Conclusion

It remains to be seen whether eucharistic piety is a form of piety that evangelicals,
broadly speaking, will incorporate into their respective forms of liturgy and piety
in the twenty-first century. Given current trends it appears likely that some, like
the Valdosta and San Jose churches, will do so to such a degree that they may no
longer identify themselves as evangelical. Others will no doubt become increasingly resistant to such changes, perhaps even to the point of militating against

---

[26] See Randall Balmer, "Why the Bishops Went to Valdosta," *Christianity Today*, September 24, 1990, pp. 19-24.
[27] See Charles Bell, *Discovering the Rich Heritage of Orthodoxy* (Minneapolis: Light & Life, 1994).
[28] Vinson Synan, *Holiness-Pentecostal Tradition*, rev. ed. (Grand Rapids, Mich.: Eerdmans, 1997).

them. A third segment, however, will increasingly find ways to include elements of eucharistic piety in life and worship while remaining fully committed to and active participants in the theological, religious and socio-cultural structures of American evangelicalism.

Twelve

Staying the Course

On Unity, Division & Renewal in
The United Methodist Church

William J. Abraham

In this essay I will address three questions: First, are there circumstances in which those committed to the classical and apostolic faith should leave The United Methodist Church? Second, what case if any can be made for remaining in The United Methodist Church and continuing to work for its renewal? Third, if we do stay in, how should we think about the nature and the historical dynamic of renewal at our present juncture? In pursuing these questions I will use as a foil some fascinating proposals by Lyle Schaller, where he calls for a new polity that would avoid schism and cater to the ideological polarization in our midst. Schaller's proposals provide, I suspect, an interesting alternative to the strategy Thomas Oden has pursued with diligence and flair over the years. The core of Oden's strategy has been to argue for and implement the vision of The United Methodist Church as a confessional church.

Before I get into these topics, however, I need to get rid of a common red herring. It is often said that by insisting on the confessional character of United Methodism a person is ipso facto fomenting division. By rejecting pluralism and insisting there really is a canonical faith to be upheld, one can readily be accused of splitting the church. Frankly, I have little patience with this charge. Clearly it is impossible to house for long all competing positions within the same denomination. People draw different lines in the sand at this point, and critics too readily overlook the lines they draw. For example, nobody would include competing positions on rape, racism or sexual harassment as officially acceptable within our church. Equally, nobody would divide over different positions on just war and pacifism or on positions for and against a national medical plan or on different theories of divine inspiration. There is room for agreement on some of the boundaries and for disagreement on a host of others. The really tough situation arises when persons hold radically different views: first, on where the boundaries lie in some contentious issues, and second, on whether the particular boundary has been breached or not.

This is where the situation currently stands. When it comes to the matter of same-sex unions and ordination of practicing gays and lesbians, some are compatibilists and some are incompatibilists. Compatibilists think that the church can sustain both positions with integrity and without loss of unity; incompatibilists do not.

The compatibilist is tempted to accuse the incompatibilist of splitting the church at this point. This is understandable—it sounds as if the incompatibilist is pitting people against each other, and it sounds as if the compatibilist is trying valiantly to hold things together. In reality the incompatibilist is doing no such thing but is simply describing the cognitive dissonance observed within the body. Further, accusing the incompatibilist of schism is wrong because those who do so seriously misunderstand the incompatibilist's position. The incompatibilist is no less committed to the unity of the church than the compatibilist. The incompatibilist claims that the church can remain united only if it holds to one position on the issue at hand. He or she claims that the church cannot have a both-and in this instance. In the end the church, it is suggested, will remain intact only if it has a single position, one way or the other. It cannot face both ways at once.

This is borne out by the events that transpired in the aftermath of the trial of Rev. Jimmy Creech in Nebraska in the early 1990s. It is clear that Creech was a compatibilist. In performing a same-sex union, he had no intention of casting out those who disagreed with his theology of sexuality and the correlative practice. If we interpret this situation generously and charitably, we see there in microcosm an effort to try a compatibilist solution by letting folk go one way or the other. So a concerted effort was made to include both positions by going ahead with a same-sex union and trusting that those who disagreed would sit tight. This did not materialize. Some left; some stayed in support or in toleration; some formed a new congregation. In these circumstances it is the compatibilist who is splitting the church. Or if this is too strong, the compatibilist is proposing a solution that has already proved to be unworkable.

These latter comments are historical in nature. They tell us when a particular denomination may fall apart or divide. They do not tell us if the denomination *should* divide or whether a person or group of persons *should* leave a denomination.

Confronting the Case for Exit

So let me now turn to this issue and try to address it head on. Are there circumstances when a person or a group should break with a denomination? I can think of three circumstances when this becomes a live option.

First, defection or division becomes a live option when it is impossible to carry out the ministry to which we have been called by Christ. In this instance there is a conflict between the law of God and the law of the denomination. God requires one set of actions; the denomination requires another. We have to choose to obey God. If our denomination prevents us from fulfilling our duty in ministry, then we will have to defy our denomination and be cast out, or we will have to leave in order to be faithful.

Second, defection or division becomes a live option when the church commits us directly or indirectly to beliefs and practices that violate our conscience as formed by the Word of God. In this instance the denomination may leave us alone and let us fulfill our ministry, yet it commits us to beliefs and actions we take to be contrary to the revealed will of God. We become party to activities we consider to be idolatrous, heretical or apostate. How far we are implicated may be a matter of degree, but the situation is relatively clear: we are forced to hold or accept beliefs and practices contrary to the gospel and to the apostolic faith.

Third, defection or division becomes a live option when the church clearly and irrevocably commits apostasy or falls into flagrant heresy or abandons the gospel and the Christian faith. This is a high standard to meet. It is not enough to point to corruption or the defection from the faith of this or that group. What we need is a clear and irrevocable rejection of the very foundations of the denomination, or a case where the foundations of the denomination are self-referentially undone. In the former case, essential elements of the Christian faith have been set aside; in the latter case the denomination has turned its back on its own constitutive commitments. In my judgment such moves must take place at the level of the canonical life of the church, that is, at the level of official, corporate, binding action.

There may well be other circumstances when we should leave or divide, but I think that these are by far the most important ones. The real crunch comes when we try to decide whether or not these conditions have been met. While relatively clear in principle, decisions in this arena are often delicate in practice. Sincere members whose integrity is unquestioned may differ in their judgments. There is also room for personal divine guidance in which someone may be called to leave and work in another part of God's vineyard.

In my judgment the Creech trial brought to the surface differences of judgment among conservatives and evangelicals in The United Methodist Church. Clearly there were those who had reached the conclusion that it was time to organize an exodus. The argument in favor of this conclusion had several components. I think the case ran something like this.

1. The real church, as opposed to the paper church, is what really goes on contingently and historically. The church is not what it is on paper in its constitutions and canons but what it is in fact as represented by the decisions of its members and leaders.

2. Attempts to renew the real church have failed over the last thirty years. Despite the efforts of Good News, The Walk to Emmaus, The Foundation for Theological Education, the presence of evangelicals on seminary faculties, the charismatic movement, The Foundation for Evangelism, The Confessing Movement, and the like, The United Methodist Church is worse off than it was in the late 1960s. Renewal has not worked and will not work.

3. The real United Methodist Church inhibits or prevents real gospel ministry. It entangles us in beliefs and practices that are contrary to the apostolic faith. It is corrupt in much of its working at the connectional level. And it is close to apostate in what it either embraces or tolerates.

4. Therefore the time has come for evangelicals to abandon renewal and to organize a corporate exodus. In the short term, every effort should be made to call the denomination to an eleventh-hour repentance and conversion, to fight for the faith and to sustain such remnants of faithfulness as exist. In the absence of a miracle of conversion, we should strategize toward forming a new Wesleyan denomination, say, at the next General Conference.

I do not think that it is an exaggeration to claim that some had hoped the Confessing Movement within The United Methodist Church would adopt this analysis and strategy. For certain individuals this conviction ran so deep that disagreement with it was thought to stem from a serious moral and spiritual lapse. Some time ago, after an address on doctrinal renewal at an Aldersgate '98 workshop in Dallas, I found myself at the center of a war of words via e-mail. What took me by surprise was not so much the misrepresentation of my views, serious as that was, but the vehemence of the attack on my motives. By not agreeing with the alternative analysis, I was charged with belonging to an evangelical establishment that refused to listen to its own constituency. Worse still, I was charged with feathering my own nest in the higher echelons of the connection. When I pursued the matter as best I could, I found underneath the attack precisely the analysis and argument I have given above.

It will come as no surprise that I did not and do not share this analysis of our situation. This is not to say that I do not respect those who take this view, even though in some cases I do not think that they really faced up to the moral attack they launched against others. Furthermore, there is clearly a gap between what we hold canonically and where we really are in fact. If there were no gap it is unlikely there would be any renewal movements in our church. A time may come when the gap between the decisions of General Conference and what we are in fact become so great that the former are simply empty and redundant. This is not, however, the case at present, nor is it likely to be the case. Cumbersome as our system can be, it is extremely difficult to undermine the actions of General Conference merely by rebellion or by resort to acts of protest. Even in the latter cases there are disciplinary measures that can be deployed.

The matter, of course, becomes more complicated when these disciplinary measures fail. Even in these circumstances, great care must be exercised before we pronounce the game over. There are several innings to be played before we know the true outcome. The total process involved takes time, and it calls for much patience and fortitude.

Making the Case for Staying the Course

We are now fully launched into our second question, namely, what case if any can be made for remaining within The United Methodist Church and continuing to work for its renewal? The case against breaking from The United Methodist Church and in favor of lively service within it is overwhelming. Let me make a laundry list of comments at this juncture.

1. The United Methodist Church is a Christian denomination as clearly laid out in its canonical commitments. It has not committed apostasy, and it has not fallen into heresy. It has not *de jure* departed in a radical way from any essential elements of the Christian faith, and it has not rejected its own canonical tradition. Because individuals and groups may have departed from the faith does not establish that the denomination has become apostate. We might reach a point where apostasy in practice is so blatant that in reality it is the same as formal abandonment of the tradition, but I do not think we have come near to reaching that point.

2. It is a commonplace of both Scripture and tradition that unity is a virtue to

be cultivated with enthusiasm, while division or schism is a vice to be avoided with diligence. Wesley himself saw this with incredible clarity; those who look to him as a mentor must take his warnings with the utmost seriousness. Decisions to leave or to divide should not be made in the heat of the moment or in the aftermath of a crisis. They should be made in fear and trembling and after much sanctified deliberation. We are far from that point in our conversation together.

3. There are millions of Christians within The United Methodist Church who need the ministry of those who are committed to its foundational vision. To abandon these people would be to leave them spiritually unfed and unprotected. They deserve, under the grace of God, the best service we can render.

4. The United Methodist Church has rendered and continues to render very significant work to God in the service of the kingdom. It would be mistaken to abandon this work. To throw away the assets given in trust by our faithful ancestors strikes me as unwarranted and unwise.

5. For the most part The United Methodist Church is open to the work, talents and convictions of those who are resolutely committed to the central components of its canonical heritage, and who are committed to historic forms of evangelism and mission.

6. To opt for division at this point would be to abandon the many valuable gains in renewal that are already in place and are yet to be reaped by sustained work. When I mentioned to one of my students that I was working on an essay on why we should stay in the church and continue the work of renewal, she immediately exclaimed, "You do not stop when you are winning!" This was from a former Baptist who is now an Episcopalian who believes in reincarnation! She is also a very shrewd politician, and I think that she is right.

7. It is unclear that a new Wesleyan body would be able to do more for the kingdom than is currently possible within The United Methodist Church. The energy diverted to creating a new denomination would be colossal.

8. I seriously doubt if we have the skill to put together a new Methodist denomination. This is not an attack on the competence of friends in renewal; it is a sober assessment of the history of Protestantism. Wesley worried at one time whether he had the ability to form a new church, and I share this kind of caution. Those who yearn for a new body rarely face up to this fact. Of course, if we are forced into this option, we can be sure God will provide all the help we need, but this is an entirely different agenda that would be a serious distraction at this point in time.

9. We need to beware a naive utopianism in our thinking about the church. Even with complete success in the work of renewal, the church will be a fragile and mixed vessel. Jesus warned us that even the kingdom will have wheat and

tares which can only be sorted out at the end of the age. Hence we should be prepared to live with all sorts of difficulties, set backs, strategic retreats and challenges. If any are discouraged, I urge them to read the writings of the fourth-century leaders. Athanasius complains that when the Arians took over his church in Alexandria, folk were frolicking naked in the baptismal fonts. Yet Athansius stayed the course, organized the faithful in exile, suffered banishment at least five times and eventually won the day for the gospel and the faith.

The upshot is we have reached the moment where we need to make up our minds about the viability of our church and get on with the job in hand. If some decide otherwise, we should respect their decisions and wish them well in their work for the kingdom. Nobody can be hostage to other people's fears or conscience on this matter. On the contrary, we need to be clearheaded and forthright in the pursuit of comprehensive renewal across the generations. We need to lay hold of the promises of God and set to work with fortitude and enthusiasm.

Noting an Alternative Proposal

It is worth noting the fascinating and remarkable suggestions recently floated by Lyle E. Schaller. Schaller can be something of a gadfly—a figure who gets us thinking along fresh and creative lines—so I think we should ponder his proposal carefully. The core of his proposal is that we should think of designing a new polity which would be compatible with ideological diversity. One way to pull this off would be to merge with another denomination that combines "a connectional polity for accountability purposes with a high degree of congregational autonomy."[1] In one version, all the national denominational offices, except the General Board of Pensions and the United Methodist Publishing House, would move to Seoul. The exact reasons for this choice are not entirely clear. I think this suggestion is really a foil. The more serious version is to develop a federation of annual conferences within The United Methodist Church.

> Thus one annual conference might be composed of Koreans and Korean-Americans, another of reconciling congregations, a third of multicultural congregations, a fourth of large downtown congregations, a fifth of small congregations served by bivocational ministers, a sixth of self-identified, theologically liberal churches, a seventh of congregations located in the same state or region, an eighth of self-identified evangelical congregations, and a ninth of Spanish language congregations.[2]

Schaller's suggestion, then, is to accept the reality of pluralism and of ideolog-

---

[1]Lyle E. Schaller, "Is Schism the Next Step?" *The Circuit Rider*, September-October 1998, p. 5.
[2]Ibid.

ical polarization, to cut through the dead hand of the past and to find a new and creative way to be United Methodist by forming a federation of annual conferences. In short, we should stop quarreling, reject schism and enlarge the tent.

What are we to make of Schaller's proposals? First, I am sure that some conservatives will be initially attracted to this proposal. Joining a likeminded annual conference would be a considerable relief to many of them. Second, it is good to see someone of Schaller's stature and astuteness come clean publicly on the challenge of division facing the church. There are indeed very deep differences in the church that harbor division. This cannot be resolved by denial, by watching passively as the polarization increases, by forming another committee to seek common ground or by encouraging congregations to leave with their property. Third, Schaller's essay is the first I have seen or read that forthrightly recognizes the social logic of pluralism. Pluralism is not the benign, cozy affair it was touted to be. In reality it is a recipe for polarization within the church. In the end it is a stop-gap arrangement that papers over deep differences.

However, I am not convinced by Schaller's proposal. First, it hinges crucially on the acceptance of pluralism as the truth about our church. It is precisely this thesis that needs to be rejected. I will not rehearse the arguments I have advanced elsewhere.[3] The truth is we are a confessional church. The challenge is not to acquiesce to a bogus pluralism but to work our way out of it and become what we are canonically and constitutionally.

Second, Schaller's thesis is set entirely in secular, nontheological or nondoctrinal categories. Differences are described as ideological polarization. Those of us who are happy to be identified as conservative or evangelical are invited to see ourselves as holding an "ideological stance." I, for one, reject this. The faith delivered once for all is not some ideology. It is an indispensable means of grace that introduces us to the mysterious reality of God. Our faith is not the dead hand of the past reaching out to squelch our creativity and hold us in check. It is a fresh and living creed which nourishes our souls, forms our identity and keeps us in continuity with the church through the ages. In a way Schaller's language shows how far we have to travel in doctrinal renewal. He does not even give a passing glance to the material on the church buried in our canonical doctrines. How are we to reconcile Schaller's proposal with the claims of our tradition when the tradition is not even invoked in the discussion?

Third, Schaller's ecclesiology does in fact shine through. It is a modified form of congregationalism. Much as I see the local congregation as the heart beat of the church—as do our Articles and Confession of Faith—and much as I want to

---

[3]See William J. Abraham, *Waking from Doctrinal Amnesia* (Nashville, Abingdon, 1995).

see the local congregation be far more active in mission and ministry, I have no desire to become congregationalist. This is really a recipe for a do-it-yourself Christianity tried and found wanting. It is a far cry from the picture in Acts where Christians hammered out the issues in council and conference. It is also a far cry from our own appropriation of that tradition down through our history.

Fourth, a practical note. Schaller's proposal has an air of exciting pragmatism about it. He has even worked out the numbers. Each annual conference would have a minimum of at least eight hundred churches with a combined average worship attendance of at least sixty thousand. Twenty percent of all congregations would be free to switch membership under certain conditions. Frankly, this scheme strikes me as totally unworkable. For example, who decides who is in the 20 percent? And who guarantees that the motley crew of conferences will hold together? Surely this scheme would be a prelude to some annual conferences bolting from the federation once it dawns on them that they really are at odds with others who are ideologically opposed to them, and once they realize that they are sending money to one more ecclesiastical bureaucracy whose job is to hold all these folk together? The scheme is a recipe for division.

Finally, I cannot help but note the acculturation at the core of Schaller's suggestion. On the one hand, The United Methodist is apparently confined to North America, as if those outside do not exist. More significantly, Schaller endorses pluralism in part because it is a contemporary fact of American culture. Surely we hope for better things for the people called United Methodists. This was exactly the mistake made in the liberal Protestant experiment of the nineteenth and twentieth centuries. It is high time we abandoned it.

The real and deep alternative to withdrawal, schism, restructuring along ideological lines and the like is clear: we need to stick to the long-haul renewal of our church.

Moving Ahead in Renewal

This takes us straight to our third question: if we do stay in, how should we think about the dynamic of renewal at our present juncture in history? More pointedly we might ask, what is the task of renewal that beckons us? Is it to "take back the church" from liberal and radical elements? Or is a deeper, more theological task at hand?

Talk of taking back the church is language drawn from the culture wars. I do not find this sort of proposal illuminating or helpful. We need a very different conceptual framework for reading our situation and for determining our strategy. Moreover, I will cast the issue in terms of the potential activity of the Confessing Movement.

The Confessing Movement has made considerable progress in its short history. It has wobbled here and there, and development of the affection and trust crucial for effective renewal has taken time. However, we are well on our way. We have found means of nurturing grassroots organizations, we have found ways to meet and make decisions, and we have kept the coalition together. We have been able to respond in a measured way to crucial developments in the church. We have furnished a lifeline to people tempted to jump overboard, and we have helped many others take a stand when they might have wilted and given up. We continue to develop a network of people who are keen to work for better days ahead. We have not achieved all our goals, but the above list is no mean accomplishment.

The most singular achievement is that we are beginning the difficult task of displacing the Quadrilateral as the core of our doctrine. For thirty years United Methodists have thought of doctrine officially and informally as those beliefs grounded in an appeal to Scripture, tradition, reason and experience. Recently, however, some bishops have nervously but openly started talking about the Articles of Religion and the Confession of Faith. This is only a start, of course, but it is amazing. There are supporters of the Quadrilateral, and there are good scholars continuing to argue its merits, but the steam has gone out of it as the substance of our identity. It is quietly being relegated to a more modest position in the life of church. We still have a long way to go in getting some conservatives to see that we really are a confessional church and that we do not need to draw up some new list of Wesleyan essentials. The deep challenge is to work for the renewal of the place of doctrine in the church. This will not be done without making initial mistakes. We will have false starts and dead ends. Hence careful and disciplined theological work is essential. We have to learn a new language, or better we have to refurbish a language we have forgotten, and we have to develop the moral and spiritual discernment essential to the teaching and appropriation of our doctrines. This will take years to achieve. Let me spell this out more fully.

Increasingly I have come to think of renewal in three phases. Phase one began in the late 1960s, a period of alienation, protest, confrontation and initial seed-sowing. Various groups sprang up to deal with, say, the primacy of Scripture, the importance of the gifts of the Spirit, the fulfillment of the Great Commission or finding better prudential means of grace in Bible study and retreats. This is where farsighted pioneers do their best work. Against great odds and facing intense criticism, they begin to identify problems and develop strategies of survival and change. The establishment ignores them, pretends they do not exist, attacks them or marginalizes them.

Phase two is a period of consolidation, deeper confrontation, painful dialogue and initial harvesting. This is a difficult time for the pioneers: they are wary of change in strategy, they have been on a long journey, and they know only too well how difficult change is. Exhausted or disillusioned, they are tempted to abandon the journey. Ironically, confronting the pioneering group head-on with the reality of withdrawal helps them to refocus and redouble their efforts to work for renewal.

It is also a difficult time for renewal newcomers because they are wary of working with people portrayed as enemies of the church by their critics. They know only too well how easy it is to be stereotyped and sidelined. Some will stand aloof, trying their own way. Through the experience of pioneers, most newcomers realize that the incubation of the seeds of renewal is pivotal in the long run. They are better prepared for the confrontation and dialogue of phase two. They are ready to shift from the trenches into positions of leadership in the church, learning as best they can to cope with the responsibilities which go with this new terrain.

While phase two is by no means confined to the Confessing Movement, the Confessing Movement is a critical catalyst and rallying point. We have learned over the years that there can be no comprehensive renewal in preaching, in the study of Scripture, in mission, in sacramental practice, in receiving the gifts of the Spirit, and the like without coming to terms with doctrinal commitments and the life of the mind. This can be done while harvesting the fruits of phase one's evangelism and mission. Focusing on doctrine richly adds to other areas of renewal. And doctrine is itself enhanced by being intimately related to renewal in worship, evangelism, disciplined living and scholarship. Consolidation and cross-fertilization provide a new lease on life for renewal in the church.

Phase two creates a new level of interaction. Church leaders cannot be as dismissive as they might desire. Defensiveness and stonewalling have to give way to engagement and dialogue. Doors previously closed are opened up. Conversations within the tradition become longer and deeper.

Phase three lies way out ahead of us. It would be premature to be predictive at this juncture, but it is helpful to speculate and dream dreams. The hope for this phase is a substantial harvesting of the seeds sown and developed in the first two phases of renewal. The fruit will take many forms: creative work in evangelism and mission on a scale scarcely imagined by the pioneers, greater confidence in the health of the church as a whole, a deepening of worship and spirituality, a marked increase in the quality and quantity of scholarly work related to the tradition, and a massive enrichment of the denomination by new ecumenical encounters. Add to this the possibility of a fresh outpouring of the Holy Spirit in a new awakening, and the possibilities are truly magnificent.

My claim, then, is that we are now well into phase two. Within the Confessing Movement the agenda is clear. We need to stick to our focus on doctrinal renewal and help our church identify, articulate and apply its deep doctrinal commitments. If we do this, we can hope over time to provide a lasting alternative to the liberal and radical options that have been attractive to many in the short term but which have not been adequate as an expression of our canonical heritage or satisfactory as a basis for evangelism or mission. The United Methodist Church has its part to play in the redemptive purposes of God. Working for renewal is a vital part of the total work that God has called us to in this generation. We should pursue that work with flair, realism and quiet hope.

We should also realize that renewal is a complex business in both its historical development and its internal structure. It is on this note that I want to finish. Stretched across history, renewal is like a three-act play. Every effective movement is a complex phenomena with diverse elements and several levels of commitment, ethos and action. This is also the case with the Confessing Movement. It is an increasingly strong coalition of United Methodists who tend in turn to be evangelical, charismatic, catholic, centrist, moderate and traditional. When it started, the bonds were quite fragile, but we have seen trust and affection deepen over the years.

The different levels are extremely interesting and important. There are those who have given extended thought to the nature and strategy of the movement and who can readily identify its virtues and strengths as well as its weaknesses and blind spots. They also understand the responsible objections made against the movement and happily acknowledge the integrity and intelligence of those who hold them. At another level are those who have made an informed decision to be involved in the Confessing Movement, and who are able to provide a fair account of their reasons for doing so, but who readily acknowledge that they cannot fully explain their position or that of their critics. They tend to fall silent or punt when confronted with tough opponents. At another level some people simply intuit or gut sense that the Confessing Movement is on the right track, and they eagerly embrace it. They tend to attack opponents rather sharply and insist that failing to become part of the movement is a moral and spiritual vice. They prefer to get out the vote rather than engage in extended debate.

Consider an analogy. In 1998 I cheered for France against Brazil in the World Cup soccer final. As is my custom I generally pick a team and become its loyal supporter. I reveled in France's virtues and in its majestic victory over Brazil, but this did not preclude a healthy respect for the Brazilian supporters or appreciation for the many fine qualities of the Brazilian team. Supporters of a soccer team constitute a movement, and they are varied in their attitudes and skill.

Some are connoisseurs who have a keen eye for the merits and strengths of their team. Yet they can also appreciate the skill of the opposing team. Other supporters are regulars who follow their team and give limited attention to the fine points of the game. Still others are more like camp followers. For them there is only one good team; they would never admit to the virtues of their opponents; and sometimes they will get involved in a brawl with the camp followers of other teams. The application to the Confessing Movement is self-evident.

In pursuing the goal of renewal we have our work cut out for us. We need both a sense of the goal we are pursuing and maturity in understanding the complexity of working for renewal. The work of Thomas Oden has been a wonderful, bracing tonic to many in this arena.

THIRTEEN

SCHISMS, HERESIES & THE GOSPEL

Wesleyan Reflections on Evangelical Truth & Ecclesial Unity

GEOFFREY WAINWRIGHT

S*chism* and *unity*: the words have reentered the internal vocabulary of a troubled Methodism as a mutually conditioning pair. *Truth* and *heresy*: the cultural situation of late modernity renders the use of these words difficult. Yet the first letter to the Corinthians makes it clear that these four terms belong in the same semantic field for Christians. "I hear that there are *schismata* among you," writes the apostle Paul, "and I partly believe it; for there must be *haireseis* among you, in order that those who are genuine among you may be recognized" (1 Cor 11:18-19). The singularity of Christ entails unity among those who have been baptized into him and his saving work (1 Cor 1:10-13; 12:12-13), but it is precisely the truth of the gospel which is the only ground of ecclesial unity (1:17—2:16; 11:23-34).

Questions of "schism" and "heresy," "unity" and "truth" are not new in the history of the church. Methodists may appropriately seek guidance from John Wesley in his circumstances, while recognizing of course the differences, both internal and external, between early Methodism as still within the Anglican ambit and contemporary Methodism as itself a denomination on the ecumenical scene.

The text in hand will deal first with Wesley on schism, then with Wesley on heresy. A third part will treat ecumenism and evangelism. The terminology of that last pair is anachronistic to Wesley, though its substance is not. In all three parts, lines will be drawn to the present.

Wesley on Schism

John Wesley was regularly accused of fomenting schism. Listen already to the minutes from his first annual conference of preachers in 1744:

Wednesday June 27th

Q.7. Do we separate from the Church [of England]?

A. We conceive not: We hold communion therewith for conscience' sake, by constantly attending both the word preached, and the sacraments administered therein.

Q.8. What then do they mean, who say, "You separate from the Church?"

A. We cannot certainly tell. Perhaps they have no determinate meaning; unless, by the Church they mean themselves; that is, that part of the Clergy who accuse us of preaching false doctrine. And it is sure that we do herein separate from them, by maintaining that which they deny.

Q.9. But do you not weaken the Church?

A. Do not they who ask this, *by the Church*, mean themselves? We do not purposely weaken any man's hands. But accidentally we may, thus far: They who come to know the truth by us, will esteem such as deny it less than they did before. But the Church, in the proper sense, the congregation of English believers, we do not weaken at all.

Q.10. Do you not entail a schism on the Church? that is, Is it not probable that your hearers, after your death, will be scattered into all sects and parties; or that they will form themselves into a distinct sect?

A. (1.) We are persuaded the body of our hearers will even after our death remain in the Church, unless they be thrust out.

(2.) We believe notwithstanding, either that they will be thrust out, or that they will leaven the whole Church.

(3.) We do, and will do, all we can to prevent those consequences which are supposed likely to happen after our death.

(4.) But we cannot with a good conscience neglect the present opportunity of saving souls while we live, for fear of consequences which may possibly or probably happen after we are dead.[1]

---

[1] *The Works of the Rev. John Wesley* (London: Thomas Jackson, 1830), 8:280-81.

Nevertheless, as the years went by, some among the Methodists favored separation from the Church of England, chiefly on the ground of the unworthiness of
many ministers in the established Church and in the conviction that ministerial
services could be more suitably provided by Methodist preachers, most of whom
were not ordained. The matter first became urgent in 1754-1755, and John Wesley
wavered somewhat but was kept loyal to the Church of England by his brother
Charles and William Grimshaw of Haworth.[2] John Wesley's paper prepared for
the Leeds conference of 1755—"Ought We to Separate from the Church of
England?"—provided the basis for his tract *Reasons Against a Separation from the
Church of England* that was published in 1758 and again in 1760 (after the case of
the Norwich preachers administering the Lord's Supper). Wesley advanced twelve
reasons why it was "not expedient"—Charles strengthened this to "not lawful"—
for the Methodists to separate from the established Church: separation would
mean going back on their repeatedly given word; it would give cause to their enemies; it would forfeit the Methodists the ear of many sympathizers; it would
hinder multitudes from hearing their preaching at all; it would cause the loss of
perhaps thousands of those now attached to them; it would occasion strife
between those who stayed and those who left; it would lead to time and energy
wasted in controversies; it would demand exorbitant effort "to form the plan of a
new church"; it would breed contempt toward the clergy in general; it was historically likely to end in sectarianism, with decline in both holiness and utility; it
would thwart God's chief design in raising up the Methodists and sending them
out, namely, to "quicken our brethren," "the lost sheep of the Church of England."[3]
These reasons against separation Wesley stood by in his sermon of 1787 "On
Attending the Church Service," just four years before his death.[4]

Nevertheless, the impression could easily be left that "Mr. Wesley, like a strong
and skilful rower, looked one way, while every stroke of his oar took him in the
opposite direction."[5] For while protesting his fidelity to the Church of England,
Wesley acquiesced, or even led, in a series of actions that gradually and almost
inevitably increased the autonomy of Methodism over against the established
Church: Frank Baker lists the formation of "independent societies, an itinerant
ministry, informal worship and field-preaching, the authorization of lay preachers,
the institution of a sacramental community, of a deliberative assembly, the erection

---

[2]See Frank Baker, *John Wesley and the Church of England* (London: Epworth Press, 1970), pp. 160-79, 326-40. There
is, of course, no telling what might have happened had the authorities of the Church of England been more responsive to the Wesleyan movement of renewal.

[3]*Works*, 13:225-32.

[4]Ibid., 7:174-85.

[5]Joseph Beaumont, cited in Baker, *John Wesley*, p. 2.

of Methodist buildings, and the undertaking of legal provisions for their security and continuity."[6] Yet Wesley refused to concede that all this amounted to "separation"—as the Large Minutes (1789) show:

> Are we not unawares, by little and little, sliding into a separation from the Church? O use every means to prevent this! (1.) Exhort all our people to keep close to the Church and sacrament. . . . (3.) Warn them also against despising the Prayers of the Church. (4.) Against calling our society, "the Church." (5.) Against calling our Preachers, "Ministers," our Houses, "Meeting-houses." Call them plain preaching-houses, or chapels. (6.) Do not license them as Dissenters. . . . (7) Do not license yourself till you are constrained; and then, not as a Dissenter, but a Methodist.[7]

Even after 1784 when he had begun to perform ordinations, John Wesley refused to admit, with Lord Chief Justice Mansfield and his own disconsolate brother Charles, that "ordination is separation."[8]

One shift that John Wesley employed was the semantic redefinition of the word *schism* to cover a reality that he condemned but did not equate with separation. In the sermon "On Schism" of 1786, he argues from 1 Corinthians 1:10-12; 11:18-21; and 12:24-25 that schism "is not a separation *from* any Church (whether general or particular, whether the Catholic or any national Church), but a separation *in* a Church." Schism within the Corinthian church was a "want of tender care for each other, . . . an alienation of affection in any of them toward their brethren, a division of heart, and parties springing therefrom, though they were still outwardly united together; though they still continued members of the same external society."[9] Now "this species of schism," says Wesley, "there will be occasion to guard against in every religious community." Yet Wesley was bound to admit that there was another sin that could "remotely" be called schism—"remotely" because the usage was "not strictly scriptural." "To separate ourselves from a body of living Christians, with whom we were before united, is a grievous breach of the law of love"; and such "schism"—schism in the "remote" sense—"is both evil in itself, and productive of evil consequences":

> It is the nature of love to unite us together; and the greater the love the stricter the union. And while this continues in its strength, nothing can divide those whom love has united. It is only when our love grows cold, that we can think of separating from our brethren. And this is certainly the case with any who willingly separate from their Christian brethren. The pretences for separation may be innumerable, but

---

[6]Baker, *John Wesley*, p. 162.
[7]*Works*, 8:320-21.
[8]Baker, *John Wesley*, pp. 256-82.
[9]*Works*, 6:401-10.

want of love is always the real cause; otherwise they would still hold the unity of the Spirit in the bond of peace.

Such separation does harm to those who leave, to those who are left behind and to "the whole world in general" in so far as—by its loveless nature and consequences—such separation or schism hardens unbelievers against the truth of the gospel. As we will see later, Wesley allows that separation may sometimes be justifiable, but only as a last resort. He did not believe that he or his British Methodists had come to that point with the Church of England; but we saw him as early as the conference of 1744 contemplating the possibility that they might be "thrust out"—which is what he believed had happened with the sixteenth-century Reformers and the Catholic Church.[10]

Now what are later Methodists—having willy-nilly become a separate body—to make of Wesley on schism? In the nineteenth century, Methodists on both sides of the Atlantic were a fissiparous people; in the twentieth century several, though not all, of the internal divisions have been repaired through denominational reunions. On the threshold of the twenty-first century, new divisions threaten, as indeed they do in the case of most mainstream Protestant churches in the Western world. The most obvious issues occur in the field of bioethics around sexuality and the beginning and ending of life. These are important enough matters in themselves, although they may also be presenting symptoms of a broader and deeper malaise involving the doctrines of creation and redemption, the status and interpretation of Scripture, and the nature and exercise of teaching authority in the church. Those of us who, as evangelicals and/or catholics, wish to maintain the identity of historic Christianity will stay as long as we can in our ecclesial location—in order, as Wesley put it, to "leaven the whole."

Three pieces of advice from Wesley may prove especially useful. First, Wesley was well aware of the problem posed in a church infected by "the ministration of unholy men." His counsel, in the light of scriptural exegesis and historical example, was "calmly to inquire, whether God ever did bless the ministry of ungodly men, and whether he does so at this hour. Here is a plain matter of fact: If God never did bless it, we ought to separate from the Church, at least where we have reason to believe that the minister is an unholy man. If God ever did bless it, and does so still, then we ought to continue therein." Theologically and pragmatically Wesley continues in the sermon "On Attending the Church Service," "the unworthiness of the minister doth not hinder the efficacy of God's ordinance": God "does not,

---

[10]According to Wesley, "Calvin and Luther, with their followers, . . . did not properly separate from it [the Church of Rome]; but were violently thrust out of it. They were not suffered to continue therein, upon any other terms than subscribing to all the errors of that Church" (*Works*, 7:182).

will not suffer his grace to be intercepted, though the messenger will not receive it himself. . . . We know by our own happy experience, and by the experience of thousands, that the word of the Lord is not bound, though uttered by an unholy minister; and the sacraments are not dry breasts, whether he that administers be holy or unholy."[11]

Second, Wesley recognized that service as salt or leaven required integrity on the part of the witness: "Let us bear a faithful testimony, in our several stations, against all ungodliness and unrighteousness, and with all our might recommend that inward and outward holiness 'without which no man shall see the Lord!'"[12]

For, third, it is such personal example that will give credibility to the exercise of discipline among both wayward clergy and laity. While discipline should always aim at the recovery of the straying, it is also necessary to the holiness that is professed of the church in the creed and described in such a passage as Ephesians 4:1-6, from which it follows, says Wesley in his sermon "Of the Church," that "not only no common swearer, no Sabbath-breaker, no drunkard, no whoremonger, no thief, no liar, none that lives in any outward sin, but none that is under the power of anger or pride, no lover of the world, in a word, none that is dead to God, can be a member of his Church."[13] Discipline is most convincingly administered when the administrators themselves abide by it.

Those, in sum, who are concerned for the church's faithfulness should as long as possible stay put for the sake of those among whom God has placed them—and they will do so relying on God's mercy rather than their own righteousness, however real. Wesley does, however, envisage cases where it may become justifiable and even necessary to separate. Sometimes he seems to have in mind the case of separation from a local church, at others times from a national church, a denominational church or even an entire confessional communion.

The Large Minutes concisely allow two cases as "exceptions." The first is, "If the parish Minister be a notoriously wicked man." Here it must have come to the point of open scandal in the character and conduct of the offender such as would pose a greater stumbling-block to evangelical witness than the act of separation. The second exception is, "If [the minister] preach Socinianism, Arianism, or any other essentially false doctrine." Notice the strength of the phrase, "essentially false doctrine." This situation will be treated in a moment under the heading of heresy. It raises, of course, the question of ministerial discipline and of teaching authority in the Church. It may also be asked whether—by acquiescence or even active approval—an entire ecclesial

---

[11]Ibid., 7:175, 184-85.
[12]Ibid., 7:185.
[13]Ibid., 6:400.

body may fall into such heresy as would justify a distancing not merely from one particular minister but from the larger corporate entity.[14]

Wesley treats the question of separation from larger ecclesiastical units toward the end of his 1786 sermon "On Schism." Here he names names—those of the Church of Rome and the Church of England, between which he does indeed differentiate; and he makes an implicit distinction between the general body of the faithful and the situation of the preacher or, more particularly, the evangelist which he himself is. The whole forthright and vigorous passage merits quotation:

> Suppose, for instance, you were a member of the Church of Rome, and you could not remain therein without committing idolatry; without worshiping of idols, whether images, or saints and angels; then it would be your bounden duty to leave that community, totally to separate from it. Suppose you could not remain in the Church of England without doing something which the word of God forbids, or omitting something which the word of God positively commands; if this were the case (but blessed be God it is not), you ought to separate from the Church of England. I will make the case my own: I am now, and have been from my youth, a member and a minister of the Church of England: and I have no desire nor design to separate from it, till my soul separates from my body. Yet if I were not permitted to remain therein without omitting what God requires me to do, it would then become meet and right, and my bounden duty, to separate from it without delay. To be more particular: I know God has committed to me a dispensation of the Gospel; yea, and my own salvation depends upon preaching it: "Woe is me if I preach not the gospel." If then I could not remain in the Church without omitting this, without desisting from preaching the Gospel, I should be under a necessity of separating from it, or losing my own soul. In like manner, if I could not continue united to any smaller society, Church, or body of Christians, without committing sin, without lying and hypocrisy, without preaching to others doctrines which I did not myself believe, I should be under an absolute necessity of separating from that society. And in all cases the sin of separation, with all the evils consequent upon it, would not lie upon me, but upon those who constrained me to make that separation, by requiring of me such terms of communion as I could not in conscience comply with. But, setting aside this case, suppose the Church or society to which I am now united does not require me to do anything which the Scripture forbids, or to omit anything which the Scripture enjoins, it is then my indispensable duty

---

[14] Ibid., 8:322. In a note dated from Bristol, July 22, 1786, and addressing the question of holding Methodist services during "church hours," Wesley allows it "when the minister is a notoriously wicked man" and "when he preaches Arian, or any equally pernicious, doctrine." He also adds cases "when there are not churches in the town sufficient to contain half the people; and, when there is no church at all within two or three miles" (see 13:257). Here the question is clearly for Wesley a *local* one; equally clearly, it is a matter of *reaching the people with the gospel.*

to continue therein. And if I separate from it without any such necessity, I am justly chargeable (whether I foresaw them or not) with all the evils consequent upon that separation.[15]

There, then, Wesley numbers three grounds for separation from a church: its imposition of acts that Scripture forbids or its omission of acts that Scripture commands; its denial of liberty to evangelize; and its requirement of false doctrine. The issues of individual separation from larger ecclesial bodies are those which, *mutatis mutandis*, individual Methodists have in turn had to deal vis-à-vis Methodist denominations themselves, once these attained historical existence. The questions recur in the present.

Wesley on Heresy

In his sermon "On Schism," Wesley pointed out that in 1 Corinthians 11:19, *haireseis* is synonymous with *schismata* in the previous verse and means "divisions" or "parties"—which, as we saw, he located *within* the Corinthian church. But he was also well aware of the historical reality of substantial errors which ran counter to the faith delivered to the saints, and the common designation of these as heresies. And while he certainly deplored the shedding of "seas of innocent blood" for the sake of "opinions, whether right or wrong,"[16] Wesley himself would have no truck with what we have already heard him elsewhere call "essentially false" and "pernicious" doctrines.

Modern Methodists—and perhaps even more so, postmodern Methodists—may need persuading that Wesley did indeed recognize the existence of what common language designates "heresy"—and that he viewed heresy as grounds for separation. Liberal or sentimental Methodists have often cited Wesley's dictum that Methodists "think and let think," but have ignored Wesley's qualification at the beginning of his tract on "The Character of a Methodist": "As to all opinions *which do not strike at the root of Christianity*, we think and let think."[17]

On "the essential doctrines of the Christian faith," the "truths of deep importance," Wesley will brook no difference. These comprise God the holy Trinity, the origin and goal of human salvation; the fallen condition of humankind and its need of redemption; the deity of Christ, and the universal scope of his atoning work; the deity of the Holy Spirit, and the transforming power of his grace. Listen to just three passages.

---

[15] *Works*, 6:408-9. I will return in the final section of this paper to Wesley's views—they are complex—on the Church of Rome in his day, and to the present relationships between Methodism and the Roman Catholic Church.

[16] Ibid., 6:404.

[17] Ibid., 8:340.

First, from the treatise on "The Doctrine of Original Sin":

A denial of original sin contradicts the main design of the gospel, which is to humble vain man, and to ascribe to God's free grace the whole of his salvation. Nor, indeed, can we let this doctrine go without giving up, at the same time, the greatest part, if not all, of the essential doctrines of the Christian faith. If we give this up, we cannot defend either justification by the merits of Christ, or the renewal of our natures by his Spirit.[18]

Second, from a letter of February 7, 1778, to Mary Bishop:

Nothing in the Christian system is of greater consequence than the doctrine of Atonement. It is properly the distinguishing point between Deism and Christianity. . . . Give up the Atonement, and the Deists are agreed with us. . . . What saith the Scripture? It says, "God was in Christ, reconciling the world unto Himself"; that "He made Him, who knew no sin, to be a sin-offering for us". . . . But undoubtedly, as long as the world stands, there will be a thousand objections to this scriptural doctrine. For still the preaching of Christ crucified will be foolishness to the wise men of the world. However, let *us* hold the precious truth fast in our heart as well as in our understanding; and we shall find by happy experience that this is to us the wisdom of God and the power of God.[19]

And third, from the sermon of 1775 "On the Trinity," where Wesley affirms the fact of the Trinity and its soteriological importance and testimony, even while confessing ignorance as to the "how" of the "Three-One God":

There are ten thousand mistakes which may consist with real religion; with regard to which every candid, considerate man will think and let think. But there are some truths more important than others. It seems there are some of deep importance. I do not term them "fundamental" truths; because that is an ambiguous word. And hence there have been so many warm disputes about the number of "fundamentals." But surely there are some which it nearly concerns us to know, as having a close connexion with vital religion. And doubtless we may rank among these that contained in the words above cited: "There are three that bear record in heaven, the Father, the Word, and the Holy Ghost. And these three are one". . . .

The knowledge of the Three-One God is interwoven with all true Christian faith, with all vital religion. . . . I know not how anyone can be a Christian believer till "he hath" (as St. John speaks) "the witness in himself"; till "the Spirit of God witnesses with his spirit that he is a child of God"—that is, in effect, till God the Holy Ghost witnesses that God the Father has accepted him through the merits of God the Son—and having this witness he honours the Son and the blessed Spirit "even as he

---

[18]Ibid., 9:429.

[19]*The Letters of the Rev. John Wesley*, ed. John Telford (London: Epworth Press, 1931), 6:297-99.

honours the Father." Not that every Christian believer *adverts* to this; perhaps at first not one in twenty; but if you ask any of them a few questions, you will easily find it is implied in what he believes.[20]

Those are the reasons why, as he reveals in a letter of July 3, 1756, to James Clarke, Wesley would "give his hand" to "no Arian, semi-Arian, or Socinian."[21]

From "essential doctrines" that allowed no variation Wesley distinguished "opinions." Some opinions might be genuinely debatable, but even here Wesley considered that some were pernicious. Even—or precisely—in the famously generous sermon on "Catholic Spirit," Wesley does not condone what he calls "speculative latitudinarianism": a catholic spirit "is not an indifference to all opinions—this is the spawn of hell, not the offspring of heaven."[22] Admittedly, however, Wesley himself could fluctuate in his reckoning of tolerable opinions. Thus in his ferocious sermon of 1739-1740 on "Free Grace" (which was never included in his "Standard Sermons"), Wesley berated predestinationism as "a direct and manifest tendency to overthrow the whole Christian Revelation."[23] And he later admitted that at the time of his break with Whitefield, he considered Calvinist teaching on predestination "not as an opinion, but as a dangerous mistake." But in writing thus to John Newton on May 14, 1765, Wesley now expressed his readiness to reclassify "particular election and final perseverance" as simply "an opinion" because his acquaintance with some who held it had shown the holding of it to be "compatible with a love to Christ and a work of grace." And with fine even-handedness, Wesley was prepared to qualify as an "opinion" his own teaching on perfection, which he told Newton was "the main point between you and me."[24] As part of his efforts toward a "union" of evangelical preachers in the 1760s, Wesley made clear that he did not envisage "an union in opinions: they might agree or disagree touching absolute decrees on the one hand and perfection on the other"; only they would "speak respectfully, honourably, kindly of each other" and "each help the other on in his work and enlarge his influence by all the honest means he can."[25]

In their ecumenical relations (and we will come to this in the final part of this exposition), Methodists have always had to face the question of what is essential doctrine, what is tolerable opinion and what is downright error. The matter arises also, however, internally to the Methodist churches, sometimes more acutely than at other times. The turn of the twentieth into the twenty-first century might mark such a moment.

---

[20]*Works*, 6:200, 205-6.
[21]*Letters*, 3:182.
[22]*Works*, 5:502.
[23]Ibid., 7:379.
[24]*Letters*, 4:297-300.
[25]See ibid., 4:235-39; cf. Baker, *John Wesley*, pp. 180-96.

Is the name of the triune God settled in contemporary Methodism, especially in North America? "The quaint device of styling them three offices rather than persons," wrote Wesley on August 3, 1771, to Jane Catherine March, "gives up the whole doctrine."[26] Wesley thereby signals in advance the inadequacy of "Creator, Redeemer, Sustainer" as a substitute for Father, Son and Holy Spirit: it suggests a hypostatically undifferentiated Godhead (Sabellianism, perhaps Socinianism) or the reduction of Christ and the Spirit to creatures (Arianism); in either case, the efficacy and nature of our salvation is at stake, as Athanasius and the Cappadocians persuasively showed and the councils of Nicea and Constantinople recognized. Put narratively, the substitute formula, in forfeiting the name by which the story of salvation is canonically and traditionally told and appropriated, risks distorting the principal character who is being rendered—the God and Father of our Lord Jesus Christ. In the second half of the twentieth century there took place a remarkable "ecumenical rediscovery of the Trinity," stimulated in part perhaps for a couple of decades by feminist criticism; it would be a shame if Methodism was to throw away that trinitarian gain in its informal day-by-day, Sunday-by-Sunday usage, and indeed in such a way as might loosen its official commitment to the classic name, doctrine and narrative.[27]

Another—and perhaps related—threat to Methodist and Christian doctrine comes from those theologians who are calling into question the unique status of Christ and the universal scope of his redemptive work. To reduce the confession of Jesus Christ as the Savior of the world to an exercise in poetic license is to abandon the gospel. The fact of religious pluralism was familiar enough to an apostolic generation that nevertheless preached salvation in "no other name" (Acts 4:12). Yet the draft text of the Faith and Order Commission of the World Council of Churches, "The Nature and Purpose of the Church," in reporting that "churches today differ concerning what are tolerable limits to diversity in confessing the one faith," offers as an example: "Is it church-dividing . . . to confess Christ only as one mediator among others?"[28] My answer would be yes: A body that so taught would have given up any claim to be part of historic Christianity; and one might also expect

---

[26]*Letters*, 5:270.

[27]The trinitarian name was most clearly revealed by the risen Lord at Matthew 28:16-20; behind that revelation stand Jesus' self-designation as "the Son," his constant address to the One who sent him as "Abba," and his teaching about the Holy Spirit; ahead of it runs the theological reflection begun in the Epistles of the New Testament and decisively completed by the Councils of Nicaea and Constantinople. See Geoffrey Wainwright, "The Doctrine of the Trinity: Where the Church Stands or Falls," in *Interpretation* 45 (1991): 117-32; "Why Wesley Was a Trinitarian," reprinted in Wainwright, *Methodists in Dialogue* (Nashville: Abingdon, 1995), pp. 261-74; and "The Ecumenical Rediscovery of the Trinity," *One in Christ* 34 (1998): 95-124.

[28]"The Nature and Purpose of the Church: A Stage on the Way to a Common Statement," Faith and Order Paper No. 181 (Geneva, Switzerland: World Council of Churches, 1998).

many of its own members to separate from it. Yet the public utterances of prominent officials in the United Church of Canada—a member of the World Methodist Council—move in that direction, which is to depart from the founding
constitution of the Canadian church in 1925. I am not, of course, denying the value
of dialogue with adherents of other religions, but Christians—by obligation of
faith and in candor toward conversation partners—ought to place such dialogue
within the horizon of evangelization.

Ecumenism and Evangelism

In the area of faith we have seen Wesley ready, for the sake of evangelism, to com-
bine firm agreement in essential doctrines with flexibility in matters of opinion. In
the area of church order we may recall from his letter of June 25, 1746, to "John
Smith," Wesley's bold answer to his own question: "What is the end of all ecclesiastical order? Is it not to bring souls from the power of Satan to God, and to build
them up in His fear and love? Order, then, is so far valuable as it answers these
ends; and if it answers them not, it is nothing worth."[29] Yet just as Wesley expected
"a man of truly catholic spirit" to be "fixed as the sun in his judgment concerning
the main branches of Christian doctrine," so also he expected him, despite any differences in liturgical practice or pastoral government, to "worship God in spirit and
in truth" and to be united to his congregation "not only in spirit, but by all the outward ties of Christian fellowship." On those conditions Wesley invited the
addressees of his sermon "Catholic Spirit" to "join with me in the work of God; and
let us go on hand in hand." Such "unity in affection"—with its entailed mutual
assistance—should be possible even where the other differences prevented "an
entire external union."[30]

Let us look, for example, at the friendly case presented in Wesley's open "Letter to
a Roman Catholic," written at Dublin in 1749, close to the time of his sermon on
"Catholic Spirit." As a preliminary, however, it must first be conceded that Wesley in
other places had severe things to say about superstitious and idolatrous practices in
Roman Catholicism and about erroneous teaching in the Roman Church.[31] Yet in his
sermon "Of the Church" he implied that the Church of Rome was part of "the
Church catholic": "I dare not exclude from the Church catholic all those congregations in which any unscriptural doctrines, which cannot be affirmed to be 'the pure
word of God,' are sometimes, yea, frequently preached; neither all those congrega-

---

[29]*Works*, 12:80-81.
[30]Ibid., 5:492-504.
[31]See, for example, his extracted publication from Bishop John Williams of "A Roman Catechism, Faithfully
Drawn Out of the Allowed Writings of the Church of Rome, with a Reply Thereto"; and his "Popery Calmly
Considered," in ibid., 10:86-128; 10:140-58.

tions, in which the sacraments are not 'duly administered.' Certainly if these things are so, the Church of Rome is not so much as a part of the catholic Church; seeing that therein neither is 'the pure word of God' preached, nor the sacraments 'duly administered.'"[32] Nevertheless, Wesley could make it appear, as in his controversy with the Catholic bishop Richard Challoner, that "particular souls" within the Roman Church might be Christian in spite of their institutional allegiance rather than in virtue of it or by its aid.[33] Thus the issue seems at bottom to be one that theologians perennially have to face, namely, that of the relation between the church as its composition is known only to God, who looks on the heart, and the church as it assumes visible social form in the world. The practical task—which has both disciplinary and ecumenical implications—must surely consist in bringing those two entities into as close a coincidence as pastoral and spiritual insight allows.

Now to get to the concrete case of Wesley's "Letter to a Roman Catholic."[34] In an appeal for mutual respect, affection and help, Wesley sets out both "the belief" of "a true Protestant" and "the practice of a true Protestant" in terms that he considers a Catholic cannot fail to approve. The content of the faith is basically expressed in terms of the Nicene-Constantinopolitan creed, expanded in places to include Chalcedon ("he was made man, joining the human nature with the divine in one person"), the *munus triplex* of Christ as prophet, priest and king, and a fuller description of the sanctifying work of the Holy Spirit. This faith— the *fides quae creditur*—is held in a fully personal way, the *fides qua creditur*: "A true Protestant believes in God, has a full confidence in his mercy, fears him with a filial fear, and loves him with all his soul." In practice a true Protestant "worships God in spirit and in truth"; he "loves his neighbour, that is, every man, friend or enemy, good or bad, as himself, as he loves his own soul, as Christ loved us"; and "knowing his body to be the temple of the Holy Ghost, he keeps it in sobriety, temperance, and chastity." All "this, and this alone," says Wesley, "is the old religion. This is true, primitive Christianity." And the horizon of evangelism is surely opened up when Wesley then immediately exclaims: "O when shall it spread over all the earth!" At the very least a common Christian witness might be expected to radiate from all the mutual love and assistance to which Wesley summons himself and his Catholic addressee.

In "Catholic Spirit," the desired and recommended "union in affection" might not reach to "an entire external union" on account of differences in "opinions," "modes of worship" or "forms of church government." But what Wesley could not

---

[32]Ibid., 6:397.
[33]*Letters*, 4:138.
[34]*Works*, 10:80-86.

in his day envisage, the twentieth-century ecumenical movement has set as a goal in the shape of a "visible unity" that it has struggled to describe. Take, for instance, the description of "the unity we seek" approved by the third assembly of the World Council of Churches at New Delhi in 1961:

> We believe that the unity which is both God's will and his gift to his Church is being made visible as all in each place who are baptized into Jesus Christ and confess him as Lord and Saviour are brought by the Holy Spirit into one fully committed fellowship, holding the one apostolic faith, preaching the one Gospel, breaking the one bread, joining in common prayer, and having a corporate life reaching out in witness and service to all and who at the same time are united with the whole Christian fellowship in all places and all ages in such wise that ministry and members are accepted by all, and that all can act and speak together as occasion requires for the tasks to which God calls his people.

In the closing decades of the twentieth century it was perhaps the Roman Catholic Church—in the wake of the Second Vatican Council and its newly expressed commitment to ecumenism—that became the chief torchbearer for the twin causes of mission and unity that had inspired the ecumenical movement among Protestants and Orthodox in its earlier years. The old mottoes of John R. Mott's Student Christian Movement— "that they all may be one" and "the evangelization of the world in this generation," both having their roots in John 17:21—were remarkably echoed in the very title of Pope John Paul II's encyclical of Ascensiontide 1995, *Ut Unum Sint*, and the powerful paragraphs on "full unity and evangelization." Paragraph 98 reads thus:

> The ecumenical movement in our century, more than the ecumenical undertakings of past centuries, the importance of which must not however be underestimated, has been characterized by a missionary outlook. In the verse of John's Gospel which is ecumenism's inspiration and guiding motif—"that they may all be one . . . so that the world may believe that you have sent me" (John 17:21)—the phrase "that the world may believe" has been so strongly emphasized that at times we run the risk of forgetting that, in the mind of the Evangelist, unity is above all for the glory of the Father. At the same time it is obvious that the lack of unity among Christians contradicts the Truth which Christians have the mission to spread and, consequently, it gravely damages their witness. This was clearly understood and expressed by my Predecessor Pope Paul VI, in his Apostolic Exhortation Evangelii Nuntiandi: "As evangelizers, we must offer Christ's faithful not the image of people divided and separated by unedifying quarrels, but the image of people who are mature in faith and capable of finding a meeting-point beyond the real tensions, thanks to a shared, sincere and disinterested search for truth. Yes, the destiny of evangelization is certainly bound up with the witness of unity given by the Church. . . . At this time we wish to emphasize the sign of unity

among all Christians as the way and instrument of evangelization. The division among Christians is a serious reality which impedes the very work of Christ."

How indeed can we proclaim the Gospel of reconciliation without at the same time being committed to working for reconciliation between Christians? However true it is that the Church, by the prompting of the Holy Spirit and with the promise of indefectibility, has preached and still preaches the Gospel to all nations, it is also true that she must face the difficulties which derive from lack of unity. When non-believers meet missionaries who do not agree among themselves, even though they all appeal to Christ, will they be in a position to receive the true message? Will they not think that the Gospel is a cause of division, despite the fact that it is presented as the fundamental law of love?

If Albert Outler could call John Wesley's open letter of 1749 "an olive branch to the Romans,"[35] then perhaps we may designate John Paul II's encyclical of 1995 a papal olive branch to—among others—the Methodists. For the pope invites the leaders and theologians of other churches to engage with him in "a patient and fraternal dialogue" on the Petrine ministry of teaching and pastoral care which the Roman see claims to exercise by divine appointment on behalf of all Christians and their universal communion.[36] Like Paul VI, John Paul II acknowledges that the Catholic Church's conviction on this point "constitutes a difficulty for most other Christians, whose memory is marked by certain painful recollections," yet the pope also rightly observes that "after centuries of bitter controversies, the other Churches and Ecclesial Communities are more and more taking a fresh look at this ministry of unity," and he asks, "Do not many of those involved in ecumenism today feel a need for such a ministry? A ministry which presides in truth and love so that the ship—that beautiful symbol which the World Council of Churches has chosen as its emblem—will not be buffeted by the storms and will one day reach its haven?" John Paul desires a joint exploration to help him "find a way of exercising the primacy which, while in no way renouncing what is essential to its mission, is nonetheless open to a new situation."

Let me repeat here a proposal that I made at a symposium held in Rome in December 1997 on this theme and that has attracted some attention then and later. It was made in full awareness that since 1967 Methodism and the Roman Catholic Church have been engaged in official bilateral dialogue through the World Methodist Council and what is now the Pontifical Council for Promoting Christian Unity.[37] My respectful suggestion was

---

[35] Albert C. Outler, ed., *John Wesley* (New York: Oxford University Press, 1964), pp. 492-99.

[36] See *Ut Unum Sint*, paragraphs 88-97.

[37] For some account of these conversations, see my *Methodists in Dialogue*, especially pp. 19-22, 37-87.

that the Pope should invite those Christian communities which he regards as being in real, if imperfect, communion with the Roman Catholic Church to appoint representatives to cooperate with him and his appointees in formulating a statement expressive of the Gospel to be preached to the world today. Thus the theme of the "fraternal dialogue" which John Paul II envisaged would shift from the *theory* of the pastoral and doctrinal office to the *substance* of what is believed and preached. And the very *exercise* of elaborating a statement of faith might—by the process of its launching, its execution, its resultant form, its publication, and its reception—illuminate the question of "a ministry that presides in truth and love." *Solvitur ambulando!*[38]

More broadly and less ambitiously put, such a project would at least offer an opportunity for delving into what John Paul II in paragraph 79 of *Ut Unum Sint* called an "area in need of fuller study before a true consensus can be achieved," namely, "the relationship between Sacred Scripture, as the highest authority in matters of faith, and Sacred Tradition, as indispensable to the interpretation of the Word of God."

Conclusion

In bringing this study thus to a provisional conclusion, I am hinting that the issues currently agitating the United Methodist Church are by no means parochial. They are part of a profound challenge and opportunity that is confronting worldwide Christianity at the entrance to the third millennium. They concern, as always, the nature of the gospel, the content of the faith, the identity and location of the church, the pursuit of its mission, and the exercise of its discipline.

Same-sex genital relationships, abortion and euthanasia all raise profound questions of theological anthropology; to condone the practice of any of them would be to take the church down tracks it has hitherto closed off. To cease preaching, baptizing and praying in the name of the Father, the Son and the Holy Spirit would be to change the character of the gospel story beyond recognition. To refrain from confessing the Lord Jesus Christ as Savior of the world would be to renege on what the church has considered its dominical commission to make disciples of all nations. Where, geographically and culturally, the church holds fast to the Scriptures, interpreted according to the classic tradition, it appears that the Christian faith is spreading. Revisionism seems to thrive only amid decline.

---

[38]See "The Gift Which He on One Bestows, We All Delight to Prove: A Possible Methodist Approach to a Ministry of Primacy in the Circulation of Love and Truth," in *Petrine Ministry and the Unity of the Church*, ed. James F. Puglisi (Collegeville, Minn.: Liturgical Press, 1999), pp. 59-82.

FOURTEEN

THE GOSPEL PROVISO

Lessons from Twentieth-Century Theology for the New Millennium

CARL E. BRAATEN

Lutherans are known for their love affair with the gospel. Perhaps no other church tradition has made concern for the purity of the gospel so central in its self-understanding. This is not by accident, since Lutheranism has been radically dependent on Luther's theology, whose inner dynamic was driven by the gospel. Werner Elert called this drive the evangelischer Ansatz,[1] translated into English as "the impact of the gospel." As with Luther so it was with the Reformation as a whole. Elert observed, "No catchword was as suitable as this one for compressing the whole propulsive power of the Lutheran Reformation into a single concept."[2] And Lutheranism ever since has always interpreted Luther's reforming program as a "rediscovery of the gospel" or as a "return to the gospel." Furthermore, Luther's specific interpretation of the gospel left its indelible imprint on the shape of Lutheran theology, marked by antitheses not present in Roman Catholic, Calvinist, Wesleyan or other types of theology, always setting in contrast law and gospel, reason and faith, nature and grace, eros and agape, philosophy and

---

[1]Werner Elert, The Structure of Lutheranism, trans. Walter A. Hansen (St. Louis, Mo.: Concordia Publishing, 1962), p. 11.
[2]Ibid., pp. 179-80.

theology, the kingdom on the left hand of God and the kingdom on the right hand, theology of glory versus theology of the cross, and so forth.

Paul Tillich called this the "law of contrasts" in Luther's theology. The concentration on the gospel as the principle of Lutheran identity also accounts for the privileged place Paul's writings enjoy in the biblical canon, for Paul was the first to sum up the entire Christian message by the term *euangelion,* by which he meant the good news proclaimed by and about Jesus Christ. Of the seventy-six occurrences in the New Testament sixty of them appear in Paul's Epistles.[3]

The historic vocation of the Lutheran confessing movement has been to serve as faithful witness to the gospel within the one holy catholic church, especially when the church is being attracted to other gospels. Admittedly this can be carried to an extreme, as in late-sixteenth- and seventeenth-century scholasticism, as well as in the Neo-Scholasticism of the nineteenth and twentieth centuries, often giving Lutheran theologians the bad reputation of being self-appointed vigilantes, attacking the spread of heresies and heterodoxies within and beyond the walls of Lutheranism. And often Lutherans have waved the banner of the gospel as an excuse to be ecumenical spoil sports. In spite of this extreme tendency within the Lutheran confessional movement yesterday and today, I do not believe that the pendulum should swing so far in the opposite direction that Lutherans neglect their historic calling of being, if not vigilantes, at least vigilant for the sake of the gospel. Our confessions affirm not only what we believe and teach but also what we disbelieve and reject. Karl Barth wrote: "If we don't have the confidence . . . to say *damnamus,* then we might as well forget the *credimus* . . . . If the Yes does not in some way embrace the No, it will not be the Yes of a confession."[4]

One way of reading church history is to see how the gospel has fared through the ages, to judge whether or to what extent given theologies have remained continuous with the evangelical substance of faith according to the Scriptures. When they become outright discontinuous as a whole or at any point, they threaten to confuse the preaching of the gospel and misdirect the ministry of church leaders. From time to time the church has made certain epochal decisions binding on all subsequent generations of Christians. Hence, in the fourth century the church decided that for the sake of the pure understanding of the gospel Christians confess the name of the holy Trinity—Father, Son and Holy Spirit—as three persons within the one being of God. In the fifth century the church solemnly declared,

---

[3]James G. Dunn, *The Theology of Paul the Apostle* (Grand Rapids, Mich.: Eerdmans, 1988), pp. 164ff. Cf. Peter Stuhlmacher, "The Pauline Gospel," in *The Gospel and the Gospels,* ed. Peter Stuhlmacher (Grand Rapids, Mich: Eerdmans, 1991), pp. 149ff.
[4]Karl Barth, *Church Dogmatics* 1/2, ed. G. W. Bromiley and T. F. Torrance (Edinburgh: T & T Clark, 1956), pp. 630-31.

again for the sake of keeping the gospel pure, that Jesus Christ is one person who fully participates in both his divine and human natures. In the sixteenth century a great controversy erupted in the Western church on the doctrine of justification, with the Reformers framing the gospel of salvation in terms of three *solas*—*sola gratia, sola fide, solus Christus.* This doctrine has become the centerpiece of the Lutheran-Roman Catholic dialogues, the official outcome of which still remains controversial in certain theological circles.

What have we learned about the shape of the gospel in the twentieth century—its ups and downs? At the start of this new millennium it may be a good time to take an inventory of what lessons we have learned from the major paradigmatic conflicts of twentieth-century theology. The most engaging experiences in my theological odyssey have been those occasions when I have looked deeply into the inner workings of various theological options, always asking what they might mean for the sake of the gospel we are to believe in our hearts, teach our children and confess in public. It was my privilege to be at work in theology for more than half of the twentieth century in one capacity or another. I tried to examine and test every new theology on the market "in light of the gospel of the glory of Christ," as Paul put the matter in 2 Corinthians 4:4. This is what I mean by the title of this essay, "The Gospel Proviso." A proviso is a condition that qualifies the way a thing works. Hence, a theology is true provided it is good for the gospel. A theology is bad if it obscures the truth of the gospel. The trick, of course, is to know the difference. The gospel itself is the criterion whether a theology is for or against the church of Christ. One who has been marinated in the sauce of confessional Lutheranism will always look into the depths of a theology, not for what's in it for me, my religion, culture, class, color or gender, but what's in it for Christ and for the church's gospel mission for the sake of the world. This is why all the special-interest theologies have so quickly suffered the fate of fading fads and fashions.

I intend to show how at various crisis moments within twentieth-century theology the gospel was in a constant struggle to hold its own. So I will examine briefly eight critical theological disputes—paradigmatic conflicts—whose outcomes have shaped our understanding of the gospel we are prepared to transmit to future generations. If we do not adequately teach the lessons of twentieth-century controversial theology, the next generation will likely repeat its errors.

Paradigm 1: Albert Schweitzer, Martin Kähler and the Quest of the Historical Jesus Yesterday and Today

The first paradigmatic conflict on my list that has qualified our understanding of the shape of the gospel was triggered by two different assessments of the modern search for the real Jesus of history. One was by Albert Schweitzer's study *The Quest of the Historical Jesus* and the other was by Martin Kähler's shattering critique titled *The So-called Historical Jesus and the Historic Biblical Christ.* Their combined effect was to cast doubt on the historical possibility and theological legitimacy of substituting the Jesus of history, as reconstructed from behind the texts using the modern methods of historical science, for the Christ of faith, as represented by the evangelists and apostles in the Gospel texts as we have received them.

The modern critical historical approach to the life and teachings of Jesus raised a gospel issue. The attempt to get at Jesus as he really was behind the Gospels resulted in a picture of a heroic personality at odds with the way the Evangelists portrayed Jesus as the Christ. The outcome is a "so-called historical Jesus" fashioned to suit modern sensibilities and not the real living Jesus Christ of apostolic preaching. The New Testament writings are not source documents from which a scientifically reconstructed life of Jesus can be written. They are rather written from the standpoint of faith and for the sake of proclaiming and passing on the faith. Whenever the framework is deconstructed and another is superimposed from the outside, we lose the gospel in the Gospels, for the preaching of Jesus as the incarnate Word, as the crucified Messiah, as the risen Lord and as the coming Judge is an essential part of the framework.

Today we are witnessing a revival of the quest of the historical Jesus. The result is virtually the same. The historical Jesus in the works of the current crop of questers is totally void of gospel significance, whether it be that of Funk, Crossan, Borg or Spong. It finally comes down to a question of presuppositions. If we presuppose that Jesus is someone else than his best friends and followers said he was, we will discover a Jesus we have never known—a complete stranger to the gospel. We will answer Jesus' question, "And who do you say that I am?" in whatever way we may choose. Schweitzer's history of the quest showed that scholars pictured Jesus mostly in their own image. Kähler's verdict of the old quest is still valid: "The historical Jesus of modern authors conceals from us the living Christ."[5]

We can be sure there is no such thing as doing research without presuppositions. If we discount the presuppositions at work in the formation of the Gospel tradition in our scholarly approach to the historical Jesus, we will end up with a Jesus who looks very different from the individual we have in the Gospels, one who most certainly is not the bringer of the good news of the kingdom nor the content of the good news the early church proclaimed.

The real Jesus is the core of the gospel. He is the ground and content of faith,

---

[5]Martin Kähler, *The So-Called Historical Jesus and the Historic Biblical Christ,* trans. Carl E. Braaten (Philadelphia: Fortress, 1964), p. 43.

who can be truly known only by the testimony of the Holy Spirit. He is the risen Christ at work in the world today through the living voice of the gospel. He is preached and confessed by the community of believers, the church, in words and images taught and transmitted by the Bible. The real Jesus of history is the risen Christ; we cannot have one without the other. They belong indivisibly and insepararably together, as the creed of Chalcedon has taught us to say.

Paradigm 2: Adolf von Harnack and the Essence of Christianity

Our second paradigm case features the attempt of liberal Protestantism to create a new Christianity fit for modernity. Adolf von Harnack was its most sophisticated and formidable exponent. Traditional Christianity, the Christianity of the ancient creeds, had built its piety, worship and proclamation on a christological synthesis of history, kerygma and dogma, starting with the story of Jesus in the Gospels, then moving on to the Christ-kerygma of the apostles and finally to the church's dogma, putting Jesus Christ ontologically on a par with God. Harnack wanted to break down this synthesis and instead mount the essence of Christianity on only one of the three legs, namely, on the historical Jesus apart from the apostolic kerygma and christological dogma. Harnack wanted a thoroughgoing reconstruction of Christianity based on the historical scientific rediscovery of the Jesus of history minus the kerygma of the risen Lord and minus the dogma that places the person of Jesus within the being of the triune God.

Harnack's chief concern was to peel back the layers of tradition to reach the pure essence of the gospel in Jesus himself. The gospel is supposedly not what the early Christians said it was, not what Paul or John or any of the apostles claimed it to be. Distortion accordingly set in at the very earliest stage, when the simple gospel that Jesus preached gave way to the more complicated gospel about Jesus' death and resurrection. Harnack said, "The Gospel that Jesus preached has to do only with the Father, and not with the Son."[6] Creeds get in the way of the gospel; Christology was an erroneous development from the beginning. The institutional, liturgical and dogmatic developments in primitive Christianity have been dubbed by Ernst Käsemann "early Catholicism," and that for Harnack constituted a total perversion of the gospel.

Harnack faced the problem that Jesus' teaching was shot through with eschatological and apocalyptic imagery, none of which for him makes sense in our enlightened age. That poses no great problem for Harnack; all that stuff is merely the husk, the outer shell. Inside is the true kernel of Jesus' message of the Fatherhood of God, the commandment of love and the infinite value of

---

[6]Adolf von Harnack, *What Is Christianity?* trans. T. B. Saunders (New York: Harper & Brothers, 1957), p. 144.

each individual soul. That is what Harnack called the "gospel in the gospel," the foundation of the new essence of Christianity.

It was Alfred Loisy who challenged Harnack's reduction of the gospel to a kernel in Jesus himself.[7] Loisy argued that Harnack's view is not defensible, for even Harnack's kernel is something we receive only through the tradition of the early church. There is no basis in the Gospel traditions for making a distinction between kernel and husk. If anything, what Harnack dismisses as husk—namely, Jesus' sacrificial death and resurrection from the grave—is for the early church essential gospel truth. The double ending of the history of Jesus—his crucifixion and resurrection—are at the core of New Testament Christology. But Harnack says, "It is perverse to make Christology the fundamental substance of the Gospel."[8]

For Loisy there can be no question of a such a break between Jesus and the early church. Every attempt to play Jesus off against his church, against Paul and John and the whole apostolic tradition, results in losing the whole ball game, as far as the gospel is concerned. Apart from the church there is no knowledge of the historical Jesus that has the spiritual power to awaken and sustain faith. Apart from the church the true identity and meaning of Jesus cannot be experienced and confessed.

The outcome of the debate between Harnack the Protestant and Loisy the Catholic turned on whether the gospel can be separated from the church, whether Christianity can refound itself on the religion of Jesus against the early church's faith in Jesus as the Christ, the crucified Lord and risen Savior, in short, whether the early church mistook the husk for the kernel. The reaffirmation of the early church's Christology of Jesus' death and resurrection was another example of the gospel in a struggle to hold its own against the hero worship of Jesus in liberal Protestantism.

Paradigm 3: Karl Barth and the Otherness of God and His Unique Revelation

Our third case study of twentieth-century theology in conflict for the sake of the identity and meaning of the gospel features Karl Barth's struggle for the freedom of God to be God, for the utter transcendence of divine revelation and the pure gratuitousness of divine grace. He called on theology to re-inhabit the strange new world within the Bible. Theology will then learn once again that the Bible is not centered in human religion, not even the religion and ethics of Jesus, as Barth's liberal Protestant professors, such as Harnack and Wilhelm Herrmann, had taught. When Barth published his Romans commentary, he compared it to ringing the

---

[7]Alfred Loisy, The Gospel and the Church, ed. Bernard B. Scott (Philadelphia: Fortress Press, 1976), pp. lix-lxiv.
[8]Harnack, What Is Christianity? p. 184.

bell in a dark church, a summons to remember that theology is primarily about God and God's revelation. The interest of Christian faith in Jesus is not because of his remarkable religious personality and exemplary morality but rather because he is the eternal Word of God, the divine Son born of the Father before all time. And precisely for that reason Jesus the Christ is the gift of God's free grace, the core reality of the gospel coming to us from beyond the realm of human capacity.

To be sure, there is such a thing as religion. Religion is human longing for the eternal, as Schleiermacher taught. The Bible, however, is not the crowning fulfillment of this human religious potential. Religion produces idols; the Bible reveals the one true God, the God of the gospel, who is jealous of the fact of being God, tolerating no rivals. Barth wrote in his Romans commentary, "Paul is authorized to deliver—the Gospel of God. He is commissioned to hand over something quite new and unprecedented, joyful and good—the truth of God. Yes, precisely—of God. The gospel is not a religious message to inform humankind of their divinity or to tell them how they might become divine. The gospel proclaims a God utterly distinct from human beings."[9]

Barth would agree with Harnack that Jesus belongs in the gospel, but only with the proviso that Jesus first belongs in God, that he is the appearing of the Son of God sent by the Father. Thus Barth reconstructs the doctrine of the Trinity on the ruins of liberal Protestant unitarianism. Barth said, contra the liberals, "Because Jesus is the Logos, the Word of God become flesh, we apprehend God in the man Jesus. . . . There is no person Jesus existing apart from the Logos."[10]

The first verse of John's Gospel declares that the Logos was with God from the beginning, and that the Logos was truly God. And this Logos became one with the man Jesus. Here and only here in this divine-human person, in this concrete God-man, do we have the heart of the gospel. At this point the historical Jesus in the Gospels, the apostolic kerygma of Jesus as the Christ, and the church's dogma of the oneness of Jesus with his Father all come together—history, kerygma, and dogma—to provide a framework for the gospel not only in the early centuries but for theology today and on into this new millennium. For Harnack and liberal Protestant theology the gospel is to be reached by going backwards behind the dogma and even behind the kerygma, into the inner life of the historical Jesus. For Barth and classical Christianity, something that C. S. Lewis called "mere Christianity," theology must move in the opposite direction and follow the trajectory of the gospel, from the history of Jesus, always anchored in the Old Testament, to the keryg-

[9]Karl Barth, *The Epistle to the Romans*, trans. W. Montgomery (New York: Macmillan, 1956), p. 28.

[10]Karl Barth, "The Principle of Dogmatics According to Wilhelm Herrmann," in *Theology and Church*, trans. Louise Pettibone Smith (New York: Harper & Row, 1962), p. 264.

matic Christ, and finally to the lasting validity of the trinitarian and christological dogmas of the ecumenical creeds.

In every case without exception, theologies that disregard the dogma—and their number is legion—also misinterpret the kerygma and finally misconstrue as well the history of Jesus. At the bottom line there is no plus sign, only a minus sign, no gospel, instead a piling on of law upon law.

Paradigm 4: Rudolf Bultmann and the Hermeneutical Question

The fourth in a series of great theological conflicts in which the gospel hung in the balance was triggered by Rudolf Bultmann's hermeneutical project to demythologize the New Testament by way of existentialist interpretation. At first Bultmann had no great quarrel with Barth's biblical theology of the Word of God. But then the question urged itself upon him: Who today can understand the gospel since it comes wrapped in the garments of an antiquated picture of the world and the mystifying language of myth and miracle?

Bultmann's demythologizing program was immediately attractive to me and even to many of his critics who shared his passion for the gospel. Who could not fail to see in his impulse to radicalism something of Luther's spirit? His single-minded focus on the Word and faith, his stress on the *pro me* of the gospel, his *theologia crucis*, his christocentrism, his love for John's Gospel, his preference for Paul's Epistles over the others and his concern to preach the gospel in existentially poignant terms—all of these accents and motifs arise out of his Lutheran heritage. And plausibly Bultmann's attempt to separate out the gospel message from its mythological envelope was akin to Luther's radical distinction between law and gospel. Bultmann inquired into the meaning of myth to discover the kerygma analogous to the way Luther placed the law in the service of the gospel. Bultmann, like a lot of Lutherans, narrowed down his exegesis to what for him was the central theme of the New Testament, the doctrine of justification through faith alone.

Bultmann used the categories of existentialist philosophy to build a bridge from the first-century kerygma to twentieth-century experience. So what went wrong from a gospel perspective? The history—including the historical personage of Jesus—that occurred prior to and remained within the kerygma dropped out of sight. The criticism came from within Bultmann's own school, in particular from Günther Bornkamm and Ernst Käsemann. Bornkamm wrote that in Bultmann's theology "Jesus Christ . . . has ceased to be a person. He himself has no longer any history."[11] Bultmann laid all the stress on the existential meaning of the gospel

---

[11]Günther Bornkamm, "Myth and Gospel," *Kerygma and History*, trans. and ed. Carl E. Braaten and Roy A. Harrisville (Nashville: Abingdon, 1962), p. 186.

rather than get bogged down in the debatable facts of history. In Bultmann's hermeneutics, historical facts and existential meaning mix like oil and water. But in the Gospels, history and kerygma are interpenetrating; there is history in the kerygma and kerygma in the history. For Harnack the kerygma of Jesus' death and resurrection were the shell; Jesus' religion was the kernel. For Bultmann it was the other way around; the kerygma of the eschatological event of Jesus' cross and resurrection is the kernel, while the historical facts are the outer trappings that can be shucked.

The gospel issue here is that without the narrative history of Jesus, there would be no gospel in the Gospels. For the very notion of gospel, of good news, denotes a message, but it is always a message about something, or better, someone, namely, "what we have heard, what we have seen with our eyes, what we have looked at and touched with our hands" (1 Jn 1:1). There must be a fundamental continuity between the kerygmatic Christ—the Christ of faith—and the historical Jesus. To separate them, that is, to dehistoricize the kerygma, would be to repeat the docetic error of ancient Gnosticism.

Paradigm 5: Wolfhart Pannenberg and the Reclaiming of Apocalyptic Eschatology and the Historical Resurrection

If Christology is mounted on a three-legged stool—history, kerygma and dogma—it is to the lasting credit of Wolfhart Pannenberg that he rehabilitated each of them and the roles they together play in a comprehensive understanding of the gospel. Pannenberg brought his theological genius to the frontline of virtually all the problems and issues of twentieth-century theology, but in light of the gospel thematic his achievement is twofold: he recovered the positive significance of apocalyptic eschatology and within that horizon reclaimed the historicity of the resurrection of Jesus.

Pannenberg was the initiator of the "theology of hope" for which Jürgen Moltmann got the credit by popularizing it in a book with that title. Many hailed the "theology of hope" as just another fad to be superseded by others. It was far from that. The central notion in biblical eschatology is the coming of God's kingdom, including the future dimension of time. Pannenberg showed the relevance of hope to the human quest for the meaning of life. Bultmann was also concerned about the question of meaning. The difference for Pannenberg is that the question of meaning is tied to history as a structural aspect of all human life. We make sense of the present experiences of life in relation to our memories of the past and hopes for the future. If the final future of the totality of life in which we individually share is only death, then life's meaning is nullified. The prospect of total annihilation nurtures nihilism. Only the hope for life beyond death—which the resurrection promises—can gather up our earthly experiences into an ultimate structure of meaning. The gospel of Jesus' resurrection offers the basis of hope that death itself will be put to death. Apart from the resurrection unto life eternal, death would have the last word and absorb all things into itself as their final end.

Pannenberg's bold reaffirmation of biblical eschatology and resurrection hope came as a shock. Pannenberg's first lecture when he came to America was titled "Did Jesus Really Rise from the Dead?" His answer was yes. It seemed almost unbelievable that an intelligent theologian would affirm the historicity of the resurrection of Jesus. Was Pannenberg some kind of a fundamentalist? After all Bultmann had declared, speaking for many, "The resurrection itself is not an event of past history."[12] Despite Paul's appeal to eyewitnesses still alive (in 1 Cor 15), Bultmann could say, "An historical fact which involves a resurrection from the dead is utterly inconceivable."[13] Of course, theologians and pastors were told they could still indulge in resurrection talk, especially on Easter Sunday when the laity, who pay the salaries, sort of expect it. But this only means that the disciples were having a peak experience, some kind of spiritual buzz. For the existentialist theologians the resurrection did not really happen to Jesus; it happened to those who came to believe in his cause, an expression of a new experience or outlook on life. The Easter event was collapsed into the Easter experience.

This whole affair is not merely a squabble among German theologians. One of the leading exponents of American process theology, Schubert Ogden, wrote that "the bodily resurrection of Jesus would be just as relevant to my salvation . . . as that the carpenter next door just drove a nail in a two-by-four, or that American technicians have at last been successful in recovering a nose cone that had first been placed in orbit around the earth."[14]

Pannenberg had the courage to call the bluff of theologians who wished to base Easter talk on the experiential subjectivity of the first Christians. The gospel drama reaches its denouement on Easter morning, and its truth rests on two conditions—that it really happened to Jesus and that it means what the first witnesses said it meant—that in raising Jesus from the dead, God promises to give life to the dead, countering the deadliness of death with the promise of eternal life.

Paradigm 6: The Holocaust and the Canonicity of the Old Testament
Another major gospel lesson that had to be learned came out of the German

---

[12]Rudolf W. Bultmann, "New Testament and Mythology," *Kerygma and Myth*, ed. H. W. Bartsch, trans. by Reginald H. Fuller (London: S.P.C.K., 1954), p. 42.

[13]Ibid., p. 39.

[14]Schubert Ogden, *Christ Without Myth* (New York: Harper & Brothers, 1961), p.136.

church struggle against Hitler's anti-Semitic policies in the Third Reich, which led to the Holocaust. This is the most important world-historical event that has brought about a paradigm shift in the relations between Christians and Jews. The gospel issue was whether the Old Testament—the Hebrew Bible—is a coequal part of Christian Scripture and whether God's covenant with his people Israel continues to have salvation-historical significance until the end of time.

Within the German Protestant church a movement called "the German Christians" arose, all members of the Nazi party. They demanded a purified church composed only of Christians of the Aryan race. Jesus was portrayed on church murals as a Caucasian Gentile of Nordic type. Christian virtues such as humility, self-sacrifice and forgiveness were rejected in favor of the Nazi values of power, obedience to Hitler and racial purity. Any references to the Old Testament were eliminated from worship as well as everything that reminded Christians of the church's Jewish origins. Pastors who resisted were arrested and sent to concentration camps or drafted and sent to the front lines.

The story of the *Kirchenkampf*, the church struggle, the Barmen Declaration and the resistance movement that took the life of Dietrich Bonhoeffer, has been told often and in great detail. We bring it up here because we should never forget the clear lesson to be learned for the sake of the gospel that there is a high price to pay whenever the church compromises the gospel in its encounter with neo-pagan religion. But the ground for this apostasy had already been prepared in German Protestant theology, in that it dusted off the old heresy of Marcion and brought it back into currency. In the second century Marcion wrote a book to prove that the gospel and the Old Testament contradict each other. He conceived of two Gods, the God of the Jews and the God of the Christians. Every association of Christianity with Judaism had to be severed. Shades of Marcionism returned in Harnack's book on Marcion. He wrote, "The rejection of the Old Testament in the second century was an error which the great church rightly opposed; holding on to it in the sixteenth century was a destiny which the Reformation was not able to escape; but for Protestantism to preserve it since the nineteenth century as a canonical document is the result of a religious and ecclesiastical paralysis."[15]

A hundred years before that Schleiermacher taught in his dogmatics that "Christianity does indeed stand in a special historical connection with Judaism, but so far as concerns its historical existence and its aim, its relations to

---

[15]Quoted from Hans Joachim Kraus, *Geschichte der historisch-kritischen Erforschung des Alten Testaments von der Reformation bis zur Gegenwart* (Neukirchen: Verlag der Buchhandlung des Erziehungsvereins, 1956), p. 351 (translation mine).

Judaism and to Heathenism are the same."[16] Bultmann also taught that the Old Testament is not the Word of God to the people of the new covenant. It is obsolete and superseded by the New. He wrote, "For the person who stands within the church the history of Israel is a closed chapter. The Christian proclamation cannot and may not remind hearers that God led their Fathers out of Egypt . . . and so on. Israel's history is not our history, and in so far as God has shown his grace in that history, such grace is not meant for us. . . . This means, however, that to us the history of Israel is not history of revelation. The events which meant something for Israel, which were God's Word, mean nothing more to us."[17]

We can scarcely exaggerate the impact of such blasphemous teaching concerning the Old Testament on the attitudes of Christians toward Jews and their religion and its indirect contribution to the Holocaust, for which Christians are still grieving and repenting. Books and articles by the dozens have been written on what is called "post-Holocaust theology," and from many perspectives. For us there is a gospel issue at stake here. Jews are blood brothers of Jesus. Christians believe that Jesus is the Messiah whose coming was announced by the Hebrew prophets. Jesus as Jesus is the bond of union between Jews and Christians; Jesus as the Messiah is the chief point of difference.

The essence of Christianity will always be grounded in the dealings of God with his covenant people Israel. The identity and meaning of Jesus as the Messiah will always turn on the prior actions of God with Israel. Our concern for Jesus Christ, for the gospel and his kingdom, will always drive Christians into the Old Testament, and thus—contra Schleiermacher, Harnack, Bultmann and the "German Christians"—the Old Testament will always possess canonical relevance for the Christian church.

Paradigm 7: Liberation Theology and the Freedom of the Gospel

Next to the Holocaust the most traumatic world-historical event of the twentieth century is the collapse of international communism. The rapid demise of Latin American liberation theology can only be explained by its all-too-ready acquiescence to the seductive influences of Marxism. I cannot provide a lengthy account of all the pros and cons of liberation theology. I only wish to zoom in on the problem area where its theory of liberation came into conflict

---

[16]Friedrich Schleiermacher, *The Christian Faith*, trans. H. L. Mackintosh and J. S. Stewart (Edinburgh: T & T Clark, 1928), p. 60.

[17]Rudolf Bultmann, "The Significance of the Old Testament for the Christian Faith," *The Old Testament and Christian Faith*, ed. B. W. Anderson (New York: Harper & Row, 1963), p. 17.

with the Christian gospel of freedom.[18]

It was Paulo Freire who said that liberation is the "generative theme" of our epoch. He was certainly right. And there is no reason that Christians should not support and promote the legitimate worldwide strivings for liberation from all sorts of oppression and domination. The goal of liberation is that life in all its dimensions be released from conditions that deprive people of dignity, harmony and justice. The way to this laudable goal is by means of liberating praxis through social, economic and political struggles. Theology is defined as a critical theory of praxis.[19]

So what's the problem? The problem is that the freedom the gospel bestows does not come about as a consequence of liberating praxis. The gospel is a gift of divine promise—an act of God through the death and resurrection of Jesus. Liberating praxis is a task that demands of humans all the guts and gumption they can muster. The generative theme of the Reformation was justification. It spoke to the universal fallen and sinful condition of the entire human race—rich and poor, male and female, black and white, smart and stupid, or whatever. Becoming reconciled with God is something humans need even in the best of all possible worlds, because the world is shot through with sin that keeps it estranged from God. This is a condition that only God, only the gospel of God's justifying grace, can rectify.

In liberation theology sin is usually spoken of as a predicate of a social situation, characterized by systemic distortions such as classism, racism, sexism and capitalism. The place to look for sin, says Gutiérrez, is in "oppressive structures, in the exploitation of man by man, in the domination and slavery of peoples, races, and social classes."[20] That is no doubt true, yet there is an overplus of meaning in the biblical concept of sin that social change and political praxis cannot deliver.

In Reformation theology God alone is the subject of all saving activity. The gospel means freedom, the gift of "freedom for which Christ has set us free" (Gal 5:1). Salvation does not happen through liberating praxis but by grace alone, not through any change in the social situation but solely on account of Christ. Paul experienced the joy of freedom sitting in a Philippian jail.

Liberation theology is not to be faulted for its passion for justice. By no means!

---

[18]In this essay I do not intend to deal with various other forms of liberation theology. Readers may wonder why I omit mention of feminist liberation theology. The reason is that I do not believe that feminist theology as such flies in face of the gospel. There are theological feminists who fully affirm the gospel in line with the Scriptures and the classical Christian tradition. The problem with radical theological feminism, such as that of Rosemary R. Ruether, Elizabeth Schüssler Fiorenza and Sallie McFague, inter alia, is that it repeats errors of doctrine (heresies) previously conceived by white male theologians. Two that come immediately to mind are Pelagianism and Unitarianism.

[19]Gustavo Gutiérrez, A Theology of Liberation (Maryknoll, N.Y.: Orbis, 1973), pp. 6-15.

[20]Ibid., p. 175.

What it failed to express was the very heart of the message of justification framed by the three great solas—*sola gratia, sola fide, solus Christus*. The gospel of the forgiveness of sins is addressed to individual persons, not to systems and societies. To turn the absolving indicative of the gospel—"your sins are forgiven"—into a demanding ethical imperative we ought to obey or else—that is to legalize and moralize the gospel. When this happens the gospel is no longer a gift but a demand. The gospel gives its own kind of freedom, not to be confused with the goals of liberation movements.

There was much to affirm in liberation theology. Sadly, its vision was blurred when it came to marking the distinction between the transcendent freedom of the eternal gospel and the imperatives of this-worldly liberation movements.

Paradigm 8: The Second Vatican Council and the Ecumenical Movement for Church Unity

Our eighth gospel lesson emerges from the Second Vatican Council and the ecumenical movement for church unity. Vatican II set in motion the ecumenical dialogues that are still going on. It brought about massive changes within the Roman Catholic Church as well as new relations between churches. The results of ecumenical dialogue have profoundly shaped our understanding of the relation between the gospel and the church. It is noteworthy that Bishop Otto Dibelius called the twentieth century, not the Christian Century, but the "Century of the Church." It can hardly be called a Christian century, given the world wars, the Holocaust, Hiroshima, Kosovo and the like. But it can be seen as the century in which the churches rediscovered the nature of the church as essentially a part of the gospel. The church is not merely an external instrument or function of the gospel, but is ontologically the body of Christ. The church is therefore a reality within the fullness of the gospel. The gospel through Word and Sacraments conveys the real presence of Christ, the whole Christ, head and body, Christ and his church. Those who have fellowship with Christ will also have fellowship with each other. Believing in Christ and belonging to the church go together. That is the ground and motive to discover ways to express the unity of the church which is a given of the gospel, a unity now hidden behind the walls of confessional and denominational separations.

The other day I received a letter from a pastor who wrote in response to a mailing from our ecumenical center:

> I have just received your information. We do not wish to be part of an ecumenical group which promotes things not found in Scripture and interprets God's Word from man's point of view. As the pastor of this congregation I am not interested in ecumenical endeavors. I am concerned that the lost come to a saving knowledge of Jesus Christ. So please take us off your mailing list. Sincerely, in Christ Jesus.

If Christ is the Bread of Life, this poor pastor is serving his people but a thin slice of moldy bread. He does not understand that Christ and his church are one, like the head and the body are one, that the church is Christ in the form of his body of which we become members through baptism and faith. We have not yet reached the goal of the ecumenical movement. Yet here we have the best testing ground for gaining a better grasp of the gospel and its relation to the church.

If we were to extend this list of gospel-related issues of crucial significance, we would take up the pluralistic theology of religion and its ill effects on the missionary task of the church and the call to world evangelization. Why evangelize the nations if all religions are equally salvific? What does the pluralistic theory do to the Christian belief in the uniqueness of the person of Christ and the universal scope of his saving work? We are still in the trenches on this one, and it is hard to foretell how the issue will be theologically resolved in church and theology for the good of the gospel.

Conclusion

What does all this mean for us at the beginning of this new millennium? What is the one thing needful that we wish to pass on to those next in line in the succession of the apostolic faith? It is the gospel together with the fullness of the great ecclesial traditions it has engendered through the centuries,[21] and so not as one of the familiar reductionistic models of our rival confessional traditions. We should remember the lessons that emerge through the past struggles of the church for the sake of the gospel. These eight events in the history of twentieth-century theology should teach us to keep the gospel at the flaming center of all our thinking and writing. That means to do theology from the inside out rather than from the outside in, lest the gospel be controlled by alien ideologies, some isms out there that keep our theological legs moving on the treadmill of the latest trends. Ecumenically we should work together to get our churches to orbit around Christ and his gospel as the center, rather than dream about the other sheaves in the field bowing down to our sheaf. At the base of all these controversial issues is Christology, and that is understandable, for Christology is the foundation which must bear the weight of so great a salvation which the gospel promises.[22]

In seminary education we should give highest priority to what is fundamental to all churches, and value our own confessional tradition as essentially a hermeneu-

---

[21]The vision and mission of the Center for Catholic and Evangelical Theology would provide further elaboration of all that is implied by this terse statement.

[22]Centering theology in Christ is the key that opens the door to the doctrine of the Trinity. It was so in the ancient church, in the controversies leading up to and surrounding the Nicene-Constantinopolitan Creed, and it is so today in the renewal of trinitarian theology.

tic in the service of the Great Tradition common to all our churches. That means we should reverse the trend in theological education that has turned the pyramid of profound learning on its head, giving greater time and attention to what is recent and novel at the expense of what is ancient and classical.

We should never have to apologize for stressing Scripture as primal norm within Christian tradition, the great acts of the triune God from the alpha of creation to the omega of redemption as central, law and gospel as God's way of engendering faith in sinful people, the sacraments that make Christ really present, and the evangelistic mission of the church as God's bridge to a dying world. Granted, this is not the kind of stuff that will tickle the ears itching for novelties. But for the sake of keeping the ministry of the gospel front and center in the life of the church, it means that we have to teach the basics all over again, and help every new generation to learn them by heart and love them with a passion.

FIFTEEN

THEOLOGICAL HERITAGE AS HERMENEUTICAL TRAJECTORY

Toward a Nonfoundationalist Understanding of the Role of Tradition in Theology

STANLEY J. GRENZ AND JOHN R. FRANKE

T he evangelical movement harbors an ambiguous relationship to church tradition. In the modern era, postfundamentalist evangelicals viewed themselves as
preserving the "faith once delivered" in the face of the ongoing challenge of theological liberalism. In so doing, evangelicals became the guardians of the tradition,
understood as the doctrines of classical Christian orthodoxy. At the same time,
their commitment to the Reformation and to the Reformation principle of *sola
scriptura* has conditioned modern evangelicals to look askance at tradition, which
they generally see—to cite D. H. Williams's characterization—as "an artificial
product of hierarchical Catholicism and therefore a corruption of the apostolic
faith" and as "antithetical to the absolute authority of the Bible."[1]

---

[1]Daniel H. Williams, *Retrieving the Tradition and Renewing Evangelicalism: A Primer for Suspicious Protestants* (Grand
Rapids, Mich.: Eerdmans, 1999), p. 18.

Recent decades, however, have witnessed the slow gestation of what promises to be a new attitude toward tradition. This rethinking began in the 1970s, as the free-spirited, anti-institutional Christianity of the "Jesus generation" gave way to the kind of journey to the "ancient Christian faith" that led a number of influential evangelicals to set out on the Canterbury trail, walk the Roman road or traverse the highway to Constantinople.[2] This 1970s ferment climaxed in "The Chicago Call: An Appeal to Evangelicals," a manifesto signed by a group of intellectuals who urged their colleagues to rediscover their continuity with the creeds, worship and spirituality of the ancient church.[3]

Since the 1970s a growing chorus of evangelical voices has come to bemoan the ahistorical amnesia of the movement. More recently its ranks have been augmented by several prominent theologians from mainline or liberal backgrounds. Perhaps no advocate of the renewal of classic Christianity through the retrieval of ancient church tradition has been more outspoken and more influential within evangelicalism than the widely-hailed Johnny-come-lately to the movement, Thomas Oden. In the wake of his wholesale break with liberalism, Oden called his adopted theological family to develop a new paradigm that took the ancient church seriously. He articulated this agenda in his 1990 jeremiad, *After Modernity . . . What?* Oden wrote:

> The agenda for theology at the end of the twentieth century, following the steady deterioration of a hundred years and the disaster of the last few decades, is to begin to prepare the postmodern Christian community for its third millennium by returning again to the careful study and respectful following of the central tradition of classical Christian exegesis.[4]

Oden sang the refrain in his autobiographically oriented essay published that same year in the *Christian Century*, in which he boldly announced that the game involving "the attempt to find some modern ideology, psychology or sociology that could conveniently substitute for the apostolic testimony" was now over. Then in a clear polemic against the liberal fixation on activism which he himself had earlier espoused, Oden added, "No political project is more urgent for society than the recovery of classic Christian consciousness through the direct address of the texts of Scripture and Tradition."[5]

---

[2] For helpful sketches of aspects of this movement, see Robert Webber, *Evangelicals on the Canterbury Trail: Why Evangelicals Are Attracted to the Liturgical Church* (Waco, Tex.: Word, 1985); Timothy Weber, "Looking for Home: Evangelical Orthodoxy and the Search for the Original Church," in *New Perspectives on Historical Theology: Essays in Memory of John Meyendorff*, ed. B. Nassif (Grand Rapids, Mich.: Eerdmans, 1996), pp. 95-121.

[3] For a summary of the conference that led to the publishing of "The Chicago Call," see *The Orthodox Evangelicals: Who They Are and What They Are Saying*, ed. Robert Webber and Donald Bloesch (Nashville: Nelson, 1978).

[4] Thomas C. Oden, *After Modernity . . . What?: Agenda for Theology* (Grand Rapids, Mich.: Zondervan, 1990), p. 34.

[5] Thomas C. Oden, "Then and Now: The Recovery of Patristic Wisdom," *Christian Century* 107 (1990):1166-67.

The challenge to regain an appreciation for the important place of tradition in theology articulated by Oden and others raises a crucial question for evangelical theological method: What ought to be the role of tradition in the kind of theological reflection and construction that gives primacy to Scripture? Or stated in another manner, how can evangelicals embrace tradition as a hermeneutical context without losing Scripture as its norming norm? The following paragraphs take up this challenge. The goal of this essay is to draw from the contemporary nonfoundationalist turn[6] in order to outline an understanding of the role of tradition in theology that remains true to the evangelical heritage but answers Oden's call for a "postcritical orthodoxy" which acknowledges that "the pre-Enlightenment theologies had mastered disciplines now virtually lost" but knows as well "that precritical orthodoxy will not really do for the postcritical situation."[7]

"Tradition" in the Tradition of the Church

Until recently, discussions of tradition among evangelicals—if they occurred at all—routinely took place within the context of the Protestant-Roman Catholic debate regarding the status of church tradition vis-à-vis Scripture (although the Protestant critique, by extension, could well encompass the Orthodox Church as well). The answers generally given to this question reflect the foundationalist commitments of participants on both sides of the historic confessional divide within the Western church. Moreover, both sides generally operate with a modern, static view of the nature of tradition.[8]

The postmodern situation provides the occasion to move beyond this impasse. However, before delineating a nonfoundationalist understanding of tradition, we must review the development of the concept in the church which eventually led to the historical divide between Protestants and Catholics.

Scripture and Tradition Before the Reformation

In the patristic era, Scripture and tradition were not seen as mutually exclusive but as coinherent.[9] According to the early church, the church proclaims the gospel, which is contained in written form in the canonical documents and is handed

---

[6]For a summary of nonfoundationalism and its significance for theology, see Stanley J. Grenz and John R. Franke, *Beyond Foundationalism: Shaping Theology in a Postmodern Context* (Louisville, Ky.: Westminster John Knox, 2001), pp. 28-54.

[7]Oden, *After Modernity*, p. 62.

[8]Williams claims that even Thomas Oden operates under a " 'steady state' theory of orthodoxy" (Williams, *Retrieving the Tradition*, p. 33).

[9]George H. Tavard, *Holy Writ or Holy Church: The Crisis of the Protestant Reformation* (New York: Harper & Brothers, 1959), p. 22.

down in living form through church tradition. Moreover, the early patristic thinkers believed that the whole of the kerygma is found in both Scripture and tradition.
Viewed from this perspective, tradition is not an addition to the message contained
in Scripture but is the living, socially embodied expression of that message. Consequently, Scripture and tradition coinhere, and this because both arise from a common source, namely, divine revelation.

The advent of extra-scriptural tradition. Beginning with Basil the Great, however, a
transition in how the understanding of tradition is to be formulated occurred. In
his treatise *De Spiritu Sancto*, Basil states that some aspects of the Christian faith
and practice are not found in Scripture but in the tradition of the church.[10] Regarding this innovation, historian Heiko Oberman writes, "We find here for the first
time explicitly the idea that the Christian owes equal respect and obedience to
written and unwritten ecclesiastical traditions, whether contained in canonical
writings or in a secret oral tradition handed down by the Apostles through their
successors."[11]

Augustine likewise played a crucial role in the establishment of this new conception of tradition. Although Augustine reflects the coinherence of Scripture and
tradition characteristic of the early church, like Basil he also gave place to an *authoritative* extrascriptural oral tradition. According to Augustine the church "moves" the
faithful to "discover the authority of Scripture" and Scripture in turn "refers the
faithful back to the authority of the church with regard to a series of issues with
which the Apostles did not deal in writing." Noting Augustine's appeal to this
extrascriptural principle in his discussion of the baptism of heretics, Oberman
indicates the importance of this theological move for subsequent history: "Abelard
in the same manner would later treat Mariology, Bonaventura the *filioque* clause,
and Thomas the form of the sacrament of confirmation."[12]

The two traditions in the medieval debate. In the fourteenth century Basil's statement on the legitimacy of extrascriptural tradition and the two aspects of Augustine's thought gave rise to two competing conceptions as to the authority of
Scripture and tradition. Oberman labels these "Tradition I" and "Tradition II."[13]

Tradition I represents the single-source understanding in which the emphasis is
on the sufficiency of Scripture as the exclusive and final authority in the church.
Oberman explains, "The horizontal concept of Tradition is by no means denied

---

[10]St. Basil the Great, *De Spiritu Sancto*, in *Patrologia Graeca*, ed. J. P. Migne (Paris: n.p., 1857-1912), 32:188; *St. Basil
the Great On the Holy Spirit* (Crestwood, N.Y.: St. Vladimir's Seminary Press, 1980), pp. 98-99.
[11]Heiko Oberman, *The Harvest of Medieval Theology: Gabriel Biel and Late Medieval Nominalism*, rev. (Grand Rapids,
Mich.: Eerdmans, 1967), p. 369.
[12]Ibid., pp. 370-71.
[13]Ibid., p. 371.

here, but rather understood as the mode of reception of the *fides* or *veritas* contained in Scripture." With the rejection of any appeals to extrascriptural tradition, ecclesiastical tradition is not to be understood as "self-supporting" but rather "depends on its relation to the faith handed down by God in Holy Scripture."[14]

Tradition II maintains a two-source conception of authority in which both the written *and* the unwritten oral components of the apostolic message, as approved by the church, are deemed to be equally authoritative. Here the emphasis shifts from the interpreters of Scripture to the bishops, who determine the content of the authentic tradition. The church hierarchy is viewed as having its "own" oral tradition which is, to cite Oberman's characterization, "to a certain undefined extent independent, not of the Apostles, but of what is recorded in the canonical books. Ecclesiastical traditions, including canon law, are invested with the same degree of authority as that of Holy Scripture."[15]

Prior to the fourteenth century these two conceptions were held together without any conscious effort to distinguish between them or to integrate them. Nevertheless, the presence of the two competing outlooks in the church precipitated a rift between the theologians and the canon lawyers. In the fourteenth century this simmering difference came to a boil.

Throughout the early Middle Ages, canonists regularly refer to Basil's statement. In fact, the leading canon lawyer of the day, Ivo of Chartres, cited it in arguing for an equal standing for Scripture and extrascriptural oral tradition.[16] Ivo's assertion along with the Basilean passage on which it was based were, in turn, included by Gratian of Bologna in his *Decretum*. From this highly influential source the passage and its interpretation were widely disseminated into the standard textbooks of theologians as well as among canon lawyers.[17] As a result, medieval canon law came to stand not only on Scripture but also on tradition, understood as approved extrascriptural oral tradition handed down from the apostles and preserved in the church.

In contrast to the lawyers of the church, the medieval theologians clung to the understanding of theology that viewed it as the science of Scripture, as is evident in their use of the term *sacra pagina* to denote their discipline. Despite their tendency to comment on previous interpretations in such a way as to appear to give them authority, these theologians elevated Scripture as the final authority for matters of faith, and they retained a crucial distinction between text and gloss. In this way the

---

[14]Ibid., p. 372.
[15]Ibid., p. 373.
[16]Ivo of Chartres, *Patrologia Latina*, ed. J. P. Migne (Paris, 1844-1890), 161:283.
[17]Oberman, *Harvest of Medieval Theology*, p. 369.

medieval theologians were able to view the prior interpretive tradition as a vital component of theology without losing sight of the primacy of Scripture in their interpretive work. In their estimation final authority in questions of interpretation resided in the text of canonical Scripture.[18]

In the end, however, the theologians lost the battle to the canon lawyers. Oberman points out that this had as much to do with historical circumstances as with theological considerations. In the crucible of the Great Schism and during the final phase of the struggle between pope and emperor, canon lawyers were in high demand, perhaps even surpassing theologians in status at the papal *curia* and the royal courts.[19] In the later Middle Ages, Tradition II increasingly gained the upper hand, so much so that reformist supporters of Tradition I, such as Bradwardine, Wycliffe and Hus, were viewed as dangerous radicals by the church hierarchy.

The Elevation of Scripture over Tradition

By the sixteenth century the debate about Scripture and tradition had undergone further development.[20] The debate now surrounded three main schools of thought. The first, corresponding to Tradition I, maintained that all truth necessary for salvation could be found either explicitly or implicitly in Scripture, with tradition being required for the task of correctly interpreting Scripture, especially elements pertaining to salvation that were deemed to be merely implicit in the text. This is often referred to as the "classical" view. The second position, which accords with Tradition II, asserted that Christian revelation is only partly contained in the canonical text, with another part lodged in the oral traditions of the apostles passed down through their disciples. Finally, a third outlook came to prominence among curial canonists and theologians in the late Middle Ages. This view taught that the Holy Spirit abides constantly with the Catholic Church and gives new inspiration or illumination to it. Because the Spirit's work is mediated through Church leaders, the teaching of popes and councils is binding on the faithful, even when such teaching is unsupported by Scripture or the oral traditions of the apostles.[21]

The Protestant response. The increasing emphasis on extrascriptural tradition and papal authority led the northern European humanists of the fifteenth and sixteenth centuries to devise a reformist agenda characterized by the slogan *ad fontes*,

---

[18]For an outstanding study on biblical interpretation and the use of Scripture in the medieval period, see Beryl Smalley, *The Study of the Bible in the Middle Ages*, 2nd ed. (Oxford: Oxford University Press, 1952).

[19]Oberman, *Harvest of Medieval Theology*, p. 372.

[20]For an overview of the discussion on Scripture and tradition in the sixteenth century see, Yves Congar, *Tradition and Traditions* (New York: Macmillan, 1967).

[21]These three positions and their proponents are described in greater detail by Tavard, *Holy Writ*, pp. 47-66.

"back to the sources." This program gave clear priority to the teaching of Scripture as the source for Christian faith and was highly critical of the elevation of tradition in the practices of the medieval church.[22] The emphases of the humanists on the sufficiency of Scripture and the related rejection of the distorting influence of the medieval tradition were adopted by the early Reformers such as Luther and Zwingli, and provided the basis for their appeal to the principle of *sola scriptura*,[23] that is, the claim that Scripture alone was normative for the faith and life of the church.

The elevation of *sola scriptura* effectively set the agenda for what became Protestant antitraditionalism, at least as it characterized the attitude of the dissidents toward the theological developments of the patristic era and the Middle Ages.[24] Predictably, the implications of *sola scriptura* were often applied against those who were committed to the principle by other reformists who believed that one doctrine or another had been too greatly affected by tradition. Thus, Luther was criticized in this manner by Zwingli on the sacraments, Zwingli by the Zurich Anabaptists on infant baptism, and Calvin by Servetus on the doctrine of the Trinity.

The Reformers did not intend to sever themselves entirely from the Christian past. Nevertheless, since the sixteenth century, Protestants have generally looked on tradition with considerable suspicion. The polemic against the Catholic position on this issue came to be a staple of Protestant theological exposition. In many respects the denial of tradition as an authoritative source for theological construction, *contra* the Catholic dependence on tradition, has at times even constituted the Protestant *raison d'être*.

The undercutting of tradition in the Enlightenment. One further point must be made in this context. The severest attack on the concept of tradition did not come in the Reformation itself. Rather, it was launched in the Enlightenment. The appeal to reason that characterized the Age of Reason provided a powerful acid that effectively dissolved the role of tradition in theology in Protestant circles and increasingly among Roman Catholic modernists as well.

In many quarters of the Enlightenment, the reliance on received authorities, whether the Bible or the church, as a source for knowledge came to be viewed with scorn. In fact, acknowledgment of the role of such sources was even viewed by most theorists of the Age of Reason as intellectually irresponsible. The truly

---

[22]Tavard, *Holy Writ*, pp. 67-79.

[23]For an account of the influence of humanism on the Reformation, see Alister McGrath, *The Intellectual Origins of the European Reformation* (Oxford: Basil Blackwell, 1987), pp. 32-68.

[24]Jaroslav Pelikan, *The Vindication of Tradition* (New Haven, Conn.: Yale University Press, 1984), p. 11.

enlightened thinker was the *individual* who did not accept matters as true simply on the basis of pronouncements by so-called authorities. Instead, such persons would carefully scrutinize all knowledge claims, refuse to accept long-held convictions of society that have no basis except external authority, and demand that all assertions of truth be supported with rational evidence of an objective and unbiased nature.[25]

In the Enlightenment beliefs that could not be sustained by means of rational investigation were to be jettisoned as irrational or superstitious. In this context patterns of thought that embodied the intellectual traditions of the past were viewed with special suspicion. In short, the Enlightenment declared that the best approach to knowing, whether the field be theology or any other area of inquiry, is to cut oneself loose from the influence of tradition in order to pursue knowledge in an objective, dispassionate manner, unencumbered by the authorities of the past.[26]

The Renewed Conversation About Tradition

In the wake of the Council of Trent and the rise of Protestant scholasticism, the distinct Catholic and Protestant positions regarding the nature and role of tradition hardened. However, recent years have witnessed a renewal of ecumenical conversations regarding tradition. Avery Dulles reports that developments among Catholics took shape at two significant meetings, Vatican II and the Montreal Conference on Faith and Order, both held in the 1960s.

The watershed in the renewed ecumenical discussion was clearly the Second Vatican Council. Vatican II echoes Trent in affirming that both Scripture and tradition are to be "accepted and honored" with equal "devotion and reverence"[27] and affirms that the word of God exists in the twofold form of Scripture and tradition.[28] Commenting on the relationship between Scripture and tradition set forth by Vatican II, Dulles says that the Council describes tradition primarily in terms of its function, namely, that of preserving and handing on the word of God. He explains that this does not imply that tradition is not itself the word of God, or that it is merely derivative and secondary to the word of God in Scripture. Rather, Vatican II understood Scripture as formally insufficient and therefore concluded that tradition is necessary in order to gain "a sufficient grasp of the word of God, even though it be assumed that all revelation is somehow contained in Scripture." Hence, Dulles declared, "It is not from scripture alone that

---

[25]For a discussion and critique of objectivity, see Michael Polanyi, *Personal Knowledge: Towards a Post-Critical Philosophy* (Chicago: University of Chicago Press, 1958), pp. 3-17.

[26]Trevor Hart, *Faith Thinking: The Dynamics of Christian Theology* (Downers Grove, Ill.: InterVarsity, 1995), p. 168.

[27]Avery Dulles, *The Craft of Theology: From Symbol to System* (New York: Crossroad, 1992), p. 97.

[28]Ibid.

the Church draws its certainty about everything that has been revealed. Tradition is the means by which the full canon of the sacred books becomes known, and by which the meaning of the biblical text is more profoundly understood and more deeply penetrated."[29]

Dulles points out that Vatican II broke with the traditional two-source theory of revelation, while still acknowledging tradition as a conduit of revelation. The Montreal Conference on Faith and Order, in turn, acknowledged the indispensability of tradition as providing a proper context for the interpretation of Scripture.[30] In this way, Catholic scholars were able to contend against the older Catholic position that Scripture and tradition are not in fact two separate "reservoirs" each containing a certain portion of divinely revealed truth. Nevertheless, these thinkers continued to maintain, contrary to the traditional Protestant understanding of *sola scriptura*, that Christians read the Bible in the context of the Church and in the understanding of the use made of it by the Church. In their estimation, therefore, the Bible does not function alone.[31]

Dulles admits that these developments "do not totally overcome all the historic disputes between Catholics and Protestants." Nevertheless, he is convinced that they "go a long way toward reconciliation." For this reason, he concludes, "it is no longer safe to assume that either Protestants or Catholics adhere to the classical orthodoxies of their own churches, as expressed in past centuries."[32]

The Nature of Tradition

Although recent developments in the Roman Catholic understanding of tradition and Scripture represent a move in the right direction, significant difficulties still remain when the matter is viewed through evangelical eyes.[33] Yet the way forward does not lie in revisiting the question on which the discussion between Catholics and Protestants has generally focused, namely, Which of the two authorities, Scripture or church tradition, carries priority? Posing the matter in this manner is ultimately unhelpful in that it rests on a basically foundationalist understanding of the derivation of knowledge. The way forward in the midst of the impasse over tradition requires a shift to a nonfoundationalist conception.

---

[29]Ibid.

[30]Avery Dulles, "Scripture: Recent Protestant and Catholic Views," in *The Authoritative Word*, ed. Donald McKim (Grand Rapids, Mich.: Eerdmans, 1983), p. 250.

[31]Ibid., p. 260.

[32]Ibid., p. 250.

[33]For an example of the strong Catholic emphasis on the magisterial teaching office of the Church, see Aidan Nichols, *The Shape of Catholic Theology* (Edinburgh: T & T Clark, 1991), pp. 248-60. On the Protestant side the lack of engagement with tradition continues in both the mainline and evangelical contexts.

Tradition and Scripture

The Protestant principle of authority as articulated in the Westminster Confession embodies the classic Reformation link between Word and Spirit. The close connection that the Reformers sought to maintain between Word and Spirit means that the authority of Scripture is not ultimately invested in any particular quality that inheres in the text itself, but that its authority is based on the work of the Spirit who speaks in and through the text. Scripture is authoritative because it is the vehicle through which the Spirit speaks. That is to say, the authority of the Bible is ultimately the authority of the Spirit whose instrumentality it is.

This Reformation understanding of the relationship between Word and Spirit suggests the possibility of a parallel connection between the Spirit and tradition. The pathway to such an understanding, however, proceeds indirectly, via ecclesiology. The same Spirit whose work accounts for the formation of the Christian community empowers it to accomplish his purposes, which include the production and authorization of the biblical texts. This characterization of the role of the Spirit points toward an appropriate pneumatological-ecclesiological, and hence nonfoundational, understanding of tradition.

The faith community and the development of Scripture. Crucial in the development of such an understanding is an impulse from the widely held contemporary postulate as to how Scripture arose in the ancient faith communities.[34] Dulles, for example, speaks about the process of "traditioning" that began before the composition of the inspired books and continues without interruption through the ages.[35]

This observation stands as a reminder that the community precedes the production of the scriptural texts. In a certain sense the faith community was responsible for both the content of the biblical books and for the identification of particular texts for inclusion in an authoritative canon to which the community has chosen to make itself accountable. Apart from the community the texts would not have taken their particular and distinctive shape. Nor would there be a canon of authorized texts. In short, apart from the Christian community the Christian Bible would not exist.

Viewed from the historical perspective the Bible is the product of the community of faith that produced it. The compilation of Scripture occurred within the context of the faith community, and the biblical documents represent the self-understanding of the community in which they were developed. As Paul Achtemeier notes, the "major significance of the Bible is not that it is a book, but rather

---

[34]For a summary statement and its implications, see Stanley J. Grenz, *Revisioning Evangelical Theology* (Downers Grove, Ill.: InterVarsity, 1993), pp. 121-24.
[35]Dulles, *The Craft of Theology*, p. 96.

that it reflects the life of the community of Israel and the primitive church, as those communities sought to come to terms with the central reality that God was present with them in ways that regularly outran their ability to understand or cope."[36]

The Scriptures witness to the claim that they are the final written deposit of a trajectory—a traditioning—that incorporates a number of varied elements in their composition, including oral tradition and other source documents. The community of faith recognized these writings as authoritative materials, and these materials in turn were interpreted and reapplied to the various contemporary situations. Under the guidance of the Holy Spirit the community engaged in the task of preserving the canonical documents for the sake of the community's continuity. These writings contain the literary witness to the events that had given shape to the community, the prophetic interpretation of those events and the various context-sensitive instructions regarding the implications of these events to the community's ongoing life.

Awareness of the role of the community in the production of the writings of Scripture, that is, to the process of traditioning present already within the biblical era, leads to a broader concept of inspiration. Although inspiration includes the composition of particular writings produced by the biblical writers, it also incorporates the work of the triune God in the biblical faith communities leading them to bring Scripture into being. By extension the Spirit's overseeing work permeated the entire process that climaxed in the coming together of the canon as the book of the Christian community. Thus the church precedes Scripture chronologically and is responsible for its formation. Nevertheless, by its own corporate affirmation in the establishment of the canon, the church has made itself accountable to Scripture as the norming norm for its life, faith and practice. In this sense the text produces the community.

The Spirit and Scripture. What unifies Scripture and the communal tradition of the church is the Spirit. The Spirit stands behind both the formation of the community and the process of producing and compiling of the biblical documents into a single canon that forms the authoritative texts of the community.

Evangelicals readily speak about the ongoing work of the Spirit in attuning the contemporary community of faith to understand Scripture and to apply it afresh within the contemporary context. Yet the process of illumination present in the church today parallels that experienced by the ancient faith communities prior to the closing of the canon. Indeed, the Bible contains materials that represent the appropriation by the community of the writings and oral traditions of their heri-

---

[36]Paul J. Achtemeier, *The Inspiration of Scripture* (Philadelphia: Westminster Press, 1980), p. 92.

tage. At the same time a significant difference separates the experience of the ancient faith communities and the relationship of the postapostolic church to Scripture. The people of Israel and the early Christian communities engaged in the interpretive task *within* the process of the formation of the canon. Subsequent to the closure of the canon the Christian community receives the illumination of the Spirit speaking through canonical Scripture. Thus, in terms of the basic character of the relationship between Scripture and church tradition, canonical Scripture is on the one hand constitutive of the church, providing the primary narratives around which the life and faith of the Christian community is shaped and formed, and on the other hand is itself derived from that community and its authority. In the divine economy Scripture and tradition are in this manner inseparably bound together through the work of the Spirit.

For this reason, to suggest that the Protestant slogan *sola scriptura* implies an authority apart from the tradition of the church—that is, its creeds, teachings and liturgy—is to transform the formula into an oxymoron.[37] Separating Scripture and church in such a manner was certainly not the intention of the Reformers. Indeed, Oberman contends that the issue of the Reformation was not Scripture *or* tradition but rather the struggle between two differing concepts of tradition.[38] Similarly, Achtemeier declares with reference to the role of the community in the process that led to the formation and identification of Scripture, "If it is true, therefore, that the church, by its production of Scripture, created materials which stood over it in judgment and admonition, it is also true that Scripture would not have existed save for the community and its faith out of which Scripture grew. That means that church and Scripture are joint effects of the working out of the event of Christ."[39] And this "working out" is always carried on under the guidance and illumination of the Spirit.

Viewed from this perspective the authority of both Scripture and tradition is ultimately an authority derived from the work of the Spirit.[40] Each is part of an organic whole, so that even though Scripture and tradition are distinguishable, they are fundamentally inseparable. In short, neither Scripture or tradition is inherently authoritative in the foundationalist sense of providing self-evident, noninferential incorrigible grounds for constructing theological assertions.

[37]Robert Jenson, *Systematic Theology*, vol. 1: *The Triune God* (New York: Oxford University Press, 1997), p. 28.

[38]Heiko A. Oberman, "Quo Vadis? Tradition from Irenaeus to Humani Generis," *Scottish Journal of Theology* 16 (1963): 225-55.

[39]Achtemeier, *The Inspiration of Scripture*, p. 116.

[40]For a treatment of Scripture in the context of the work of the Holy Spirit, see Stanley J. Grenz, *Theology for the Community of God* (Grand Rapids, Mich.: Eerdmans, 2000), pp. 379-404.

The authority of each—tradition as well as Scripture—is contingent on the work of the Spirit, and both Scripture and tradition are fundamental components within an interrelated web of beliefs that constitutes the Christian faith. To misconstrue the shape of this relationship by setting Scripture over against tradition or by elevating tradition above Scripture is to fail to comprehend properly the work of the Spirit. Moreover, to do so is, in the final analysis, a distortion of the authority of the triune God in the church. A nonfoundational understanding of Scripture and tradition locates ultimate authority only in the action of the triune God. If we must speak of a "foundation" of the Christian faith at all, then we must speak of neither Scripture nor tradition in and of themselves, but only of the triune God who is disclosed in polyphonic fashion through Scripture, the church and even the world, albeit always in accordance with the normative divine self-disclosure through Scripture.[41]

Tradition and Theology

The Spirit who guided the community in the process of the composition, compilation and canonization of Scripture continues to direct the contemporary embodiment of that community by speaking through Scripture. In this way the Spirit enables the church to fulfill its task of living as the people of God in the various historical and cultural locations in which it is situated. This broader conception of the Spirit's illumination in the production of Scripture and the ongoing life of the community leads not only to a more adequate understanding of the process by which Scripture came into being, but also to a greater appreciation for the theological significance of the tradition of the Christian community. More particularly, tradition provides an important reference point as well as a deposit of resources for the contemporary community in its quest to understand the meaning of Scripture and engage in the task of theology in the context of the complex issues that characterize the present age.

The concept of tradition. Viewing tradition as carrying theological significance and acknowledging tradition as a reference point for the community raises again the question as to what is meant by the designation "church tradition." That is, it leads us back to the concept of tradition itself.

According to Alasdair MacIntyre, a tradition begins with some contingent historical starting point, most often a text or a set of related texts, and develops from this starting point as a historically extended, socially embodied argument as to

---

[41]On the development of the notion of God as the foundation for theology in the thought of Karl Barth, see William Stacy Johnson, *The Mystery of God: Karl Barth and the Postmodern Foundations of Theology* (Louisville: Westminster John Knox, 1997).

how best to interpret and apply the formative text(s).[42] From this conception of tradition in general, we can conceive of the Christian tradition as the history of the interpretation and application of canonical Scripture by the Christian community, the church, as it listens to the voice of the Spirit speaking through the text. More specifically, we might define the Christian tradition as the ongoing historical attempts by the Christian community to explicate and translate faithfully the first-order language, symbols and practices of the Christian faith—by means of the interaction among community, text and culture—into the various social and cultural contexts in which the community has been situated.

In this understanding tradition is viewed not as static but as a living, dynamic reality in which development and growth occurs. A tradition grows as it confronts new challenges and faces new situations over the course of time and in various contexts. The Christian tradition is thus characterized by both continuity and change, as the faith community under the guidance of the Spirit grapples with the interaction between Scripture and the particular challenges of changing situations. D. M. Williams offers this helpful summary of the implication of the dynamic understanding of tradition: "If it is true that the Tradition is what it is because of its active development within concrete, living communities, then the Tradition will itself be a construction of how the church addressed its present circumstances by utilizing what it has received. In other words, the Tradition is always in process of dialoguing with itself as it encounters each new crisis that confronted the church in history."[43] In short, tradition entails the bringing of the resources from the past into the service of the church in the present.

Tradition as biblical reflection and biblical beliefs. One crucial "resource from the past" is the wealth of historical reflection on the biblical texts preserved in the church's liturgy and literature, especially as this reflection focuses on Jesus Christ as the incarnate Word. Williams once again offers an insightful comment: "In the final analysis, then, the Tradition denotes the acceptance and the handing over of God's Word, Jesus Christ (*tradere Christum*), and how this took concrete forms in the apostles' preaching (*kerygma*), in the Christ-centered reading of the Old Testament, in the celebration of baptism and the Lord's Supper, and in the doxological, doctrinal, hymnological and credal forms by which the declaration of the mystery of God Incarnate was revealed for our salvation."[44]

This historical deposit puts us in contact with the wisdom and insights that

---

[42]Alasdair MacIntyre, *Whose Justice? Which Rationality?* (Notre Dame: University of Notre Dame Press, 1988); and *Three Rival Versions of Moral Enquiry: Encyclopaedia, Genealogy, and Tradition* (Notre Dame: University of Notre Dame Press, 1990).

[43]Williams, *Retrieving the Tradition*, p. 37.

[44]Ibid., p. 36.

resulted from the Spirit-guided reflection on Scripture that characterized our fore-bears in the faith. As Gabriel Fackre rightly notes, this gift of the Christian commu-nity "comes to us in creed and council, catechism and confession, dialogue and proclamation. It meets us in the ancient lore of the Church and the present learnings of the Christian community. This common life and its wisdom, brought to us by the constant activity of the Holy Spirit, is a fundamental resource in our engagement with the biblical source."[45] Insofar as church tradition is the product of the ongoing reflection of the Christian community on the biblical texts, it is in many respects an extension of the authority of Scripture. Thus, Oden suggests that the history of the-ology may be viewed in large measure as the history of biblical exegesis.[46]

In addition to mediating the *kerygma*, the narrative of God's redemptive action toward human beings, Scripture also provides a record of some of the basic Chris-tian teachings and practices that developed in the earliest church. The canonical documents bear witness both to these teachings as well as to the concern of the early church that these basic teachings be communicated from one generation of Christian believers to the next. The narratives of God's redemptive activity together with the basic teachings and practices of the early Christian community constitute what Scripture calls "the faith which was once for all delivered to the saints" (Jude 3). The sense of passing on the teachings of the community from gen-eration to generation is the most basic expression of the operation of tradition.

Tradition as engagement with the historical-cultural context. Although the commit-ment to pass on "the faith once delivered to the saints" is an important component of the Christian tradition, it can also be misconstrued and as a consequence used as the basis for oversimplifying a complex phenomenon. The assumption that tra-dition comprises an unchanged body of Christian doctrines articulated by the ancient church for all time, while in one sense true, all-too-readily exchanges the dynamic character of tradition for an erroneous, static conception.

The dynamism of tradition, in contrast, emerges out of its very nature within the life of the faith community. From its inception the Christian community has been concerned with the task of proclaiming its message to the ends of the earth, so that all humankind might know and experience the love of the Creator. In keeping with this concern the church has undertaken the mission of establishing communities of believers throughout the world. As a consequence the Christian church as been located in a wide variety of social, historical and cultural con-texts, and it has faced the numerous challenges presented by these various situa-

---

[45] Gabriel Fackre, *The Christian Story: A Narrative Interpretation of Basic Christian Doctrine*, 3rd ed. (Grand Rapids, Mich.: Eerdmans, 1996), p. 18.
[46] Thomas C. Oden, *Systematic Theology: The Living God* (San Francisco: Harper & Row, 1987), p. xiii.

tions. These challenges have called on the Christian community to exercise wisdom and creative judgment in addressing questions in a manner that best promotes its mission. A canonical example of this activity is the Jerusalem Council (Acts 15), which was occasioned by the need for the church to address the cultural issues raised by the conversion of Gentiles and their coexistence in the community of the new covenant with ethnic Jews who were concerned to preserve their social distinctiveness. Viewed from this perspective tradition is an ongoing deposit of "wisdom" emerging from the dynamic movement of the community under the Spirit's guidance.

The multicultural character of the Christian community alerts us to an additional insight regarding tradition. All expressions of the faith are contextualized. This includes not only the confessions, creeds and theological constructions of the church, but also the content of the biblical documents themselves. All texts of the Christian faith were formulated within the social, cultural, linguistic and philosophical frameworks of the times in which they were produced. Rather than detracting from the authority of Scripture as the inspired and canonically constitutive standard of the Christian community, this observation merely alerts us to the incarnational character of the Bible and the challenges of contextualizing its message into new, varied and changing settings. But it also calls for a nuanced understanding of the tradition of the church as a source for theology.

Tradition as Theological (Re)source

These considerations lead us finally to the central question: How then does tradition serve as a theological (re)source? In what manner does tradition, viewed from a nonfoundationalist perspective, take its rightful place in theological construction?

Tradition as the Hermeneutical Context for Theology

Stated simply, the proper role of tradition is to serve as the hermeneutical context for theological engagement. Church tradition is not the final arbiter of theological questions, as would be the case if tradition were the foundation for Christian theology. Ultimately, the role of arbiter must be reserved for the Spirit, and more specifically for the Spirit speaking in Scripture. Nevertheless, tradition contributes to the process as it forms the hermeneutical trajectory in which the task of theological discourse transpires. Moreover, tradition provides this context as constructive theologians examine the history of Christian worship, the history of Christian theology and past theological formulations, for the sake of articulating the Christian belief mosaic in the contemporary context.

The history of worship. One of the most significant components of the Christian tradition is the history of worship and liturgy. Throughout the history of the church, worship—both in content and in form—has provided a context in which theologians carried out their work, and it has offered insight into the primary commitments of the church throughout the ages.

Recently, a renewed emphasis on the role of personal faith in the theological task has reminded us that theologians neither produce systems of theology in isolation from the community nor apart from their involvement in the worshiping life of the community. On the contrary, theologians are part of a particular community that prays and worships, and this context informs the nature and shape of their theological reflection and their theological constructions.

The phrase *lex orandi, lex credendi* ("the way you pray determines what you believe") encapsulates the intimate connection between the life of prayer and the content of faith. More importantly in this context, it points toward the crucial interaction between theology and all dimensions of worship. What Christians believe shapes the content and approach of their worship, and their worship reflects what they believe. This alerts us to the importance of liturgical history as providing insight into the first order commitments of the Christian community that have shaped its theological reflection.

Certain strands of contemporary theology have evidenced a renewed interest in the relationship between worship and theology. Of special importance here is the work of Geoffrey Wainwright, whose systematic theology is written from the perspective of the liturgical forms of the church.[47] Wainwright examines the connection between liturgy and theology and draws attention to the ways in which the earliest Christian communities incorporated theological motifs into their worship. He points out that the liturgy of the church is neither simply nor purely emotive in character, but that it also includes intellectual elements and that the connection between the intellectual and the emotive is entirely natural. Wainwright suggests that doing theology from a liturgical perspective serves to ground theology in the life and faith of the historical and ecumenical Christian community by pointing to the beliefs and concerns that have been expressed through the forms and practices of Christian worship.

The history of theology. Another aspect of the tradition of the Christian church that is particularly beneficial for the theological enterprise is the complex and multifaceted story of theological history that describes the responses of the Christian community to past challenges. Throughout its history the church has continually sought to understand and proclaim the gospel in the context of the specific cultural situations in which it has been situated. The story of theological history is the nar-

---

[47]Geoffrey Wainwright, *Doxology: The Praise of God in Worship, Doctrine, and Life* (New York: Oxford University Press, 1980).

rative of the attempts by the Christian community to explicate the gospel message within these shifting historical circumstances.[48]

This theological history is important for a number of reasons. Previous theological models and constructions are helpful for theology in that they provide the present community with a record of some of the failures of past efforts that have emerged over the course of time. Ideas have consequences. But the long-term consequences of ideas are seldom fully discernible. The history of theology provides the opportunity to observe the long-term consequences of various theological formulations and approaches to theology in a number of different contexts.

Some of these formulations and approaches have clearly failed to sustain the community throughout its history. For example, overly accommodationist understandings of the relationship between theology and culture have had devastating long-term consequences for the church. Perhaps the most telling example of such accommodation has been the close linking of Christian faith with the goals and aspirations of particular nationalities or political ideologies at the cost of faithfulness to the gospel and the integrity of the community.[49]

The history of theology also brings us into contact with another type of failure, namely, what has traditionally been labeled *heresy*. The Christian community did not simply receive orthodox belief and pass it on in a static fashion. Rather, throughout its history the community has struggled to determine the content and application of orthodoxy in ways that are faithful to the canonical narratives. This process grew through the challenges presented by those whose teachings were eventually deemed heretical. To cite one especially important example, understanding the development of orthodox conceptions of the Trinity requires that we grasp those views that both prompted and shaped the formation of the early conceptions of this doctrine. Awareness of those thinkers whose formulations of the faith have been rejected by the Christian community remains instructive for contemporary theology. As Roger Olson rightly concludes, it is "almost impossible to appreciate the meaning of orthodoxy without understanding the heresies that forced its development."[50]

Another significance of the history of heresy is the realization that, paraphrasing Luther, God sometimes strikes significant blows with a crooked stick. Those who have held views that have been declared heretical by the church have often

---

[48]For an excellent recent account of the narrative of theological history, see Roger Olson, *The Story of Christian Theology: Twenty Centuries of Tradition & Reform* (Downers Grove, Ill.: InterVarsity Press, 1999).

[49]For a fascinating study of this phenomenon as it manifested itself in Nazi Germany, see Robert P. Ericksen, *Theologians Under Hitler: Gerhard Kittel, Paul Althaus and Emanuel Hirsch* (New Haven, Conn.: Yale University Press, 1985).

[50]Olson, *Story of Christian Theology*, p. 21.

been of great importance in the development of theology. One of the most striking examples of this is the work of the early Alexandrian theologian Origen, who has been hailed as the first systematic or constructive theologian in the history of the church. Although many of his ideas were declared unorthodox after his death, his speculative theology provided the impetus for much of the theological reflection of the early Christian community, and his essential vision of the Christian faith has remained highly influential throughout the history of the church.

Classic theological formulations and symbols. In addition to the negative role of warning against past failure, the history of theology fulfills the positive function of pointing out directions that hold promise for the contemporary attempts of the community to fulfill its theological calling.

Especially important in this respect are those formulations and symbols that have come to be regarded as "classic" theological statements. These have survived the test of time and thereby have remained an integral part of the community's life in its various cultural locations. For example, the near universal acceptance by the worldwide Christian community of ecumenical statements such as the Apostles' Creed and the Nicene Creed serves to make these "classic" symbols of the faith a vital resource for theology. Gabriel Fackre highlights this aspect of the tradition viewed as an ecumenical consensus inherited from the past.

> Found in both official documents and formal statements of the undivided Church, such as the Apostles' and Nicene Creeds, the doctrines of the Person of Christ and the trinity, the patterns of affirmation implicit in the worship and working of faith of the church universal, tradition is a weighty resource in Christian theology.[51]

These classic statements and symbols of the historical community stand as milestones in the thought and life of the church universal and therefore have a special ongoing significance for the work of theology.[52]

The role of classic theological formulations is brought into sharper relief when we recall the broader historical implications of Christian confessions of faith for our own theological affirmations. Throughout the history of the church, Christian believers from successive generations and representing various social, cultural locations have confessed faith in the God revealed in Christ. In this act they have participated in the faith of the one church and have been coconfessors with all who have acknowledged the one faith throughout the ages. So also in confessing the one faith of the church in the present, we become the contemporary embodiment of

---

[51]Fackre, *Christian Story*, p. 18.

[52]For a compilation of such "milestones" in the history of the church in its various expressions see John Leith, *Creeds of the Churches: A Reader in Christian Doctrine from the Bible to the Present*, 3rd ed. (Philadelphia: John Knox Press, 1982).

the legacy of faith that spans the ages and encompasses the host of faithful believers. Rather than standing alone in this act, we confess our faith in unison and solidarity with the whole company of the church universal. Hence, although our expression of faith is to be contemporary, in keeping with our task of speaking the biblical message to the age in which we live, it must also place us in continuity with the faith of the one people of God, including both our forebears who have made this confession in ages past and our successors who will do so in the future. When we engage in the second-order task of theology, therefore, we do so conscious that we stand in the context of a community of faith that extends through the centuries and that has engaged in this task before us. Because we are members of this continuous historical community, the theological tradition of the church must be a crucial component in the construction of our contemporary theological statements, so that we might maintain our theological or confessional unity with the one church of Jesus Christ.

Statements that have stood the test of time and have received broad affirmation among Christians of many generations and in many contexts comprise a type of "ecumenical theology." This ecumenical theology has come to expression in the great corpus of theological literature written over the centuries. The library of theological writings can be read with great benefit in the contemporary context, providing a considerable resource for the task of theology that, with few exceptions, has been largely untapped in Protestant theology.[53]

One caveat must be voiced here, however. Despite their great stature and the important role they play as a theological resource, past creeds, confessions and theological formulations in and of themselves are not binding on subsequent theology or on the church. Nor dare they usurp the place of canonical Scripture as the community's constitutive authority, for they must always and continually be tested by the norming norm, the Spirit speaking in and through Scripture. In addition, in our reading of the great theological literature we must keep in mind the culturally situated nature of all such statements and hence that they must be understood within their particular historical and cultural contexts. For this reason it is the *intent* of the creeds, confessions and formulations, and not the specific construction and order of their wording, that is significant for contemporary theology.

Tradition as a Hermeneutical Trajectory

A nonfoundationalist conception of tradition views the tradition of the church

---

[53]A fine example of engaging the resources found in this body of historical theological literature to address contemporary theological issues is Ellen Charry, *By the Renewing of Your Minds: The Pastoral Function of Christian Doctrine* (New York: Oxford University Press, 1997).

above all as the hermeneutical trajectory in the context of which the theological task of the community is pursued. What remains to be noted are the central characteristics of tradition when the concept is viewed from this perspective. The non-foundationalist turn suggests that church tradition provides a hermeneutical trajectory for theology that is open-ended, eschatologically directed and performatively operative.

Tradition as an "open" trajectory. The first characteristic of tradition emerges from the caveat that was voiced at the conclusion of the previous section. The acknowledgment that all theological formulations are culturally embedded stands as a challenge to those Christian confessional bodies and denominations that ascribe the kind of defining authority to past confessional statements which demands complete subscription to these formulations as a prerequisite for participation in the fellowship. Such groups run the risk of transforming their creeds, even if unofficially or unintentionally, into *de facto* substitutes for Scripture. Furthermore, in the interest of securing an absolute authority in the church beyond the Scriptures themselves, this approach can actually hinder such a community from hearing the voice of the Spirit speaking in new ways through the biblical text.

One especially significant confessional group that should be noted in this context is the broader Reformed tradition. Reformed denominations are often strongly confessional, sometimes to the point of falling into the ironic position of evidencing methodological commitments similar to the medieval Catholic position rejected by their Reformation forebears. At the heart of the Reformed tradition, however, is the principle that the truly Reformed church must always be reforming itself in accordance with the teaching of Scripture. As Jan Rohls points out in contrasting the Reformed and Lutheran traditions, in Lutheranism "the process of confessional development came to a conclusion with the Formula of Concord (1577) and the Book of Concord (1580). On the Reformed side there is nothing that corresponds to this conclusion."[54]

The crucial distinction Rohls highlights is akin to the differentiation Jack Stotts draws between open and closed confessional traditions. According to Stotts, closed traditions hold "a particular statement of beliefs to be adequate for all times and places." An open tradition, in contrast, "anticipates that what has been confessed in a formally adopted confession takes its place in a confessional lineup, preceded by statements from the past and expectant of more to come as times and circumstances change."[55] Stotts then adds that an open confessional tradition understands

---

[54] Jan Rohls, *Reformed Confessions: Theology from Zurich to Barmen*, trans. John Hoffmeyer (Louisville, Ky.: Westminster John Knox, 1998), p. 9.
[55] Jack L. Stotts, "Introduction: Confessing after Barmen" in Rohls, *Reformed Confessions*, p. xi.

its obligation to develop and adopt new confessions in accordance with shifting circumstances. Although such confessions are "extraordinarily important" for the
integrity, identity and faithfulness of the church, "they are also acknowledged to be
relative to particular times and places." In addition, he adds that the "occasional"
nature of confessions is a reminder "that statements of faith are always subordinate
in authority to scripture."[56]

The concept of an open confessional tradition brings into relief the major function of tradition in the task of theology. In contrast to the demand for a strict subscription to a particular symbol or confession characteristic of a "closed"
confessional tradition, a nonfoundational tradition is by its very nature "open." And
this openness in turn preserves the dynamic nature of tradition.

Tradition's eschatological orientation. We have argued that the tradition of the
Christian community provides the context in which to hear the Spirit's voice
speaking through the canonical texts of Scripture in continuity with the church
universal. This context, we added, comprises the Spirit-directed hermeneutical
trajectory for theological reflection. Furthermore, in keeping with the Reformation commitment to Tradition I (to cite Oberman's category), we claimed that
the hermeneutical trajectory is not institutionalized, as Roman Catholic theologians have argued, but must be discerned through participation in the fellowship
of the Christian community and in its practices of worship, prayer, Bible reading
and service as well as through study and reflection on the symbols and literature
of the tradition.[57] That is to say, the task of Christian theology begins with commitment to, and participation in, the ongoing life of the church.[58] To participate in
the fellowship of the Christian community, however, is to participate in its hermeneutical trajectory and to embrace the shared responsibilities of maintaining continuity with the community of the past and addressing the context in which the
community is situated.

All this, however, must be viewed in accordance with the eschatological directedness of the dynamic called "church tradition." The church is a pilgrim people en
route to the eschatological consummation of the divine work in the world.
Throughout the ebb and flow of the history of the church, the Spirit is at work
effecting the divine program and bringing the people of God into a fuller compre-
hension of the implications of the gospel. Until the consummation the church
must grapple with the meaning and implications of the biblical message for its

---

[56]Stotts, "Introduction," p. xi.

[57]On the importance of participating in the practices of the Christian community as crucial for engagement in the
task of theology, see the works of James Wm. McClendon, particularly *Systematic Theology: Ethics* (Nashville: Abingdon, 1986).

[58]Hart, *Faith Thinking*, pp. 192-94.

ever-changing context as its listens patiently and expectantly for the voice of the Spirit speaking afresh through Scripture, but also in continuity with the Spirit-guided trajectory of Christian tradition. This eschatological perspective serves as a reminder that to understand the tradition of the church as providing a hermeneutical trajectory is to acknowledge the importance of tradition without elevating it to a position of final authority.

The unfolding of the ongoing trajectory of the church is a dialectic involving continuity and change. In his overview of the history of theology Roger Olson tells the story of the conversations and conflicts between "traditionalists," who were particularly concerned with maintaining the continuity of the faith, and "reformers," whose concern was primarily focused on correcting past formulations and addressing their particular context.[59] Church tradition has taken shape within the to-and-fro movement of these conversations in the midst of the life and ministry of the Christian community. But this process continues throughout the entire penultimate age in which we are living. Gabriel Fackre describes the on-going theological dynamic that characterizes the life of the church and contributes to the development of church tradition prior to the consummation:

> The circle of tradition is not closed, for the Spirit's ecclesial Work is not done. Traditional doctrine develops as Christ and the Gospel are viewed in ever fresh perspective. Old formulations are corrected, and what is passed on is enriched. The open-endedness, however, does not overthrow the ancient landmarks. As tradition is a gift of the Spirit, its trajectory moves in the right direction, although it has not arrived at its destination.[60]

In short, at the heart of tradition and of the role of tradition in theology is the eschatological directedness of the Spirit's work in guiding the community of faith into the purposes and intentions of God that comprise a divinely given *telos* that is ultimately realized only at the consummation. The eschatological-directedness of the community as a whole gives a similar character to the theological reflection that becomes church tradition.

Tradition and performance. One final aspect of the function of the hermeneutical trajectory in the task of theology remains to be noted, a dimension that emerges from the metaphor of performance.[61] Tradition provides an interpretive

---

[59]This dialectical tension is highlighted in the subtitle of Olson's work *The Story of Christian Theology: Twenty Centuries of Tradition & Reform.* Olson has also used this distinction between traditionalists and reformers to characterize current tensions in contemporary evangelical theology (Roger Olson, "The Future of Evangelical Theology," *Christianity Today* [February 9, 1998], pp. 40-48.)

[60]Fackre, *Christian Story,* pp. 18-19.

[61]For the development of the metaphor of performance with respect to Scripture, see Frances Young, *The Art of Performance: Towards a Theology of Holy Scripture* (London: Darton, Longman & Todd, 1990).

context for the task of living out or *performing* the deepest intentions of an established, historical community.

The ultimate purpose of theology is not simply to establish right belief but to assist the Christian community in its vocation to *live* as the people of God in the particular social-historical context in which they are situated. The goal of theology is to facilitate and enable authentic performance of the Christian faith by the community in its various cultural locations. Tradition provides an essential component in this process.

Like the performance of a Mozart symphony that has only one score but many possible interpretations, the text of Scripture has been subject to numerous interpretations over the centuries. The score of the symphony is, of course, authoritative. Nevertheless, it demands performance if it is to realize the intention for which it was produced, and performance requires interpretation. At the same time, not all interpretations of Mozart have equal integrity in the history of the performance of his works; some are too radical or idiosyncratic. Determinations as to the legitimacy or illegitimacy of particular interpretations and performances emerge in the context of tradition.

Frances Young offers a helpful perspective on the performative metaphor. She writes, "For classic performance, tradition is indispensable. A creative artist will certainly bring something inspired to the job, but an entirely novel performance would not be a rendering of the classic work. Traditions about appropriate speed and dynamics are passed from master (or mistress) to pupil, from one generation to another, and a radical performance will be deliberate reaction against those traditions if it violates them."[62] The tradition of the Christian community functions in much the same manner. It establishes a context for authentic interpretation and performance of the biblical message and its implications, which allows for creativity in addressing new situations while providing a basis for identifying interpretation which is not consonant with the historic position of the community.

N. T. Wright suggests a model of biblical authority that moves along similar lines.[63] He uses the analogy of a five-act Shakespeare play in which the first four are extant but the fifth has been lost. In this model the performance of the fifth act would be facilitated not by the writing of a script that "would freeze the play into one form" but by the recruitment of "highly trained, sensitive, and experienced Shakespearean actors" who would immerse themselves in the first four acts and then be told *"to work out a fifth act for themselves."*[64] The first four acts would serve as

---

[62]Ibid., p. 45.
[63]N. T. Wright, "How Can the Bible be Authoritative?" *Vox Evangelica* 21 (1991): 7-32.
[64]Ibid., p. 18.

the "authority" for the play, but not in the sense of demanding that the actors "should repeat the earlier parts of the play over and over again." Instead, the authority of these extant acts would consist in the fact of an as yet unfinished drama that contained its own impetus, its own forward movement, that demanded to be concluded in the proper manner but which required of the actors a responsible entering in to the story as it stood, in order to first understand how the threads could appropriately be drawn together, and then to put that understanding into effect by speaking and acting with both *innovation* and *consistency*.[65] Wright then suggests that this model closely corresponds to the pattern of the biblical narrative.

Extending the performance model to encompass not only Scripture but also tradition brings into focus the role of church tradition in the task of theology. A key component of Wright's model, although not one he emphasizes, is the role of tradition. His actors were not only immersed in the first acts of the play, the textual authority, but also in the Shakespearean interpretive *tradition*, which also functions in an authoritative fashion, albeit a secondary one, in the performance of the final act. Viewed in the light of the Christian life as performance, the Christian tradition becomes the historically extended, socially embodied context in accordance with which the contemporary community is being called to interpret, apply and live out—that is, to perform in the here and now—the communally formative narratives given in the canonical texts.

To conclude: The Protestant movement in general and evangelicalism in particular have rightly maintained that the Spirit speaking in and through Scripture is the norming norm for Christian faith and life. Although Scripture retains the position of primacy, the tradition of the community provides a crucial and indispensable (re)source for theology. Tradition forms the hermeneutical context and trajectory for the construction of a contemporary theology that is faithfully Christian. Tradition therefore plays a crucial, albeit nonfoundational, role in every theological construction that fulfills Thomas Oden's vision for an orthodoxy that is not only "postcritical" but also truly Christian.

---

[65]Ibid., p. 9.

Sixteen

Theology as Worship

The Place of Theology
in a Postmodern University

ALAN G. PADGETT

If you are a theologian, you will pray truly. And if you pray truly, you are a theologian.
EVAGRIUS PONTICUS

Divine theology brings into harmony the voices of those who praise God's majesty.
DIADOCHUS OF PHOTIKE

I t is an honor and a privilege to contribute to Thomas Oden's *festschrift*. He was my favorite teacher in systematic theology at Drew University, and I have learned so much from him over the years. It was wonderful to be at Drew among his students, just as he was publishing his *Agenda for Theology* and working out his new position in "postmodern orthodoxy."[1] From Professors Oden and James Pain I first learned to honor and study the great mothers and fathers of the first ecumenical centuries of Christian thought, and this orientation has never left my theological reflection.

In this chapter I will take a page from Oden's "postmodern" orientation to classic Christian sources, asking the questions "What is the true nature of theology?

---

[1]Thomas C. Oden, *Agenda for Theology* (San Francisco: Harper & Row, 1979). This was later revised as *After Modernity . . . What?* (Grand Rapids, Mich.: Zondervan, 1990).

Where is the true home of theological reflection?"[2] This is not a question about geography, but a spatial metaphor for revisiting the "agenda of theology." In particular, I wish to explore theology's self-understanding of its nature and purpose. In brief, my answer will be that *theology is a form of worship.* Perhaps I ought to say, good theology can and should be a form of worship, a form of giving glory to God. In developing this view of the nature of our theological task, I will also discuss the role theology thus understood can play in a postmodern university.

Theology as Worship

What is theology all about? I believe no reasonable answer to this question can be given until we settle what the aim, goal or *telos* of theology is. Philosophy of science has taught me that our understanding of methods and principles in science is dependent to a great deal on our grasp of the *aims* of that science. Our first question then is this: What is the aim of theology? I am going to defend a traditional answer: The goal of theology is to praise and worship God.[3]

Theology is concerned with knowing God and with the study of God. But for too long that study has been isolated from the spiritual and religious quest to know God in a personal way. The spiritual and religious quest, this hunger for God and for the truth of God, is the true root of theological reflection. One example of the divorce between knowing God in a spiritual and in a "scientific" way is the division between Protestant orthodoxy and Pietism in the seventeenth century. The roots of this breach go back to the founding of university faculties of theology in Europe. But this is a story we cannot detail here.[4] After the end of the Enlightenment project, in our postmodern times we have been given the opportunity to heal this breach in the heart of theology. Once again, we can seek to know God truly in both an existential and an academic way.[5] Only this holistic approach will, in the end, satisfy our spiritual and intellectual needs. I am in full agreement with the Westminster Divines when, in their Shorter Catechism (question one), they taught that the chief end of humans is to know God

---

[2] Earlier thoughts on this topic were stimulated by three summers with the Consultation on Teaching Theology (1996-1998), Wabash College, funded by the Lilly Endowment through the Wabash Center for Teaching and Learning in Theology and Religion. Many thanks to Raymond Williams, William Placher, Lucinda Huffaker and Sherry Macy for their hospitality, and to my colleagues and friends in the consultation for their stimulating discussion.

[3] See also Geoffrey Wainwright, *Doxology* (New York: Oxford University Press, 1980); Dan Hardy and David Ford, *Praising and Knowing God* (Philadelphia: Westminster Press, 1985); and Frans Jozef van Beeck, *God Encountered*, vol. 1: *Understanding the Christian Faith* (Collegeville, Minn.: Liturgical Press, 1989), chap. 7.

[4] See one version of this story in Edward Farley, *Theologia* (Philadelphia: Fortress, 1983). Another version is found in David Kelsey, *Between Athens and Berlin* (Grand Rapids, Mich.: Eerdmans, 1993).

[5] See David Kelsey, *To Understand God Truly: What's Theological about a Theological School* (Louisville, Ky.: Westminster John Knox, 1992)

and enjoy him forever. This point has deep roots, going back to Aquinas and Augustine. Both of them argued that the ultimate human happiness lies in the knowledge and love of God.[6] As Augustine states in *On Christian Doctrine:*[7]

> For the divinely established rule of love says, "you shall love your neighbour as yourself" but God "with all your heart, and with all your soul, and with all your mind" so that you may devote [confero] all your thoughts and all your life and all your understanding to the one from whom you actually receive the things that you devote to him.

I propose to follow Augustine and locate the proper home of theology in the greatest commandment, that is, in the commandment to love the Lord with all our mind (among other things). Even before Augustine, Clement of Alexandria taught that the true Christian theologian (gnostic) "is before all things a lover of God."[8] The purpose of the section of his unfinished *Stromateis* from which this quote is taken was "to prove that the gnostic alone is holy and pious, worshipping the true God as befits him; and the worship which befits God includes both loving God and being loved by him" (*Stromateis* 7.3). I think we are within our rights to interpret Clement's "Christian Gnosis" as the discipline of Christian theology itself, for our day.

The thesis I am putting forth, then, has deep roots in the classical Christian tradition. This basic ecumenical understanding of the knowledge of God grounded in the love of God leads to my larger point: the knowledge of God comes within the life of prayer, worship, praise and obedience that is the spiritual life of the church. For these things are the way that the church loves God. Thus the knowledge of God, and so also theology, finds its proper home in the worship of God.[9]

The praise and worship of God, in both Scripture and in our Christian liturgy, includes telling the wonderful deeds of the Lord and extolling his glorious divinity. The Psalms are filled with such theology, and we find it often in Paul and in the book of Revelation. Take Psalm 8, an early hymn of praise, as an example. Mixed together in this psalm are both the praise of God and a truth-telling about the majesty and glory of God. The name of the Lord is majestic in all the earth, and the psalmist praises God as Creator of all: the starry heavens, the human race and all living things. This hymn ends as it began: "O Lord, our Lord, how majestic is your name in all the earth!" Notice that the praise of God is grounded in the truth about

---

[6]Aquinas *Summa Theologiae* Ia-IIae.Q3; Augustine *City of God* 19.26.

[7]Augustine *De Doctrina Christiana* 1.22, ed. R. P. H. Green (Oxford: Clarendon Press, 1995), p. 30.

[8]Clement *Stromateis* 7.4; in *Alexandrian Christianity*, ed. J. E. L. Oulton and H. Chadwick, Library of Christian Classics 2 (Philadelphia: Westminster Press, 1954), p. 95.

[9]I am in great sympathy with Ellen Charry's notion of the sapiential and salutary function of theology in *By the Renewing of Your Minds* (New York: Oxford University Press, 1998).

God, that is, in theology. To rightly worship God, we need to know the story of God. Right worship implies sound theology, and sound theology can and should be a kind of worship. The purpose of theology, I am pressing, is to know God, to tell the truth about God and to give glory to God: in short, to worship God.

The English word *worship* is related to the word *worth*. To worship someone is, etymologically, to tell of their worth, esteem, honor and renown. In biblical language the concept of worship is conveyed for the most part either in bodily terms, such as "bowing down before" (e.g., Gen. 22:5, John 9:38), or it comes under words like *glorify* or *praise* (e.g., hallelujah). Like the English word for worship, the biblical terms *to glorify* or *to praise* also suggest a telling of the wonderful honor, esteem and magnificence of the one who is to be praised.[10]

This basic point is also clear in the history of Christian liturgy and hymnody. First-class hymns are also first-class theology! The best liturgy has always been grounded in and expressed the best theology. To take just one example from the service of Holy Communion: in the Great Thanksgiving there is a long section on the mighty deeds of God in Jesus Christ which form the foundation of the sacrament. My argument is that this giving of glory to God in Jesus Christ is the proper place of theology. Theology is best done, one might say, before the Word and Table in the worshiping community of faith. This is, I am arguing, the true home of theology.

I have learned a great deal from Geoffrey Wainwright and accept his basic point in *Doxology* that "worship, doctrine and life," all three, intend the praise of God.[11] I cannot agree with him, however, when he makes liturgy itself the primary language of Christian worship, moving theological language to the role of a secondary reflection upon "the primary experience" of worship.[12] Theology too is an integral aspect of the liturgy and worship and praise of God. *Prayer, sermons, hymns, worship and liturgy are already theology.* I find the separation between theology and worship to be rather artificial.

The fact that theology is worship raises the issue of the truth about God. To worship is to proclaim the worth, to ascribe the glory and to describe the worthiness of someone. Unlike flattery or marketing, worship is interested in the *truth* about the one we worship. True worship can only be grounded in the truly wonderful things about the one we worship. True worship then is grounded in truth. Schubert Ogden correctly insists that the Christian witness of faith carries with it

---

[10] I have in mind here the Hebrew roots *halel* (הָלַל) and *yadah* (יָדָה) and the Greek words *aineō* (αἰνέω) and *doxazō* (δοξάζω).

[11] Wainright, *Doxology*, p. 10.

[12] Ibid., p. 21.

an implicit truth claim. "Any act of Christian witness, just like any other act of human praxis, necessarily implies, even if it may not express, certain claims to validity."[13] Unfortunately, Ogden goes on to find those claims to validity primarily in a pseudo-universal "common sense" rationality. Here I must disagree.[14] The truth as we know it in the story of God and most of all in Jesus Christ must be allowed the freedom to correct our common human reasonings. These are, after all, distorted by sin—as most of the Christian tradition has affirmed.

I am arguing, then, that theology is not merely a "critical reflection" on some other kind of experience or language or rationality that is "primary." Theology is a reflection only in the sense that it is a response: a response to the love of God, to the priority of God's action in salvation and creation. Theology as I see it is fundamentally a participation in the worship of God by telling the truth about God. It is grounded in the quest to know God in a deeply personal way: in the words of Clement, to love and to be loved by God. Theology, of course, does have many tasks and dimensions, including critical reflection. But theology should not be reduced to *academics*.

This understanding of theology is not far from what we find in Karl Barth, especially in the first part of his *Church Dogmatics*. Barth explicitly begins by stating, "theology is a function of the Church. The Church confesses God as it talks about God."[15] But Barth goes on to talk about theology as a science, which he sees as "the third, strictest, and proper sense of the word."[16] Barth rightly sees that the Church itself "puts to itself the question of truth."[17] He then goes on to state, "Theology follows the talk of the Church to the extent that in its question as to the correctness of its utterance it does not measure it by an alien standard but by its own source and object," namely the Word of God. So Barth understood this latter, proper task of dogmatics to be "the task of testing, criticising and correcting the actual proclamation of the Church at a given time."[18] The basis for this criticism, of course, is the Word of God. And this Word, for Barth, is clearly established only in Jesus Christ, the Word made flesh. In a late essay on the relationship between the-

---

[13]Schubert Ogden, "Process Theology and the Wesleyan Witness," in *Wesleyan Theology Today*, ed. Theodore Runyan (Nashville: Kingswood, 1985), p. 65, reprinted from the *Perkins Journal* 37 (1984): 18-33, and newly reprinted in *Thy Nature and Thy Name Is Love: Process and Wesleyan Theologies in Dialogue*, ed. Bryan Stone and Thomas Oord (Nashville: Kingswood, 2001). See further Schubert Ogden, *On Theology* (San Francisco: Harper & Row, 1986), esp. pp. 3-21. Note this telling remark in the latter book: "[theology's] appeal in support of this claim [to truth] is to no other conditions than those universally established with existence as such" (p. 20). I would love for Ogden, or any philosopher, to spell out convincingly just exactly what those conditions are!

[14]See further my essay, "Putting Reason in Its Place," in Stone and Oord, eds., *Thy Nature and Thy Name Is Love*.

[15]Karl Barth, *Church Dogmatics*, I/1 (1932; English translation, Edinburgh: T & T Clark, 1975), p. 3.

[16]Ibid.

[17]Ibid., p. 4.

[18]Ibid., p. 288.

ology and philosophy, Barth wrote, "In Jesus Christ the free grace of God summons the gratitude of the human being, and the free gratitude of the human being answers the grace of God, not the reverse!"[19]

I agree fundamentally with Barth's notion of theology as a free response of gratitude toward the work of God, especially in Christ. I also agree with Barth that revelation must, for the theologian, be the primary source of insight into the God whom we worship. But I do not and cannot agree that the "third sense" of theology, the critical or "scientific" task, is the most proper sense of theology as an academic discipline. As Barth correctly argued, theology as an academic discipline must take as its axiom the First Commandment, to worship the one true God, and him alone.[20] But this implies that the critical moment for theological reflection is secondary to the primary aim of telling the truth about God, that is, praising the Lord.

I have been arguing that the proper and primary goal of theology is worship: the praise of the one true God. If I am right, several serious questions, which come from our Enlightenment heritage and which we cannot ignore, raise their head. How can theology be a rigorous academic discipline? How can theology as an academic discipline ("science") legitimate its truth claims? How does theology as a discipline relate to the other arts and sciences of the university? It is to these questions we now turn.

Three Audiences for Theology

David Tracy argues that theological literature has three "publics," or audiences: the church, the academy and the broader culture or society.[21] Tracy's work regarding the rhetorical audience of theological works (written or spoken) is important for answering the question of the "scientific" character of theology. But my argument so far suggests a very different set of answers to the question, Who is addressed in theological discourse? The first audience is neither the church nor society, but God. This is because theological literature, like so much (but not all!) of our worship, is a linguistic form of the praise of God. The blessed Trinity is the first audience for our theological literature.

---

[19] Karl Barth, "Philosophy and Theology," in *The Way of Theology in Karl Barth*, ed. H. M. Runscheidt (Allison Park, Penn.: Pickwick, 1986), p. 90, originally published as "Philosophie und Theologie" in the Festschrift for his brother, Heinrich Barth, who was a philosopher. See *Philosophie und christliche Existenz*, ed. Gerhard Huber (Basel: Helbing & Lichtenhahn, 1960).

[20] Karl Barth, "The First Commandment as an Axiom of Theology," in Rumscheidt, *The Way of Theology*; German original, "Das erste Gebot als theologisches Axiom," in *Theologische Fragen und Anworten: Gessamelte Vorträge*, Band 3 (Zurich: Theologischer Verlag Zürich, 1957).

[21] David Tracy, *The Analogical Imagination* (New York: Crossroad, 1981), p. 21.

The second audience, then, is the community of all those who, alongside us, praise and worship the one true God. They will, as cocelebrants with us in the life of worship, be interested in the truth about God as we understand it. I, for one, do not believe this community is coextensive with the visible church.

In principle, the third audience includes all of humanity, for it is all those interested in "the Christian thing." All people of reason and good will, interested in knowing about Christians and their God, comprise this third audience. And it may well be that the theologian, from time to time, needs to address this audience directly, to explain the substance of gospel truth and Christian practice to the wider culture of our own time and place. This may be the very best kind of apologetics. But nevertheless even such apologetic writings are written to the glory of God and in fact have God as their primary audience. We know that at least God will read what we write if no one else does!

What then about the so-called criteria for truth, meaning and adequacy in theology? If God is our first audience, we will want most of all to be true to God's own revelation. The majority of Christian theologians would affirm that God is revealed in history (and to a lesser extent in nature and reason), with the acme of this historical revelation being in Jesus of Nazareth. The Scriptures are the primary witness to this revelation. They embody this revelation in textual form. Therefore, they form the first, or primary, source and norm for theological reflection. The Wesleyan Norms (or Quadrilateral) would also include ecumenical, orthodox tradition as a second norm, followed by reason and experience. These norms are also concerned to discover the truth about God, wherever it may be found. The theologian draws on all of these sources, *in this order*, in order to speak the truth in praise of God (to be clear: the order of the Wesleyan norms is a methodological, not a chronological one).

Tracy, along with many others, allows the terms of theological meaning to be dictated to by the third audience, that is, by our broader society. "The theologian," he states, "should argue the case (pro and con) on strictly public rounds that are open to all rational persons."[22] There is a sense in which we can and should agree here. Theological works should be understandable and clear so that our second and third audiences may grasp what it is we are saying. Yet our ultimate source of truth, meaning and coherence comes from revelation, not a supposed universal human experience or rationality (*pace* Tracy and Ogden).

Theology and the Postmodern University

There is and must remain a critical moment, a self-searching, for theological litera-

---

[22]Ibid., p. 64.

ture, even understood as a type of worship. We want to do the very best for God, and in the realm of the intellect this means searching out the truth with diligence, vigor and clarity. Anything less would not honor the One who is the Truth. Because theology is a kind of worship, we are interested in the truth about the One we worship. This truth can indeed come from many sources, including other academic disciplines. Still, many theologians go wrong in making the other arts and sciences of the university too independent of the truth as we know it in Christian revelation and faith. Barth argued as he did only because, for him, philosophy, science and the rest could only begin their work apart from faith. On this specific point both Ogden and Barth follow Kant, Schleiermacher and indeed most of the Enlightenment. Modernism insisted on the importance of independent faculties of arts and science: independent, that is, of church dogmas and regulations. Schleiermacher, ever the preacher, put it this way:

> Unless the Reformation from which our church first emerged endeavors to establish an eternal covenant between the living Christian faith and completely free, independent scientific inquiry, so that faith does not hinder science and science does not exclude faith, it fails to meet adequately the needs of our time.[23]

There is a sense in which we should agree with Schleiermacher, and a sense in which we cannot and should not follow him down this path. We can and should agree that all of the university, all the arts and sciences, are free of political control by Christians. Indeed, they should be free of all merely political (as opposed to ethical) controls, of any ideology or faction. Science and art must be free to pursue the truth as they know it. But this freedom is not and cannot be completely independent of all philosophical or religious issues. As I have argued elsewhere, the modernist myth of a purely value-free science is the nightmare of the twentieth century.[24] Scientific pursuit and technological innovation, apart from ethical concerns, are destructive to the planet and harmful to all living things, including human beings. Apart from these humanistic and ethical limitations, however, theology and the church should support the freedom of the arts and sciences to pursue and publish the truth as they see it.

However, no academic discipline is free of presuppositions, nor are they self-interpreting. This "freedom" we cannot allow the arts and sciences, since they in fact are dependent in exactly these areas. No science or academic discipline is value free or neutral: all are based on certain presuppositions, and all have results that

---

[23]Friedrich Schleiermacher, *On the Glaubenslehre*, trans. J. Duke and F. S. Fiorenza (Chico, Calif.: Scholars Press, 1981), p. 64.

[24]See my "Advice for Religious Historians: On the Myth of a Purely Historical Jesus," in *The Resurrection*, ed. S. T. Davis, D. Kendall and G. O'Collins (Oxford: Oxford University Press, 1997).

can and should be more fully interpreted within a particular worldview (and its associated tradition).[25] This implies that there is room for a faith-based approach to any academic discipline, including physics, art criticism, computer science and the rest. What I am talking about here is Christian learning, or Christian scholarship.[26]

Enlightenment thinkers like Kant would argue that the very idea of a Christian approach to science or art would be a betrayal of the rigor and intellectual discipline of that subject. This understanding of the rigor of academic pursuit has been called into question by philosophers as diverse as Søren Kierkegaard, Abraham Kuyper and Wilhelm Dilthey. In the last century, thinkers as diverse as Heidegger, Polanyi, Kuhn, Gadamer and Habermas would reject a "value free" or "neutral" understanding of what counts as good academics (*episteme, scientia* or *Wissenschaft*), and rightly so. The distinction between science and theology is not found in the difference between reason and faith or knowledge and myth or some other muddle-headed confusion. Both the sciences and theology draw on faith and reason. The *aim* of the arts and sciences on the one hand and theology on the other dictates differences in what counts as data and good methods in each. The true differences lie in the goals of each discipline. All are rational in their own way, however, and all are grounded in certain basic commitments that they cannot fully justify on their own. The Enlightenment ideal of a universal rationality has to be abandoned because it simply failed to achieve its goals according to its own principles (whether those are empiricist, Hegelian, Cartesian, etc.)

A postmodern approach to science and higher education will avoid the errors of Enlightenment rationality, but I am likewise unwilling to abandon the pursuit of truth as the goal of science and the university. Academic disciplines pursue truth in the areas of their interest and focus, based on certain value judgments they *own* but cannot *ground*. Such virtues as honesty, humility, attention to detail and rigorous testing of theories are commitments that come to each discipline from the broader culture: we might say, from a worldview.[27] Yet at the same time the postmodern academy should not be committed to any one religion, philosophy or worldview. The Christian too is committed to "welcome the stranger" and appreci-

[25]See further my essay "The Mutuality of Theology and Science," *Christian Scholar's Review* 26 (1998): 12-35.

[26]See, among recent expositors, George Marsden, *The Outrageous Idea of Christian Scholarship* (New York: Oxford University Press, 1997); and Nicholas Wolterstorff, "Public Theology or Christian Learning?" in *A Passion for God's Reign*, ed. Miroslav Volf (Grand Rapids, Mich.: Eerdmans, 1998); cf. Wolterstorff's earlier *Reason Within the Bounds of Religion*, 2nd ed. (Grand Rapids, Mich.: Eerdmans, 1984).

[27]For some early reflections on the nature of worldviews (*Weltanschauung*) and their role in philosophy, academic disciplines and life, see Wilhelm Dilthey, *Selected Writings*, ed. H. P. Rickman (Cambridge: Cambridge University Press, 1976).

ate the great variety of voices and perspectives within the academy and culture. While a postmodern university should allow diversity and embrace difference, the various disciplines are still committed to the pursuit of truth and scholarship according to the epistemic practices of that discipline's tradition. To learn chemistry, for example, or film criticism is to be tutored into particular epistemic practices and to be initiated into a particular tradition of inquiry. These various traditions of academic inquiry assume certain values and principles, which they cannot and do not pretend to justify. Furthermore, the results of these sciences and arts must still be interpreted and reflected on within the broader culture and within specific worldviews. Aspects of our worldviews both make the academic disciplines possible and place them into a broader perspective in which they are interpreted and applied.

Christian theology then has two roles in the postmodern, public academy. First, Christian theology is a key part of the Christian worldview, which in turn informs Christian scholarship in the postmodern academy. Christian scholarship or Christian learning is scholarship informed by, grounded in and interpreted within the Christian worldview. This worldview in turn arises out of Christian tradition, practice and faith. Not only the theologian but the economist, scientist and poet should, if they are Christians, approach their work in a way that is informed by Christian commitments. This should not lead to shoddy scholarship. On the contrary, since this intellectual work, too, is done to the glory of God, only the best scholarship is admissible. What counts as good data, excellent methodology and acceptable theory is determined by each discipline.

The Christian enters into this method of inquiry with a specifically Christian grounding for the value judgments and presuppositions that make it possible. Christian scholars may well be guided by their ultimate concerns in choosing a topic for intellectual study. The Christian scholar also will interpret the results of this academic discipline within a broad Christian worldview. Finally, I have argued elsewhere that Christian scholars are right to accept that theory which is most in consonance with their faith when two or more theories are equally sound according to the standards of their discipline. In fact, the Christian scholar may wish to defend that theory as "best"—not on the basis of special revelation or faith, but on the basis of what counts as good evidence and argument in that discipline.[28] Of course, Christian scholarship is only one form of scholarship, but it should be allowed within a pluralistic, postmodern academy along with the many other voices and perspectives. So this is the first role of Christian theology in a postmodern university: as a key element in a Christian worldview that informs and inter-

---

[28]Padgett, "Mutuality," pp. 24-25.

prets Christian learning in all the arts and sciences.

From this perspective religious studies is just like any other academic faculty in a pluralistic university. Christians may be experts in Islam or Taoism, in Hebrew studies or early Christianity. The roles can also be reversed, with fine Jewish scholars in New Testament studies and the like. The many academic disciplines that make up "religious studies" will determine what counts as excellence in scholarship in any of these specializations. Christian professors in religious studies departments will do their best to explain, without advocating, the religion in which they are academic specialists (even if that religion is their own). A pluralistic and open academic context would not allow the advocacy of any one religion. In such a context the activity of Christian theology as the worship of the one true God, in proclamation and praise, can only be described in the classroom. It cannot be engaged in within the classroom and academy of a postmodern, pluralistic university.

This leads to the second role for Christian theology in a pluralistic university. The primary audience in such a context will be the third audience for Christian theology, that is, all people of reason and good will interested in the Christian thing. The Christian theologian may well be employed in such a context as an expert in Christian or biblical studies. Here the Christian theologian must focus primarily on the third audience for theology, but without forgetting the first and second audiences. Christian theology in all its variety can and must be described and evaluated but not advocated within this context. Even in this context, however, Christian religious studies professors will seek to glorify God in excellent academic description and evaluation of Christianity. In other contexts outside the pluralistic academy and classroom, they are free to worship God more openly in their academic work. They will not (if they are wise) lose sight of the true goal and primary audience of their scholarly productions.

A corollary of my argument is that Christian theology can be fully articulated and taught only within a faith-based institution of higher learning. This turns on my previous point, that the true home of theology is at Word and Table, in the worshiping community. When seminaries understand their scholarly production flows from preaching and liturgy, then some healing of the unfortunate state of our theological schools (at least the mainstream Protestant ones) may begin. Whether these are Christian universities or theological seminaries, *the full and complete teaching and learning* of Christian theology is not possible in a pluralistic context. Again this has to do with the aim of theological work. Of course people, anywhere, can engage in Christian theology in the privacy of their own study. We should be allowed to write and publish as we see fit. But these facts are irrelevant to my point, which is about corporate teaching and learning. Teaching and learning Christian theology as a worshipful activity can only take place in a fully Christian context, that is, in the context of the worship and praise of God in a Christian university, college or seminary.

In a recent volume titled *Taking Religion to School: Christian Theology and Secular Education*, Stephen Webb argues that the teaching of religion is always itself a religious act.[29] I am in full agreement with this viewpoint. But he insists that by way of empathetic engagement, the religion scholar can appreciate and present a variety of religions in the classroom. Further, he argues that each religion teacher should come clean with respect to their own religious biases, which we are usually bad at hiding from bright students anyway. The classroom then becomes a safe place for a diversity of religious perspectives, including the teacher's own, but without imposing any one religion as the true one. I find this book to be a refreshing essay on its topic and agree with the main points. But my point is that teaching theology *as theology* requires advocating the truth of a particular religion, and this can only be done in a faith-based context. The pluralistic context that Webb is discussing can and should embrace his proposals. *But he is not suggesting we advocate a particular religion as the true one in class.* That advocacy is what I find unique about theological education in the strict sense and why a faith-based context is vital to it. Will such a "confessionalism" not lead to irrational, nonacademic religious instruction? That is the next question to explore.

The Academic Character of Theology

We are now in a better position to answer the question of the "critical moment" in theological reflection. In what way is theology "scientific" or academically sound? How can theology meet the needs of modern intellectuals without losing itself? In my work on the problem of induction, I argue that there are no univocal, universal standards of good informal arguments.[30] Instead, there are "family resemblances" among the standards in various traditions of inquiry. The standards of argument, inference and evidence must be contextualized by each discipline, given its aims and focus of study.[31] What counts as a "good argument" or "evidence" or "coherence" differs slightly from discipline to discipline. These values and criteria do exist in a general way, but they are vague and need to be spelled out within each tradition of inquiry.

Theology is no different from the other academic disciplines in this regard.

---

[29]Stephen Webb, *Taking Religion to School: Christian Theology and Secular Education* (Grand Rapids, Mich: Brazos, 2000).

[30]See my essay "Induction After Foundationalism," published as an appendix in my book *Science and the Study of God: A Mutuality Model for Theology and Science* (Grand Rapids, Mich.: Eerdmans, forthcoming).

[31]Formal systems of reason such as mathematics and symbolic logic are more universal. But even they must be applied properly in each context.

What counts as clear, coherent and sound arguments will need to be assessed in part by the criteria of intelligibility found in the Christian religion, including its way of life, history, creeds, sacred texts, religious practice and worldview. On the other hand, there will be parallels and analogies in method and logic that theology will borrow from other disciplines. Textual criticism in biblical studies will be pretty much the same as the textual criticism of other literature. What counts as coherent within theology may be similar to what counts as coherent in a particular philosophy. The list can be extended. My point here is that theology must be true to its first source and norm, that is, revelation. Theology must always remember its first audience. These commitments will very often alter and shape the methods, criteria and data brought to theology from other disciplines. Theology should strive to honor reason, but not a supposed universal rationality. Rather, reason in theology is in the service of faith; our minds seek to love the one true God. We are not interested in mind in the abstract, but rather "the mind of Christ" (1 Cor 2:16).

Because theology is about God, including the work of God in the world, it will always be interested in the results of the other arts and sciences. Theology does not stand alone here, however, but depends on Christian scholarship. Christian theology will be done in cooperation with Christian learning, that is, with the best Christian scholarship in the other arts and sciences. Theologians will take on board truth as it is known in other disciplines, but they will depend on Christian experts in those disciplines to fund and interpret this "truth" in a Christian manner. So I argue, against Barth, that theology is based on "revelation and Christian scholarship," and not revelation alone.

Barth himself seems to allow for this in his article "The First Commandment as an Axiom of Theology." He gives three cautions to those who would add the little word "and" to revelation. First, we must speak of revelation "with a notably heightened seriousness and interest, and by speaking of that other criterion only secondarily and for the sake of revelation."[32] Second (and this sounds very much like what I am calling Christian scholarship) theology expresses its commitment to the first commandment by "interpreting those other things according to revelation and not the other way around."[33] Third, theology must permit "no possibility . . . of intermixing, exchanging, or identifying the two concepts in this relation."[34] I believe all these cautions are well taken. Yet there is plenty of room here for theology to be based not simply on revelation but on any truth that bears upon our knowledge of God. The quest for truth about God demands that theology look also to Christian

---

[32]Barth, "The First Commandment," p. 73.
[33]Ibid., p. 74.
[34]Ibid., p. 75.

scholarship in all the disciplines as its guide and helper. This would include both philosophy and natural science understood within the Christian worldview.

In a recent lecture on spiritual and practical theology, Randy Maddox argued that there are four "dimensions" or senses of the word theology.[35] First, there is theology in the life and thought of the individual believer, often tacit and undeveloped. This kind of theology is practical and living, including the mind of Christ and the fruit of the Spirit at work in the life of the believer. This is an important sense of "theology" that I admire and believe to be important but have not emphasized here. A second sense is the Eastern Orthodox notion that liturgy—the worship of God in the community—is theology. This is the emphasis of my chapter. A "second order" kind of theology exists, which is the third sense. This is academic, critical theological reflection. I have not emphasized this, although I do accept it and value it. Finally, the fourth dimension of theology is theological method and apologetics, which Maddox calls "third order" theology. This too is crucial. Put in terms of this expansive notion of what "theology" is, my thesis that "theology is worship" I understand to be true for all four dimensions, but especially for the second one.

There is clearly an important place for second and third order reflection on the primary theological data (on the individual and on the worshiping community). Christian theology is an academic discipline because it seeks to know the truth about its focus of study in a rational, rigorous manner. But Christian theology does not allow its notions of rationality to be dictated to it from the outside. That, I think, is the great danger of third-order theological reflection, that is, theological method and apologetics. Rather, even in this domain, as long as it is truly Christian theology it seeks to know and love the One who has revealed himself in Jesus Christ and in all creation as Lord. And it uses methods and standards of reason that are appropriate to this goal, and are likewise clear and coherent. Reason, evidence and argument are not foreign to theology, but they must conform to the standards of faith and revelation to be acceptable. In this way, theology honors the God who is the source of all truth. At the same time, theology retains its proper nature as the worship and praise of God.

---

[35] Randy Maddox, "Spiritual and Practical Theology: Trajectories toward Reengagement," *Association of Practical Theology, Occasional Papers* 3 (1999): 10-16.

SEVENTEEN

RESURRECTION

The Ultimate Hope

WOLFHART PANNENBERG

The integrity of individual existence in the act of salvation will be finally achieved in the resurrection, which is the ultimate hope for the individual. As such, it is not in competition with the hope for the kingdom of God, which is the comprehensive concept of the final accomplishment of God's creation. The hope for the resurrection of the dead can be accounted for as an application of the hope for the kingdom to the individual life of the creatures, especially of human beings. It is connected with the hope for the kingdom, however, in the idea of a general resurrection at the end of history for all humankind together with a final judgment that occurs at the entrance into the kingdom of God.

The general resurrection of the dead is indeed an act of God in the dynamics of history, an act that will be concerned with the completion of all history. In the same way, the resurrection of Jesus was an act of God in history, an act of decisive importance for the Christian faith and comparable, according to Paul, only to the act of creation from nothing (Rom 4:17).

The Christian proclamation of Jesus' resurrection met with unbelief since the very beginning—unbelief among the Jews, because they didn't expect a resurrection to occur to an individual person in the midst of history, before the general end of the world; and unbelief among the Gentiles of the Hellenistic culture, because they couldn't imagine that the body could partake in eternal life. In modern times this unbelief has increased, because educated people no longer believed in miracles. Miracles were considered to amount to violations of the laws of nature, and a resurrection of the dead would constitute the extreme case of such a miracle. Therefore, David Hume dismissed the idea of such a miracle as most absurd because it is contrary to all experience and to the customary course of nature. Until this day most people—especially in Western culture—are persuaded of the impossibility of miracles and therefore dismiss the Christian affirmation of the resurrection of Jesus as well as the hope for a future resurrection of the dead. This is the main reason why even Christian historians and biblical exegetes declare that the resurrection of Jesus could never be regarded as a historical event, whatever else it might have been. And many preachers have difficulty telling their congregations at Easter what really had happened, except perhaps in the imagination of the disciples.

Meanwhile, natural scientists have become much more cautious, because they do not claim that our knowledge of the laws of nature a priori excludes the possibility of events that we cannot explain on the basis of our present knowledge. Most scientists no longer conceive of the universe in terms of a closed deterministic process, but rather in terms of an open process where the natural laws function in a somewhat elastic way as they allow new qualities of events and new forms of reality to emerge. Still, scientists are not comfortable with the idea of events that don't happen regularly but remain unique. Nevertheless, the claim of secular historians that our knowledge of natural laws would rule out the possibility of a resurrection from the dead in principle is not based on science but on a now obsolete concept of a deterministic universe.

Christians, therefore, in proclaiming the resurrection of Jesus need not be afraid of the authority of science. But they should have good reasons otherwise for what they have to say on this issue, historical reasons as well as reasons for the general expectation of a resurrection from the dead. In the time of the early Christian proclamation of the Easter event, the more general expectation of a resurrection from the dead was part of the plausibility structure, and this was one reason why as early as the second century Christian apologetic theology in the world of Hellenistic culture focused on this issue. Correspondingly, I will start the following discussion with some remarks on the relationship between resurrection hope and the Greek belief in the immortality of the soul. Secondly, I will go on to discuss the roots and the different forms of the Jewish and Christian expectation of a general resurrection of the dead. Finally, I will briefly examine the Christian Easter tradition and its fundamental importance to our Christian faith.

Immortality and Resurrection

In the second century several treatises were written on the resurrection. Most prominent among them is the treatise of Athenagoras from Alexandria. He argued that the salvation of human persons would be incomplete if only related to the soul, since a human being consists of soul and body. The body is not something accidental, but the soul is essentially soul of a body. At this point the Christian authors felt closer to Aristotle than to Plato, because Aristotle had described the soul not as an independent entity but as the form of a body.

According to Plato the soul is by itself immortal since like the immortal gods it nourishes itself by contemplating the eternal ideas. In that activity the soul moves itself, while all bodily movement is caused by something else. Immortality and the divine nature of the soul are closely connected. Embodiment is not its nature. Rather, the body is the prison of the soul. The soul was imprisoned in a body as a consequence of a fall, when it turned away from the eternal ideas. When the body dies, the soul escapes. But it will be imprisoned again in another body. Thus Plato believed in the transmigration of souls.

For a number a reasons the Christian theologians could not accept this doctrine. In the first place, according to the Scriptures human beings were created as body and soul. Second, the soul is not divine by nature, though it may participate in divine eternity by grace. The soul—or rather the human being—is indeed destined to immortality, but only by grace. Therefore, Christian theologians could accept the idea of an immortal soul only with qualifications, that is, as depending on the design of the Creator. Furthermore, since the soul together with the body is meant to be part of the individual human person, a particular soul is created for each individual. Accordingly, the transmigration of souls is rejected. This was a modification of decisive and far-reaching importance regarding the conception of human nature. It was the proclamation of the eternal value of the individual.

The immortality of the platonic soul did not mean the immortality of the human individual, since that soul lives on through many individual biographies. It was only the Christian reformulation of this platonic idea that turned it into an idea of the eternal value and destiny of the individual person, who comes into existence at birth and ends at death. Death separates the soul from the body until at the resurrection of the dead it receives a new body. In between, the soul was not thought to exist as a complete human being, but nevertheless the function of diminished existence of the soul secured the continuity of the person between death and resurrection. Thus in some way the identity of the soul served as a guarantee of the identity of the person who will be raised on the last day with the person who lived on earth some time ago, perhaps a long time ago.

The original body would long be decomposed. How could there ever be the same body raised from the dead on the last day? It was a question that disturbed the early Christian theologians no less than later Christian thinkers. The most ingenious answer was provided by Thomas Aquinas. He considered the soul to contain and preserve the information for the reproduction of the body. Thus in the resurrection of the dead the soul would function like a computer program in the restoration of the body.

In modern theology the Christian reformulation of the platonic immortality of the soul has come under serious criticism, especially by Paul Althaus and Oscar Cullmann. Both theologians correctly pointed out that the biblical hope in a bodily resurrection is quite different from the platonic idea of an immortal soul. It is also closer to the outlook of contemporary anthropology that emphasizes the unity of human existence in terms of bodily existence, where the soul is only a function of the body and cannot exist separate from the body after a person dies. Nevertheless, the modern critics also noticed the function of the soul in the history of Christian thought, a soul that can be separated from the body at death and bridges the gap between death and the resurrection. The question is whether Christian theology needs the idea of a separate soul for this purpose.

In my personal judgment, our Christian belief in God's eternity renders the assumption of a separate soul superfluous for this purpose. While in the hour of death our life ceases to exist in relation to ourselves and to others, it does not pass away in the memory of God, to whom all things are present and remain present. With that information God can very well recreate the same human person at the resurrection of the dead, if he wishes to provide that person once again with a bodily and independent existence. It all depends on our belief in God the Creator.

Roots and Forms of the Expectation of a Future Resurrection

The belief in a future resurrection of individual persons developed in postexilic Judaism. Its emergence was less dependent on Persian ideas than earlier scholarship suspected. Apparently it arose as a solution to problems within the Jewish tradition itself. In ancient Judaism ideas about a future life of the individual beyond death did not arise as long as the individual was predominantly perceived as a member and function of the community. The individual would live on in the memory of posterity like the forefathers did. But after Jerusalem was defeated and destroyed by the Babylonians in 587, the righteousness of God in his actions in history was questioned, and Ezekiel declared that in the future each person would receive his or her fate individually according to his or her own merit. Experience, however, did not confirm this rule. It rather showed that the wicked live on happily, while good people suffer.

At this point belief in the justice of God required an adjustment beyond the death of the individual person. Whoever had not received their due reward in this life could expect compensation by divine judgment after their death, and in order to receive their judgment they had to be restored from their tombs. In this sense Daniel 12:2 expected a future resurrection of the dead: "many of those who sleep in the dust of the earth shall awake, some to everlasting life, and some to shame and everlasting contempt." The same idea, but with more detail, occurs in Syrian Baruch 50. There it is said explicitly that those who are raised from the dead return in exactly the same form so that they can be recognized by others. After the act of judgment, however, a transformation takes place, the glorification of the good and a deterioration in the condition of the wicked (syr Bar 51). In this conception of a future resurrection of the dead, then, the resurrection functions as a presupposition of the act of judgment, the consequence of which will be either glorification or deterioration. In the New Testament, this conception can be found in Revelation 20:12ff.

According to another conception of resurrection, however, that event itself means salvation and life. It occurs only to the righteous ones. Thus Isaiah 26:19 says of the faithful: "Thy dead shall live, their bodies shall rise," while of the wicked it is said, "They are dead, they will not live; they are shades, they will not arise" (26:14).

Among the Pharisees, some adhered to this conception of the future resurrection of the dead, others (like Hillel) adhered to the one which considered resurrection simply a precondition of judgment. In the New Testament the apostle Paul speaks of resurrection in terms of the Christian hope (1 Cor 15:35-56). Here, resurrection as such means participation in eternal life. Therefore, resurrection itself takes the form of a transformation into a spiritual body, a form of life that is completely penetrated by the power of the life-giving Spirit.

A similar conception of resurrection is expressed in Jesus' answer to the question of the Sadducees where he says that the God of Abraham, Isaac and Jacob "is not a God of the dead, but of the living" (Mk 12:27). Here again resurrection, as such, means transformation into a new form of life: "For when they rise from the dead, they neither marry nor are given in marriage but are like angels in heaven" (12:25), like Daniel said with regard to the righteous and wise ones: "they shall shine like the brightness of the firmament and like the stars" (Dan 12:3).

The root of this second conception of the resurrection of the dead can be identified, perhaps, not so much in the idea of God's justice but in the hope for everlasting communion with God, even beyond the event of death. This hope is expressed most profoundly in Psalm 73, where God is said be the only reliable and abiding companion of the faithful: "My flesh and my heart may fail, but God is the strength of my heart and my portion forever" (73:26). The communion of faith with this

God will be eternal like God himself. It will therefore survive our death and carry us into his eternal life beyond the death of our bodies.

The Resurrection of Jesus

The resurrection of Jesus is the most prominent manifestation of the power of God's future in the dynamics of history. That this event really happened in the midst of our human history is the cornerstone of the Christian faith, for Paul says: "if Christ has not been raised, then our preaching is in vain and your faith is in vain" (1 Cor 15:14). As early as the time of Paul, there were people at Corinth who insisted "that there is no resurrection of the dead" (1 Cor 15:12). It is not known whether from this general assertion they drew the conclusion that neither could Jesus have been raised. It was Paul who exposed this consequence: "if there is no resurrection of the dead, then Christ has not been raised" (15:13).

This, however, was exactly the argument of David Hume in his famous section "Of Miracles" in his *Inquiry Concerning Human Understanding*, 1748. It is not a historical argument against the plausibility of the Christian claim, but rather an a priori consideration. Hume was right, of course, that in ordinary human experience resurrections of dead persons do not occur. More questionable was his assumption that such an event would constitute a break in the order of nature. Contemporary understanding of the concept of natural law emphasizes, contrary to Hume, the elasticity and openness of the order of natural events. Whether or not an event took place in the past can only be decided by historical argument. Nevertheless, a priori reasoning concerning the nature of reality strongly influences the judgment of historians to the present day, even among Christian historians who want to do their job according to secular standards.

In fairness to those Christian theologians who feel overwhelmed by the difficulties in this matter, it may be said that the plausibility of the Christian claim is conditioned by whether or not a person believes in the God of the Bible or at least admits the possibility of his existence, the possibility also of his omnipotent action. Jesus argued against the Sadducees that those who deny a future resurrection of the dead do not know "the power of God" (Mk 12:24). It is the omnipotent power of the Creator God in whom Abraham trusted, the God "who gives life to the dead and calls into existence the things that do not exist" (Rom 4:17). Even if the reality, or at least the possibility, of this God is duly taken into consideration, however, judgment of the Christian claim that Jesus was raised from the dead still depends on a historical examination of the Easter tradition.

The early Christian reports on appearances of the risen Jesus to a number of persons (many of whom had been his disciples before, while others—Paul and perhaps James—became disciples in consequence of the appearances that occurred to them) are rarely rejected. But the appearances usually are explained as hallucinations, although such an explanation is not easy since it requires the assumption that preconditions for hallucinations did in fact exist, especially in the case of Peter and Paul. It is not easy to show with plausibility that this was the case, unless one starts by postulating that this is the only way to explain the reports on those appearances. Reconstructions of the psychological mechanism that supposedly led to these "hallucinations" have been attempted. However, the reconstructions are more fantastic than the biblical reports themselves, and one often wonders how easily critical historians, who examine their sources with a great deal of skepticism, believe their own imaginations without checking the historical plausibility of their intuitions with comparable rigor.

The most vehement attacks are directed against the biblical reports of the empty tomb of Jesus. They are often dismissed as late legends, although the reports in their basic substance do not clearly show the literary marks that are typical of legends, and some details could not easily occur in a late legend, for example, the role of women who were not considered effective witnesses in the Jewish tradition. In addition, the risen Jesus does not appear in connection with the discovery of the empty tomb. A late legend would more effectively argue that Jesus' disciples discovered the tomb and that Jesus appeared to them there. Many modern critics, however, agree that the tomb of Jesus may have been unknown to the disciples; the critics suppose that after the crucifixion the disciples fled to Galilee and later on, after their return to Jerusalem, they were not interested in where Jesus had been buried. A very incredible thesis, indeed, since everybody agrees that at Jerusalem the disciples started to proclaim the resurrection of Jesus. Since according to Jewish belief the resurrection of a person requires that his or her tomb "returns" the body, it is hardly conceivable that the early Christians would proclaim the resurrection of Jesus at Jerusalem without public evidence that his tomb was empty. That fact alone, of course, did not substantiate the claim of the Christian proclamation. That the tomb was empty could be explained in different ways, and the Gospels give some indications of how the adversaries of the Christians' proclamation explained that fact: They said that the body was stolen by the disciples themselves (Mt 27:28). The empty tomb—taken by itself—is not the decisive evidence for the Christian claim that Jesus had been raised from the dead. But without admitting that friend and foe at Jerusalem knew that the tomb was empty, the situation of the early Christian proclamation of Jesus' resurrection at Jerusalem, of all places, is historically not conceivable.

Given the subordinate value of the empty tomb in the Christian proclamation of the resurrection of Jesus, it is astonishing that the criticism of the Christian Easter tradition focused so much on this particular report in order to deprive it of its credibility. The reason becomes clear, however, when one considers the relevance of the empty tomb for the interpretation of the apostolic experiences of the risen Lord: It seems easier, then, to explain the appearances as products of hallucinations without the empty tomb. One could, of course, argue that hallucinations took place precisely in consequence of the discovery of the empty tomb. But that could not be the case with Paul, and after all, the question would remain where Jesus' body had disappeared.

The empty tomb and the reports on appearances strengthen each other mutually. The historical examination of the Christian Easter tradition yields nothing that would prevent the conclusion that the resurrection of Jesus was a historical event, an event in human history. It was, of course, not a mere resuscitation of a corpse, not a return into this mortal life. The new, eschatological life into which Jesus' body was transformed is not of this world. Nevertheless, the event of his resurrection occurred in our human history.

There remains one difficulty with the empty tomb story that should not go unmentioned. That is the absence in this detail of analogy with the future resurrection according to the Christian hope. With regard to other details, Paul stressed the analogy between our future resurrection and the resurrection of Jesus Christ. Thus he says in Philippians 3:21 that the Lord Jesus Christ "will change our lowly body to be like his glorious body." But after our death, our bodies will decay in the earth and the hope for our resurrection does not depend on the continuity of that bodily substance with the future spiritual body. At this point the case of Jesus is different if his resurrection has to be understood in connection with his empty tomb. In my judgment, however, this lack of analogy is a further indication for rather than against the historicity of the empty tomb.

The significance of Jesus' resurrection for the Christian faith can hardly be overemphasized. In the first place it meant the divine confirmation of Jesus' pre-Easter teaching in the face of the ambiguities concerning his own person that had caused his rejection and finally his death on the cross. In the light of Easter, Jesus' communion with God the Father, as Son of this Father, was confirmed, and since such a communion with the eternal God is itself eternal, the early Christian belief in his preexistence immediately followed, and consequently the belief that the eternal Son had been sent by the Father to become incarnate in Jesus for the salvation of humankind. Without his resurrection, his crucifixion would only have been the final disaster of Jesus' career. In the light of Easter, however, the cross was to be understood as a saving event, suffered for the sins of others. There is no saving significance of the death of Jesus on the cross without his resurrection. But his death and resurrection together provide the Christian faithful with the chance that their communion with Jesus now, especially with his death by the act of baptism, gives the assurance of future participation in the life of his resurrection. This hope of participating in the eternal life of God through communion with Jesus constitutes the core of the Christian confidence. Forgiveness of sins is included in such communion with Jesus and with God, not the other way around. Communion with God removes by implication whatever separated a person from God. Therefore, in his earthly ministry, admission of "sinners and publicans" to the meal that Jesus celebrated as a symbol of communion in the kingdom implied the forgiveness of sins.

If early Christian spirituality, then, was centered around the proclamation of Jesus' resurrection from the dead and of the Christian hope to share in that new life beyond our death, did not Christianity then originate with a strong otherworldly twist? That is certainly true, and rather than being easily dismissed, this fact should raise a question to us modern Christians, who are proud of our worldliness. The early Christian spirituality was not escapist, however. It involved a positive attitude toward the world as God's creation, but also a certain aloofness because of the Christian certainty of an ultimate accomplishment beyond this present and mortal life. The life to come is the strength of this life, the liberal German theologian Ernst Troelsch said ("Das Jenseits ist die Kraft des Diesseits"). Contemporary secular men and women have lost this strength. The Christian proclamation should once more make it available to them and that could be done if only we contemporary Christians would ourselves recover the authentically Christian confidence in a life beyond death, in communion with our risen Lord and with the eternal life of God the Father in his kingdom to come.

EIGHTEEN

C. S. LEWIS
IN THE PUBLIC SQUARE

RICHARD JOHN NEUHAUS

The similarity in the vocations of Thomas Oden and C. S. Lewis may not be self-evident to the reader. But I hope this reflection on Lewis will make apparently unlikely connections plausible, if not self-evident. As others in this collection will no doubt discuss in detail, there was a time when Tom Oden eagerly awaited the latest news from the culture in order to respond with an appropriate theological update, thus demonstrating the determined and sometimes desperate "relevance" of Christianity. Some in the mode of Paul Tillich called this "correlation," with the world asking the questions and Christian theology providing the answers. On the ecumenical front the World Council of Churches adopted the slogan "The world sets the agenda for the church." That was a long time ago, and for his part in such wrong-headedness Tom Oden has long since issued his *mea culpa*.

Tom Oden wrote in an introduction to a volume on systematic theology that he hoped the reader would find nothing new in the book. That, of course, was a slight indulgence of hyperbole. As Oden well knows, the truth that St. Augustine called "ever ancient, ever new" always calls for and lends itself to fresh expression. But the fresh expression of that truth will not be understood unless people are familiar with that truth in the first place. Not in Protestant theology *only* but in Protestant theology *particularly*, Oden realized that "the church had lost its story" and was therefore increasingly incapable of remedying the circumstance discussed in the following essay, namely, the world's loss of its story. Tom Oden found his theological vocation in narrating the story of the church's reflection on the story of the world and of, quite simply, everything—for God's revelation in Jesus Christ is the story of everything. He has concentrated most productively on the patristic reflection on that story, thus recovering treasures long neglected by the desperate relevancies of much of modern theology. In his devotion to the persuasive telling of the story, I would suggest, is the important if not entirely self-evident connection with the vocation of C. S. Lewis, to which I now turn.

The first thing I should say at the outset is that I am not a Lewis scholar. The second thing is that, from what I understand of the man, he would likely be amused that there are people called Lewis scholars. There are simply those who can stop reading Lewis, and those who can't. After a while, some of the latter find that they are thought to be Lewis scholars. The third thing I should say is that I am very much aware that anybody who knows much about Lewis might think the title of this paper—"C. S. Lewis in the Public Square"—highly improbable.

The phrase "public square" evokes images of the political arena with its partisan games and intense debates over public policy. Lewis did occasionally, very occasionally, address what are ordinarily called political issues. One thinks of his reflections on the Second World War, on pacifism and belligerency, on laws regarding obscenity, and on the nature of criminal punishment. But for the most part Lewis is understandably viewed as a determinedly apolitical, even private, man. Indeed, in many ways he took his stand, and encouraged others to take their stand, over against politics—especially politics as dominated by the machinations of the modern state. He was on the side of reason, myth, splendor and virtue, in the hope that such vital elements of life might "still trickle down to irrigate the dust-bowl of modern economic Statecraft." This might be called the C. S. Lewis trickle-down theory of politics.[1]

His skepticism with respect to the modern state was emphatic:

Christianity, with its claims in one way personal and in the other way ecumenical and both ways antithetical to omnicompetent government, must always in fact . . . be treated as an enemy [by the state]. Like learning, like the family, like any ancient and liberal profession, like the common law, it gives the individual a standing ground against the State.[2]

As in Augustine's two cities—the *civitas terrena* and the *civitas Dei*—Lewis

---

[1] C. S. Lewis, "Myth Become Fact," in *God in the Dock* (Grand Rapids, Mich.: Eerdmans, 1970), p. 64.
[2] C. S. Lewis, "On the Transmission of Christianity," *God in the Dock*, p. 118.

insisted on clear distinctions and was not intimidated by the risk that distinctions may turn into antinomies. Of course the city of God is not immediately available to us, and we have to make do with the earthly cities we have. Like Augustine who preferred the ancient Romans to those of his own day, Lewis recognized the need to make comparative judgments between political regimes, but insisted we should do so without delusions. "The practical problem of Christian politics," he wrote, "is not that of drawing up schemes for a Christian society, but that of living as innocently as we can with unbelieving fellow-subjects under unbelieving rulers who will never be perfectly wise and good and who will sometimes be very wicked and very foolish."[3]

The kind of people we are is more important than what we can do to improve the world; indeed, being the kind of people we should and can be is the best and sometimes the only way to improve the world. Society is ever so much more important than the state, and mores more important than laws. "The law must rise to our standards when we improve and sink to them when we decay."[4] Better, therefore, to attend to standards than to laws. This overlooks, we may observe, the ways in which laws influence standards, but it reflects Lewis's studied skepticism toward the search for political or legal fixes for human problems. His disdain for the public excitements generated by what he derisively referred to as "the news" is well known. Amidst the incessant declarations of public crises about this, that and the other thing, C. S. Lewis looks very much like an "escapist." After all, he spent a large part of his life writing fairy tales for children, didn't he?

Nevertheless, I think I will stick with my title, "C. S. Lewis in the Public Square." Lewis was anything but the isolated and privatized individualist whom the Greeks called an "idiot." If we do not think of Lewis's work as public, it is probably because of our shriveled definition of "public" that equates "public" with the "political," and further equates the political with the governmental. Lewis was a public man. For even the most reclusive author, to publish is to go public. The recluse or the "idiot" publishes what is *private*, which is a form of exhibitionism. Lewis frequently published what is *personal*, always in the expectation that it would engage the like experience of other persons who are, broadly speaking, the public. Lewis wrote in the service of public conversation. Throughout his writings, one detects between the lines the inquiry posed to his readers, "Is it not true? Don't you find it to be so?"

His effort was to engage, inform and elevate what is today called "public discourse," although I doubt if he ever used the term. He was, I think, inclined to

---

[3]C. S. Lewis, "The Humanitarian Theory of Punishment," *God in the Dock*, pp. 292f.
[4]C. S. Lewis, "Sex in Literature," in *Present Concerns*, ed. Walter Hooper (San Diego: Harcourt Brace, 1988), p. 105.

assume that his experience was the common experience. In this sense, although he cherished excellence, he was not an elitist. Anything but. We might even risk calling him a populist. Whether it was "mere" Christianity or "mere" sex or the "mere" companionship of friends, his purpose was to elicit what is already there, if only we would open our eyes to see it—the wonder disguised in the "mere." In this he was at one with Chesterton, who declared that the only sin is to call a green leaf gray. Epiphanies did not await the occurrence of something extraordinary or out of the way. They are to be discovered in the ordinary, and ordinary people are capable of that discovery.

To Elicit What Is Already There, and Bring It to Fuller and Finer Expression

I was recently reading Edward Norman's magnificent history of Christian architecture, *The House of God*, and came across this:

> The other religions of the ancient world had incorporated some sense of God's presence but it remained latent and descriptive. Christ came among men with a simple ministry of teaching whose main purpose was to confirm that the kinds of ways in which God had been understood in Natural religion, and the very language used to express those insights, were broadly right. Yet he came also—and this was the unique gift of Revealed religion—to redeem men and the world which was their home. . . . Hence the Incarnation. God literally became a man in order that the human categories of spirituality could be recognized as truly divine, and not the mere invention of a frightened race seeking some means of converting a miserable and ephemeral existence into a dignified and permanent purchase upon the existence of the universe.[5]

I expect Lewis would approve of that way of putting the matter.

Far from being private and idiosyncratic, Lewis's métier was the public, as in universal. He was in the fullest and finest sense a humanist. He was a Christian humanist, to be sure, but he could say with the pre-Christian Terence, "I am a man: nothing human is alien to me." Being a *Christian* humanist was in no way a limiting factor. Quite the opposite is the case, if Christ is the *logos* who informs, sustains and fulfills all that is. Lewis frequently used "humanism" and "humanitarian" as pejoratives, but only because in common usage those terms reflected smug liberal prejudices that were not nearly humanistic enough. For Lewis, "The Great Fact" is that God became a human being, and you cannot get more humanistic than that.

In discussions of the universally human, the universal is frequently pitted against the particular, but this was not the case with Lewis. This is underscored by Gilbert Meilaender, one of the most insightful readers of Lewis, in a recent essay,

---

[5]Edward Norman, *The House of God* (London: Thames & Hudson, 1990), p. 19.

"The Everyday C. S. Lewis."[6] He cites John in *The Pilgrim's Regress*, who has finally made his way back to Mother Church and sings:

> But Thou, Lord, surely knewest Thine own plan
> When the angelic indifferences with no bar
> Universally loved but Thou gav'st man
> The tether and pang of the particular.

"The Tether and Pang of the Particular"

Although it is not Meilaender's point, and perhaps not Lewis's point in the verse quoted, I would suggest that it is through this particular that we discern the universal. The experience of the particular is itself universal. The experience of the particular is the tether that ties us to the universal, even as there is the pang of its remaining particular, of its not being fully shared with others—at least for now. One day that sharing, that communion, will be consummated. With respect to the tether and pang of the particular, one detects again the implicit inquiry to the reader: "Is it not true? Do you not find it to be so?"

Meilaender notes that in his religious writings Lewis frequently drops the aside that he is not a theologian and that what he says is subject to correction by real theologians. Meilaender suggests that we should "recognize this for what it is: a smart rhetorical strategy that gets the reader on his side over against the presumably elitist theologians." He notes that, in fact, Lewis had read more theology than many theologians, but nonetheless his writing is better described as "religious" than as "theological." Religious language, he notes, is closely related to poetic language, as distinct from both "ordinary" language and "scientific" language. I do not disagree with Meilaender on that, but there is a trap here that should be clearly marked.

Theology, at least in the great tradition, claims to be about truth. It makes cognitive claims about the way things really are. It is one of the great secularizing achievements of modernity to have created the category we call "religion." Questions about God, judgment, purpose, sin and redemption are all put into a sandbox labeled "Religion," leaving the rest of the public square for the deliberation of questions dealing with "the real world." This is evident in our universities where theology has long since been replaced by—at best, or perhaps at worst—"religious studies." For two hundred years theologians retreating from the advance of scientific and philosophical debunkings have taken refuge in the sphere that modernity graciously set aside for religion as a subcategory of poetic expression. Lewis is sometimes viewed as joining that retreat, and there are elements of his work that

---

[6]Gilbert Meilaender, "The Everyday C. S. Lewis," *First Things*, August-September 1998.

can be cited in support of that view, but I think that was not his intention. On the contrary, he wanted to call a halt to the retreat. He wanted to persuade us that the religious and particularly Christian construal of reality is more encompassing, has more explanatory power, and is, in a word, true. While presenting himself as a religious thinker rather than a theologian, he was attempting to do the authentically public thing that many theologians had lost the nerve to do.

Alan Jacobs of Wheaton College is another close reader of Lewis, and he suggests that the Lewis project is of limited usefulness today. "Lewis wrote in a time when, among the educated British public if not among their professional philosophers, there was considerably more agreement than there is now about what constitutes a valid and rational argument for a given case." He says Lewis might have paid more attention to Screwtape in the very first letter where Screwtape says that the time has passed in which "the humans still knew pretty well when a thing was proved and when it was not." Lewis's apologetic works, writes Jacobs, "presuppose, and rarely make any argument for, the criteria for rationality." Almost fifty years later, deconstructionism and antifoundationalism have done their wasting work. Under the tutelage of today's academy, unbelievers are skeptical about the very notion of "evidence," and they chatter cleverly about plausibility structures and paradigm shifts, leading them to offer the relativistic response to the most convincing of arguments, "That's great if it works for you." Or as it is said in England, "Right you are if you think you are."[7]

In short, it is suggested that Lewis has no standing in the deconstructed public square. His arguments have no public purchase. It is not that the cleverly educated of today disagree with his arguments. On the contrary, they agree with his argument that modernity's methodological skepticism logically leads to precisely where he says it leads. Except the endpoint that he views as catastrophe they welcome with a frisson of nihilistic delight. Consider one of the most rhetorically admirable passages in the entirety of Lewis's work. It comes at the very end of *The Abolition of Man*:

> But you cannot go on "explaining away" for ever: you will find that you have explained explanation itself away. You cannot go on "seeing through" things for ever. The whole point of seeing through something is to see something through it. It is good that the window should be transparent, because the street or garden beyond it is opaque. How if you saw through the garden too? It is no use trying to "see through" first principles. If you see through everything, then everything is transparent. But a wholly transparent world is an invisible world. To "see through" all things is the same as not to see.

---

[7]Alan Jacobs, "The Second Coming of C. S. Lewis," *First Things*, November 1994.

To which today's clever academic says with patronizing glee, "Exactly, old man. Except for your last line, for to see through all things is to see precisely what is to be seen, precisely what is there, which is to say—nothing!" It is hard to know how seriously we should take the fashionable nihilism of our time. In *The Closing of the American Mind*, Allan Bloom called it "debonair nihilism," which might be described as a flirtation with nothingness that has nothing as a consequence. Bright young things look over the edge into the abyss and gigglingly pronounce it to be "intriguing." It has been remarked that suicide is the most sincere form of self-criticism. With respect to the nihilism so enthusiastically embraced by today's herd of independent minds, one might take it more seriously if more of them leaped over the edge. Of course there are such as Michel Foucault who follow the lethal illogic to its end, but there are many times more who, like Richard Rorty, declare that "truth" (in quotation marks) is socially constructed "all the way down," yet go on living in pleasantly genteel irony, just as though the quotation marks were not there.

Postmodernism and C. S. Lewis

In any event, there is no denying that this intellectual world, commonly called postmodern, is very different from the world that C. S. Lewis sought to convince with arguments that could only be denied at the price of violating the law of non-contradiction. In today's intellectual climate, self-contradiction is deemed a small price to pay for liberation from the limits of reason. It is no surprise that Richard Rorty's heroes are—contradictorily, as one might expect—John Dewey and Walt Whitman. Rorty's liberals respond with Whitman: "Do I contradict myself? Very well then I contradict myself, (I am large, I contain multitudes.)" One might say that Lewis has addressed multitudes, but he did so one reasonable person at a time. I expect he would be somewhat at a loss—as are we all—when faced by postmodernist interlocutors quite unembarrassed by being caught in self-contradiction. To the most conclusive of knock-down arguments, they cheerfully respond, "Right you are if you think you are, Mr. Lewis."

The self-described "madness" of postmodernists who have domesticated Nietzsche to the comforts of the faculty lounge may be dismissed as being simply silly. But, as Richard Weaver understood, silly ideas, too, have consequences. Postmodernism may be a temporary aberration, but "temporary" may be a long time. It is an intellectual posture well suited to the well situated in a time of affluence and relative tranquillity. In circumstances of personal crisis we may be sure that the most ironic of Rorty's liberals will insist on the most foundational of rationalities. Nobody wants a postmodernist surgeon in the operating room. Slight comfort can be derived, however, from such occasional reversions to sanity. No point is scored.

The retort is ready at hand: "Do I contradict myself? Very well then I contradict myself."

As Dr. Johnson said of hanging, so some great social or political or military crisis might concentrate the minds of our intellectual elites, shocking them back into sanity. But hard core postmodernists are for the most part securely ensconced in the academy where the reality principle has long been suspended and real-world irruptions short of the cataclysmic cannot penetrate. In a circumstance of real social crisis, however, the irrationalists might be isolated and prevented from spreading the poison of debonair nihilism throughout the culture, as they do at present. But I expect that for the foreseeable future the indulgence of intellectual decadence will hold sway. At least we should be braced for that prospect.

Given this circumstance, what might C. S. Lewis do today? I rather hope that he would continue to do what he did so very well; that he would persistently, persuasively and winsomely make his arguments, engaging people one by one with the questions, Is it not true? Do you not find it to be so? One keeps at this in the confidence that there is such an irrepressible thing as human nature, and people may at some point be shamed into not denying—maybe even admitting—the obvious. Or at some point they may be faced by a question of great personal consequence that requires a yes-or-no, true-or-false, answer. Or best of all, they may weary of trashing their own dignity as creatures endowed with the divine gift of reason.

So I would hope that in the postmodern wilderness Lewis would keep on making his arguments, in the confidence that people can be brought to recognize that the rules of reason such as the law of noncontradiction are not the iron cage of outmoded rationalism but reason's royal road to discovering what is true. Like solipsism and related sophomoric indulgences, the hermeneutical skeptic's dalliance with nihilism soon becomes tiresome. "Yes, my dear," one is inclined to say, "we see you playing on the edge of the abyss. Now either jump or come away and let's get on with the conversation. It is really most annoying when you keep interrupting by announcing your discovery of nothing. Everything either is or is not nothing; and if it is, it is nothing. So whatever you may say, you really cannot have discovered it."

Telling Stories

In addition to making arguments, I expect that Lewis today would continue to tell stories. In fact I am certain he would, for it was central to his thought that discursive reason is inseparable from myth as a medium of truth. One recalls that decisive September evening in 1931 when Tolkien explained that "the story of Christ is simply a true myth: a myth working on us in the same way as the others, but with this tremendous difference that it really happened: and one must be content to accept it in the same way."[8] Of course, in today's postmodernist climate "stories" are very popular; you have your story and I have my story, and we both know that we are just making it up as we go along. Lewis knew no such thing. As he then insisted that discursive reason is inseparable from myth, he would today, I expect, insist even more emphatically that myth is inseparable from discursive reason.

Lewis's confidence in human nature, with its capacity for reason and susceptibility to myth, gave him a measure of patience with those who did not see the truth or saw it only dimly. It is a patience premised on confidence that might well be emulated by admirers of Lewis who too much relish him in his courtroom style, when he smites the unbelieving opponent hip and thigh, delivering knock-out arguments with a forensic brilliance that leaves the audience breathless. It is true that Lewis could be wickedly clever with liberals who stripped the faith of its substantive truth claims while still thinking of themselves as Christians. But unlike some of his admirers today Lewis did not insist that such liberals should fish or cut bait. Rather, he encouraged them to hang around the Christian thing, so to speak, in the hope that it might edge them toward the truth in ways better than they could understand.

> A man who disbelieved the Christian story as fact but continually fed on it as myth would, perhaps, be more spiritually alive than one who assented and did not think much about it. The modernist—the extreme modernist, infidel in all but name—need not be called a fool or hypocrite because he obstinately retains, even in the midst of his intellectual atheism, the language, rites, sacraments, and story of the Christians. The poor man may be clinging (with a wisdom he himself by no means understands) to that which is his life.

Myth and fact are inextricably entangled, and a person is not necessarily a more authentic Christian by being more firmly grasped by the one or the other: "For this is the marriage of heaven and earth: Perfect Myth and Perfect Fact: claiming not only our love and our obedience, but also our wonder and delight, addressed to the savage, the child, and the poet in each one of us no less than to the moralist, the scholar, and the philosopher."[9]

I should say that in public conversation today I do not think the word *myth* is useable, and it was probably less than helpful fifty years ago. Outside the circles of literary criticism *myth* connotes falsehood. Speaking of a "true myth" may catch attention, but it is also misleading for most people, suggesting that the truth in the myth is something less than *really* true. The word *story* is better. Despite postmodernism's story-telling games, people more readily recognize that stories can be true

---

[8] J. R. R. Tolkien, quoted in A. N. Wilson, *C. S. Lewis* (New York: Fawcett Columbine, 1991), p. 126.
[9] Lewis, "Myth Became Fact," p. 67.

or false. But I expect the still better word is *narrative*. I may have a difference with Lewis here (one day, God willing, we will find out), but I wonder whether his relentless effort to open people to the truth-disclosing genre of myth did not, because of the connotations surrounding the word *myth*, obscure the truth he most wanted to be disclosed. In some contemporary writings inspired by Lewis, the reader may get the impression that the fact of Bethlehem and the myth of Narnia, the fact of Christ and the myth of Aslan, are, at the end of the day, pretty much the same thing. Of course they are the same thing in part, but in much more important part they are not. I quickly add that Lewis should not be held accountable for all that is done by writers who claim his inspiration.

I should also say that Lewis anticipated some of the concerns addressed here. Somewhere he says that imagination is the organ of meaning and reason is the organ of truth. At least according to some interpreters, after the encounter with Anscombe at the Oxford Socratic Club, he lost confidence in reason and turned to imagination and myth. I expect it is more accurate to say that he came to more clearly recognize the interdependence of reason and imagination. He did ponder the difference between story and myth in the exercise of imagination. My modest suggestion is that, in today's intellectual culture, there is near insurmountable resistance to proposing truth under the title of "myth." "Story" is better, and "narrative" is better still.

A Two-Pronged Apologetic

In what might be called his two-pronged apologetic, Lewis employed argument and story, discursive reason and narrative, to powerful effect. In the public square of today and tomorrow, that strategy meets with even greater obstacles than it did in Lewis's time. I have already discussed the concerted attack on reasonable argument. In that department Lewis could take much more for granted than we can today. But there is also an attack on story, or perhaps it is less an attack than a trivializing of story. The story of postmodernism is the story of how, in Robert Jenson's fine phrase, "the world lost its story."[10] All too briefly and in broad strokes, I will say what I think that means. The late Hans Frei of Yale persuasively contended that the modern world's typical way of understanding human life was through "realistic narrative." A realistic narrative is, as Aristotle taught, a sequence of events that in retrospect "had" to happen or could happen in the real world. The realistic narrative of the West—and the West has been the driving force of world-historical change for almost a millennium—was the story that the Bible tells, the story of God with his creatures, from creation, through the election of Abraham, the com-

---

[10]Robert W. Jenson, "How the World Lost Its Story," *First Things*, October 1993.

ing of the Messiah and the eschatological promise of the feast of the Lamb.

As is now generally acknowledged, modernity fed off that realistic narrative for a long time. The myth of historical progress and ideological schemes such as Marxism were secularized riffs on the biblical story. But the story-line could not be sustained without its Author and Chief Protagonist, namely, the God of Abraham, Isaac, Jacob and Jesus. What we today call postmodernism is the long-delayed general dissemination of what, in the earlier part of this century, appeared in the arts under the title of "modernism." Surrealism, dadaism, the writings of James Joyce and, later, Samuel Beckett—all proclaimed a world that has lost its story and, along with its story, its coherence, purpose and promise. We no longer live in what might be called a "narratable world" (Jenson). Of course C. S. Lewis was aware of "modernism" in the arts, but it was then on the edges of the public square, presenting itself as the avant-garde. Today, under the title of "postmodernism," it bids fair to take over the public square in its entirety.

Postmodernism dissolves the controlling master story or metanarrative into disconnected fragments, just as modernist painting, sculpture and fiction exulted in turning art forms into formless fragments. In the absence of the metanarrative, other narratives are crippled in their capacity to disclose truth. Consider allegory, for instance. To speak figuratively is to assume a knowledge of that which is figured. The word *allegory* is from the Greek *allos*, meaning other, and *agorein*, to speak publicly in the *agora*, meaning the public square. Lewis assumed, and reasonably so, that his allegories would resonate in a public square over which and around which hovered the metanarrative of the biblical story. He wrote allegorically in the expectation that at least the thoughtful reader would "get it." That cannot be assumed today, and even less will we be able to assume it tomorrow. The modern world, now become the postmodern world, has lost its story.

Postmodernists are incapable of allegory because allegory requires a known story to which it is "other." With debonair desperation they multiply the telling of stories, making them up as they go along, in the hope of finding one with which, as it is said, they are "comfortable"—at least for the time being, until they feel the need for another that will, as it is said, meet their needs. The resulting cacophony in the public square is called multiculturalism. In such a world, Lewis's talk about a "true" story strikes many as quaint. "Right you are if you think you are, Mr. Lewis."

So what are we to do—we who are convinced that we know the realistic Narrative that, in the words of Dante, moves the sun and all the other stars, the narrative of God's love with his creatures? We cannot, we must not, withdraw from the public square. I suggest that we firmly reject the counsel of those who say that we live in a post-Christian age and should prepare ourselves for a return to the catacombs. If the Narrative is true, if Christ is Lord, it follows that no age can be post-Christian. We might better say that our world is not post-Christian but proto-Christian, awaiting, whether it realizes it or not, the story by which it might, as though for the first time, know itself. Were I giving another paper, I would go on to explain why the community that bears the story of the world must itself more clearly exemplify that story. The story must be told by the life of the church, and by the Eucharist, which is the source and summit of the life of the church and therefore of the world. Lewis had relatively little to say about liturgy and the ecclesial dimension of Christian faith. I expect he might sense the urgency of saying more today. Church and Eucharist are the story of the world, the *axis mundi*, the center of all that is, the recapitulation of all that ever has been, the anticipation of the promised feast of the Lamb. The church must more manifestly *be* what in fact she is, the story of the world. But, as I say, that is the subject of another paper.

For the moment and in answer to the question, What are we to do? I suggest that we should also do what C. S. Lewis did so very well. As Christian humanists in the public square, we should persist in making the very best arguments that we can. Not in order to score points but in order to elicit the capacity for critical thought; being confident, as Lewis was confident, that human beings are hardwired for reason in search of truth. And we should tell better stories that winsomely, even seductively, reintroduce the great Story; being confident, as Lewis was confident, that the pagans then and now, in the fine phrase of Edward Norman, got it "broadly right." We must help them to tell their story, for whether they know it or not their story is the story of God's ways with his creatures, the story of salvation.

In the freedom and confidence that come from knowing and being known by the Truth, we join the everyday C. S. Lewis in the public square—patiently and imaginatively engaging our interlocutors, one by one, and asking, Is it not true? Do you not find it to be so? As Lewis well understood, a salutary touch of polemic is in order from time to time—to catch the listener's attention or to clear the air of cant. But the Christian humanist knows that at its heart the conversation with the world is a love affair; to elicit what is already there and bring it to fuller and finer expression in what is, finally and simply and wondrously, the truth.

I am confident that Thomas Oden, who has found his vocation in telling, in ever greater depth and detail, the story of the church's reflection on that truth, would agree.

Nineteen

A Poem of
Saint Bonaventure

Daniel B. Clendenin

O ne of my fondest memories of Tom Oden, and one that fills me with a
sense of deep gratitude, recalls a meeting of the Evangelical Theological Society
in New Orleans. I was one of a number of people who had helped Tom by reading through the rough draft for his massive third volume of his systematic theology, *Life in the Spirit,* and he wanted to thank us. So he treated our group to
breakfast, but that was just the beginning. As it was Sunday, our group then
moved to Tom's room, where he led us in a short service, based on the Book of
Common Prayer.

For me this memory captures something essential for the Christian scholar,
something that Tom has incarnated in his own life and in so doing bequeathed to
us as a gift: the integration of intellectual rigor with personal piety. Any number
of people excel in one of these areas; Tom has in both.

At a meeting in Atlanta, Bob Fryling, publisher of InterVarsity Press, read a poem
by Saint Bonaventure (1221-1274) that I found especially powerful for those of us
who, like Tom, care deeply about both the life of the mind and the heart. Bonaventure was a professor who studied and taught at the University of Paris, a pastor and
later general of the Franciscan Order, but perhaps most of all he is remembered as a
mystic. In 1273 he was elected as the Cardinal Archbishop of Albano.

Bonaventure's poem is found in one of his most famous works, *The Journey of the Mind Toward God:*

> Do not assume that mere reading will suffice without fervor, Speculation without devotion, Investigation without admiration, Observation without exaltation, Industry without piety, Knowledge without love, Understanding without humility, And study without divine grace.

For people committed to the life of the mind in the context of the university, and to the growth of the soul in the community of the church, I find his advice salutary. Bonaventure cautions us against two extremes and points us to a holistic life that combines rather than separates intellectual endeavor and spiritual fervor.

On the one hand, Christians who are scholars must struggle against the deep impulses of anti-intellectualism that disregard, disparage, oversimplify and generally fail to appreciate the calling to intellectual contemplation and abstract thought. Related to this, of course, are the frightening and even broader cultural currents of loss of literacy described in the analyses of critics like Neil Postman, Morris Berman, Robert Kaplan, Benjamin Barber and others.[1] As Richard Hofstadter showed in his Pulitzer prize-winning book *Anti-Intellectualism in American Life* (1964), our overall culture is biased toward pragmatic concerns and an egalitarian spirit that often exhibit outright disdain for intellectual work. Hofstadter also identified "the evangelical spirit" as a third cause of our culture's anti-intellectualism.

Anti-intellectualism can be especially acute within the church. Despite numerous advances of evangelicalism within American culture—in politics, education, social status, increased wealth and the like (remember, *Time* magazine characterized 1976 as "The Year of the Evangelical")—overall, Mark Noll has shown how and why our fundamentalist-evangelical heritage has been a disaster when it comes to first-order intellectual work. Ask yourself, why isn't there a single evangelical institution in a list of the top fifty colleges and universities in our country? There are a number of reasons for this, as Noll documents in his book *The Scandal of the Evangelical Mind* (1994), but the result can often be that the Christian who is an intellectual often feels disenfranchised even by our evangelical church culture.[2]

---

[1] Neil Postman, *Amusing Ourselves to Death* (New York: Penguin, 1985); Morris Berman, *The Twilight of American Culture* (New York: W. W. Norton, 2000); Robert Kaplan, *An Empire Wilderness: Travels into America's Future* (New York: Vintage, 1999); and Benjamin Barber, *Jihad Versus McWorld* (New York: Ballantine, 1995).

[2] See also Nathan Hatch, *The Democratization of American Christianity* (New Haven, Conn.: Yale University Press, 1989); and two of the many works by George Marsden, *Fundamentalism and American Culture* (New York: Oxford University Press, 1980), and *The Soul of the American University* (New York: Oxford University Press, 1994).

Bonaventure's own life is a reminder how the scholarly life of the mind can be a sacred calling. In his work he emphasized that the created world is a rational world open to intellectual inquiry by people created in God's image. Reason and knowledge are divine gifts. He reminds us that one of the ways we fulfill the greatest commandment to love God is by loving him "with all of your mind" (Mark 12:30). Tom Oden's intellectual legacy, in its substance but perhaps even more powerfully in its method of what he calls paleo-orthodoxy, is a wonderful model of intellectual rigor that is fully comfortable as a sacred service to the kingdom.

On the other hand, within the university context Christian scholars often face the opposite extreme, a sort of rationalistic reductionism that allows no place for religious devotion or cultivation of the soul. If Huston Smith is correct in his book *Why Religion Matters* (2001), "the modern university is not agnostic toward religion; it is actively hostile to it." Tom also experienced the full force of these currents, laboring away for almost his entire career at a liberal arts university all too prone to the shibboleths of a politically-correct "fundamentalism" of its own secular sort. Bonaventure's poem draws special attention to this hazard. For Bonaventure, and likewise Tom, human reason is a divine gift to be celebrated, but the health of the soul is a human necessity that must be cultivated.

Recently I reread Henri Nouwen's book *Finding My Way Home* (2001). He speaks to this second danger. After teaching at Yale and Harvard, for the last ten years of his life Nouwen lived and ministered at Daybreak near Toronto, a home for people with severe mental and physical disabilities. There, he says, he learned that ultimately the life of the heart is more fundamental to being human than the life of the mind:

> Somehow during the centuries we have come to believe that what makes us human is our mind. Even those unfamiliar with Latin know Seneca's definition of a human being as a reasoning animal: *rationale animal est homo*. . . . [But] what makes us human is not primarily our minds but our hearts; it is not first of all our ability to think which gives us our particular identity in all creation, but it is our ability to love. . . . I am speaking here about something very, very real. It is about the hidden mystery of the primacy of the heart in our true identity as human beings.

In Bonaventure's vision the ultimate journey we are on is to union with God and not merely rational inquiry or intellectual achievement. Tom was not only an able scholar in the Wesleyan intellectual tradition; he was a living example of its wonderful emphasis on the primacy of the heart.

Human knowledge and academic inquiry are precious gifts that can help us toward our ultimate goal. We must never disparage them, but instead honor and enjoy them. Nor should we ever separate faith and reason or play one off the other. But to reach our final goal, says Bonaventure, to our speculation, investigation and observation we must add devotion, admiration and exaltation. To our industry, knowledge and understanding we need to include piety, love and humility. Undergirding it all, in our study we seek divine grace.

Contributors & Acknowledgments

William J. Abraham is Albert Cook Outler Professor of Wesley Studies at Perkins School of Theology, Southern Methodist University.

Carl E. Braaten is executive directory of the Center for Catholic and Evangelical Theology. His essay was delivered in the spring of 1999 to the Pacific Lutheran Theological Seminary, Berkeley, California.

Daniel B. Clendenin is a staff member of InterVarsity Christian Fellowship Graduate & Faculty Ministries at Stanford University.

John R. Franke is associate professor of theology at Biblical Theological Seminary.

Stanley J. Grenz is Pioneer McDonald Professor of Baptist Heritage, Theology and Ethics at Carey Theological College, Vancouver, B.C. The Grenz and Franke essay is adapted from their book *Beyond Foundationalism* (2000) and is used by permission of Westminster John Knox.

Vigen Guroian is professor of theology and ethics at Loyola College in Maryland. His essay appeared in the March 2001 issue of *Second Opinion* and is used by permission.

Christopher A. Hall is associate professor of biblical and theological studies at Eastern University, St. Davids, Pennsylvania, and associate editor of the Ancient Christian Commentary on Scripture. His essay was given at the American Academy of Religion, Eastern Orthodox Studies Group, Orlando, Florida, November 1998.

Thomas Howard, until he retired, was professor of English at St. John's Seminary College in Boston. His essay originally appeared in the summer 1993 issue of *Touchstone* and was delivered in Oklahoma City to The Fellowship of St. Barnabas in July 1993.

Robert W. Jenson is senior scholar for research, Center of Theological Inquiry, Princeton, N.J. His essay appeared as "Jesus in the Trinity" in *Pro Ecclesia* 8, no. 3 (1999).

Ancient & postmodern Christianity

David Mills is director of publishing for Trinity Episcopal School for Ministry and senior editor for *Touchstone* magazine. His essay appeared in *Touchstone* (March 2002).

Bradley Nassif is a professor at the Institute for Orthodox Studies, Cambridge University; professor of historical and systematic theology, Antiochian House of Studies, Balamand University, Lebanon; and founder and president of the Society for the Study of Eastern Orthodoxy and Evangelicalism.

Richard John Neuhaus is editor-in-chief of *First Things*. An earlier version of his essay appeared in *First Things* (December 1998).

Amy E. Oden, Tom Oden's niece, is professor of church history at Oklahoma City University. Parts of her essay first appeared in her *And You Welcomed Me* (Abingdon, 2002). Used by permission of Abingdon Press.

J. I. Packer is the Board of Governors' Professor of Theology at Regent College, Vancouver, B.C. His essay was delivered in part to a September 1999 meeting of the Society for the Study of Eastern Orthodoxy and Evangelicalism in Irvine, California.

Alan G. Padgett is a professor of systematic theology, Luther Seminary, St. Paul, Minnesota.

Wolfhart Pannenberg is emeritus professor of systematic theology, Protestant faculty, University of Munich, and director of the Institute for Fundamental Theology and Ecumenics. His essay was first delivered in N. Washington in September 1999.

Edmund Rybarczyk is adjunct professor of religion at Vanguard University of Southern California.

Joel Scandrett is translations project coordinator for the Ancient Christian Commentary research team at Drew University.

Kenneth Tanner is ordained in the Charismatic Episcopal Church and serves on the staff of *Touchstone: A Journal of Mere Christianity*.

Geoffrey Wainwright is Cushman Professor of Christian Theology at The Divinity School, Duke University. His essay was delivered at the Stover-Ward Lecture at the St. Paul School of Theology, Kansas City.

Robert E. Webber holds the William R. and Geraldyne B. Myers Chair of Ministry at Northern Baptist Theological Seminary, Lombard, Illinois. His essay was previously delivered to the summer 2000 conference of the Center for Catholic and Evangelical Theology, Collegeville, Minnesota.